BOOKS BY MICHAEL FIELD

Michael Field's Cooking School

Michael Field's Culinary Classics and Improvisations

All Manner of Food

Cooking With Michael Field

The Michael Field Egg Cookbook

ALL MANNER OF FOOD

ALL
MANNER
OF
FOOD

MICHAEL
FIELD

The Ecco Press
New York

First published by The Ecco Press in 1982
18 West 30th Street, New York, New York 10001
Published simultaneously in Canada by
George J. McLeod Limited, Toronto
The Ecco Press logo by Ahmed Yacoubi

The articles in this book have appeared in different form
in *McCall's* and *Holiday* magazines.

Library of Congress Cataloging in Publication Data

Field, Michael, 1915-1971.
    All manner of food.

    Reprint. Originally published: 1st ed. New York:
Knopf, 1970.
    Includes index.
1. Cookery, International.   I. Title.
TX725.A1F47   1982   641.5   82-2321
ISBN 0-88001-013-4
ISBN 0-88001-014-2 (pbk.)

For my son, Jonathan

Contents

Introduction

All the essays in this book—but only a handful of the recipes—have appeared during the past few years in substantially different forms in *McCall's* and *Holiday* magazines. My intent then was to explore in depth various categories of foods, some familiar and others only vaguely known, if at all. I was concerned at that time not with recipes as such but with the foods themselves: their chemistry and composition, how to find and recognize them, how to buy and assess their qualities and, finally, how to cook with them. After each essay appeared I received countless letters, almost all of them requests for specific recipes for the unusual—and even the better-known—dishes I had either mentioned in passing or had discussed in general terms.

All Manner of Food began as a reply, as it were, to these queries. However, along the way, it led me to further exploration and to the discovery that cross-relationships of course inevitably occurred: lemons combined with garlic, wine with cheese, nuts with chocolate, roots with potatoes, and members of the onion family with everything but the ingredients for desserts. As a result, the book began to take on a life of its own; it has now become a cohesive whole made up of many diversified but independent parts.

To ensure the success of each dish, I have written my recipes as I teach them, emphasizing a pitfall here and a warning note or alternative there; and I never take anything for granted. Some of the recipes may seem inordinately long (and when read in succession, somewhat repetitious as well), but I have presented them to you in this fashion deliberately. I long ago discovered from questions shyly asked by my cooking-class students that supposedly simple culinary procedures were misunderstood and often not understood at all. Since all the recipes in this book cover a wide spectrum of cuisines, they often require techniques unfamiliar to even experienced American cooks. These, and my own innovations, I have also explained in detail. To enable you to use this book to its greatest advantage, I have included at the end a series of recipe categories and a few personal menus as guides to light your way.

In *All Manner of Food* I write of all *kinds* of food; but when all is said and done, it is the manner that is my message.

GARLIC

gARlic

"It is not really an exaggeration," wrote the great chef Marcel Boulestin, "to say that peace and happiness begin, geographically, where garlic is used in cooking." As a Frenchman, he meant, of course, France, and more specifically the south of France, where he was born. There, and in adjacent Italy, garlic is used as naturally and spontaneously as salt to flavor food. Since Boulestin's pronouncement some forty years ago, the garlic frontiers of the world have expanded enormously and, if this has not exactly brought peace and happiness to man, it has, at least, improved his eating habits.

A member of the lily family, garlic—or scientifically, *Allium sativum*—is a singularly innocent-looking bulb consisting of an unpredictable number of tightly clustered, narrow, spoon-shaped cloves. Individually sheathed in deceptively delicate skins—silvery white, pale green, or streaky mauve—they give no hint of the power they pack when peeled. Unlike its shyer relatives—onions, scallions, leeks, and shallots—garlic has a voice that is loud and clear. For thousands of years it has made itself heard as have few other foods or flavorings known to man.

References to the use of garlic crop up persistently throughout recorded history, even as far back as the Old Testament. As if the Israelites hadn't had enough to worry about during their journey through the wilderness of Sinai, we hear them crying out in despair to Moses (Numbers XI: 5) for their favorite foods: leeks, onions, and garlic. And in ancient Egypt, according to Herodotus, laborers stopped work on the great Pyramid of Cheops when deprived of their daily ration of garlic. Because Egyptians of all classes invoked garlic in oaths and literally worshipped it, their priests considered it an abomination and denounced its use as blasphemous. Despite this prohibition, garlic often served as a medium of exchange, and such was its worth that fifteen pounds of it could buy a healthy male slave.

Unlike the Egyptians, the fastidious Greeks of Herodotus' time were not enthusiastic about garlic and seldom used it in their cooking. They considered it vulgar; so vulgar, in fact, that those who had eaten it were forbidden to worship in the temples of the great mother goddess Cybele. The more sensual Romans, on the other hand, consumed staggering amounts of garlic, not because the refinements of their cooking particularly required it but because they considered the bulb a potent aphrodisiac. This wishful concept, with no basis in fact, persisted throughout the centuries, trailing in its wake other equally fanciful notions. Pouches filled with garlic were worn around the neck as a preventive against the plague. Moreover, the cloves were considered powerful enough to ward off the evil eye and protect the wearer against the machinations of witches. From the earliest days of antiquity until almost a century ago, raw garlic was fed to soldiers, athletes, and even fighting cocks to give them strength and courage to meet their adversaries. And during the sixteenth century, the Elizabethans, like the Romans, were convinced that eating garlic not only sharpened the appetite for lovemaking but led to a larger drinking capacity as well. Thomas Nash, a satiric poet of the period, wrote, "Garlic maketh a man winke, drinke, and stinke." Whatever reservations one may have about the first two claims, there can surely be none about the last: the odor of garlic is an incontrovertible fact. To this so-called alliaceous odor must be ascribed, in great part, the diversity of garlic's roles, not only in food, but in myth, magic, and medicine as well.

On the principle that the more penetrating the odor of a plant or herb, the more therapeutic its value, early medicine, from the days of Hippocrates on, employed garlic as a pharmaceutical in the treatment of diseases as disparate as tuberculosis and leprosy. Pliny, the Roman naturalist, listed sixty-one diseases garlic was supposed to cure and appended the information that "garlic has such powerful properties that the very smell of it drives away serpents and scorpions."

And lest it be assumed that only the ancients had such primitive notions, there are those among us, even today, who are just as sanguine. In the United States, garlic pills are sold in health-food stores, for they are supposed to have a salutary effect on arthritis. The pills have no medical sanction whatsoever, but afflicted Americans continue to buy them by the thousands. That the Russians are not above such medical hocus-pocus is revealed in a dispatch from the Soviet Union, dated April 4, 1965, reporting that Russian newspapers advised their readers to munch raw garlic as a safeguard against contagion during the influenza epidemic raging there at the time. There is no medical basis for eating garlic as a flu preventative, according to most reputable doctors, but they half seriously admit garlic's value in forcing people to keep their distance, thus lessening the possibility of contagion.

But keeping one's distance in some situations—while performing in a play, for example—is often difficult. According to a well-known director, finicky actors, overwhelmed by a fellow performer's garlic fumes, have been known to change their lines or forget them entirely and improvise new business in order to keep as far from the offender as possible. Performances in these circumstances are not always the most polished. Perhaps Shakespeare was aware of this when he had Bottom, in *A Midsummer Night's Dream,* tell his cast, "And most dear actors, eat no onions nor garlic for we are to utter sweet breath." On the other hand, some actors are made of sterner stuff. The realistic Lunts take a more practical stand, telling their casts, "We don't mind garlic or onion on the breath—but we do object to the smell of liquor."

Man's attempts to cope with the odor of garlic have from earliest times proved fruitless. Mouthwashes, chewing gums, toothpastes, and such old-fashioned countermeasures as chewing raw parsley or watercress after garlic-flavored meals have only the slightest palliative effect, and even that is temporary, for the odor lingers. In fact, the director of one of the country's largest pharmaceutical houses has stated flatly that nothing at all can be done about it.

But if modern scientists can't do anything about it, they now at least know why they can't. The *American Journal of Medicine* describes experiments that prove conclusively that the volatile oils of garlic do not cling to the teeth, tongue, and palate, as was commonly supposed, but enter the lungs instead. There they are exhaled with every breath—and through every pore, too—and persist until the action of the oils ceases. The potency of these oils can be more easily understood when one realizes that, by scientific estimate, one millionth of an ounce is detectable in a single sniff of air.

Unaware of these findings thirty-five years ago, the English writer Ford Madox Ford tells a charming, if improbable, tale about garlic in his travel book, *Provence.* In brief, it is the story of a beautiful young model who so adored garlic that neither her fellow workers' complaints

nor threats of being fired would make her give it up. In desperation,
hoping to surfeit her need once and for all, she decided to take a leave
of absence for a week and eat nothing but food cooked with garlic in
every form she could think of. After a week of utter bliss she returned
to the shop and to her amazement encountered none of the hostility
that had greeted her entrances in the past. As Ford describes it, "At the
studio there had been no outcry, and there she had been congratulated
on the improvement, if possible, of her skin, her hair, and her carriage."
And, he goes on to explain, "She had solved the great problem; she had
schooled her organs to assimilate, not to protest against the sacred
herb."

Such an apocryphal story could only have been told by a writer
obsessed with Provence. For it is there that garlic can be truly called
the "sacred herb." Although various areas in France, Italy, Spain,
Greece, Russia, and China, among others, have produced individual
garlic dishes of great originality, only Provence has created a cuisine in
which garlic is more often than not the indispensable ingredient. On
occasion there may be some doubt as to whether a dish cooked *à la
provençale* necessarily contains tomatoes—an important element in
Provençal cooking—but one thing is certain: the dish will almost always be made with garlic, and lots of it.

Paradoxically, the amount of garlic in a dish doesn't always determine the strength of its flavor; *how* it is cooked is the controlling factor. A clove of garlic can be peeled, bruised, sliced, chopped, minced,
crushed, mashed, or pressed. Garlic can be combined with food raw, or
it can be poached, boiled, steamed, sautéed, or roasted with food. These
forms and processes produce a spectrum of garlic flavors of which few
American cooks are aware.

Uncompromising and vigorous, to say the least, are the great Provençal sauces in which only raw garlic is used. *Aïoli, pistou, rouille*—
their names alone evoke the sun-drenched, explosively colored land-
scape of Provence and its groves of gnarled olive trees climbing the
terraced hillsides. The native olive oil and garlic form the basic sauce
(some say it is the soul) of Provençal cooking—called *aïoli*. This thick,
garlic-laden mayonnaise, *aïoli* (*ail* means "garlic") is as necessary to
Provençal cooking as butter is to ours; in fact, *aïoli* is often called the
butter of Provence. It is used as a sauce for hot or cold vegetables; combined with fish stock for the classic fish soup, *bourride;* or served plain
over steamed salt cod. Often it is spread copiously over cold eggs,

meats, lobster or other shellfish; and, in secret, probably eaten straight. There is scarcely a household in Provence that doesn't regularly have a bowl of *aïoli* on hand. If the cooks of Provence have not yet devised a dessert with *aïoli*, it is only because they just haven't gotten around to it.

Other cuisines have their own versions of *aïoli*. In Spain it is called *ali-oli* and is, despite the hyphen and the different spelling, exactly the same sauce as the Provençal original. The Greeks, naturally, have another name for it. Greek cooks toss into their *aïoli* a handful of ground almonds, a few fresh bread crumbs, and a little chopped parsley and call it *skordalia*. There are other Greek versions too, and an especially good one is made with freshly mashed potatoes, olive oil, and, of course, great amounts of chopped garlic. Considerably thicker than the Provençal *aïoli*, *skordalia* in all of its forms is usually served with cold eggs and vegetables. A typical Greek salad may consist of hard-cooked eggs, sliced tomatoes, sliced beets, black Mediterranean olives, radishes, and a bowl of *skordalia*. I have given both versions of this pungent sauce on pages 14 and 15. Your own taste will determine which of the two you prefer; I can't choose—I like them equally.

Even if the natives of Provence can rightfully claim *aïoli* as their own, they find it painful to admit that they are indebted to the neighboring Italians for another uncooked garlic sauce. *Pistou* is its name, and it derives from the Genoese *pesto*, which I discuss in the pasta chapter, page 111. The composition of both sauces—a paste of garlic, basil, cheese, and olive oil—is almost as similar as their names. But one difference is that the French *pistou* does not have the crushed pignolias —or sometimes walnuts—that the Italians add to their *pesto*. In Provence, *pistou* is most often stirred into a vegetable-bean soup, *soupe au pistou*, and is seldom used for any other purpose. In Genoa, on the other hand, *pesto*, although occasionally added to minestrone, is almost always used as a sauce for pasta.

When I was in Provence recently, I tried to analyze the original Provençal flavor of their *soupe au pistou*, which comes from the extraordinary quality of the vegetables—the slightly salty tomatoes, for instance—and the soup that is water- rather than meat-stock-based and tastes fully of vegetables. I feel I have recaptured that taste in the recipe I evolved, see page 15.

Provençal cooks perform culinary sleight of hand with garlic by cooking whole cloves of it—and seldom less than thirty at a time—in a soup called *soupe à l'ail*. Because the garlic cloves are cooked whole and care is taken not to bruise them, their volatile oils condense within the cloves themselves. During this process, the oils undergo a mysterious transformation, and their final flavor is a fine and subtle one that has neither the characteristic taste nor the odor of garlic as we usually experience it. I almost maliciously served my *soupe à l'ail*, as described on page 20, to people who had insisted for years that they couldn't eat garlic, that it made them ill, that they couldn't stand the aftertaste. But these friends innocently consumed three bowls of the soup, were stunned when they discovered what they had eaten, and delighted that they felt no discomfort that night nor the next day.

Not only in Provence but in other areas of France as well, a chicken (or sometimes a goose) is also cooked with thirty or more cloves of garlic. This dish has a variety of names but is most frequently called chicken *béarnaise* or chicken *dauphinoise*—the first, a roast chicken; and the second, a sauté.

For the *béarnaise* version, anywhere up to two pounds of whole, peeled garlic cloves are stuffed into the chicken. The cloves of garlic saturated with the juices of the chicken, are served as a garnish almost as if they were, to use Ford Madox Ford's metaphor, *haricots blancs* or white beans, in this case mashed to a purée. The only difference between the *béarnaise* and *dauphinoise* versions is that the chicken *dauphinoise* is cut up, lightly browned, and then cooked with the garlic. The garlic retains a hint of its personality, but so transmuted as to be nearly unrecognizable. You may blanch if you are suddenly confronted with six or seven whole cloves of garlic nestled next to the drumstick on your plate, but you should have the courage to eat them, for they have a sweet, nutlike flavor quite unlike any other vegetable and, an unexpected dividend—they leave no odor of garlic on your breath.

We in the United States tend to associate Italian food with the strong flavor of garlic, but almost the reverse is true. Apart from the rich, aromatic tomato sauces and fish soups of southern Italy, the Italians use garlic in their cooking with considerable restraint. Few of their roasts, stews, or even their famous salamis are flavored with garlic to a noticeable degree. In more aristocratic Roman and Florentine circles, garlic is positively frowned upon.

I must say, however, that when the Italians cut loose with garlic, they do so with abandon. Even in Provence there are few dishes that compare in alliaceous intensity to spaghetti *all'aglio e olio*, the Nea-

politan pasta dish sauced wholly with straight garlic and olive oil. Pied-
mont, too, has its celebrated garlic masterpiece, *bagna cauda* (literally,
"hot bath"). There are two versions of this dish—one, a heavily gar-
licked sauce made of hot cream, butter, and anchovies, and flavored
with white truffles, and another which omits the cream and combines
the butter, anchovies, truffles, and garlic with olive oil. I have given
you both versions on pages 25 and 26. They are perhaps the most original dishes in the Italian cuisine. Into the sauce, which is kept warm in
a casserole, all sorts of icy-cold raw vegetables are dipped, and in Pied-
mont it is consumed on every possible occasion. It makes an excellent
hors d'oeuvre and I have often served it with cocktails before dinner—
a large platter of colorful vegetables, cut for easy handling, surrounding
a bowl of the aromatic *bagna cauda,* kept warm on a table heater. Mi-
lan, not to be outdone, has its very own garlic dish, *osso buco.* Properly
prepared, this lusty dish, composed of short veal shanks braised with
vegetables, white wine, and tomatoes, is seldom actually cooked with
garlic, but, before being served, is heavily garnished with *gremolata,* a
colorful mélange of chopped raw garlic, lemon peel (and in my recipe
orange peel), and parsley. Needless to say, in *osso buco* the presence of
the raw garlic is unmistakable before, during, and after you eat it.

Many Italians, like their Roman ancestors, are even today great
believers in the medical efficacy of garlic. They think nothing of crush-
ing handfuls of it in garlic presses and drinking a draught of the raw
juice as a cure for anything from headaches to hypertension. According
to its Italian and Swiss manufacturers, the garlic press was devised
originally for medicinal purposes, and its use in cooking was secondary.
When the presses were exported about twenty years ago, Americans
bought them by the millions. This, in part, may account for the tremen-
dous increase in our use of garlic over the past dozen years. Unfortunately, the garlic press, while it may have made us more garlic con-
scious, can be the most insidious of culinary instruments. Many cooks
do not realize that one small clove of garlic, put through a press, is the
approximate equivalent of three garlic cloves of similar size minced or
chopped. Food flavored with pure garlic juice, even for the most rabid
enthusiast, can be too much of a good thing.

Our increased consumption of garlic during the past decade is due,
also, to its availability in commercial forms. It can be bought in every
possible dehydrated state—powdered, ground, minced, chopped,
sliced, or puréed. Certainly these products do well enough in a pinch,

but any sound cook knows that there is little excuse for using them when fresh garlic is so easily found everywhere. Manufacturers quite reasonably claim that their dehydrated garlic is easier to use, less messy to work with, and more precisely measurable than fresh garlic. They may be right, but frankly I would simply avoid making any great garlic flavored dishes if *fresh* garlic were not available. *Bagna cauda* made with sliced dehydrated garlic or *skordalia* spiked with garlic powder would have little resemblance to the original dish—and, moreover, would be disturbingly indigestible.

Dehydrated garlic, however, does play an interesting role in the processed-food industry. Many of you who profess a horror of garlic may be amused, or perhaps alarmed, to learn that a good proportion of the bottled, canned, and packaged food you buy contains a high percentage of dehydrated garlic: soups, ketchup, mayonnaise, prepared mustard, sandwich meats, sausages, pickles, salad dressings—the list is almost endless. And though the garlic flavor in these foods is seldom apparent as such, were it omitted many of the products would lose what little flavor they have. Delightfully enough, dehydrated garlic is also an important ingredient in canned dog foods. Apparently dogs adore garlic, as dog-food manufacturers have discovered to their immense profit. In periodic feeding trials (the larger companies have special kennels for just this purpose), dogs have been observed to sniff with disdain at bland, garlicless food set before them.

People, too, seem to be developing similar sensibilities. Salad bowls are rubbed with garlic, legs of lamb are spiked with it, loaves of buttered French bread drip with it. We are using more and more of it each day. If Marcel Boulestin was right, peace and happiness in America must surely be right around the corner, and in the following recipes, I hope to help you find it.

Aïoli

makes about 2 cups

1 tablespoon dry bread crumbs
1 tablespoon wine vinegar
4–6 large cloves garlic, *peeled
　　and coarsely chopped*
3 egg yolks

1½ cups olive oil
1–2 tablespoons boiling water
½ teaspoon salt
⅛ teaspoon cayenne
1–2 tablespoons lemon juice

Soak the bread crumbs in the vinegar for 2 or 3 minutes. Squeeze the crumbs dry in a corner of a towel and combine them with the chopped garlic in a mortar or small wooden bowl. With a pestle or the back of a spoon, mash the garlic and crumbs together until you have a smooth paste—and it *must* be smooth. Now add one of the yolks. Mix and pound it into the paste, then add the other yolks. Mix, pound again, and scrape the paste into a large mixing bowl.

With an electric mixer, rotary beater, or wire whisk, start beating in the olive oil about ½ teaspoon at a time. Beating constantly, add the oil at this rate until you have used about ½ cup. Beat in the remaining oil somewhat more rapidly. The *aïoli* should now be thick and creamy. Beat in a tablespoon of boiling water (more, if you prefer the sauce thinner), then taste the *aïoli* and season with salt and cayenne and as much lemon juice as you like. Serve with hot or cold vegetables or hard-cooked eggs; instead of butter with boiled or baked potatoes; or with hot or cold fish.

Bourride

serves 8–10

2 cups *aïoli* (see above)

6 egg yolks, reserving the whites
　　for some other purpose if you
　　wish

Bourride

THE COURT-BOUILLON

The heads and trimmings of the
fish listed below, amplified if
possible with more heads or
trimmings, to make about 3
pounds
6 cups water
2 cups dry white wine
2 tablespoons white wine vinegar
2 medium onions, *peeled and
thinly sliced*
2 leeks, *the white parts and about
2 inches of the green tops
thoroughly washed to rid
them of sand, then thinly
sliced*

A paper-thin strip of orange peel,
about 6 inches long and 1
inch wide, *removed from the
orange with a swivel-bladed
vegetable peeler*
2 medium bay leaves
2 stalks fresh fennel, *thinly sliced,*
if available; or use 2 teaspoons fennel seeds, *lightly
bruised with a mortar and
pestle (or wrap them in a
towel and run a rolling pin
back and forth over them)*
2 teaspoons salt

THE FISH

A mixture of any firm white-
fleshed fish such as haddock,
pollack, perch, bass, rockfish,
or halibut, among others, *fil-
leted and skinned, then cut*

*crosswise into approximately
3-inch-wide chunks;* the total
weight of the fish after the
trimming and the filleting
should be 5 to 6 pounds

Salt
White pepper
Lemon juice
12–16 one-inch-thick slices of

day-old French or Italian
bread, *lightly toasted*
(*croûtes*)

1 recipe *rouille* (optional) (page
17)

The *aïoli* may be made at any time. When it is finished, spoon about
⅔ cup of it into a small sauceboat, cover with plastic wrap, and refrigerate the *aïoli* until you are ready to serve it. Put the rest of the *aïoli*
(about ⅓ cup) into a 2-quart enamel or stainless-steel saucepan, and
with a whisk, beat in the 6 egg yolks, one at a time. Set aside.

To make the best *court-bouillon*—one with an intense, concentrated flavor—cajole your fishman into giving you not only the trimmings of the fish you have just bought but as many other fish heads and spines (avoiding the oilier fish like mackerel, bluefish, and salmon) as he has on hand. Wash them thoroughly and place them in a 4- to 6-quart enamel or stainless-steel pot with the water, wine, vinegar, onions, leeks, orange peel, bay leaves, fennel or fennel seeds, and the salt. Bring the *court-bouillon* to a boil over high heat, skim it of all the foam and scum rising to the surface, and reduce the heat to low. Simmer undisturbed, partially covered, for about 40 minutes. Then strain the stock through a fine sieve set over a 6- to 8-quart casserole, pressing down hard on the fish trimmings and vegetables with a spoon to extract all their liquid before throwing them away.

Because the *bourride* should be served the moment it is done, plan on about 15 minutes to complete it from this point on. Bring the stock in the casserole to a boil over high heat and add the fish. Bring the liquid back to the boil, then reduce the heat to moderate and cook the fish fairly briskly, uncovered, for 4 to 8 minutes, or until the flesh is firm to the touch. Be careful not to overcook the fish, and have a large heated platter ready to receive them the moment they are done. Carefully remove the pieces with a slotted spoon and arrange them attractively, side by side, on the platter. Cover the top loosely with foil to keep the fish warm while you make the sauce.

Lower the heat under the casserole and remove about a cupful of the stock. Stirring with a whisk, slowly pour it into the *aïoli* and egg mixture. Then, in a slow stream, pour the now-fluid mixture back into the simmering casserole, stirring all the while. Then, with a wooden spoon, stir for 3 to 4 minutes, or until the soup is thick enough to coat the spoon lightly. Under no circumstances let the soup come to a boil or it will curdle irretrievably. Taste, and add as much salt, white pepper, and lemon juice as you think it needs. Quickly pour the soup into a large tureen and bring it to the table with the platter of fish, the sauceboat of *aïoli*, the *rouille* (if you have decided to include it), and the *croûtes*. Place a slice of toasted bread in the middle of individual soup plates, lay two pieces of the fish on top, and ladle the soup over them. Pass sauceboats of *aïoli* and *rouille* separately, each diner adding it to the *bourride* to taste. Or, if you prefer, serve the soup with the toasted bread separately as a first course, and then the fish on fresh plates accompanied, of course, by individual sauceboats of *aïoli* and *rouille*.

Skordalia with Almonds
makes about 1¼ cups

2 cups *aïoli* (page 11)
¼ cup fresh white bread crumbs,
    made from French or Italian
    bread, *trimmed of crusts and
    pulverized in a blender, or
    torn apart and shredded with
    a fork*
¼ cup blanched almonds, ground,
    *pulverized in a blender or
    ground in a Mouli grater*

Parsley (preferably the flat-leaf
    Italian type), *enough to
    make 3 tablespoons finely
    chopped*
Salt
Cayenne pepper
Fresh lemon juice

Spoon the *aïoli* into a small glass bowl and stir into it the bread crumbs, almonds, and parsley. Taste and season with as much salt, cayenne, and lemon juice as you think it needs. Serve with a large platter of cold vegetables, sliced ripe tomatoes, black Mediterranean olives, and black or white radishes. Covered with plastic wrap or aluminum foil, the *skordalia*, if refrigerated, will keep for as long as 2 days.

Skordalia with Potatoes
makes about 1 cup

1 pound baking potatoes, *peeled
    and cut into 2-inch pieces
    (about 2 cups)*
Peeled garlic cloves, *enough to
    make 1 tablespoon finely
    chopped*

1 teaspoon salt
2 egg yolks
½–¾ cup olive oil
2 tablespoons fresh, strained
    lemon juice
Freshly ground black pepper

Drop the potatoes into at least 3 quarts of rapidly boiling salted water and boil, uncovered, until they can be pierced easily with the tip of a small sharp knife. Don't overcook them or they will absorb too much water. Drain the potatoes at once in a sieve, return them to the pan, and shake them over moderate heat until they are dry and mealy. Force them through a potato ricer, then mash them to a smooth purée with an electric mixer or a fork. Cover the bowl with foil to keep the potatoes warm.

Pound the garlic and salt to a smooth paste with a mortar and pestle or mash it in a heavy bowl with the back of a large spoon. Then beat the paste into the warm potatoes and, still beating, add the egg yolks one at a time. Beating constantly, pour in the oil in a slow, thin stream, adding as much as you need to make a smooth, dense mixture that will hold its shape almost solidly in a spoon. Stir in the 2 tablespoons of lemon juice and a liberal amount of freshly ground black pepper. Taste for seasoning. It will probably need more salt and possibly more lemon juice. Serve the *skordalia* at room temperature with either the chilled vegetables suggested for *skordalia* with almonds or with a fried vegetable (such as eggplant) or poached or fried fish.

Soupe au Pistou   serves 10–12

THE BEANS

4 cups water
1 cup dry white beans (Great

Northern, marrow, or navy
beans)

THE PISTOU

Peeled garlic cloves, *enough to make 1 tablespoon finely chopped*
½ teaspoon salt
Fresh basil, *enough to make ½ cup (firmly packed), finely cut,*

or 5 tablespoons dried basil, *crumbled*
6 tablespoons tomato paste
Imported Parmesan cheese, *enough to make ½ cup grated*

THE SOUP

6 tablespoons olive oil
1 large onion, *to make 1 cup coarsely chopped*

2 pounds fresh, ripe tomatoes, *peeled and coarsely chopped (about 3 cups)*

Soupe au Pistou

3½ quarts water

1 tablespoon salt

2 medium carrots, *scraped, to make 1½ cups thinly sliced*

About ½ pound boiling potatoes, *to make 2 cups (½-inch cubes) diced*

About 1 pound leeks weighed with their tops, *to make 1 cup well-washed, coarsely chopped, including about 1 inch of the green tops*

½ cup celery leaves, *coarsely chopped*

2 cups fresh string (green) beans, *cut into 2-inch pieces*

2 cups unpeeled but scrubbed zucchini, *diced (½-inch cubes)*

½ cup uncooked vermicelli, *broken into 2-inch pieces*

⅛ teaspoon powdered saffron, or saffron threads, *pulverized with a mortar and pestle or with the back of a spoon*

Imported Parmesan cheese, *enough to make 1 cup grated*

The Beans:

The beans may be soaked in cold water overnight or softened more easily in the following fashion: bring 4 cups of water to a rapid boil in a 2- to 3-quart pot, add the beans, and boil briskly for 2 minutes. Turn off the heat and let the beans soak for an hour. Then bring the water to a boil again, lower the heat, and simmer slowly, partially covered, for about 1 to 1½ hours, or until the beans are quite tender but still intact. Drain the beans in a colander set over a bowl and save the bean stock.

The Pistou:

Pound the garlic with the salt to a smooth paste with a mortar and pestle, or mash it in a heavy bowl with the back of a large wooden spoon. Pound or mash in the basil about a tablespoon at a time, alternating it with the olive oil. When the mixture becomes a fairly smooth purée (do not use an electric blender—it will make the purée *too* smooth), stir in the tomato paste and the ½ cup of grated cheese. The *pistou* may be prepared at any time and put aside until the soup is ready.

The Soup:

Warm 6 tablespoons of olive oil over moderate heat in a 6- to 8-quart heavy casserole or soup pot. Add the onions and, stirring frequently, cook for about 8 minutes or until they become transparent and have just begun to color. (Don't let them really brown.) Stir in the tomatoes, raise the heat, and cook briskly for 2 or 3 minutes, stirring constantly before pouring in the 3½ quarts of water and the tablespoon of salt. Bring the casserole to a turbulent boil and drop in the carrots, potatoes, leeks, and celery leaves, lower the heat to moderate, and cook, uncovered, for 10 to 15 minutes, or until the carrots and potatoes are almost but not quite tender. Then add the string beans, zucchini, and vermicelli, and stir in the saffron. Continue to cook fairly rapidly, still uncovered, for another 10 minutes, or until the vegetables are tender but not too soft. Finally, add the drained beans (and as much of the reserved bean stock as you wish if the soup seems too thick) and simmer only long enough to heat the beans through. (At this point the soup may be put aside and reheated for a few minutes whenever you wish.)

Just before serving, ladle ½ cup of the soup stock into a small bowl. Beat into it about half the *pistou* and stir the mixture back into the soup. Taste for seasoning. Then pour the soup into a heated tureen and serve. Pass the remaining *pistou* and the cup of Parmesan cheese separately and suggest that each diner add them to the soup to taste.

Rouille

½ cup (packed down) fresh bread crumbs, *made in the blender, using French or Italian bread, or torn apart and shredded with a fork*

¼ cup cold water

6–8 large cloves garlic, *peeled and finely chopped*

2 teaspoons dried hot red-pepper flakes

½ teaspoon salt, preferably coarse salt

3–5 tablespoons olive oil

Soak the bread crumbs in the water for about 5 minutes, then squeeze them thoroughly dry. With a mortar and pestle or the back of a spoon in a heavy bowl, pound the garlic, pepper flakes, and salt to as fine a paste as you can. Slowly pound in the soaked bread crumbs, and when they are entirely incorporated, stir and pound in the olive oil, a tablespoon at a time. Use as much of the oil as you need to make a smooth paste that will just about hold its shape in a spoon. The *rouille* may now be used as it is. Or, if you have the time, rub it completely through a sieve with the back of a large spoon. Because of the *rouille's* fiery potency (in France, the red pepper with which it is made is called *piment enragé,* or "enraged pepper"), it should be used with extreme discretion. *Rouille* is characteristically served with French fish soups like *bouillabaisse* and *bourride,* but there is no reason why it couldn't be served with the Italian fish soup (which follows) as well.

Italian Fish Soup with Fried Saffron Croûtons

serves 8–10

THE FISH STOCK (The *Brodo*)

Fish heads and trimmings of the fish listed below with enough of the trimmings, if possible, to make about 3 pounds
3 cups cold water
1 cup dry white wine
1 medium onion, *peeled and thinly sliced*
2 leeks, the white parts and 2 inches of the green tops, *thoroughly washed to rid them of sand, then thinly sliced*

1 medium carrot, *scraped and thinly sliced*
2 celery tops with leaves
1 large bay leaf
1 pound fresh tomatoes, *coarsely chopped (about 1½ cups)*
2 large unpeeled garlic cloves, *crushed with the flat of a large knife or cleaver*
½ teaspoon dried thyme, *crumbled*

THE VEGETABLE MIXTURE (The *Soffrito*)

1 medium onion, *peeled*
1 large carrot, *scraped*
2 stalks celery
2 leeks, white parts only, *thoroughly washed*

4 large garlic cloves, *peeled*
6 tablespoons olive oil
1 pound fresh tomatoes, *peeled, seeded, and finely chopped (about 1½ cups) (page 109)*

Italian Fish Soup with Fried Saffron Croûtons

1 teaspoon dried oregano, *crum-bled*

2 teaspoons salt

Freshly ground black pepper

⅛ teaspoon powered saffron

THE FISH

A mixture of firm-fleshed fish such as haddock, cod, snapper, mackerel, halibut, perch, pollack, among others, *scaled, gutted, heads removed and*

the fish cut crosswise into 3-inch-wide chunks; the total weight of the fish after cleaning should be about 5 pounds

THE FRIED BREAD

10–12 one-inch-thick slices of French or Italian bread, *fried with the oil and saffron as described on page 249*

Flat-leaf parsley, *enough to make 2 tablespoons finely chopped*

The Fish Stock:

For the fish stock, or *brodo* as the Italians call it, combine in a 4- to 6-quart enamel or stainless-steel saucepan, the well-washed fish heads and trimmings, the water, wine, sliced onion, leeks, carrot, and the celery tops, bay leaf, tomatoes, garlic, and thyme. Bring to a boil over high heat, skim the surface of all foam and scum, and lower the heat. Partially cover the pan and simmer undisturbed for about 40 minutes. Then strain the broth through a fine sieve set over a deep bowl, pressing down hard on the fish trimmings and vegetables with the back of a spoon to extract all their liquid before throwing them away.

The Vegetable Mixture:

Chop the onion, carrot, celery, leeks, and garlic together as finely as you can with a large sharp knife. Or, less traditionally, first chop the vegetables separately, and then together. Heat the 6 tablespoons of olive oil in an 8-quart casserole (the size of the casserole is important; the fish which will be added later should not be crowded) over moderate heat, and add the mixture of chopped vegetables, called the *soffrito*. Cook for about 8 minutes, stirring occasionally, until the vegetables are soft but not brown. Then add the tomatoes and oregano and bring the *soffrito* to a boil over high heat. Stirring constantly, cook briskly for about 3 minutes, or until the tomato juices have completely evaporated and the *soffrito* is thick enough to hold its shape in a spoon. Pour in the fish stock and add the 2 teaspoons of salt, a liberal grinding of black pepper and the saffron. Bring to a boil, lower the heat, and simmer, partially covered, for about 10 minutes. Taste for seasoning and either cool and refrigerate until ready to use or proceed at once to cook the fish.

The Fish:

Because the *zuppe de pesce* should, ideally, be served the moment it is done, plan on 15 to 20 minutes from this point to complete the cooking. Bring the soup to a boil and drop in the fish, arranging them so that each piece is well covered with the broth. When the soup boils again, reduce the heat to moderate, half cover the casserole, and cook for 10 to 15 minutes, or until the fish turns opaque and is firm to the touch. Do not overcook. If smaller pieces appear to be done before larger ones, simply remove them with a slotted spoon from the casserole to a plate and then return them to the soup when the larger pieces are done. In any case, handle the pieces of fish gently; they break and fall apart easily.

Serve the fish soup directly from the casserole; ladle the soup over the fried bread into the deep, individual soup plates, and place a piece of fish on top. Or you may, if you like, arrange the fish on a large platter, pour the soup into a tureen and serve it separately over the fried bread. In either case, sprinkle the soup and fish with a little chopped flat-leaf parsley.

Soupe à l'Ail

serves 6

Peeled garlic cloves, *enough to make ½ cup*
2 tablespoons butter
4 tablespoons olive oil: *1 table-*

spoon to simmer the garlic, and the rest for the thickening mixture
4 cups chicken stock, fresh or

Soupe à l'Ail

canned (the French tradi-
tionally use water, but the
stock, to my mind, gives the
soup more character)
3 egg yolks
½ teaspoon salt
⅛ teaspoon cayenne pepper

A few gratings of whole nutmeg
6 slices (½-inch thick) of French
or Italian bread, *lightly
toasted*
Parsley, *enough to make 1 tablespoon finely chopped*

The simplest way to peel the garlic cloves without bruising them (and they must remain intact) is to drop them into a pan of boiling water, let them cook for a minute, then drain them in a sieve. Run cold water over them to cool, and slip off their skins with the aid of a small sharp knife.

Over low heat, melt the 2 tablespoons of butter with the 1 tablespoon of olive oil in a 2-quart enamel or stainless-steel saucepan. Drop in the garlic and cook over low heat for about 15 minutes, turning the cloves frequently with a wooden spoon; they must not brown. Pour in the chicken stock (or water, if you prefer), raise the heat, and bring it to a boil. Then half cover the pan, lower the heat, and simmer the soup undisturbed for about 20 minutes.

Meanwhile, in a small bowl, beat the egg yolks with a whisk or rotary beater for 2 or 3 minutes, or until they thicken. Pour in the remaining 3 tablespoons of olive oil, ½ teaspoon at a time, beating until the mixture becomes a dense mayonnaise. Now slowly stir into the mayonnaise 2 or 3 tablespoons of the simmering soup, and return this mixture in a slow stream and stirring continuously to the rest of the soup. Heat almost to the boiling point (beyond it, the soup will almost surely curdle), then pour the entire contents of the saucepan, garlic, and all into a sieve set over a heated tureen. With the back of a wooden spoon, rub and mash the garlic through the sieve into the soup. Briskly stir in the salt, cayenne, and freshly grated nutmeg, and continue to stir until the garlic purée and the soup are thoroughly amalgamated. Taste for seasoning. Ladle into soup plates over the rounds of bread and serve, sprinkled with a little chopped parsley.

Roast Chicken Béarnaise   *serves 4*

6 cups water
Unpeeled garlic cloves, *enough to make 1 cup*
8 tablespoons butter (¼ pound, 1 stick), *softened*
1 teaspoon dried rosemary, *crumbled*
Salt
Freshly ground black pepper

A 4-pound roasting chicken
8 tablespoons olive oil
1 large onion, *peeled and thickly sliced*
1 large carrot, *scraped and cut into 1-inch pieces*
1 cup chicken stock, fresh or canned

Bring 6 cups of water to a boil in a 2-quart saucepan, drop in the unpeeled garlic cloves, and boil briskly for 10 minutes, or until a clove, pressed gently between the fingers, yields ever so slightly. Drain at once in a colander and run cold water over the garlic to cool it quickly. Slip off the skins with the aid of a small sharp knife and try not to bruise or cut into the cloves themselves. Cream the softened butter, beating and mashing it against the sides of a bowl with a large spoon until it is smooth and fluffy. Beat in the crumbled rosemary, salt and pepper to taste, and gently fold the mixture into the garlic cloves, turning them about until they glisten with the herbed butter. Then stuff them into the cavity of the chicken and lace or sew up the openings securely. Truss the chicken with kitchen cord and, with a pastry brush, coat the bird's skin thoroughly with 2 tablespoons of the olive oil. Reserve the remaining oil for basting.

Preheat the oven to 475 degrees.

Choose a shallow roasting pan just large enough to hold the bird comfortably. Place the chicken on its side on a rack set in the middle of the pan and roast undisturbed for about 10 minutes, brushing the chicken with 1 tablespoon of the remaining olive oil after the first 5 minutes.

Turn the chicken on its other side and roast 10 minutes longer, again brushing with olive oil as before. Finally, turn the chicken on its back, baste it with the remaining oil and sprinkle liberally with salt.

Scatter the onions and carrots over the bottom of the pan and turn the oven down to 375 degrees. Roast the chicken on its back for about 1 hour longer, basting it every 15 minutes or so with pan juices. Test the chicken for doneness by piercing the fleshy part of the thigh with the point of a small sharp knife. The juice that trickles out should be pale yellow; if it is tinged with pink, roast the bird about 5 or 10 minutes longer. Transfer the chicken to a carving board and let it rest for 8 minutes or so for easier sectioning and carving.

Meanwhile, pour the cup of stock into the roasting pan and bring to a boil over high heat, scraping into it all the brown sediment clinging to the bottom of the pan. Let it boil briskly until its flavor is intense and definite. Skim off and discard as much of the surface fat as you can; then strain the sauce into a sauceboat and serve with the chicken.

NOTE: After carving the chicken, serve the garlic cloves as a vegetable, or, in the kitchen, mash it to a purée with the back of a spoon and spread it on rounds of lightly toasted French bread. Or, mash the garlic, beat it into the reduced and strained pan juices and serve it as a sauce for the chicken.

Sautéed Chicken Dauphinoise   *serves 4*

Peeled garlic cloves, *enough to make ½ cup*
A 2½- to 3-pound chicken, *cut into 4 to 6 serving pieces*
Salt
Freshly ground black pepper
2 tablespoons butter
3–4 tablespoons olive oil
Fresh rosemary, *enough to make*
1 tablespoon *finely cut,* or 1 teaspoon dried rosemary, *crumbled*
1 bay leaf
Parsley (preferably the flat-leaf Italian type), *to make 1 tablespoon, finely chopped*
Fresh lemon juice
Crisp watercress

The simplest way to peel the garlic cloves without bruising them (and they must remain intact) is to drop them into a pan of boiling water, let them cook for a minute, then drain them in a sieve. Run cold water over them to cool, and slip off their skins with the aid of a small sharp knife.

Sautéed Chicken Dauphinoise

Pat the chicken pieces dry with paper toweling (they won't brown well if they are damp), and sprinkle them liberally with salt and a few grindings of black pepper. Choose a 10-inch heavy frying pan or sauté pan that has a tightly fitting cover, and in it melt the butter with 3 tablespoons of the olive oil over high heat. When the butter begins to turn ever so slightly brown, add the chicken pieces, skin-side down. Regulate the heat so that they brown fairly rapidly without burning. Turn them with tongs and brown the other sides for a somewhat shorter period, adding a little more oil to the pan if necessary.

Push the chicken to the side of the pan and add all the garlic cloves. Sprinkle the cloves with the rosemary and turn them about in the hot oil for a moment or two, but don't let them brown. Then, with a bulb baster or large spoon, remove all but a thin film of oil from the bottom of the pan and arrange the chicken pieces, skin-side up, over the garlic. Add the bay leaf, cover the pan tightly and cook the chicken over the lowest possible heat for 30 to 40 minutes. Baste well with the oil every 10 minutes or so—after a while, enough liquid will collect in the pan so that you can baste the chicken with its own juices. Test the chicken for doneness by piercing the fleshy part of the leg or thigh with the point of a small sharp knife. The juice that trickles out should be a light yellow. If it is still pink, cover the chicken and cook a few minutes longer, but be careful not to overcook it.

To serve, arrange the chicken on a large heated platter, and if you have the courage, scatter the garlic cloves over the chicken and moisten them with the pan juices. Sprinkle with the chopped parsley. As an alternative, mash the cooked garlic into the pan juices, beat with a whisk and season the sauce lightly with a little extra salt, pepper and a few drops of lemon juice. Then pour it over the chicken and sprinkle with parsley. Or, if you must, simply scoop out the garlic cloves with a slotted spoon and throw them away. Add the chopped parsley to the juices remaining in the pan, season with a little salt, pepper, and lemon juice, and pour over the chicken. In any case, surround the chicken with watercress before serving.

Bagna Cauda with Cream and White Truffles

makes about 1 cup

THE VEGETABLES

8–12 scallions, including 2 inches of the green tops, *all trimmed to the same length*

2–3 carrots, *scraped and cut into matchlike strips about 2 inches long*

1 green and 1 red pepper, *seeded, deribbed, and cut into matchlike strips about 2 inches long*

8–12 celery stalks, *cut into matchlike strips about 2 inches long*

A small head of raw cauliflower, *broken into flowerets*

8–12 well-washed black, red, or white radishes

2 cucumbers, *peeled, seeded, and cut into matchlike strips*

THE BAGNA CAUDA

2 cups heavy cream

4 tablespoons (½ stick) unsalted butter, *cut in ¼-inch pieces*

Peeled garlic cloves, *enough to make 2 teaspoons finely chopped*

8–10 canned flat anchovy fillets,

drained, rinsed in cold water, and finely chopped (about 1 tablespoon)

⅛ teaspoon cayenne pepper

1 large canned white truffle, *drained and finely chopped*

The Vegetables:

A few hours before you plan to serve them, prepare the vegetables and soak them in a large bowl of ice water for at least an hour. When they are cold and crisp, drain and pat them thoroughly dry with paper toweling. Arrange them decoratively on a large attractive platter, cover with plastic wrap, and refrigerate until ready to serve.

The Bagna Cauda:

Pour the cream into a 6- to 8-inch enamel or stainless-steel skillet, bring it to a rapid boil, uncovered, until the cream has thickened heavily and reduced to about 1 cup. This may take up to 15 minutes, and it is a wise precaution to stir constantly as it begins to thicken and to turn down the heat as the cream reaches the appropriate amount lest it burn. Set it aside.

In a 2-cup saucepan or heatproof earthenware pot, melt the butter over the lowest possible heat, add the garlic, and simmer for about 5 minutes, lifting the pan from the heat and returning it every few minutes in order to interrupt the simmering and prevent the garlic from browning. Stir in the anchovies and simmer 2 or 3 minutes, mashing them into the butter with the back of a fork. Now gradually stir in the reduced cream, the cayenne and chopped truffle. Heat almost to the boiling point, stirring constantly, then taste for seasoning. Keep the *bagna cauda* hot (without letting it boil) over an alchohol burner, or lacking that, a candle warmer or even an electric hot tray, and pass the platter of vegetables for dipping. Other raw (or, for that matter, cooked) vegetables than the ones suggested above may be used. And try dipping Italian bread sticks into the *bagna cauda* too.

NOTE: Should you wish to make the *bagna cauda* earlier, cool it to room temperature and refrigerate it covered with plastic wrap. It may separate after a few hours. All you need do then before reheating it is to beat it vigorously with a whisk to recombine it.

Bagna Cauda with Butter and Olive Oil

makes about 1 cup

¼ pound unsalted butter, *cut into ¼-inch pieces*
½ cup olive oil
Peeled garlic cloves, *to make 1 tablespoon finely chopped*

8–10 anchovy fillets, *drained and finely chopped (about 1 tablespoon)*
2 or more canned white truffles, *drained and finely chopped*

OPTIONAL

½ teaspoon fresh lemon juice
Flat-leaf parsley, *enough to make 1 tablespoon finely chopped*

Freshly ground black pepper

This *bagna cauda* is an earthier, lustier dipping sauce than the one made with cream. It is really a matter of taste which of the two you prefer.

In a heavy casserole or earthenware pot, melt the butter with the olive oil over the lowest possible heat and skim off the foam with a large spoon as it rises to the surface. Add the garlic and simmer for about 5 minutes, lifting the pan from the heat and returning it every few minutes to prevent the garlic from browning. Stir in the anchovies and simmer for 2 or 3 minutes longer, mashing them into the mixture with the back of a fork, then stir in the truffles if you have decided to use them. Traditionally, the *bagna cauda* is now ready to serve in the same manner and with the same vegetables as described in the recipe for *bagna cauda* with cream. However, you may depart from tradition, as I occasionally do, and add the optional lemon juice, parsley, and a few grindings of black pepper for a new and piquant note.

Osso Buco   *serves 4–6*

1 medium onion, *peeled*
1 medium carrot, *scraped*
1 leek, the white part and 2 inches of the green stem, *thoroughly washed to rid them of sand*
2 celery stalks
2 large garlic cloves, *peeled*
3 tablespoons butter
1 pound ripe tomatoes, *peeled, seeded tomatoes, and finely chopped* (page 109), or use 1½ cups *drained and finely chopped* canned tomatoes
1 tablespoon fresh basil, *finely cut,* or 1 teaspoon dried basil, *crumbled*
4–5 pounds meaty veal shanks, *sawed into 6 to 8 pieces, each about 3 inches long, and tied with string around their circumference to hold the meat in place*
1 tablespoon salt
Freshly ground black pepper
Flour
4–8 tablespoons olive oil
½ cup dry white wine
½–1 cup beef stock, fresh or canned
1 paper-thin strip lemon peel, about 2 inches long and ½ inch wide
A bouquet consisting of 6 sprigs parsley and 1 bay leaf, *tied together with string*

Osso Buco

GREMOLATA

Flat-leaf parsley, *enough to make 4 tablespoons finely cut*

Lemon peel, *enough to make 1 tablespoon finely chopped: the peel should be removed with a swivel-bladed peeler and chopped as described on page 154*

Orange peel, *enough to make 2 teaspoons finely chopped: the peel removed as described for the lemon above*

Peeled garlic cloves, *enough to make 1 tablespoon finely chopped*

With a large sharp knife, chop the onion, carrot, leek, celery, and garlic together as finely as you can. (Or, if less traditionally, first chop the vegetables separately and then together.) This *soffrito,* as the Italians call it, should, when packed down, come to about a cupful; if it is noticeably less, add a chopped small onion and celery stalk. Choose a deep, heavy casserole just about large enough to hold the upright pieces of veal side by side snugly. In it, melt the butter over moderate heat and add the *soffrito.* Stirring occasionally, cook for about 8 minutes until the vegetables are soft but not brown. Then add the tomatoes and basil and bring to a boil over high heat. Stirring constantly, cook briskly for about 3 minutes, or until the tomato juices have completely evaporated and the *soffrito* is thick enough to hold its shape in a spoon. Set the casserole aside, off the heat, while you brown the veal.

Sprinkle the shanks evenly with the tablespoon of salt. Grind a discreet amount of black pepper over each shank, coat each one thoroughly with flour, then shake vigorously to remove any excess. Heat 4 tablespoons of oil in a heavy 8- to 10-inch frying pan set over high heat. When the oil almost reaches the smoking point, add 3 or 4 pieces of the veal at a time. Regulate the heat so that the meat browns fairly quickly but deeply on all sides without burning. Add more of the oil if the pan seems too dry at any point. As each piece reaches a rich brown color, transfer it to the casserole, placing it upright on the *soffrito* to prevent its marrow (for most Italians, really the whole point of the dish) from falling out. Fry the remaining veal in similar batches and when all the pieces are brown and reposing in the casserole, pour off and discard most of the oil from the frying pan and add the wine. Bring it to a boil over high heat, meanwhile scraping into it all the brown sediment clinging to the bottom of the pan. Continue to boil the wine until it has almost completely cooked away, then stir in ½ cup of stock. Pour the liquid over the meat in the casserole, add the lemon peel and the bouquet of parsley and bay leaf, and bring to a boil over high heat. Turn the heat to its lowest point, cover the casserole tightly (use foil to reinforce the cover if it doesn't fit securely) and simmer the veal slowly for about an hour until the meat is very tender and almost but not quite falling away from the bones. If at any point during this period the liquid in the casserole seems to be cooking away, add the remaining stock by the tablespoon.

While the veal is simmering, make the *gremolata* by combining the parsley, chopped lemon and orange peels, and the garlic in a small bowl. Toss together lightly with a spoon, cover the bowl with plastic wrap and set aside.

To serve, carefully transfer the *osso buco* from the casserole to a large platter, making sure that the marrow doesn't fall out in transit and cover with foil to keep the meat warm. Taste the sauce. If it seems thin or lacking in flavor, bring it to a rapid boil over high heat and continue to boil, uncovered, until the sauce thickens slightly and reaches the intensity of flavor you like. Pour it over the *osso buco* and sprinkle the *gremolata* evenly over the top. Or if you like, serve the *gremolata* separately and suggest that it be added to the *osso buco* to each diner's taste.

cooking with cheese

cookiNq wiTh chEESE

Of all the foods created by man, cheese is surely the oldest. References to it reach as far back as the Old Testament, and if we can't with certainty trace its genesis any further, we can at least assume that wherever man began to drink the milk of domesticated grazing animals, he soon learned to make cheese. For all cheese is made of milk, be it the milk of cows, sheep, goats, horses, buffaloes, camels, reindeer, or llamas.

Hundreds of varieties of cheese are produced throughout the world today, and all of them, theoretically at least, can be cooked. Cooking cheese is essentially a matter of melting it to one degree or another; a cheese that couldn't be melted would be a singular cheese indeed.

Some cheeses are more suitable for cooking than others. Their usefulness is determined by how easily and smoothly they melt, how much heat they can tolerate, how much flavor and character they retain, and how well they combine with other foods. Although there are a number of cheeses that qualify satisfactorily when put to these tests, the one that behaves most predictably, perhaps, is Parmesan.

For more than eight hundred years Parmesan has dominated Italian cooking, and with good reason. No matter to what degree of heat it is subjected, Parmesan seldoms turns stringy, and its flavor remains constant and incomparable. Even when it isn't cooked at all but simply sprinkled over hot pasta or minestrone, it dissolves almost instantly without becoming rubbery, or *gommoso*, as I have heard the Italians so contemptuously and graphically describe the performance of inferior cooking cheese.

But what the Italians mean by Parmesan is a far cry from the cheese most of us in the United States call by that name. Not that a fine

Parmesan can't be bought here. It can, if you know what to look for. Unfortunately, the name Parmesan is not protected by law in the United States as are the names of such imported products as Roquefort cheese and Cognac. Trustingly asking for Parmesan by name, therefore, isn't much help. In fact, it often compounds the difficulty. Shops are full of bottled and packaged domestic cheese products labeled Parmesan, Parmesan-Romano, Italian-Style Parmesan, and the like, and most of them have little to do with the real thing. To ensure getting an authentic Parmesan, find a dealer you can trust and do as I do. Examine on the spot the cheese you want to buy. Learn to recognize the characteristic rind, grain, color, and taste. All true Parmesan is enclosed in a smoky black rind and the cheese itself is a pale golden yellow, delicately honeycombed and closely grained. Indeed, it is because the graining is so typical and characteristic that Italians call their Parmesans *grana,* or grainlike. Each has a second name—Reggiano, Parmigiana, Lodigiana, and others—to indicate its place of origin.

The two Parmesans you are most likely to find on sale in the United States are Grana Padano and Parmigiano-Reggiano; there are others equally authentic. But knowing the best names is not as much help as it might be; often the lettering stenciled on the rind is cut away as the cheese is sectioned for sale.

For all cured cheeses used in cooking, age is an important consideration, and Parmesan is no exception. The older the cheese, the better its flavor, and because old Parmesan is comparatively rare, its price, like that of fine Cognac, increases in direct proportion to its years. But even young Parmesan (that is, a cheese about two years old) is distinguished by a characteristic taste unlike that of any other cheese; aromatic and earthy, and at the same time piquant and sweet. Once you have tasted it, no other so-called Parmesan will do.

There are, of course, many other cheeses used in Italy for cooking; a few of the firmer varieties resemble Parmesan to some degree and, in the United States at least, are often mistaken for it. Romano, the most popular, has the black rind and rocky texture of Parmesan, but there the resemblance ends. Made from ewe's milk rather than cow's milk, Romano, or Pecorino Romano to give it its proper name, is a sharp, salty, and often, when young, a rather sullen cheese. It is used extensively by Southern Italians who prefer it to Parmesan to season their tomato-sauced pasta dishes. Northern Italian cooks, if they use it at all, usually temper its bite by combining it with a large proportion of Parmesan.

For different reasons entirely, the French also use Parmesan in conjunction with other cheeses, notably Switzerland cheese and their own Gruyère. French chefs add it to their cheese-flavored cream sauce *mornay*, to give it the lift it so often needs, and they long ago discovered that apart from its extraordinary seasoning powers, Parmesan cheese had other powers as well. It made their lighter-than-air cheese soufflés even lighter (as you will see when you make my crabmeat and Parmesan cheese soufflé on page 224), their crisp *beignets* crisper, and it gave their celebrated gratinéed dishes a finer crust and better flavor than buttered bread crumbs or grated Gruyère alone ever did. And Parmesan, the most Italian of Italian cheeses, is surely as necessary an accompaniment to French onion soup as it is to pasta. With infallible taste as always, French cooks know precisely what they are doing; Gruyère and Parmesan are unquestionably the greatest cooking cheeses in the world.

The Swiss are as proud of their Switzerland cheese as the Italians are of their Parmesan. (The authentic cheese is always called Switzerland cheese, you might note, not Swiss cheese.) Although the cheeses are almost totally different, they somehow complement each other. It is as if the delicate, curiously sweet Switzerlands were the feminine counterparts of the rugged, masculine Parmesans. And this may well be the reason they get on so well. In the various dishes in which they are used together—and not by any means in the French cuisine alone— they create an impressive unity in which the flavor of each supports the other.

Switzerland cheese cooked alone is something else again. Capricious and quixotic, it can behave more unpredictably than any other cheese; in the classic Swiss fondue it can, in fact, be positively treacherous. Cooking a Swiss fondue is essentially a simple affair: grated Switzerland cheese mixed with a little flour or cornstarch, is tossed by the handful into barely simmering wine, stirred with a fork to dissolve it, seasoned with salt, pepper, and a jigger or two of Kirsch and used as a sauce for dunking small pieces of bread. We are constantly being assured by the Swiss that there is nothing to it. And indeed there isn't— when it works. But when it doesn't and the cheese, without warning, turns into a granitic mass which can neither be stirred, dissolved again, nor eaten in any form, exasperated cooks seriously begin to question either their technique or the quality of the cheese. As it turns out, both can be at fault and the only way to cope with the problem is to find out more about the singular nature of Switzerland cheeses and the proper way to cook with them. Few Americans appear to be aware of the many types of Switzerland cheese available to them in the United States. Generally, they are content to ask for "a pound of Swiss" and let it go at that, little realizing that merely calling a cheese Swiss means nothing except, perhaps, that it is a cheese with holes.

It is the fate of great cheeses to be copied everywhere and usually badly. Ohio and Wisconsin cheesemakers imitate Switzerland cheese better than most—but only when they make it in wheels and by traditional Swiss methods. The Swiss reluctantly admit that these cheeses, when you can find them, are superb and are almost indistinguishable from a true Switzerland. But for the most part, other Swiss cheese imitations are pressed into rindless blocks; whether they are manufactured in the United States, Finland, or Denmark, they are seldom worth the eating or the cooking.

Fortunately, because its name is stenciled all over its rind, true Switzerland cheese is easily and precisely identifiable. After you have come that far, discovering the three varieties imported here in significant quantities is only a few steps farther. Among knowing cooks, each cheese has its partisans, and it is really a matter of taste which of the three you prefer.

Emmenthal, the most popular, has the largest eyes, ranging from one to one and a half inches in diameter. Its flavor has been rather fancifully compared to that of the walnut, but nutty or not, Emmenthal has a distinct sweetness that distinguishes it from Gruyère, a cheese with somewhat more tartness and bite and the one I really prefer. Gruyères of both the French and Swiss types (French Gruyère, by the way, is excellent) have holes approximately the size of peas. Appenzell, the last of this noble trinity, has almost imperceptible holes (cheese dealers call the cheese "blind") and is the most intensely flavored of the three. For this reason, Appenzell is seldom used in cooking and, when it is, only in small amounts to fortify the flavor of blander cheeses.

The blandness of a cheese, at least of the great ones like Switzerland cheese and Parmesan, is determined, more often than not, by its youth. But distressingly I note that generally the youngest Emmenthals and Gruyères are shipped to the United States simply because misinformed Swiss exporters I have been told are under the illusion that we prefer them that way. Perhaps a few of us do favor these blander cheeses and more is the pity; but flavor apart, cooks should remember that young Switzerland cheeses don't melt as well as older ones. They are, in fact, to a very large degree responsible for the disasters that occur when we make our fondues. The Swiss themselves always shop for the oldest cheeses they can find for their fondues and even then put the cheese aside to age a while longer.

But the Swiss tell me (evidently they are not entirely immune to fondue disasters either) that apart from the condition of the cheese, there can be another reason for failure. They maintain that only wines high in acid (Swiss mountain whites like Fendant or Dézaley, a French Muscadet, or a California Johannisberg Riesling among others) will ensure a perfect fondue. For reasons they are unable to explain, the excess acid in the wine supposedly prevents the cheese (whatever its age) from separating into rubbery strands when it melts. As added insurance against a failure, they will often add a tablespoon of fresh lemon juice (or more, if the cheese is very young) to the most acid of wines to increase its acidity further. The taste of lemon juice, they say, is never apparent in the finished fondue. I don't entirely agree. I almost always make my fondues successfully without it unless, as has happened on occasion, I can't find the properly aged cheese I want. In my recipe for the classic fondue Neuchâteloise on page 44 I leave the inclusion of lemon juice entirely up to you.

No such problem confronts the cook with a more reliable version, an Italian fondue made with milk and eggs rather than wine. Called a *fonduta,* it is a dish of incomparable elegance especially as it is served in Italy during the truffle season, the golden, melted cheese covered with thin slices of fresh white truffle and surrounded with triangles of hot buttered toast. The fontina cheese with which it is made is not unlike Swiss Gruyère, but it is creamier, richer, and has superior melting powers. Fontina is at its best somewhat aged, at least for cooking purposes. Again, like many great cheeses, it has its imitators, and I find almost all of them bad. And the worst, unfortunately, is also called fontina. The only way to make certain of getting a good fontina is to ask for it by its proper name, fontina d'Aosta. Make sure its rind is a light, bright brown, not red, and the cheese itself soft and a delicate ivory rather than hard and yellow.

Other cuisines have their fondues too, and surprisingly good ones are made in England. With their typical no-nonsense attitude, English cooks simply grate one or a mixture of their superb aged cheeses like Cheddar, Caerphilly, Cheshire, or Dunlop into a pan of hot buttered ale or beer (or milk, if the cook is a teetotaler), melt it to a thick cream, season it highly, and without any more ado serve it over hot buttered toast. For reasons that elude me and even the English, whether the dish will be called an English monkey, a Welsh rabbit, or a golden buck will depend upon the cook's having added to it, at any point, bread crumbs, flour, eggs, or cream. But satisfying as these cheese dishes can be, they cannot compare in refinement with their Swiss, French, or Italian counterparts. Nevertheless, they are simple, rough, and hearty and have a certain charm when served without pretension, on family or other informal occasions. And the same might be said of the English cheese sausage recipe I have given you on page 58.

The Italians, with their love of the unexpected, have devised a number of cheese dishes so surprising and delightful they might almost be described as witty. To make them, cheese is either hidden in bread, wrapped in pasta, or stuffed into meat or chicken breasts (or, for that matter, concealed in almost anything edible that will hold it); the combination package is then cooked until the cheese melts.

One of the most successful and spectacular of these dishes is a Roman specialty called *spiedino alla romana*. Small squares of bread are intersected with slices of mozzarella (and sometimes paper-thin slices of prosciutto as well), soaked in a batter and cautiously reshaped into what appears to be a solid loaf of bread. Rolled in bread crumbs, threaded on a long *spiedino*, or skewer, the loaf is fried in olive oil until a thick outer crust is formed, enclosing the now almost-liquid cheese within it.

There is a recipe for *spiedino alla romana* in an earlier book of mine, *Michael Field's Cooking School*. Needless to say many other versions of cheese *spiedini* exist, some of which are considerably less bothersome to make than the Roman variety. Try the simple Swiss-Italian one on page 48 of this book. I discovered this enchanting dish recently in a small restaurant in Lugano and my re-creation of it can be put together in a matter of minutes.

A less sophisticated version of this dish is made by Sicilians and called, charmingly enough, *mozzarella in carrozza*, or literally mozzarella in a carriage. Somewhat the same technique as for the *spiedino* is used to make it, the only difference being that the cheese enclosed in bread is fried in the form of individual sandwiches instead of a loaf. Because the flavor of the mozzarella is so bland, these dishes are often accompanied by a highly seasoned anchovy-butter sauce. But with a sauce or without it, when either of these bread-and-cheese concoctions makes its appearance the effect is always dramatic.

Equally dramatic but considerably more involved are the Italian dishes of stuffed meat or chicken. One, for example, requires that veal be pounded to almost transparent thinness and cut into squares approximately four inches by four. Each slice is then covered with a smaller square of cheese, usually mozzarella, and topped with another square of veal. The plump little packages—or "pillows of veal," as they are called—are hermetically sealed by pounding the thin outer edges of the meat together with a mallet. They are then dusted with flour and sautéed in some butter and oil until the meat is done and the cheese completely melted.

There are variants of this dish by the dozen, some including ham and others mushrooms. A few are considerably less demanding. Particularly attractive and simple is the *petti di pollo alla bolognese* on page 50.

Although we consume prodigious quantities of mozzarella with our versions of pizza, veal parmigiana, eggplant parmigiana, and the like, this oddly shaped little cheese is not as well understood as it should be by most American cooks. At its best and freshest (ideally, mozzarella is meant, like all fresh cheeses, to be eaten the day it is made) it bears little resemblance either in texture or flavor to the rubbery, factory-made mozzarellas and so-called pizza cheeses now available everywhere. Regrettably, we can't possibly duplicate the mozzarella the Italians still sometimes make in Italy with buffalo milk as they have done for centuries, but many skillful cheesemakers can now produce almost identical cheeses here with cow's milk.

Large specialty stores or small grocery stores in Italian neighborhoods are likely to have these fresh, moist mozzarellas delivered to them every day and, because of their extraordinary delicacy and superior melting quality, the fresh cheeses are worth making a determined effort to find. Should there be any mozzarella left over after you have cooked with it, the cheese is delicious eaten as the Italians do, in strips, with salt, freshly ground black pepper, unsalted butter, and crusty bread.

When you can't find fresh mozzarella, other semi-soft Italian cheeses do quite well as substitutes and, in fact, sometimes better. Among the best are Bel Paese, fontina, and the less well known taleggio. Because they are rich, buttery cheeses with not only superior melting qualities but distinctive flavor as well, they are especially useful in bland dishes which often need a little more character than even a good mozzarella can give them. And if the imported taleggios and fontinas are sometimes difficult to come by, it might be reassuring to note that the domestic Bel Paeses made in Wisconsin are almost as good as those imported from Italy.

Native American cheeses are, with a few notable exceptions, too mass and mechanically produced to achieve much distinction for cooking—although the so-called processed cheeses, whatever their limitations in flavor, have extraordinarily predictable and reliable melting qualities. However, we do have in the United States fine, fresh country cheeses—cottage cheese, farmer cheese, pot cheese, cream cheese, and the domestic version we make of Italian ricotta. Most of these cheeses, like ricotta, have their parallels in fresh country cheeses of other countries, and like them are used in a variety of dishes from the rustic simplicities of cottage-cheese pancakes to the sublime glories of cheesecake.

Cheesecake appears insistently enough throughout culinary history to give it a universality shared by no other cheese dish. We know that the ancient Greeks baked and ate it, because their poets sang of it passionately. In *The Deipnosophists*, an anthology written about A.D. 230 by Athenaeus, a whole section is devoted to cheesecakes, and the actual recipes have a surprising quality of contemporaneity. Although present-day cooks don't go so far as molding their cheesecakes in the shape of a woman's breast as described by Athenaeus, they have created some fine, if more conventional, cheesecakes of their own. Most cuisines today have their specialties, and whether one prefers the smooth cheesecakes of the Americans, the elaborate pot cheese *pashkas* of the Russians, the unsweetened *gougères* of the French, or the generally over-sweet ricotta pies and cheesecakes of the Italians is, of course, a matter of taste. My friend, the gifted chef John W. Clancy, has, to my mind, devised the best American one of them all. You will find the recipe for his cheesecake on page 54.

Cheesecakes are on the whole really no more difficult to make than other cakes and cookbooks, good and bad, give recipes for them by the dozen. But cheese being what it is, baking a cheesecake—whether it is

John Clancy's or another recipe—should be approached warily, and more than usual attention paid to temperatures, baking times, and the like.

You will have no such technical difficulties when you make a Sicilian cheesecake, *cassata*, which isn't baked at all and which I describe in detail, recipe and all, in *Michael Field's Cooking School*. With typical Italian ingenuity the *cassata*, or literally box, is constructed by putting together thinly sliced layers of sponge or pound cake, spreading them first with ricotta, the cheese flavored with bits of chocolate and chopped candied fruit, and the cake doused with liqueurs. Thoroughly masked with chocolate or vanilla icing, the cake—to all intents and purposes now a solid, uncut loaf—is then allowed to "ripen," as Italians describe it, for at least a day. When the *cassata* is sliced, the moist cake and creamy cheese will have merged to form a texture not quite cake and not quite cheese but an extraordinary mélange of both.

It is upon the success of such artful culinary transformations that good cooking with cheese depends. Think of all the cheeses we can so satisfyingly and simply eat—with bread, a bottle of wine, with fruit. Unless you as a cook can justify changing the cheese from its original form to another, there seems to me little reason to cook it at all.

Cheese Beignets or Fritters *serves 4–6*

4 tablespoons (½ stick) butter, *cut into small pieces*
¾ cup water
¾ cup flour
3 large eggs, not extra-large or jumbo
1 teaspoon salt
1 teaspoon prepared mustard, preferably the French Dijon type

Switzerland cheese, preferably Gruyère, *enough to make ½ cup coarsely grated*
Imported Parmesan cheese, *enough to make ½ cup grated: ⅓ cup for the beignet batter and the rest for sprinkling over the finished beignets*
Vegetable oil or melted shortening for deep frying

Combine the butter and the water in a 1- to 2-quart enamel or stainless-steel saucepan. Over high heat, bring the water to a turbulent boil, stirring constantly until the butter is completely melted. Remove the pan from the heat and immediately dump in all at once the ¾ cup of flour. With a large wooden spoon, stir vigorously until the flour is absorbed and the mixture comes away from the sides of the pan in a dense mass. With your spoon, make a small well in the center of the paste and drop in the first egg. Stir vigorously. The mixture will spread into moist ribbons, then come together solidly again. Add the second egg and beat as before, and then finally the third egg, continuing to beat until the paste (*pâte à choux,* the French call it) is shiny, smooth, and thick.

Now beat in the salt, mustard, the Switzerland cheese, and ⅓ cup of the Parmesan cheese. Don't expect the cheese to dissolve thoroughly, but beat it vigorously nonetheless to combine the ingredients well. Taste for seasoning. The *pâte à choux* should be sharply flavored; add more salt and even a little more mustard (but not *cheese*) if necessary. It can now safely rest, covered with plastic wrap, unrefrigerated for anywhere up to 4 hours before frying.

Preheat the oven to 200 degrees. Line a shallow baking pan with a double thickness of paper toweling and set aside.

Heat at least 3 inches of the oil or fat in a deep fryer until it reaches a temperature of 375 degrees on a deep-frying thermometer. Drop the paste, a heaping teaspoon at a time, into the pan, pushing it off the spoon with another spoon, or with the tip of your finger. Fry 6 or 8 *beignets* at a time, turning them with a large slotted spoon (theoretically, they are supposed to turn over by themselves as they brown but they often don't, so it is best to help them along) until they have puffed into a symmetrical shape—part of their charm, I think—and are crisp and brown on all sides. Don't undercook them or their centers will be gummy. As each batch is done, transfer them to the paper-lined baking dish and place it in the oven to keep warm while you proceed to fry the remaining *beignets*. They can remain in the oven for about 10 minutes at the most, but, ideally, they should drain on paper toweling and be served almost immediately. In any case, sprinkle the *beignets* with the reserved Parmesan cheese before serving them. They make delightfully piquant accompaniments to drinks of all kinds.

Cottage-Cheese Pancakes   *serves 2–4*

1 cup creamed cottage cheese (about ½ pound)
4 eggs
6 level tablespoons flour
8 tablespoons butter, *melted but not browned: 6 tablespoons,* cooled, for the batter and 2 tablespoons to cook the pancakes
Pinch of salt
Powdered sugar and/or strawberry jam

With the back of a large spoon, rub the cottage cheese through a fine sieve set over a small mixing bowl. Beat the eggs with a fork or whisk only long enough to combine them, and stir them little by little into the cheese. When they are completely absorbed, beat in the flour, a tablespoon at a time, then stir in 6 tablespoons of the melted butter and the pinch of salt. If the mixture appears too fluid (which is unlikely)—it should hold its shape lightly in a spoon—stir in a little more flour, a teaspoon at a time, until the batter reaches the proper consistency.

Cottage-Cheese Pancakes

With a pastry brush, spread about a tablespoon of the remaining butter over the bottom of a heavy 10- to 12-inch skillet, one with a non-stick surface preferably, and place it over high heat. When a drop of cold water flicked across it splutters and evaporates instantly, drop in the cheese mixture, a large tablespoon at a time—leaving about an inch between pancakes—and flatten each slightly with a small metal spatula. Lightly brown the pancakes for about 2 minutes on each side, turning them over gingerly with the spatula. Add a little more butter to the pan if necessary.

Serve at once for breakfast or as a dessert, sprinkled lightly with powdered sugar and accompanied with a bowl of strawberry jam.

Cheese Fondue Neuchâteloise   *serves 6–8*

¾ pound Switzerland Emmenthal or Gruyère cheese, or a combination of both, *grated in an electric blender or shredded with a Mouli grater or hand grater (about 3 cups packed down)*

2 level tablespoons flour

1½ cups dry white wine: preferably a Swiss Fendant or Dézaley, a French Muscadet, or a California Johannisberg Riesling

1 tablespoon fresh, strained lemon juice (optional)

1 large garlic clove, *peeled and slightly bruised with the flat of a large knife*

Salt

Freshly ground black pepper

2–4 tablespoons Kirsch, the imported variety, preferably

1 loaf French or Italian bread, *first cut into 1-inch-thick slices, then each slice cut into 1½-inch cubes with at least one side of crust left on*

A fondue at its best should be served the very moment it is made. Place the grated cheese in a large mixing bowl and add the flour. Toss the two together with your hands until all trace of the flour disappears. A few moments before making the fondue, light the burner of whatever heating element you own for keeping the fondue hot. (A small gas table stove is really best, but a chafing-dish warmer does the job almost as well.) Place the bread cubes in a basket and lay out fondue forks if you own them or use ordinary table forks. Have plenty of napkins on hand and even little plates (the Swiss would find this amusing) for the more fastidious of your diners.

Pour the wine into your fondue or chafing dish (and the lemon juice, if you want to play it safe—see page 37), add the garlic clove, and over high heat bring the wine to a boil on the stove in your kitchen. Then turn the heat down to moderate and, handful by handful, toss in the cheese, stirring constantly with a fork. The mixture should soon turn into a slowly bubbling smooth cheese sauce: that is, if the cheese you have used is a fine aged one. Taste it and add as much salt and freshly ground pepper as you think it needs, and remove and discard the garlic clove. Then stir in 2 tablespoons of the Kirsch, taste again, and stir in up to 2 or more tablespoons of Kirsch if you like its flavor. Quickly place the fondue on your burner, regulating the heat so that the fondue simmers slowly without ever coming to a boil. Start the ball rolling by securely spearing a chunk of bread on your fork, swirling it around in the fondue, and eating it without any more ado. Your fellow diners will soon get the point.

The Swiss are by no means unanimous about what to drink with fondue. Some say tea, *never* wine, beer, or any other cold liquid. For my part, I would suggest ignoring the advice of the purists and drink with it what you like. But definitely *not* water.

Welsh Rabbit

serves 4

8 slices fresh white bread, *trimmed of their crusts and lightly toasted*
2 tablespoons butter
½ cup flat beer or ale
2 teaspoons Worcestershire sauce
½ teaspoon dry mustard
⅛ teaspoon cayenne pepper
1 pound aged sharp domestic Cheddar cheese, or Caerphilly, Cheshire, or Dunlop if you can find them, *coarsely shredded with a Mouli grater or a hand grater*
2 egg yolks (*reserving the whites for another purpose if you wish*)
Salt

Welsh Rabbit

Preheat the broiler to its highest point and arrange toast slices side by side in two's in separate shallow ovenproof baking dishes or ramekins. Over moderate heat, melt the butter (without letting it brown) in a 2- to 3-quart enamel or stainless-steel saucepan. Pour in the beer, stir in the Worcestershire sauce, mustard, and cayenne, then bring the mixture almost but not quite to a boil. Now, handful by handful, stir in the cheese, and simmer, still stirring, until it has completely melted and is thick and smooth. Off the heat, beat in the egg yolks, one at a time, with a whisk, and simmer again for 5 to 10 seconds, but don't allow the mixture to boil. Taste for seasoning and enliven the mixture, if you like, with salt (which it probably won't need because of the saltiness of the cheese), more Worcestershire sauce, mustard, or cayenne. Pour the rabbit over the toast, dividing it among the ramekins as evenly as you can. Slide the dishes under the broiler (about 2 inches from the source of the heat) for a few seconds to brown the cheese lightly. Serve at once.

NOTE: In place of individual baking dishes or ramekins, you may arrange the toast slices side by side in a shallow baking dish just large enough to hold them comfortably. Pour the hot rabbit over the slices, masking them completely, and broil as described above. You may also find it useful to know that any leftover rabbit can be reheated fairly successfully (but not boiled). If it appears to be too thick after reheating, thin it with a little flat beer and simmer the rabbit a few seconds longer before pouring it over fresh pieces of toast, then browning it.

Mozzarella in Carrozza with Anchovy Sauce
serves 4–6

THE SAUCE

8 tablespoons (¼ pound, 1 stick) unsalted butter

1 tablespoon capers, *drained and coarsely chopped*

4 flat anchovy fillets, *drained of all their oil and coarsely chopped*

1 tablespoon fresh, strained lemon juice

Parsley (preferably the flat-leaf Italian variety), *enough to make 2 tablespoons finely chopped*

THE CHEESE SANDWICHES

Vegetable oil or shortening for deep frying

1-pound loaf of French or Italian bread, *cut into ¼-inch-thick slices (see* NOTE *at the end of the recipe)*

1 pound fresh mozzarella cheese, *cut into ¼-inch-thick slices*

¼ pound prosciutto, *very thinly sliced, or use very thinly sliced Smithfield or Virginia ham*

4 eggs

1 cup plus 2 tablespoons milk

First prepare the sauce by melting the butter in a small saucepan or skillet. Watch carefully, and don't let it brown or burn. Stir in the capers, anchovies, and lemon juice and simmer until the bits of anchovy completely dissolve. Add the parsley and taste for seasoning. The sauce should be tart and definite in flavor; add more lemon juice, and even another chopped anchovy or two if you like. Set the pan aside.

In a large deep-fryer, heat about 3 inches of oil or shortening until it reaches a temperature of 375 degrees on the deep-frying thermometer.

With a cooky cutter or small glass, cut the slices of bread into crustless rounds. The size of the rounds you make will vary with the size of the loaf, but they should be no less than 2 inches in diameter. Trim the slices of cheese and prosciutto slightly smaller than the rounds of bread, and make neat, compact sandwiches of the bread, cheese, and ham.

Pulverize the bread crusts, a handful at a time, in the jar of an electric blender. (If you don't have the time or a blender, you can, of course, use ordinary dry bread crumbs, but the results will not be ideal.) Spread the crumbs on a sheet of waxed paper. In a small mixing bowl, beat the eggs with a whisk or fork until they are well combined, then beat in 2 tablespoons of the milk. Pour the remaining cup of milk into another bowl.

One at a time, dip the sandwiches into the milk briefly and seal the edges of each sandwich by gently pressing them with your fingers all around their circumference. Coat the flat surfaces of the sandwiches with the crumbs, and roll the sandwiches like cartwheels through the crumbs to coat the sides as well. Dip the sandwiches, one at a time, into the egg mixture, and arrange them side by side on a long strip of waxed paper. Deep-fry 2 or 3 sandwiches at a time for 3 or 4 minutes, turning them occasionally with a slotted spoon until they are golden-brown on both sides. As they brown, transfer them with a slotted spoon to paper toweling to drain while you deep-fry the rest. Serve the sandwiches while they are very hot or the cheese will turn rubbery, and spoon a little hot anchovy sauce over each of them.

NOTE: Loaves of French and Italian bread vary widely in weight and size, and you may have to improvise as best you can with the loaf you are able to buy. The ideal loaf for this recipe should weigh 1 pound and be about 3½ to 4 inches in diameter at its largest point. Somewhat smaller loaves may be used for the sandwiches, but in that case, the amounts of mozzarella and prosciutto will vary accordingly. Good American white bread can be used in a pinch, but the sandwiches made with them, although attractive enough, will lack that special quality only French or Italian bread will give them.

Spiedini of Bread, Anchovies, and Mozzarella Cheese in the Lugano Manner

serves 6

3 loaves of French or Italian bread

Fresh mozzarella cheese, *cut into 12 chunks about 1½ inches long and ¾ inch wide* (buy about a pound of cheese, although after trimming you will have scraps left over; use them for other purposes as described on page 39)

12 flat anchovies (2-ounce can), *drained of all their oil*

½ pound unsalted butter, *melted but not browned* (1 cup), *hot*

Spiedini of Bread, Anchovies, and Mozzarella Cheese

The only tricky aspect of this simple but unusual dish is the construction of the *spiedini*. You will need 6 metal or bamboo skewers, each 9 to 10 inches long. Cut 1½ inches off the tapered ends of each loaf, then slice the rest of the bread crosswise into 5-inch-long pieces. On a board, one at a time, stand each section upright and cut away all the crusts but the bottom ones. (To do this neatly, use a sharp, preferably serrated, knife.) Then trim each of these loaves down to rectangles, 2 inches wide by 5 inches long. Crust-side down, divide each piece into 3 cubes, by cutting down to—*not through*—the crust at about 1½-inch intervals, thus creating three cubes of bread still attached to their crust.

Now, spreading the cut sections of each *spiedini* apart accordionwise, insert a chunk of mozzarella into each opening. Gently, but firmly press the cut sections together and force a skewer, lengthwise, through the center of each long *spiedini*. Crust-side down, lay the skewered *spiedini*, side by side, in a shallow baking dish large enough to hold them comfortably. Arrange 2 anchovies lengthwise on top of each *spiedini* and set aside, covered with plastic wrap or foil (for as long as 4 to 6 hours, if you like) until you are ready to bake them.

Preheat the oven to 500 degrees. Pour the hot melted butter over the *spiedini*, moistening each piece of bread evenly. Bake in the center of the oven for about 8 to 10 minutes, or until the cheese has melted and the bread is brown and crisp. Using a bulb baster or spoon, baste the *spiedini* every few minutes or so with the butter in the bottom of the pan. Be careful not to overcook the *spiedini* or the cheese will turn rubbery.

To serve, place the *spiedini*, still on its skewer, on heated individual serving plates, spoon a little butter over them, and suggest that each diner slide the *spiedini* off the skewers with a fork onto the plate.

Chicken Breasts with Prosciutto and Parmesan Cheese in the Bolognese Manner

PETTI DI POLLO ALLA BOLOGNESE   *serves 4*

2 whole chicken breasts about 1 pound each, *skinned, boned, and cut in half lengthwise*

Salt

Freshly ground black pepper

¼ cup flour

5 tablespoons butter: *1, softened, to butter the baking dish; 3 to sauté the chicken; and 1, cut into small pieces, for the final baking*

2 tablespoons vegetable oil

About ¼ pound prosciutto or any good smoked Virginia ham, *cut into 6–8 paper-thin slices*

About ½ pound imported fontina or Bel Paese cheese, *cut into 8–12 ⅛-inch-thick slices*

Imported Parmesan cheese, *enough to make 3 tablespoons grated*

6 tablespoons chicken stock, fresh or canned

Spread the chicken breasts, smooth sides up, on a board and with a long thin carving knife, slice each one horizontally. (If this appears too formidable a task to contemplate, ask your butcher, if he is friendly, to do it for you.) Place 4 slices of breast at a time about 2 inches apart on a long strip of waxed paper, lay another sheet of waxed paper over them, and pound the breasts gently with the flat of a cleaver or even the bottom of a small heavy saucepan to flatten them slightly. Remove them from the waxed paper and, with a sharp knife, trim each breast slice neatly, and to approximately the same size.

With a pastry brush, spread 1 tablespoon of softened butter over the bottom of a shallow baking dish just about large enough to hold the chicken breasts side by side in one layer. Sprinkle both sides of the breasts liberally with salt and more generously with black pepper, then dip them, one at a time, in the flour, shaking them gently to remove any excess.

Melt 3 tablespoons of butter and the oil in a heavy 10- to 12-inch skillet over high heat. When the fat begins to turn ever so lightly brown, add the breasts (don't crowd them; you can sauté the breasts in 2 batches, if you must) and brown them lightly for about 2 minutes on each side, turning them over with tongs. Regulate the heat so that they color quickly and evenly without burning.

Arrange the breasts in the buttered baking pan and lay a slice of ham on each, trimming the slices to match the contours of the breasts, thus masking them completely. (You may patch any ragged pieces of ham together on the breasts if the ham slices are too uneven to handle —which often happens.) Now lay the slices of cheese over the ham, and make sure they are not only large enough to cover the breasts completely but let them come slightly down over the sides as well. (As with the ham, you may patch here too, if you must.) Sprinkle the Parmesan cheese evenly over the top of each breast. The dish may now be covered with plastic wrap and refrigerated until you are ready to bake the breasts, or you may proceed with the final cooking operation at once.

Preheat the oven to 350 degrees.

Slowly pour the chicken stock down into one side of the baking dish, tipping it slightly to spread the stock evenly. Dot the top of each breast with a few specks of the remaining tablespoon of butter, and place the baking dish in the upper third of the oven. Bake undisturbed for about 10 minutes, or long enough, depending on the reliability of your oven, for the cheese to melt completely and brown lightly.

To make it even browner (and to add to the flavor) slide the dish under the broiler for a few seconds before serving.

Pillows of Veal in the Italian Manner

serves 6

2 pounds veal scallops, *sliced ⅜ inch thick and pounded a little less than ¼ inch thick, then cut into 24 4-by-4-inch squares*

About ½ pound fontina or Bel Paese cheese, *cut into 12 3½-inch-square slices about ⅛ inch thick*

Pillows of Veal in the Italian Manner

About ¼ pound prosciutto or other
    good cooked, smoked ham,
    cut into 12 paper-thin 3-inch-
    square slices
Salt
Freshly ground black pepper

½ cup flour
4 tablespoons (½ stick) butter
3 tablespoons olive oil
½ cup dry white wine
1 cup chicken stock, fresh or
    canned

Make neat sandwiches of the veal, cheese, and prosciutto by placing a cheese slice and a square of prosciutto on each one of 12 scallops and topping them with the remaining scallops. The veal should cover the cheese and ham completely. Pinch or press the edges of the veal together firmly; to seal them more securely pound the edges with the flat of a cleaver, the handle of a large chopping knife, or the bottom of a heavy bottle. (The "pillows" may now be wrapped in plastic wrap and refrigerated for as long as a day, or until you are ready to use them.)

Promptly before sautéing them, sprinkle each pillow sparingly with salt and more discreetly with pepper, dip them in the flour on all sides, and shake them gently to remove any excess flour.

Over high heat, melt the butter and the oil in a 10- to 12-inch heavy skillet, preferably one with a non-stick finish. When the butter begins to turn ever so lightly brown, add the pillows and sauté them 6 or so at a time for about 2 minutes or so on each side, turning them over gingerly with a metal spatula. Transfer the browned pillows to a plate and continue browning the remaining veal precisely as before, adding more butter and oil to the pan if necessary.

When the 12 pillows are browned, pour off all but a thin film of fat from the skillet and in its place pour in the wine and ½ cup of the stock. Bring the liquid to a boil over high heat, meanwhile scraping into it any brown particles clinging to the bottom of the pan. Continue to boil briskly, uncovered, until the liquid has cooked down to ½ cup or to approximately half its original amount. Now lower the heat, return the veal pillows to the skillet, and cover tightly. Simmer undisturbed for about 5 minutes, then gently turn the pillows over and simmer for 5 minutes longer.

Working quickly, transfer the pillows to a heated serving platter and stir the remaining ½ cup of stock into the skillet. Bring to a boil and, stirring constantly, boil the sauce briskly, uncovered, for 2 or 3 minutes or until it thickens slightly. Taste for seasoning, then pour it over the veal pillows and serve at once.

NOTE: It is useless to embark on this deceptively simple dish unless you have a butcher who is able (and, even more important, willing) to cut and pound the veal (of the best quality) to the sizes I so precisely specify. Attempting to execute these anatomical maneuvers yourself is of course possible, but the going can be rough unless you have the sharpest of knives and the surest of hands.

Ricotta Pie

serves 6–8

A partially baked 10-inch shell (as described on page 285)
Save the leftover pastry scraps for the lattice topping
2 tablespoons butter, *softened*
½ cup sugar, the superfine type, if possible
1½ pounds ricotta cheese
½ teaspoon ground cinnamon
1 tablespoon candied citron, *coarsely chopped*
1 tablespoon candied orange peel, *coarsely chopped*
1 teaspoon each of fresh orange and lemon peel, *the fruits peeled with a swivel-bladed*
vegetable peeler, then finely chopped
Pinch of salt
2 tablespoons raisins, *soaked in ¼ cup Marsala wine for 15 minutes or so, then drained*
6 egg yolks: *5 for the filling and 1 for the glaze (reserve the whites for another purpose if you wish)*
2 tablespoons slivered, blanched almonds, or 2 tablespoons pignolia nuts
1 tablespoon heavy cream
12–15 whole candied cherries

Preheat the oven to 375 degrees.

In a large bowl, cream the butter and sugar together by mashing and beating them against the sides of the bowl until light and fluffy. Rub the ricotta cheese through a sieve with a large spoon directly into the butter mixture and beat thoroughly, scraping up with a rubber spatula any butter that may be clinging to the bottom of the bowl. Now stir in the cinnamon, the candied fruits, the chopped fresh orange and lemon peels, a pinch of salt, and the drained raisins. Stir in 5 of the yolks, one at a time. When the ingredients are well combined, pour the mixture into the pastry shell and spread it out evenly with the spatula. Scatter the slivered almonds or pignolia nuts evenly over the top.

On a lightly floured board, gather the leftover strips of pastry into a ball and roll it out into a ⅛-inch-thick rectangle. With a sharp knife or a pastry wheel, cut the rectangle into 10 to 12 (fewer if you prefer) strips about 12 inches long and ½ inch wide and place them on top of the pie, crisscrossing them latticewise and pressing the ends securely to the rim of the shell. Beat the remaining egg yolks with the heavy cream and use this mixture to paint the lattice strips lightly before baking. This will give them a golden glaze.

Place the pie tin on a cooky sheet or jelly-roll pan and bake the pie for 45 minutes, or until the top is brown and the filling firm. Unmold the pie as described on page 262 and cool to room temperature. Place a candied cherry in each lattice opening and serve.

John W. Clancy's Cheesecake
serves 8–10

THE CRUST

5 tablespoons unsalted butter: 2 tablespoons softened for greasing the pan; 3 tablespoons, melted and cooled, for the crust

½ cup graham crackers, *finely crumbled or wrapped in a* towel *and crushed with a rolling pin*

1 tablespoon sugar
1 teaspoon ground cinnamon
2 tablespoons ground walnuts, *pulverized in an electric blender or ground in a Mouli grater*

THE FILLING

4 four-ounce or 2 eight-ounce packages cream cheese, *softened to room temperature*

2 tablespoons unsalted butter, *softened*

¾ cup granulated sugar, *preferably the superfine type*

3 eggs, *separated*

1 cup (½ pint) sour cream

3 level tablespoons flour

1 teaspoon vanilla extract
2 teaspoons fresh, strained lemon
      juice
2 teaspoons lemon peel, *the*

lemon thinly peeled with a
swivel-bladed vegetable
peeler, then finely chopped

With a pastry brush, spread the 2 tablespoons of softened butter over the bottom and sides of a 7-inch spring-form pan that is 3 inches high. Then, in a mixing bowl, stir together the crumbled graham crackers, sugar, cinnamon, and ground walnuts, and pour in the 3 tablespoons of melted butter. Knead the mixture with your fingers until the particles more or less adhere; if they seem too dry to cling together, add a little more melted butter. Now dump the mixture into the buttered pan and pat it evenly on the bottom and sides of the pan with your fingers. You will probably have some trouble making the crumbs adhere to the sides of the pan, but don't be concerned if the coating appears uneven or if patches occur here and there—this won't affect the cheesecake itself. Place the pan in the refrigerator and let it chill while you make the filling.

Preheat the oven to 350 degrees.

In a large, deep bowl, cream the cheese, the 2 tablespoons of the softened butter, and the sugar together by vigorously stirring and mashing them against the sides of the bowl until the mixture is smooth and fluffy. (This can be done more easily in an electric mixer if you own one equipped with a paddle or pastry arm.) Then add the egg yolks, one at a time, beating well after each addition. When all traces of the egg yolks disappear, add the sour cream, flour, vanilla, lemon juice, and chopped lemon peel, and beat vigorously for a few seconds longer.

Now beat the egg whites (in an unlined copper bowl with a balloon whisk, if possible) until they are stiff enough to grip the beater firmly and their small white peaks stand upright on the beater when it is lifted from the bowl. Thoroughly mix about ½ cup of the whites into the cheese mixture and, with the aid of a rubber spatula, gently but thoroughly fold in the remaining whites.

Immediately pour the filling into the crumb-lined pan and spread the top out evenly with the spatula. Bake the cake undisturbed in the center of the oven for an hour. Then open the oven door, turn off the heat, and let the cake remain in the oven until cool. It will probably sink in the center somewhat as it stands, but then again it may not. In either case, its texture and flavor will remain the same.

After the cake has rested for its allotted time in the turned-off oven, remove it and let it cool to room temperature. Just before serving, unhinge the sides of the pan and carefully remove them. Don't attempt to remove the cake itself from its metal base unless you have a very large spatula or unless you are especially courageous. To be on the safe side, simply place the cake, base and all, on a circular cake plate and serve.

NOTE: Don't refrigerate this delicate cake at any point before serving it. Any leftover cake, however, may be refrigerated overnight, covered with plastic wrap—but let it return to room temperature before you serve it again.

Cheese and Bacon Tart

OR MY VERSION OF A HIGHLY
UNTRADITIONAL QUICHE LORRAINE   *serves 6–8*

A partially baked 10-inch pastry shell (as described on page 285)

1 pound lean packaged bacon slices, *left unseparated and cut crosswise into ¼-inch strips*

4 eggs: *2 whole eggs and 2 egg yolks combined for the custard, saving the two remaining whites for another purpose if you wish*

1½ cups heavy cream

Imported Parmesan cheese, *enough to make ½ cup grated: 2 tablespoons to sprinkle over the finished tart and 6 tablespoons for the tart filling*

¾ teaspoon salt

Freshly ground black pepper

1 teaspoon dry mustard

1 tablespoon butter, *cut into small pieces*

Parsley, *enough to make 1 tablespoon finely chopped*

Preheat the oven to 375 degrees. Place the bacon (without bothering to separate the cut strips if they stick together) in a cold 10- to 12-inch heavy skillet. Fry over moderate heat, stirring the bacon until the strips separate, render their fat, and become a golden color and slightly crisp. Immediately drain the bacon in a sieve and discard the fat. Spread the bacon on a double thickness of paper toweling to drain.

Drop the 2 whole eggs and the 2 yolks into a large mixing bowl and whisk only long enough to combine them. Then add the cream, the 6 tablespoons of cheese, the salt, a few grindings of black pepper, the mustard, and approximately half the reserved bacon. Stir together thoroughly and taste for seasoning. The mixture may need more salt but that will depend on the saltiness of the cheese and bacon. Use your discretion.

Place the prebaked pastry shell (still in its pan) on a cooky sheet or jelly-roll pan. Ladle the entire contents of the mixing bowl into the shell and dot the top with the tablespoon of butter bits.

Bake the *quiche* undisturbed in the center of the oven for about 30 minutes, or until the custard is firm (but not too firm, the center should move slightly when the pan is shaken) and the top lightly browned. Follow the directions for unmolding the tart on page 262. Serve at once, or if you prefer, let it cool to lukewarm. In either case, sprinkle the finished tart evenly first with the rest of the bacon, then the 2 tablespoons of grated cheese, and finally, the chopped parsley.

NOTE: The cheese and bacon tart may be baked ahead, allowed to cool and set aside, unrefrigerated, for a few hours. Reheat in a preheated 350-degree oven for about 10 minutes before serving. It will lack something of the pristine quality of the freshly baked tart but it will be nonetheless quite edible.

Cheddar-Cheese Soup in the English Manner

serves 4–6

4 tablespoons (½ stick) butter
1 medium onion, *to make ¾ cup finely chopped*
1 scraped carrot, *to make ½ cup and finely chopped*
1 medium stalk celery, *to make ½ cup finely chopped*
1 small green pepper, *to make ⅓ cup finely chopped*
4 level tablespoons flour

Cheddar-Cheese Soup in the English Manner

4 cups chicken stock, fresh or canned: *if you use the con-centrated canned type, dilute it with an equal amount of water*

1 pound aged Cheddar cheese, preferably Vermont Cheddar,

coarsely grated in a Mouli grater or with a hand grater (about 4 cups, packed down)

1 teaspoon dry mustard

⅛ teaspoon cayenne pepper

⅓–½ cup heavy cream

Salt

Melt the butter over moderate heat (without browning it) in a 2- to 3-quart enamel or stainless-steel saucepan. Add the onions, carrots, celery, and green pepper and, stirring frequently, cook them for about 10 minutes until they are quite soft but not brown. In fact, they must *not* brown, so regulate the heat accordingly. Now add the flour and stir until it is completely absorbed, then pour in the chicken stock. Stirring constantly with a whisk, bring the soup to a boil over high heat. When it has thickened somewhat, reduce the heat to low and simmer the soup with the pan partially covered for about 30 minutes. Then strain the entire mixture through a fine sieve into a bowl, pressing down hard on the vegetables with the back of a spoon before throwing them away. Return the strained soup to its saucepan and bring to a simmer over moderate heat. Handful by handful, stir in the cheese and simmer—still stirring—until it has melted completely. Add the mustard and cayenne, stir in ⅓ cup of the cream, and pour in the remaining cream if you prefer the soup thinner. Taste for seasoning. It is quite unlikely that you will have to add any salt because of the natural saltiness of the cheese, but you may want to liven up the soup's flavor a bit with a little more mustard or cayenne pepper. Serve at once.

Deep-Fried Cheese Sausages in the English Manner

makes about 12 rolls
to serve 4–6

½ pound aged sharp Cheddar cheese, *grated or shredded with a Mouli grater (about 2 cups, packed down)*

3 cups fresh bread crumbs, *made from fresh white bread crumbs (crusts removed), pulverized in a blender or the*

Deep-Fried Sausages in the English Manner

bread bunched together, then finely shredded with a fork (dried crumbs will not do): 2 cups for the filling and 1 cup to coat the rolls
2 tablespoons scallions, *finely chopped, including about 2 inches of the green tops,* or use 2 tablespoons onions, *very finely chopped*
Parsley (preferably the flat-leaf type), *enough to make 2 tablespoons finely chopped*
1 teaspoon dry mustard
⅛ teaspoon cayenne pepper
1 teaspoon salt
Freshly ground black pepper
4 eggs: *the yolks for the filling and the whites for the coating*
2–6 tablespoons cold water
Vegetable oil or shortening for deep frying
Sharp prepared mustard

In a large mixing bowl, combine the cheese, 2 cups of the bread crumbs, the scallions or onions, the parsley, mustard, cayenne, salt, and a generous amount of freshly ground black pepper. With a large spoon or your hands, toss the ingredients together until they are well mixed, then stir in the egg yolks one at a time. Add 2 tablespoons of the water and knead the mixture with your hands until it can be gathered into a compact ball. If it crumbles (and this will depend to a large extent on how moist or dry your particular cheese is), knead in more water by the teaspoon until the particles firmly adhere.

Now pick up 2 tablespoons of the mixture and roll it between your palms into a sausage-like shape. In the same fashion, make sausages of the rest of the mixture, lining them up side by side on a long strip of waxed paper.

With a whisk or fork, beat the egg whites for a few seconds or until they run off the beater fairly smoothly—don't overdo this. (In fact, you may even omit beating them altogether but the whites will be easier to handle if you do.) Spread out the remaining bread crumbs on another strip of waxed paper. One at a time, dip the sausages in the egg whites (coating them thoroughly), then roll them in the bread crumbs until the entire surface of the sausage is covered with a fairly substantial layer of crumbs. As you proceed, sausage by sausage, place them on a wire cake rack or any other rack you may have on hand. Chill in the refrigerator for at least an hour before frying them. (If you are in a hurry, the sausages may be fried without chilling them, but the results will be more predictable if you allow the coating to dry out a bit.)

Heat the oil or shortening in a deep-fat fryer until it reaches a temperature of 375 degrees on a deep-frying thermometer. Drop in the sausages about 4 or 5 at a time and fry them for about 3 or 4 minutes, or until they turn a deep golden-brown. Remove them from the fat with a slotted spoon and let them drain on a double thickness of paper toweling while you fry the rest. (If they must wait, the sausages can be kept warm in a preheated 200-degree oven for 10 minutes or so before serving.) Serve as an accompaniment to drinks or as a first course. In either case, sharp prepared mustard should accompany them.

NOTE: If you prefer, you may fry the sausages in a 10- to 12-inch skillet filled with about 1 inch of hot, but not smoking, oil or melted shortening. Cook them over moderate heat, turning them over with a spatula and regulating the heat so that they brown quickly and evenly without burning.

Cheese Straws   *makes about 30 straws*

4 tablespoons unsalted butter, *cut into tiny bits and chilled*
Aged sharp Cheddar cheese, *enough to make ⅓ cup finely grated*

1 cup flour
½ teaspoon cayenne pepper
1 egg yolk
2 tablespoons iced water

In a large mixing bowl, combine the butter bits, cheese, flour, and cayenne and toss them about with your hands. Then rub them together until they blend and look like flakes of coarse meal. The dough should remain fairly dry; don't overmix or it will become oily.

Drop the egg yolk and the 2 tablespoons of water into a small bowl and beat them with a fork for a few seconds. Then pour the mixture over the dough and toss together with your hands or a fork until it can be gathered into a compact ball. Wrap the dough in waxed paper and refrigerate for at least an hour, or until fairly firm.

Preheat the oven to 400 degrees. On a lightly floured surface, roll the dough (let it soften a bit at room temperature if it is too firm and resistant) into a rectangle approximately 4 inches wide and 15 inches long. With a small sharp knife or a pastry wheel, trim the edges of the rectangle neatly and cut the pastry crosswise into strips 4 inches long ½ inch wide. Transfer the strips with a spatula to 1 or 2 ungreased baking sheets. Bake in the center of the oven for about 10 minutes until the straws are firm to the touch. Don't let them brown. Cool the straws to room temperature on a wire cake rack before serving. They make fine accompaniments to drinks.

NOTE: You may vary the flavor of these fragile, crisp straws by stirring 1 or 2 teaspoons of sesame or caraway seeds into the dough before you add the egg-yolk–water mixture.

MUSHROOMS

MUSHROOMS

Neither flower, fruit, grain, nor vegetable, mushrooms inhabit a dark, mysterious world of their own. They have nothing in common with the conventional foods we eat, and it is perhaps for this reason that many cooks I know approach them with so much uncertainty. That the fragile mushroom has survived our culinary assaults, its popularity undiminished, is the measure of its extraordinary appeal.

Although wild mushrooms have been a universal food through the centuries, the cultivation of mushrooms was undertaken successfully only two hundred years ago. It began in France, and in the United States it is an even more recent phenomenon. Since its beginnings here at the turn of the century, the American mushroom industry (for that is what it has become) has proliferated with such rapidity that you can find cultivated fresh mushrooms at any time of the year and at almost every supermarket or greengrocer.

The characteristic of mushrooms (and of all fungi, in fact) that makes them unique in the vegetable kingdom is that they lack chlorophyll, the green coloring matter present in all other plants. That, and the store of folklore, superstition, and the real and imagined dangers surrounding mushrooms, may well account for many of our misconceptions about them.

Of the numberless varieties of fungi known to botanists, we need be concerned, practically at least, with only one: the common field mushroom, *Agaricus campestris bisporus,* to give it its scientific name. The cultivation of various mushrooms has been attempted often both here and abroad, but this is the only type that has been domesticated successfully. If you know how to cope with its fragility and learn the

secrets of cooking it, the *Agaricus campestris* can be a mushroom
of incomparable flavor and texture.

There are many hardy, wild mushrooms that can withstand fairly
rough handling, but you must approach the cultivated mushroom
with some knowledge of its special sensibilities. Subjecting it to a bath,
for example, is an indignity it doesn't easily tolerate. Instead of shed-
ding the water, as those of you who seldom cook them might reasonably expect, the mushroom will absorb the water like a sponge; and
vindictively, as it were, throw it off at the first sign of heat. Anyone
who has attempted to sauté thoroughly soaked mushrooms has surely
noted with dismay a pool of water in the pan where none had been
before. It might relieve you to know, on the other hand, that unwashed
mushrooms behave quite differently and retain most of their natural
moisture as they should.

For the overly fastidious, wiping a mushroom lightly with a
dampened towel may be considered, but it is hardly worth the effort
except, or course, when you know they have been picked and pawed
by careless shoppers. Most cultivated mushrooms are grown in steril-
ized synthetic composts these days and the only part of the mushroom
which comes in contact with the soil at all is the base of its stem. And
even this is left behind when the mushroom is harvested. The cut
end of the stem (commonly mistaken for the mushroom's root) often
hardens after exposure and you may slice it off or not. But if the mushrooms you are about to buy are really fresh, why bother with this extra
and quite unnecessary chore?

The mushroom's cap is the only other area in which grit, soil, or
dust might conceivably lodge. However, this need cause you no con-
cern. The caps of growing mushrooms are always closed, and superior
mushrooms are harvested, packed, and shipped long before they open.

Peeling a mushroom demeans it as much as washing it. Although
the mushroom will not react as dramatically to the affront as to being
washed, its flavor will never be the same. Its texture, too, will suffer,
for it is the "skin" which gives the mushroom its particular texture.
Of course, a badly discolored or brown mottled cap can be camou-
flaged to a point by peeling it, but you should never buy mushrooms
in this condition in the first place. Today, baskets of fresh white mushrooms are available everywhere and there is little excuse for buying
poor ones. Although most of us can recognize an overripe melon, a

pulpy tomato, or a sprouting potato, oddly enough, few of us know
what to look for in a mushroom. An obvious indication of freshness,
even to the uninitiated, would appear to be a smooth, white, un-
blemished cap, but in reality, that is only part of the story.

A fresh, young mushroom will show no space between the inverted rim of its cap and its stem. As it matures, and its moisture
evaporates, the cap will open, exposing on its underside a wide ring of
velvety, accordian-like pleats called gills. These can range in color
from the most delicate pink to blackish-brown and are, to the practiced
eye, an indication of the mushroom's age and tenderness. Mushrooms
with slightly open caps should be bought only if they are to be used
at once, but older specimens with widely spread caps and blackish
gills should be avoided. They may still be edible but they will turn
quite dark after they are cooked and have a musty flavor besides. I will
admit that I know some cooks who like this flavor. I don't. By all means,
experiment with these older specimens and make up your own mind.

Contrary to popular supposition, the size of a mushroom's cap
has nothing to do with its quality. The United States Department of
Agriculture says so in effect, by grading mushrooms as U.S. # 1, and
then simply classifying them as small, medium, large, and extra large.
Nor is the price affected by size. Unless you wish to use whole mushrooms as a garnish (they are spectacular if you have learned to groove
or flute them), or intend to stuff them as I suggest on pages 72–4, the
size of the mushrooms you buy is of little consequence. A more important consideration is the length of its stem.

Mushrooms stems are perfectly edible, but they sometimes lack
the tenderness of the cap. And not infrequently, they tend to be fibrous;
for this reason alone, try to find short stemmed mushrooms. Whatever
their length, however, mushroom stems have a variety of uses, and
unless they are too pulpy, don't ever throw them away.

The number of experienced household cooks I know who are not
only guilty of wasting mushroom stems and who continue to wash,
peel, and trim the cap never ceases to astonish me. And incredible to
relate, this includes those paragons of the kitchen, the French. The
bible of French gastronomy, *Larousse Gastronomique,* solemnly ad-
vises its readers to thoroughly wash, and peel cultivated mushrooms
before cooking them. Conceivably, this may be a carryover from the
days when mushrooms were cultivated in the far from sanitary caves

and abandoned quarries surrounding Paris. Be that as it may, ignore these misleading instructions however authoritative the books in which they appear.

You can serve cultivated mushrooms in a variety of ways (and I have given you representative recipes for them at the end of this chapter), either raw or cooked; whole, cut up, sliced, or chopped; broiled, sautéed, deep-fried in batter—by themselves or with other foods. In fact, if you become obsessed with mushrooms as I sometimes do, you can serve them day after day for weeks on end as an hors d'oeuvre, a soup, a sauce, a main dish, or salad, and never repeat a recipe.

To the French must be given the credit for perhaps the greatest of all mushroom preparations, *duxelles*. Created in the late 18th century by the celebrated La Varenne, *chef de cuisine* to the Marquis d'Uxelle, *duxelles* is quite simply a hash of finely minced mushrooms combined with shallots or onions and slowly cooked in butter until all its moisture has evaporated. (Don't take the easy way out by first squeezing the mushrooms in a towel before cooking them as many professional cooks recommend; in this admittedly expedient process you will also squeeze out most of the mushrooms' flavor.) Because a perfectly made *duxelles* is a dry mixture, with an intense mushroom taste and no residual moisture, you can add it to sauces without diluting them, mix it into stuffings without softening them, and use it as a stuffing itself for fish, fowl, or meat. Moreover, the *duxelles* can be transformed into a *sauce duxelles* by simply adding to it a little cream, wine, or stock. And if that weren't versatility enough, *duxelles* can be stored for at least a week without spoiling, freezes well, and can be made economically with mushroom stems alone, thus freeing the more desirable caps for other purposes.

If you are an enterprising cook, raw or cooked stuffed mushrooms offer you many opportunities for culinary inventiveness and display. The raw caps may be stuffed with anything from the simplest cream-cheese mixture flecked with fresh minced herbs to an extravagant steak Tartare topped with grains of fresh black caviar. In France's Touraine, large broiled mushroom caps come to the table, in the words of Waverly Root, "riding inverted on little rafts of toast, brimming with *beurre d'escargot*." Not quite as elaborate as it sounds, this is just butter mixed with garlic (lots of it), chopped shallots and parsley, and I have given you my version of it on page 72.

Less extravagantly, you may fill mushroom caps with any cooked vegetable, fish, or meat, first chopped or puréed, then amplified with fresh bread crumbs and cream, topped with a speck of butter and baked or broiled till done. These make fine first courses, or inexpensive but impressive cocktail accompaniments. I have discussed this technique in some detail on page 74 and given you specific stuffing recipes as well.

As opposed to the comparative complexity of many of the procedures I describe, serving raw mushrooms in salads is simplicity itself. All you need do is slice the mushrooms, thinly, then add them to a green salad. Although Americans, for some obscure reason, claim the dish as their own, the French, if their early cookbooks are to be believed, appear to have been eating raw mushrooms in salads long before the American Republic was founded. But whoever discovered it first, I think it still an inspired notion. I often simply dress raw sliced mushrooms with olive oil, white wine vinegar, and a sprinkling of fresh herbs and produce a salad you don't easily forget. The mushrooms can be combined with other ingredients too: julienned strips of cold tongue, chicken, turkey, duck, beef, cheese, or whatever you will. The choice is limitless. For those of you who have never tasted raw mushrooms, their flavor may come as something of a delightful shock, particularly after all the overcooked, sodden mushroom dishes you have probably been eating all your life. Even served in the middle of winter (when cultivated mushrooms, surprisingly, are at their most plentiful), you may discover that the fresh, vibrant taste of the raw mushroom seems a harbinger of spring.

Although their consistency will be different, cooked mushrooms, in whatever style you prepare them, should have as fresh a quality as raw ones. And you can accomplish this simple culinary feat by cooking the mushrooms as quickly as possible: 10 minutes at the most if they are whole, and 5 minutes or less if they are sliced or quartered. Famous French dishes like *boeuf bourguignon, coq au vin, blanquette de veau, veal marengo,* and others, which are garnished with the classic *garniture à la bourguignonne* of small white onions and fresh mushrooms, should be precisely timed so that the raw mushrooms are added to the dish about 10 minutes before you serve it. (There are exceptions to this, of course, but not many.) Only then will the mushrooms retain their resiliency as they are meant to do.

Despite the quality of our cultivated mushrooms, to say nothing

of their absolute safety and availability, there are intransigent groups
of mushroom lovers who insist that wild mushrooms are in every way
superior to the domesticated ones. Mushroom manual and basket in
hand, they will tramp indefatigably through forest and glade in search
of edible fungi, often forgetting in their enthusiasm that the odds in
this hobby are heavily against the collector. For those of you fortunate as I sometimes am in having experts pick the trumpet shaped
chanterelle, the spongy morel, or the almost overpoweringly flavored
boletus or *cèpe*, the cultivated mushroom does indeed seem a trifle
pallid by comparison. But if amateur mushroom hunters would remember that these well-known wild mushrooms can much too often be
mistaken, except by experts, for a poisonous variety of the same genus,
they would be less likely, in the words of a famous mushroom authority,
"to gamble the price of a mess of mushrooms against doctor and hospital
bills."

Of small solace to wild mushroom fanciers may be the canned
wild mushrooms imported from France, Switzerland, and Germany,
and sold at astronomical prices in our plushier food stores. For my
taste, however, they have little relation to the real thing. I find canned
chanterelles, for example, almost always overcooked, unpleasantly
flaccid, and often quite bitter. As for the canned *cèpes* and *morelles*,
they aren't much better. If you must have them, avoid the sauced
varieties like the oily *cèpes à la bordelaise* and the *morelles* in dubious
cream sauce. Instead, buy the canned mushrooms in their simplest,
most natural form. At least they will have retained a slight vestige of
their original character.

Preferable in every way are dried *cèpes* and *morelles*. Imported
from Europe, they are almost, but not quite as expensive as the canned
varieties but well worth the price. What they lack in texture is more
than compensated for by their flavor. Because they are virtually in-
destructible and, unlike fresh mushrooms, can be cooked for long
periods of time without coming to any harm, they are a common de-
nominator in many otherwise disparate cuisines. The Russians and
Chinese, particularly, have found them indispensable to their cooking.
Indeed, the success of such traditional dishes as mushroom barley
soup or winter melon soup depend upon the quite-difficult-to-find
large black Chinese mushrooms; and the soups don't taste quite as they
should when cultivated mushrooms are substituted. Our daring might
be well repaid were we to use dried mushrooms in our longer-cooking

soups and stews when, for whatever reason, fresh mushrooms are not easily available.

The new frozen mushrooms make more than tolerable substitutes served either alone or in dishes in which they can be cooked very quickly. They lack the intensity of the dried mushrooms, and the delicacy of the fresh ones, but compared with other frozen foods are quite extraordinary. As a technical achievement alone they must be loudly applauded. Contrary to what one might expect, they maintain their color and consistency with remarkable fidelity after they are cooked, and if their uses are limited, they create the illusion of the fresh mushroom as canned mushrooms never do.

With millions of pounds of fresh mushrooms at our disposal, many of us have come a long way from the days of the early Egyptians whose Pharaohs thought mushrooms much too rare and delicate for common palates and, by edict, reserved them exclusively for their own use. But considering the carelessness with which too many of our cooks treat our mushrooms, I sometimes think the Pharaohs may have had a point.

Broiled Mushrooms   *serves 4–6*

24 firm fresh mushrooms, each 2   Salt
    to 3 inches in diameter   Freshly ground black pepper
2 tablespoons butter, *melted*

To prepare the mushrooms for broiling, carefully remove the stem from each mushroom by holding the cap securely in one hand and gently bending back the stem with the other until it snaps free. If any part of the stem still adheres to the inside of the cap, cut it away with the point of a small sharp knife, thus enlarging the cavity. Do not scrape away any of the gills. And under no circumstances wash the caps, but if you wish, lightly and gently wipe the mushrooms with a slightly dampened towel.

Remove the grid from your broiling pan, and preheat the broiler to its highest point. Using a pastry brush, coat the mushrooms inside and out with a light film of butter, then arrange them, side by side, cap sides up, on the grid. Slide the mushrooms under the broiler about 4 inches from the source of heat and broil undisturbed for about 2 minutes. Turn the caps over with tongs, brush the upturned cavities with a little more butter, and broil for 2 or 3 minutes, or until the mushrooms are lightly brown. Under no circumstances, overcook them. They should still retain their shapes when done, and be slightly resistant to the gentle pressure of your thumb and forefinger. Sprinkle each mushroom liberally with salt, and more discreetly with pepper, and serve at once.

Broiled Mushrooms Stuffed with Garlic Butter on Toast   *serves 8–10*

24 firm fresh mushrooms, each 2   8 tablespoons (¼ pound, 1 stick)
    to 3 inches in diameter   unsalted butter, *softened*

1 teaspoon fresh, strained lemon
   juice
2 teaspoons *very finely chopped*
   scallions, including about an
   inch of their green stems
Peeled garlic cloves, *enough to*
   make 2 teaspoons very finely
   chopped
Parsley (preferably the flat-leaf

type), *enough to make 1 ta-*
   blespoon finely chopped
Salt
Freshly ground black pepper
1 tablespoon vegetable oil
8–10 rounds French bread, each
   about 4 to 6 inches in diameter, *lightly toasted*

Prepare the mushrooms for broiling as described on page 72 and set them aside.

In a large mixing bowl, cream the butter by stirring and mashing it against the sides of the bowl with a large wooden spoon until it is light and fluffy. Beat in the lemon juice a few drops at a time, then stir in the scallions, garlic, and parsley. Taste for seasoning and add as much salt and freshly ground pepper as you think it needs.

Remove the grid from your broiler and preheat the broiler to its highest point. With a pastry brush, coat the mushrooms inside and out with a light film of the vegetable oil. Then arrange the mushrooms, side by side and cap sides up, on the grid. Slide the mushrooms under the broiler about 4 inches from the source of the heat. Broil them undisturbed for about 2 minutes. Turn the caps over with tongs and stuff each mushroom with as much of the garlic butter as it can hold, leaving a ¼-inch space exposed around the rim to prevent the butter from spilling over as it melts. Return the mushrooms to the broiler and broil for 2 to 4 minutes or until the butter has melted and the mushrooms are slightly brown. Under no circumstances, overcook them or they will collapse and the butter will escape.

To serve, place one or two pieces of the toast on individual heated plates. With a spatula, carefully transfer 2 or 3 of the butter-filled mushrooms to each piece of toast, and serve at once.

Baked Mushrooms Stuffed with Duxelles

serves 4

12 firm fresh mushrooms, each 2
to 3 inches in diameter

THE DUXELLES

About ½ pound mushrooms, *to
make 2 cups very finely
chopped*
4 tablespoons (½ stick) butter
About 5 medium shallots or 4 me-

dium scallions (white parts
only), *to make ⅓ cup finely
chopped*
2 tablespoons dry Madeira

THE BÉCHAMEL SAUCE

1 tablespoon butter
2 level tablespoons flour
¾ cup milk

Imported Parmesan cheese,
*enough to make 1 tablespoon
grated*
1 tablespoon butter, *cut into tiny
bits*

Salt
Freshly ground black pepper

Prepare the mushrooms as described on page 72, and save the stems.

The Duxelles:

Chop the ½ pound fresh mushrooms as finely as possible to make 2 cupfuls. Melt the 4 tablespoons of butter over moderate heat. When it has melted completely, but not begun to brown, add the shallots or scallions. Stirring constantly, cook for about 3 minutes until the shallots or scallions soften. Immediately stir in the chopped mushrooms, and cook, stirring constantly, until the mushrooms have begun to release their liquid. Lower the heat and, stirring every now and then, cook the mixture anywhere from 10 to 20 minutes, or until the mushrooms are dry but not brown. Pour in the Madeira, raise the heat to high and, stirring constantly, cook the wine away completely. Remove it from the heat and set aside.

The Béchamel Sauce:

To make the *béchamel* sauce, melt the tablespoon of butter over low heat in a small saucepan. Off the heat, stir in the flour to make a *roux,* and when it is quite smooth, immediately pour in the milk. Beat with a whisk to dissolve the flour partially, then return the pan to high heat and bring the mixture to a boil, meanwhile whisking constantly until the sauce thickens heavily and is perfectly smooth. Wait to season.

The Stuffing:

For the stuffing, stir the *béchamel* into the *duxelles,* 2 or 3 tablespoons at a time, using enough to make a filling dense enough to barely hold its shape in a spoon. (Save any remaining *béchamel* for other uses. Covered with plastic wrap, it will keep, refrigerated, for at least a week.) Now add as much salt and pepper as you think the sauce needs, and stuff as much of the filling into each mushroom as it will hold, mounding it slightly. Sprinkle the mushrooms with a little of the grated cheese, and place one or two bits of butter on each.

Preheat the oven to 350 degrees. Arrange the stuffed mushrooms, side by side, in a shallow, lightly buttered baking dish just large enough to hold the mushrooms compactly. Bake in the center of the oven for 10 to 15 minutes, or until the top of the filling is lightly brown and the mushrooms are tender but not falling apart. If the filling is not brown enough to suit you, slide the mushrooms briefly under the broiler to brown them further. Serve at once.

NOTE: The 2 fillings following may be used in place of the *duxelles* and the procedure for stuffing and baking the mushrooms, is precisely the same.

CRABMEAT FILLING

3 tablespoons butter: 2 for *sauté-ing the shallots and 1, cut into tiny bits, for dotting top of mushrooms*

3 medium shallots or 3 scallions, including an inch or so of their green stems, *to make 3 tablespoons finely chopped*

Baked Mushrooms Stuffed with Crabmeat

1 cup crabmeat, fresh, frozen
  (but thoroughly defrosted
  and drained), or canned,
  shredded finely and any bits
  of cartilage or shell discarded
¾ cup béchamel sauce (page 75)

¼–½ teaspoon strained, fresh
  lemon juice
Salt
White pepper
1 tablespoon dry bread crumbs

Melt the butter in a heavy 10-inch skillet set over high heat. When the butter is thoroughly melted, add the shallots or scallions, reduce the heat to moderate, and cook for about 5 minutes, stirring constantly, until the shallots or scallions are soft but not brown. Stir in the shredded crabmeat, and toss it with the shallots or scallions over moderate heat for a few minutes or so until the mixture is fairly dry. Remove from the heat and immediately stir in the *béchamel* sauce, 2 or 3 tablespoons at a time, using enough of it to make a filling dense enough to barely hold its shape in a spoon. Now add as much of the lemon juice, salt, and pepper as you think it needs, and stuff the filling into the mushrooms, mounding it slightly. Sprinkle each mushroom with a little of the bread crumbs and place one or two bits of butter on top. Bake as described previously in the recipe for baked mushrooms with *duxelles*.

SPINACH FILLING

2 tablespoons butter: *2 for sauté-*
  ing the shallots and 1, cut
  into tiny bits, for dotting top
  of mushrooms
About 5 medium shallots or 3
  scallions, including about an
  inch of the green stems, *to*
  make ⅓ cup finely chopped
1 cup fresh cooked spinach, *finely*
  chopped, squeezed, and
  firmly packed (about 1

pound), or 2 ten-ounce
  packages of frozen chopped
  spinach, *defrosted, squeezed*
  dry, and chopped again
¾ cup béchamel sauce (page 75)
Salt
Freshly ground black pepper
Imported Parmesan cheese,
  enough to make 1 tablespoon
  grated

Melt the butter in a heavy 10-inch skillet set over high heat. When it is thoroughly melted, add the shallots or scallions, reduce the heat to moderate, and cook for about 8 minutes, stirring constantly, until the shallots or scallions are soft but not brown. Stir in the chopped spinach and mix it with the shallots and scallions over high heat until the mixture is quite dry and begins to stick to the bottom of the pan. Remove from the heat and stir in the *béchamel* sauce, 2 or 3 tablespoons at a time, using enough of it to make a filling dense enough to barely hold its shape in a spoon. Taste for seasoning, and add as much salt and pepper as you think it needs. Stuff the filling into the mushrooms, mounding it slightly. Sprinkle each mushroom with a little of the cheese and place one or two bits of butter on top. Bake as described in the recipe for baked mushrooms with *duxelles*.

Mushrooms à la Grecque *serves 6*

3 cups chicken stock, fresh or canned: *if you use the concentrated canned type, dilute it with an equal amount of water*
1 cup dry white wine
1 cup olive oil
½ cup fresh, strained lemon juice
6 parsley sprigs
2 large garlic cloves, *peeled and coarsely chopped*
½ teaspoon dried thyme, *crumbled*
10 whole black peppercorns
1 teaspoon salt
1 pound firm, fresh mushrooms, *left whole if small, quartered or thickly sliced if large*
Parsley (preferably the flat-leaf type), *enough to make 2 tablespoons finely chopped*
Lemon slices or quarters

For the marinade, combine the stock, wine, olive oil, lemon juice, parsley sprigs, garlic, thyme, peppercorns, and salt in a 3- to 4-quart enameled or stainless-steel saucepan. Bring the mixture to a boil over high heat, then turn down the heat to low, and partially cover the pan. Simmer, undisturbed, for about 45 minutes, then strain through a fine sieve set over a large bowl, pressing down hard on the garlic, parsley, and peppercorns with a large spoon before throwing them away.

Return the strained marinade to a saucepan, drop in the mushrooms and, over high heat, bring the marinade to a boil. Reduce the heat to low, cover the pan, and simmer for 5 minutes or less. The mushrooms must not overcook and should retain more than a hint of their original firmness when they are done.

Now pour the entire contents of the pan into a shallow glass or enameled baking dish, and taste for seasoning. Stir in more salt if you think it needs it. Place the baking dish in the refrigerator to cool the marinade quickly, then cover it with plastic wrap, and marinate the mushrooms anywhere from 4 hours to 4 days, turning them over now and then.

To serve, remove the mushrooms from the marinade with a slotted spoon and arrange them on a chilled platter. Moisten them with a little of the marinade, sprinkle with the chopped parsley, and garnish them with slices or quarters of lemon.

Mushroom Barley Soup in the Middle-European Manner
serves 6–8

4 tablespoons butter: *2 for sauté-ing the vegetables and 2 for the roux*

1 small onion, *to make ½ cup finely chopped*

½ medium carrot, scraped, *to make ¼ cup finely chopped*

½ stalk celery, *to make ¼ cup finely chopped*

2 quarts chicken stock, fresh or canned: *if you use the concentrated canned type, dilute it with an equal amount of water*

8 to 10 dried mushrooms, *coarsely chopped*

½ cup pearl barley, *washed in a sieve under cold running water until the draining water runs clear*

2 level tablespoons flour

Salt

Freshly ground black pepper

Fresh dill or parsley (preferably the flat-leaf Italian type), *enough to make 2 tablespoons finely chopped*

Melt 2 tablespoons of the butter in a 3- to 4-quart casserole set over high heat. When the butter is completely melted, add the onions, carrots, and celery. Lower the heat to moderate and cook, stirring frequently, for about 10 minutes, or until the vegetables are soft but not

Mushroom Soup with a Garnish of Raw Mushrooms

brown. Pour in the chicken stock, and bring it to a boil. Turn the heat down to low and stir in the mushrooms and the barley. Partially cover the casserole and, stirring occasionally, simmer the soup slowly for about 1 hour.

Approximately 10 minutes before the soup is done (you will know, if you taste the barley), melt the remaining 2 tablespoons of butter in a small skillet set over low heat. Stir in the flour to make a *roux*. Raise the heat a bit and, stirring constantly, cook the *roux* for about 10 minutes, or until it turns a delicate golden-brown. Watch carefully for any signs of scorching, and lower the heat if necessary. With a rubber spatula, scrape the *roux* into the soup and stir it gently with a whisk until it dissolves. Now simmer the soup for about 20 minutes longer. It will become fairly thick. If it is too thick for your taste, thin it with a little stock or water and simmer for a few minutes longer.

Taste for seasoning, and serve the soup from a large tureen. Sprinkle the soup with the dill or parsley or pass either of the herbs in an individual bowl to be added to the soup at each diner's discretion.

Mushroom Soup with a Garnish of Raw Mushrooms

serves 6-8

8 tablespoons (¼ pound, 1 stick) butter, *softened*
About 12 scallions, including about 4 inches of their green stems, *to make 2 cups finely chopped*
2 level tablespoons flour
5 cups chicken stock, fresh or canned: *if you use the concentrated canned type, dilute* *it with an equal amount of water*
¾ pound firm, fresh mushrooms: *½ pound (2 cups), finely chopped, for the soup, ¼ pound (1¼ cups), cut into paper-thin slices, for the garnish*
1-1½ cups heavy cream
Salt
Freshly ground black pepper

In a large bowl, cream the butter by stirring and mashing it vigorously against the sides of the bowl until it is light and fluffy.

Mushroom Soup with a Garnish of Raw Mushrooms

Stir in the scallions, and with a rubber spatula, transfer the entire mixture to a 3- or 4-quart enameled or stainless-steel casserole. Set the pot over low heat, cover tightly, and simmer for 15 to 20 minutes, stirring occasionally, until the scallions are soft but not brown. In fact, they must *not* brown, so watch them carefully, and lower the heat if necessary.

Stir in the flour to make a *roux*, and simmer, uncovered, for a minute or so, then pour in the stock. Raise the heat and bring the soup to a boil, stirring constantly with a whisk until it thickens lightly. Add the 2 cups of chopped mushrooms, turn down the heat to low, and simmer, partially covered, for about 10 minutes.

Pour the soup into a food mill or sieve set over a large bowl and purée it (with the back of a spoon if you are using a sieve) as finely as you can. (Do not use a blender, enticing as it may be; it will purée the mushrooms too much.)

Return the purée to the casserole and stir in the cream, ½ cup at a time, using as much as you need to give the soup the consistency you like. Ideally, it should not be too thin.

Taste for seasoning. To serve, place the 1¼ cups of sliced mushrooms in the bottom of a large tureen and pour the hot soup over them. Serve at once. The texture of the barely heated-through raw mushrooms will surely delight you as it does me.

Deep-Fried Mushrooms in a Beer Batter
serves 4–6

The beer batter on page 139
24 firm white mushrooms, 1 to 2 inches in diameter, stems left in or snapped out

Vegetable oil or melted shortening for deep frying
Lemon wedges

Prepare the batter precisely as I describe it on page 139. A few minutes before frying the mushrooms, beat the egg white (in the beer-batter recipe) until it forms firm, unwavering peaks, and carefully fold it into the batter.

Deep-Fried Mushrooms in Beer Batter

Heat at least 3 inches of the oil or shortening in a deep fryer until it registers 375 degrees on a deep-fat frying thermometer. Drop the mushrooms into the batter and turn them about gently until they are well coated. With a slotted spoon, drop 6 or 7 of the batter-coated mushrooms into the hot fat and fry them for about 5 minutes, turning them occasionally with a spoon until they are brown and crisp. Drain them on a double thickness of paper toweling while you deep fry the remaining mushrooms in similar batches.

The mushrooms will be at their best and crispest if they are served almost immediately after they are all done. But they may be kept warm in a 250-degree oven for 5 or 10 minutes or so if they must wait. Serve garnished with lemon wedges.

NOTE: There are many variations possible with this recipe: before coating and frying the mushrooms, you may marinate them for an hour or so in a mixture of equal parts of lemon juice and olive oil, seasoned to your taste with salt and freshly ground black pepper. Make sure to pat them dry with paper toweling, however, before dropping them into the batter. Or, instead of coating the mushrooms with beer batter, try the batter on page 288 instead. It is somewhat lighter in texture, and you may prefer it.

PASTA

PASTA

Of the foreign dishes that make up so much of our national cuisine, few are as popular as those of the Italians. Supermarket and grocery-store shelves are laden with such "Italian-style" products as Chicago prosciutto, Wisconsin provolone, and California Italian plum tomatoes. And our fancier stores carry the imported varieties of these foods and others, in great profusion. But despite this largesse, mention Italian food to the average American and his immediate association will be pasta—and, more often than not, simply spaghetti. If proof were needed, pasta outsells all other foods of Italian origin manufactured in the United States today.

Fortunately for us, most American pasta (or macaroni, to give it its interchangeable name) is produced in factories owned, controlled, or managed by Americans of Italian descent. Surely, it is for this reason that our domestic pasta and noodle products are as good as most of their Italian counterparts.

Grateful as we are for this technical achievement, I must confess that our expertise in pasta-making is not matched by our ability to cook it. Rare, indeed, is the dish of pasta ordered in an Italian or American restaurant that doesn't come to the table carelessly drained and blanketed with a dubious tomato sauce. That we consume so much of it prepared in this fashion indicates that we know less about pasta cooking than we suppose.

Contrary to common supposition, pasta, whatever its type, is distinguished not by its taste but by its texture. As well it might be, for it is composed of nothing more than semolina—a special grind of durum wheat—mixed with water. The resultant dough, before being processed as pasta—in the United States, at least—is enriched with thiamin, riboflavin, niacin, and iron. In Italy, any attempt to tamper with traditionally made pasta, however beneficial to health, is looked upon as heretical.

For centuries Italians have used pasta dough to create all manner of decorative and fanciful shapes. That this made a daily diet of pasta (some families in southern Italy actually eat it seven or eight times a week) less monotonous can also be assumed. Few natural objects have escaped immortalization in this simple, tasteless dough. Among the more fanciful of the smaller forms, there are stars, melons, rings, seeds, roses, and tiny snail shells; these, Italians consider to be at their best served as pasta *in brodo,* that is, in a clear soup. Heavier pasta, molded into seashells, conch shells, cocks' combs, wheels, butterflies, twisted strings and ribbons, is designed to be served more elaborately, with richly seasoned sauces.

American macaroni companies, following the lead of their Italian competitors, have lately begun to enlarge their pasta repertoires with such rapidity that the American housewife begins to find herself left behind. Confronted in supermarkets with box upon box of *mezzani* (tubes), *fettuccelle* (ribbons), *maruzzelle* (shells), *rigatoni* (ribbed bent tubes), *tufoli* (large tubes), and *fusilli* (wires), to mention only a few, in her panic she is likely to reach defensively for the nearest box of spaghetti, a can of tomato sauce, and a jar of grated cheese and let it go at that.

But the possibilities for the pastas she has passed by are enormous. Once she becomes aware that the shapes, apart from their decorative aspects, have practical uses, experimenting with them—can become an exciting and rewarding experience.

Most of us are able to cope, more or less with the better-known string and ribbon pastas, like spaghetti, the thinner spaghettini, flat *linguine,* and broad *lasagne.* But few of us know what to do with the tubular *manicotti* and *tufoli* or the pouch-like *conchiglie,* or giant shells. In reality, they are all easy to prepare and whatever their shape or size, need only be cooked in vast quantities of salted boiling water until tender, then filled with a cooked meat, vegetable, or cheese stuffing. Baked with a previously prepared sauce, these make substantial main courses for lunch, dinner, or supper, with the added advantage that, unlike most other pastas, they can, if necessary, be prepared ahead and baked just before serving.

Of the many tubular pastas available, three lend themselves best to stuffing: *manicotti*, literally "small muffs," each about 4 inches long; *tufoli*, smaller and narrower tubes, about 2 inches long; and *conchiglie*, or giant shells deep enough to hold an overflowing tablespoon of stuffing easily. Although it takes some effort, I often prepare all three in large quantities for buffet parties and rather than limit myself to one filling, stuff them with three varieties: a cheese filling, a spinach, mushroom, and prosciutto filling, and a veal and sausage filling. The cheese filling is especially easy to make because, unlike the others, its ingredients require no previous cooking whatsoever. Ricotta, Parmesan, and mozzarella cheeses are simply combined with fresh herbs, salt, pepper, and egg yolks, spooned into a pastry bag fitted with a large plain tip (by far the most sensible way to handle the filling), then piped into the previously parboiled pasta. Among the many advantages of this delicate but definitely flavored filling is that any good, dry country cheese you may have at hand such as pot cheese or farmer cheese can be used in place of the ricotta or even combined with it for an interesting effect. In fact, the drier American cheeses are to be preferred to many of the tasteless and overly moist commercial varieties of ricotta being produced in the United States today.

But whatever the stuffing and however well a particular pasta has been cooked, its success depends, finally, on the sauce with which it is served. Italians, of course, know that all pastas taste alike, but they insist—and rightly so—that each can be given a life of its own if it is served with the proper sauce. They proceed on the assumption that the proper sauce for a particular pasta should be determined by the shape, and even more importantly, by the lightness or heaviness of the pasta itself.

Maruzzelle—or small unfilled shells—*rigatoni, ziti,* and the like should be served with a dense sauce flavored highly enough to be savored through the thickness of the pasta and plentiful enough to fill the hollows of each shell or tube. Such a sauce might be a robust Bolognese meat sauce or *ragù Bolognese* as it is called. With its base of chopped prosciutto, onions, carrots, beef, pork, and chicken livers all slowly simmered in beef stock and wine, this classic northern Italian sauce has the vigor and character to stand up assertively to literally any heavy pasta however convoluted its shape. To soften its impact a bit, Bolognese cooks will often either enrich the *ragù* with heavy cream or use it in tandem with *besciamella*, a cream sauce similiar to the French *sauce béchamel*. Few pasta dishes are quite as luxurious and opulent as this stuffed pasta immersed in a *ragù Bolognese,* masked with a nutmeg-flavored *besciamella,* and gratinéed with a golden crust of freshly grated Parmesan cheese.

Yet *ragù Bolognese,* remarkable as it is, would be unthinkable with more delicate string pastas like vermicelli, for example. Because of its comparative fragility, I feel, it requires a more nuanced sauce if its special texture is to be perceived at all. When fresh ripe tomatoes are at their best and fresh basil available, I make a sauce composed of the youngest of sliced scallions, green stems and all, fresh basil, Italian flat-leaf parsley, and peeled, seeded, and chopped fresh tomatoes, all lightly cooked in butter for only a few minutes. Its fresh fragrance is such that the name I fancifully bestowed on it, *salsa primavera,* seems especially appropriate each time I taste it. This simple, innocent sauce is really at its best, I think with barely cooked and lavishly buttered vermicelli, but spaghettini, *linguine,* and similar pastas do almost as well.

Classic Italian sauces, unlike those of the French, are scarcely known for their refinement. But they are considerably easier to prepare, have fewer pitfalls and possess a vitality French sauces frequently lack. And not all Italian sauces are made with tomatoes, as is so often assumed. Some of the best and most original, in fact, use none at all.

Among the latter, and one of the most useful for the thinner pastas, is a sauce consisting wholly of soft butter, Parmesan or Romano cheese, salt, and freshly ground black pepper. Because I make it often I have discovered a device which I think important; instead of melting the butter and stirring it into the pasta, as the Italians do, I cream the butter first—that is, I beat it with a spoon until it is light and pale, then, still beating, add to it a few tablespoons of heavy cream before combining it with the cheese and seasonings. Prepared in this fashion, as I describe it precisely on page 110, the creamed butter never becomes oily, melts evenly without separating and coats each strand of pasta with a golden velvety sheen.

With the greatest of ease, if not economy, Italians transform this simple dish into an elegant, sophisticated one by adding to it, at the last moment, grated or thinly sliced fresh white truffles. Regrettably, fresh white truffles are not available here, but the canned ones serve the purpose almost as well, although their slightly gamey flavor is not to everyone's taste.

More robust than butter and cheese, and therefore suitable for

somewhat heavier pastas like spaghetti, is the sauce Italians describe as
all'aglio e olio, or garlic and oil sauce. Made by lightly cooking chopped
garlic—and lots of it—in good olive oil and then mixing it into the hot,
drained pasta, this is a preparation to delight any garlic lover's heart,
if not his immediate neighbor's.

The northern half of Italy eats pasta sparingly, but the southern
half eats so much that understandably enough the tomato, a typically
Mediterranean vegetable, forms the basis for many, though by no
means all, of their heavier pasta sauces.

Best known, perhaps—particularly in the United States, with its
large southern-Italian American population—is the Neapolitan marinara, or mariner's, sauce. In Naples, it often is prepared with fresh
tomatoes; but our marinara sauces are always made with canned tomatoes and usually too much tomato paste as well. But whether the tomatoes are canned or fresh, an ideal marinara sauce should be smoothly
textured and lightly scented with olive oil, herbs, onions and anchovies.

Served over thoroughly drained, buttered hot pasta, a wine-dark
marinara sauce makes an admirable dish particularly if the Parmesan
cheese (from Italy) is really from Italy, is well aged, freshly grated,
and plentiful.

Among the many advantages of a good marinara sauce is its use
as a base for an endless number of other sauces. The famous *spaghetti
alle vongole,* or spaghetti with clams and tomato sauce, so much beloved by the Romans, is made by cooking well-scrubbed clams in a
thick marinara sauce. When the clams open, their juices not only thin
the sauce appropriately but flavor it as well. *Spaghetti alle vongole*
is seldom eaten with cheese, but, like other sauces of this type, is liberally strewn with chopped fresh Italian parsley before being served.

Mushrooms, shellfish, chicken, fish, or meat may be cooked in a
previously prepared marinara sauce, and although these sauces suffer
from a certain similarity because of the tomatoes, they nonetheless
offer the enterprising cook many opportunities for experimentation
with little extra work.

With the help of an electric blender it is now possible to make perhaps the most original of all Italian pasta sauces, the Genoese *pesto.*
Because it is distinctive without being overpowering and subtle without being bland, *pesto* can be used successfully with almost every type
of pasta.

It would take more athletic prowess than most of us could muster if we had to make it—in the traditional Genoese way—pounding the basil, garlic, and pine nuts in a mortar, then stirring in the olive oil drop by drop. Done in a blender, *pesto* can be made in a matter of minutes, and if the result is not exactly what you might get in a Genoese household or restaurant, it approximates it to a remarkable degree. But however you make the *pesto*, when it is thinned with a little spaghetti cooking water and stirred into a bowl of hot buttered pasta, it will turn the pasta a brilliant, speckled green, the fresh fragrance and bright color combining to make this a memorable pasta dish, indeed.

But memorable as this is, there is another world of fascinating and original pasta dishes, based on old-fashioned, homemade noodle dough. Although it is similar to factory-made pasta doughs, its significant difference is that it is made with eggs and, of course, almost always by hand. Most Italian cooks, professional or not, are able to produce it with the greatest of ease. It is so simple to do, in fact, that it can be quickly learned by cooks without any particular gift for pastry-making.

Flour, eggs, and a minimal amount of water are mixed to form a firm, rough dough, which is then kneaded unmercifully until it becomes elastic enough to be rolled out to an almost transparent thinness. Then the dough is cut into strips, sheets, squares, or rectangles, each of them destined to become the basis for any number of simple or intricate pasta dishes.

The simplest dish of them all, called *fettuccine Alfredo* in Rome and *tagliatelle al burro* elsewhere, has for the past number of years earned a renown in the United States it most assuredly deserves. Consisting of nothing more than ½- or ¼-inch-wide strips of freshly made noodle dough, classically dressed with butter, cheese, salt, and pepper, it is one of the few pasta dishes in the United States you can be reasonably sure of enjoying in a restaurant if you can find one that makes it well. Generally, its cost is absurdly astronomical, but at its best it is worth it. The silky, suave texture of the paper-thin noodles is extraordinary, particularly if the noodles are cooked no longer than five or six minutes, or until they reach that desirable state of doneness the Italians so graphically describe as *al dente,* or slightly resistant to the bite.

Much more complicated, but still within your capabilities if you are an ambitious cook, are the rectangles, squares, and circles of homemade dough which Italian cooks, seemingly without effort, transform into amazing pasta constructions. Folded around stuffings, twisted into hats, formed into pouches, tortured into coils—there is apparently little Italian cooks can't do with this delicate, pliable dough.

Perhaps the most practical of these pastas for you to attempt are ravioli—little square envelopes containing any one of a number of possible fillings. I have given my recipes for them; if you have the time, they are decidedly worth learning to make. Skillful Italian cooks, not content with ravioli alone, often playfully vary or carry the procedures a few steps farther. They cut the ravioli into circles instead of squares and call them *cappelletti,* or little hats. And *cappelletti* become *tortellini* by folding the stuffed circles in half and bringing the points of the half circles together, twisting them loosely around the finger to form little rings. When they are skillfully made, they look like navels, as the Italian insist they do.

Understandably, it takes determination and a certain amount of practice to produce these morsels. But Italian technology has at last produced a machine that transforms pasta-making into the most elementary of operations and, in effect, makes the rolling pin obsolete. Quite suddenly and without fanfare, there have appeared in American stores small, manually operated, chromium pasta machines, about six by seven inches. They are comparatively inexpensive, and they are capable of kneading, rolling, and cutting an easily made egg-and-flour dough into *fettuccine,* vermicelli, or any number of other types of noodle. The pasta machine can't make ravioli, *cappelletti,* or *tortellini,* but it can make the dough for them. All you need do is take it from there.

Enticing as this may appear, it is, of course, not essential to make your own pasta in order to enjoy it. And it may be consoling to learn that many Italians (and knowing Americans, as well) really prefer the firmer commercial pastas to the softer homemade type.

But whatever the pasta, with so many superb varieties and sauces to choose from, it would seem a pity to continue cooking, saucing, and serving it as carelessly and monotonously as so many of us do. After all, pasta is a dish of great simplicity—and it invites creative embellishment.

THE COOKING, SAUCING, AND SERVING OF PASTA

One pound of pasta of most types is generally adequate for four people if it is served, Italian fashion, as a separate course before the main dish of a meal. But as a main course, as many Americans like it, 1½ pounds would be a more reasonable amount. In either case, 6 to 7 quarts of turbulently boiling water plus 2 tablespoons of salt are indispensable to the successful cooking of pasta, as is a capacious pot large and deep enough for the pasta to swirl around freely as it cooks and rid itself of all its starch. And a tablespoon of olive or vegetable oil added to the water is useful to prevent the heavier pastas, especially, from sticking to each other in the pot. Despite all these precautions, it is wise to stir the pasta from time to time with a long handled fork, never a spoon—lest you entangle the pasta hopelessly and mash it as well.

How long to cook pasta (some types, like *cappello d'angeli*, take as little as 3 seconds, and others, like *rigatoni*, up to 20 minutes) depends on the pasta and finally on your own taste. Most pastas, it is agreed, are at their best cooked *al dente* (or in other words fairly firm to the bite), and to make sure your pasta doesn't go irretrievably beyond this state, taste it frequently as it cooks. Cooking times listed on most packaged pastas tend to be too long and should not be followed precisely, but they can at least be used as a general timing guide. On the other hand, because it is more delicate, homemade pasta takes considerably less time to cook than commercial varieties.

To whatever point you cook your pasta, however, it is imperative that you drain it in a large sieve or colander the very moment it is done. And it is quite unnecessary to run hot or cold water over it to wash away the starch; the ample quantities of water in which the pasta should be cooked will take care of that. Remember, too, that hidden rivulets

of water in the draining pasta should be drained off to prevent any
thinning of the sauce when it is mixed with the pasta. Shake the sieve
or colander vigorously as the pasta drains, and with two forks help the
process along by lifting and separating the pasta until you are certain
all the water is gone.

No time should be wasted between the draining of the pasta and
its saucing and serving. Like a well-puffed soufflé, freshly cooked pasta
must be served the moment it is done. Except for the stuffed and baked
varieties, it can not be reheated nor allowed to stand for more than a
moment or two or it will become gummy and unmanageable.

To expedite the serving of your pasta, have available a heatproof
bowl, a large deep serving platter, and individual serving plates, and
warm them in a 200-degree oven while the pasta is cooking. Have ready
4 to 6 tablespoons of hot melted butter (for 1 to 1½ pounds of pasta;
naturally, omit this if your sauce is a heavily buttered one like the one
on page 108) and heat the sauce, such as the marinara sauce on page
98, if it has been made earlier. The moment the pasta is done, drain it,
and drop it into the heated bowl. Pour in the melted butter and toss
the pasta together with two forks until each strand glistens. Now add
the sauce and toss again, lifting the pasta up from the bottom of the
bowl to coat it thoroughly. The final step, and one too often omitted,
surprisingly, by even practiced cooks, is to taste the pasta before serving it. Almost inevitably, it will need more salt and usually a few more
grindings of pepper as well. Add it courageously, and don't serve the
pasta until it is seasoned to your taste. There is nothing more discourag-
ing to the palate than underseasoned pasta no matter how good its
sauce.

Freshly Made Pasta

(BY HAND)   *makes 1½ pounds*

3 cups all-purpose flour   1 teaspoon salt
3 eggs   4–8 teaspoons lukewarm water
1 tablespoon olive oil

Dump the flour into a large mixing bowl and form a deep depression in the center. Drop in the eggs, add the olive oil and salt, and, with your fingers, gradually mix the flour into the eggs, continuing to mix until the eggs have been completely absorbed and the mixture becomes a somewhat damp and crumbly dough. Sprinkle over it 4 teaspoons of the lukewarm water and toss together with your hands to moisten the dough as evenly as possible. Then knead and press the dough against the bottom and sides of the bowl until it can be gathered into a compact ball. If the dough continues to crumble, add more water, a teaspoon at a time, and mix until the particles adhere. (If you miscalculate the amount of water and the dough becomes too sticky to handle, knead in a little more flour; alternatively, if you have used too much flour, add a little more water.)

Now transfer the dough to a lightly floured surface and knead it by folding it end to end, pressing it down, and pushing it forward with the heels of your hands. Move the dough a quarter turn, clockwise, and repeat the folding, pressing, and pushing process, adding a little more flour from time to time to prevent the dough from sticking to the board. After about 10 minutes of energetic kneading, the dough should be smooth, satiny, and elastic. Let it rest for about 10 minutes before rolling it out.

Divide the dough into 3 or 4 pieces. Place one piece on a lightly floured surface and flatten it with the palms of your hands into an oblong about 1 inch thick. Dust its surface lightly with flour, and with a heavy rolling pin, roll the dough into a long strip. (Because of its elasticity, the dough will be quite resistant at this point, but it will become more pliable as you proceed.) Turn the sheet of dough so that a long side faces you and again roll it out to widen it. Continue this rolling procedure, precisely, flouring the dough lightly from time to time, until you have a large rough rectangle as tissue-paper-thin as you can get it. Roll out the remaining pieces of dough similarly.

To cut into strips most easily, roll each sheet, jelly-roll fashion, into a long compact cylinder. Then, with a large sharp knife, slice the rolls crosswise into the pasta widths of your choice: ⅛-inch-wide rounds for *tagliarini,* ¼-inch-wide rounds for *fettucine* or *tagliatelle,* and 1½- to 2-inch-wide rounds for lasagne. One at a time, unroll the tightly coiled rounds and spread them out on a lightly floured kitchen towel to dry for 15 minutes to ½ hour at room temperature before cooking them. Although they won't be at their best if they wait much beyond that, the noodles may be covered with plastic wrap and refrigerated for as long as 24 hours. Or they may be packed in freezer bags and frozen. Follow the general directions for cooking and saucing the pasta as described on page 92.

Freshly Made Pasta

(MADE IN A PASTA MACHINE) *makes 1½ pounds*

NOTE: The Italian pasta machine imported to this country is always accompanied by a booklet explaining how its mechanism works. Read it carefully.

Make the ball of dough as described in the preceding recipe for hand-made pasta but instead of kneading the dough by hand, knead it in the machine. It will do the job more easily and efficiently.

Set the gauge of the machine at the first or widest notch of the rollers. Feed a small handful of the dough through the opening and roll it into a rough, ragged sheet. Fold the sheet in half, dust it lightly with flour, and run it through the machine again. Continue the folding, flouring, and rolling procedure until the dough is a smooth, short elastic sheet. In fact, it should finally make the sound of a snapped rubber band when it has been kneaded sufficiently. (To reach this point, you may have to put it through the roller four or five times.) Dust the sheet lightly with flour, lay it on a long strip of waxed paper, and knead the remaining dough, folding, flouring and rolling into similar sheets, then laying them down side by side on the paper.

Now roll out the dough, a sheet at a time, in the following fashion: move the gauge one notch toward you, thus bringing the rollers a little closer together. Insert a sheet of the kneaded dough (don't double it now or thereafter), and roll it through the machine. Move the gauge another notch, and roll out the dough again. Continue this process, moving the notch so that the rollers are increasingly closer together and the dough is as thin as you like it. However thin your final sheets of dough, flour each sheet lightly and let it dry for about 10 minutes before putting it through the cutting rollers.

To cut the pasta into flat strings, insert one sheet of dough at a time into either the ⅛-inch or ¼-inch cutter. The first will produce *tagliarini* and the second, *fettucine*. For pastas of other widths, follow the hand-cutting technique I describe in the preceding recipe for freshly made pasta by hand.

Ravioli

*makes about 40 ravioli
if pasta is machine-made;
about 30 if hand-made*

THE PASTA

2 cups all-purpose flour	½ teaspoon salt
2 eggs	3–6 teaspoons lukewarm water
2 teaspoons olive oil	

THE FILLINGS

Any of the fillings on pages 103–6

Prepare the pasta dough as described on page 94, but with the proportions listed above. If you intend to roll the dough by hand, divide it exactly in half. On a lightly floured surface, roll the first half into a large, rough rectangle as tissue-paper-thin as you can get it. Then cover it with a lightly dampened paper towel to prevent it from drying out, and roll the second half of dough into approximately the same size and thickness. (To roll the dough in a pasta machine, follow the directions on page 95, putting the dough finally through the fifth notch. Because of the width of the machine, the sheets will of course be narrower than those described above, and consequently there will be many more of them. As you feed the dough into the machine, use the same amount for each sheet: they should all be approximately the same size.)

Begin making the ravioli by trimming and straightening the edges of one of the pasta sheets with a small sharp knife or a pastry wheel. Drop a scant teaspoon of the filling 1½ inches apart across the surface of the pasta, checkerboard fashion, and with a small pastry brush (or your finger) dipped in cold water, paint damp lines lengthwise and crosswise between the spoonfuls of the filling. Then carefully lift up another sheet of pasta and lay it on top. Trim the edges and run your finger down the layer of dough where it meets the previously moistened lines, pressing down firmly to secure the two layers. With a plain or serrated pastry wheel or small sharp knife, cut the pasta into 1½-inch squares. If you are at all fearful that the edges of the ravioli are not firmly enough secured (and they must be), press the back side prongs of a fork all around the sides to secure them further. Then lift the ravioli up with a small spatula and arrange them side by side on a tray or baking sheet covered with a lightly floured kitchen towel. Ideally, the ravioli should be cooked soon after they are made, but if they must wait for an hour or two, drape them with a lightly dampened towel to keep them slightly moist. For a wait longer than 2 or 3 hours, cover them with plastic wrap and refrigerate.

To cook the ravioli, drop them one by one into 6 to 7 quarts of rapidly boiling salted (2 tablespoons) water. Reduce the heat a bit to prevent the water from churning too rapidly and boil the ravioli uncovered for about 8 minutes or until they are cooked to your taste. Stir them with a spoon (not with a fork, lest you pierce them) from time to time to prevent them from sticking to each other or to the bottom of the pan. When they are done, remove the ravioli from the water with a large slotted spoon and place them side by side on a double thickness of paper toweling or a dry kitchen towel to drain. Serve hot either with melted butter and freshly grated Parmesan cheese or with marinara sauce (page 98) or *ragù Bolognese* (page 106) and grated cheese.

Marinara Sauce

*enough for 1–1½ pounds
of pasta to serve 4–6*

4 tablespoons olive oil
1 large onion, *to make 1 cup
    finely chopped*
1 scraped carrot, *to make ½ cup
    finely chopped*
2 teaspoons dried basil, *crumbled*
Parsley (preferably the flat-leaf
    variety), *enough to make 2
    tablespoons finely chopped*
1 medium bay leaf

2-pound-3-ounce can Italian plum
    tomatoes
1 tablespoon tomato paste
Freshly ground black pepper
3 flat anchovies, drained, *rinsed
    in cold water, and finely
    chopped* (*about 1 teaspoon*)
¼ teaspoon hot red-pepper flakes
    (optional)
Salt

Barely heat the olive oil in an 8- to 10-inch heavy frying pan. Add the onions, and stirring occasionally, cook them over low heat for 8 to 10 minutes until they are soft and translucent but not brown. Stir in the carrots, cook for 3 or 4 minutes longer, then add the basil, parsley, and bay leaf. Simmer a moment or two, stirring constantly, and drop in the tomatoes with all their liquid. Raise the heat and bring the mixture to a boil, meanwhile mashing and breaking up the tomatoes with the back of a large spoon. Stir in the tomato paste and a liberal grinding of black pepper. Cook the sauce over moderate heat (it should cook fairly briskly, not simmer) for 30 to 45 minutes, or until most of the liquid in the pan has evaporated and the sauce has become a coarse purée thick enough to hold its shape lightly in a spoon. (Watch carefully for any signs of burning, and lower the heat a bit if necessary.)

Now purée the sauce in a food mill (*not* a blender, which would liquefy it too much), or, with the back of a large spoon, rub it through a sieve set over a bowl. Discard any vegetable debris remaining in the mill or sieve and return the sauce to the pan. Bring it to a simmer over low heat and stir in the chopped anchovies and, if you like your sauce highly seasoned, the pepper flakes. There should be about 2 cups of smooth thick sauce in the pan; if there is more, and it seems thin or watery, boil rapidly, uncovered, stirring frequently, until it thickens further and has cooked down to 2 cups. Taste for seasoning. Despite the salty anchovies, it will probably need at least ¼ teaspoon more salt.

Marinara Sauce with Italian Sausages

enough for 1–1½ pounds of pasta to serve 4–6

2 cups marinara sauce (page 98)
½–¾ pound sweet or hot Italian
    sausages, or a combination of
    both

Freshly grated imported Parmesan
    cheese

In a 2- to 3-quart heavy saucepan, bring the previously prepared marinara sauce to a simmer over low heat. Let it simmer, half covered, while you blanch the sausages in the following fashion to rid them of their excess fat.

Pierce the sausages in two or three places with the tip of a small sharp knife and place them in a 10- to 12-inch frying pan. Cover them completely with cold water, bring to a boil, then reduce the heat to moderate. Simmer for 5 to 8 minutes, pour off the cooking water, and place the sausages on paper toweling to drain. Then cut the sausage into rounds, ½ inch thick, and drop them into the simmering sauce. Simmer for 10 to 15 minutes, and pour the sauce—sausages and all— over freshly cooked, drained, and buttered spaghetti (see page 92) or any other fairly substantial pasta. Serve with a bowl of freshly grated Parmesan cheese.

Marinara Sauce with Lobster

enough for 1–1½ pounds
of pasta to serve 4–6

2 cups marinara sauce (page 98)
1½-pound live lobster
3 tablespoons olive oil

Freshly grated imported Parmesan
cheese (optional)

In a 2- or 3-quart heavy casserole, bring the previously prepared marinara sauce to a simmer over low heat. Let it simmer, half covered, while you prepare the lobster.

Before killing the lobster, see page 216 for reassurance. Wash the lobster under cold running water, then lay it on its back on a chopping board. Place a towel over its torso and, holding the lobster firmly with one hand, with a large sharp knife cut off the tail section at the point where it joins the body. Slice the tail, crosswise, into 3 or 4 sections, twist off the claws, and cut the body in half lengthwise. Remove and discard the gelatinous sac (the stomach) behind the eyes and the intestinal vein attached to it, but leave the green tomalley (the liver) and any black coral (the roe) intact in the shells. With a sharp blow of the knife, make a gash on the underside of each claw to facilitate removing the claw meat later.

In a 10- to 12-inch heavy frying pan, heat the olive oil over high heat until it almost reaches the smoking point. Add the lobster and cook it briskly for 2 or 3 minutes, turning it about in the oil with tongs until the shells become bright pink.

Transfer the lobster and the liquid in the pan into the simmering marinara sauce. Half cover the casserole, and over the lowest possible heat, simmer the lobster for about 10 minutes. Then remove the lobster from the sauce with tongs, pick all the meat from the shells with a lobster fork, and cut it into ½-inch dice. Return the lobster meat to the sauce and simmer for a moment or two to heat it through. Serve with freshly cooked, drained, and buttered *linguine*, spaghetti (see page 92), or any other string pasta. Serve with or without freshly grated Parmesan cheese.

Marinara Sauce with Clams or Mussels

enough for 1–1½ pounds
of pasta to serve 4–6

2 cups marinara sauce (page 98)
1 dozen small hard-shell clams,
   thoroughly washed and
   scrubbed, or 1 dozen mussels,
   thoroughly washed, scrubbed,

and their black, ropelike
tufts removed (page 220)
Freshly grated imported Parmesan
   cheese (optional)

In a 2- to 3-quart heavy casserole, bring the previously prepared marinara sauce to a simmer over low heat and drop in the prepared clams or mussels. Cover the casserole securely and simmer for 5 to 8 minutes, or until the shells open. Give them a few minutes longer, then discard any that don't open. Either remove the clams or mussels from their shells and return them to the sauce, or serve them with it, shells and all, poured over freshly cooked, drained, and buttered pasta of virtually any type. Serve with or without grated Parmesan cheese.

Stuffed Pastas

HOW TO STUFF, SAUCE, AND BAKE THEM

Manicotti:

These are fairly thick tubes of pasta about 4 inches long and 1 inch in diameter. Like all pasta meant to be stuffed, *manicotti* must be partially cooked, then stuffed while warm. To do this most effectively, drop 8 *manicotti* into 6 quarts of rapidly boiling salted (2 tablespoons) water and cook them briskly, uncovered, for about 8 minutes, or until they soften somewhat but still retain their tubular shapes. Add a quart of cold water to the pot to cool the *manicotti* a bit, then, one at a time, remove them from the water, pat them dry with paper toweling, and stuff them with one of the three fillings on pages 103–6. (Any of the three fillings will be sufficient for 8 *manicotti,* or enough to serve 8 people as a first course and 4 as a main course.) To stuff the *manicotti* easily (or, for that matter, to stuff all tubular or pouchlike pastas), use a large pastry bag fitted with a ¾-inch (No. 9) or slightly smaller plain tip. Lacking this, a long-handled iced-tea spoon will do almost as well. The stuffed *manicotti* should be baked in a shallow baking dish just large enough to hold them snugly in one layer and may be sauced in any of the following ways:

Spread a thin coating of *besciamella* sauce (page 108) on the bottom of the baking dish and arrange the stuffed *manicotti* on it. Cover the *manicotti* with a layer of either *ragù Bolognese* (page 106) or the marinara sauce (page 98), and spread the remaining *besciamella* lightly over the top. Or omit the *besciamella* sauce altogether and use only the *ragù Bolognese* or marinara sauce. But however you sauce the *manicotti,* sprinkle the last layer of sauce evenly and liberally with freshly grated Parmesan cheese. Bake in the middle of a preheated 350-degree oven for about 30 minutes, or until the sauce begins to bubble. Slide under the broiler for a few seconds to brown the top (being careful not to let it burn) and serve it directly from the baking dish.

Tufoli:

These are small tubular pastas 1½ inches long and about 1 inch in diameter, and may be precooked, stuffed with one of the fillings on pages 103–106, sauced and baked precisely as the *manicotti* described previously. Any of the three fillings will stuff about 32 *tufoli,* enough to serve 8 people as a first course or 4 as a main course.

Conchiglie, or Giant Shells:

These are deep, shell-shaped pastas 1½ to 2 inches long, and may be precooked, stuffed with one of the fillings on pages 103–6, sauced, and baked precisely as the *manicotti* described previously. Any of the three fillings will stuff 24 to 28 shells, enough to serve 6 people as a first course or 4 as a main course.

Lasagne:

These are long strips of pasta, usually about 2 inches wide and 9 to 10 inches long and are available with either straight or rippled edges. Unlike *manicotti, tufoli,* or *conchiglie,* the following—somewhat untraditional—version of baked *lasagne* is rolled rather than stuffed.

Drop 12 *lasagna* strips, one at a time, into 6 quarts of rapidly boiling salted (2 tablespoons) water, add a tablespoon of olive oil if you wish, and boil the *lasagne,* uncovered, for about 20 minutes, or until they are tender but not too soft. Stir occasionally with a large spoon to prevent the *lasagne* from sticking together or to the bottom of the pot. When the *lasagne* are done, let a thin trickle of cold water run into the pot until the *lasagne* have cooled, then transfer them, one by one, placing them side by side on towels to drain. Fill them with one of the fillings on pages 103–6 in the following fashion: with a rubber spatula, spread each strip of *lasagna* evenly, with about 3 tablespoons of the filling of your choice. Then, starting at the bottom end, roll each strip, like small jelly rolls, into plump, neat cylinders, smoothing the open ends with a rubber spatula. Place the stuffed *lasagne,* seam-sides down, in a baking dish, and sauce and bake them precisely as for the previously described *manicotti.* Twelve stuffed *lasagne* will serve 6 people as a main course, 12 as a first course.

NOTE: Homemade pasta (page 94) may be cut into *lasagna*-sized lengths and filled as the version described above. They should be precooked, however, no longer than 6 or 7 minutes and drained on paper toweling as described above.

THREE FILLINGS FOR STUFFED PASTAS OF ALL TYPES

Four-Cheese Filling   *makes about 2 cups*

½ pound pot cheese or farmer cheese
½ pound ricotta cheese
Imported Parmesan cheese, *enough to make ¼ cup freshly grated*

Peeled garlic cloves, *enough to make ¼ teaspoon finely chopped*
½ teaspoon salt
Freshly ground black pepper

Four-Cheese Filling

3 large or 4 small egg yolks,
    *reserving the whites for some
    other purpose if you wish*
Chives, *enough to make 2 table-
    spoons finely cut,* or green
    scallion tops, *enough to make
    2 tablespoons finely chopped*

Parsley (preferably the flat-leaf
    variety), *enough to make 1
    tablespoon finely chopped*
¼ pound fresh mozzarella, *cut
    into ¼-inch dice*

With a large spoon, beat the pot or farmer cheese in a large bowl
until smooth, then, little by little, beat in the ricotta. Add the Parmesan
cheese, garlic, salt, a liberal grinding of black pepper, and the egg
yolks, one by one, beating well after each addition. Then stir in the
chives or scallion tops, the parsley and mozzarella, and taste for seasoning. The filling should be quite definite in flavor; add more salt, pepper,
and even some more chives or scallions if necessary. Cover with plastic
wrap or foil and refrigerate for at least an hour. Use as a stuffing for
pasta, following the directions on page 101.

Spinach and Mushroom Filling

makes about 2 cups

6 tablespoons (¾ stick) butter:
    *4 for sautéing the onions and
    2 for sautéing the mushrooms*
1 small onion, *to make ½ cup
    finely chopped*
Peeled garlic cloves, *enough to
    make 1 teaspoon finely
    chopped*
2 packages frozen spinach,
    *thoroughly defrosted,
    squeezed dry by the handful,
    and finely chopped,* or 1
    pound fresh spinach, *cooked,
    drained, squeezed dry, and
    finely chopped*

½ pound mushrooms, *to make 2
    cups coarsely chopped*
2 eggs
Imported Parmesan cheese,
    *enough to make 4 tablespoons
    grated*
⅛ pound prosciutto or other
    smoked ham, *coarsely
    chopped*
¼ pound mozzarella, *cut into
    ¼-inch dice*
¼ teaspoon salt
Freshly ground black pepper

Over moderate heat, melt 4 tablespoons of the butter in a 10-inch heavy frying pan. Add the onions and garlic and, stirring frequently, cook for 5 minutes without letting them brown, then add the spinach. Raise the heat and cook, stirring constantly, until all the moisture in the pan evaporates and the spinach begins to stick lightly to the pan. With a rubber spatula, scrape it into a large mixing bowl.

Melt the remaining butter in the frying pan and add the mushrooms. Cook over moderate heat for 2 or 3 minutes, until they begin to give off their liquid, then raise the heat and rapidly boil away almost all their moisture. Now scrape the mushrooms into the mixing bowl. Stir the mixture for a few minutes to cool it, then, with a wooden spoon, beat in the eggs, one at a time. Stir in the Parmesan cheese, prosciutto, mozzarella, salt, and a few grindings of black pepper. Taste for seasoning and add more salt and pepper if you think it needs it. Use as a stuffing for pasta, following the directions on page 101.

Veal and Sausage Filling   *makes about 2 cups*

2 tablespoons olive oil
½ small onion, *to make ¼ cup finely chopped*
½ pound sweet Italian sausages, *stripped of their casings and finely crumbled,* use half sweet and half hot sausages or any well-seasoned pork sausage meat, *similarly stripped (if cased) and crumbled*
½ pound lean veal, *ground*
6 tablespoons dried bread crumbs, *made preferably from stale Italian or French bread*

¼ cup heavy cream
2 eggs
Parsley (preferably the flat-leaf variety), *enough to make 2 tablespoons finely chopped*
¼ teaspoon dried rosemary, *crumbled*
Lemon peel: *the lemon thinly peeled with a swivel-bladed vegetable peeler, then finely chopped—enough to make ½ teaspoon*
¼ teaspoon salt
Freshly ground black pepper

Veal and Sausage Filling

Heat the oil in a 10- to 12-inch heavy frying pan, add the onions and cook them over moderate heat for about 5 minutes, stirring frequently. When they have barely begun to color, add the sausage meat. Raise the heat and, mashing the sausage constantly with the flat of a fork to break up any lumps, cook until it has rendered most of its fat and turned a light brown. Quickly add the veal, and again mashing it with the fork, cook it for 3 to 4 minutes over high heat until it has turned from pink to brown and separated into small granules. Scrape the entire contents of the pan into a sieve and drain the meat of all fat.

Soak the bread crumbs in the heavy cream in a large bowl for 3 or 4 minutes, and add the drained meat. Beat together with a large spoon until the mixture is fairly smooth, then beat in the eggs one at a time. Stir in the parsley, rosemary, lemon rind, salt, and a few grindings of pepper, and taste for seasoning. Use as a stuffing for pasta, following the directions on page 101.

Ragù Bolognese

BOLOGNESE MEAT SAUCE   *makes about 3½–4 cups*

1 large onion, *to make 1 cup coarsely chopped*

1 medium celery stalk, *to make ½ cup coarsely chopped*

½ medium carrot, *to make ¼ cup coarsely chopped*

¼ pound prosciutto or any other good smoked ham, *coarsely chopped*

6 tablespoons (¾ stick) butter: *4 for sautéing the ham and vegetables and 2 for sautéing the chicken livers*

½ pound lean beef chuck and ¼ pound lean pork, *ground together twice through the finest blade of a meat grinder*

½ cup dry white wine

1½ cups beef stock, fresh or canned

1 pound ripe tomatoes, *peeled, seeded, and finely chopped (1½ cups)—see page 109;* or use 1½ cups drained and finely chopped canned tomatoes

Parsley (preferably the flat-leaf variety), *enough to make 1 tablespoon finely chopped*

¼ pound chicken livers, *trimmed of their fat and cut into ¼-inch dice*

Salt

Freshly ground black pepper

Freshly grated nutmeg   ½–1 cup heavy cream (optional)

Combine the onions, celery, carrots, and ham on a chopping board, and, with a large sharp knife, mince them together as finely as possible, almost to a paste, in fact. In a 10- to 12-inch sauté pan or 2-quart enameled or stainless-steel casserole, melt 4 tablespoons of the butter over moderate heat and add the vegetable mixture, or the *soffritto*, as the Italians call it. Cook, stirring frequently, for about 8 minutes, or until the vegetables and ham are lightly brown. Add the ground beef and pork, mashing it into the *soffritto* with a large spoon, and continuing to mash until all the lumps have disappeared and the meat has separated into small granules. Raise the heat and fry briskly for 3 or 4 minutes to brown the meat lightly.

Add the wine, bring it to a boil, and, stirring constantly, cook until it has almost completely evaporated. Stir in the beef stock, chopped tomatoes, and parsley, bring to a boil again, then reduce the heat to its lowest point. Half cover the pan or casserole and simmer the sauce for about 1 hour, stirring every now and then. By this time, most of the liquid will have cooked away and the sauce should be thick and intensely flavored. However, if it seems the slightest bit watery or pallid to the taste, bring it to a boil over high heat and, stirring constantly, boil it rapidly, uncovered, until the liquid has reduced and thickened to an almost syrupy consistency. Let the sauce simmer slowly, uncovered, while you prepare the chicken livers.

In an 8-inch frying pan, melt the remaining 2 tablespoons of butter over high heat. When it has begun to turn ever so lightly brown, add the diced livers and, stirring them constantly with a spoon, sauté them for 2 or 3 minutes, or until they are lightly brown but still faintly pink inside. Scrape them into the sauce, half cover the pan, and simmer for another 5 minutes. Taste for seasoning and add as much salt, freshly ground black pepper, and freshly grated nutmeg as you think it needs. The *ragù* may now be used exactly as it is or you may stir into it ½ to 1 cup of cream for more richness. Simmer a moment or two to heat the cream through and taste again for seasoning.

Bolognese sauce may be served with any of the more substantial types of pasta, following the directions on page 101. For most tastes, 2 cups are adequate for 1 to 1½ pounds of pasta. The remainder may be refrigerated, tightly covered, for 3 to 4 days. Or it may be successfully frozen for future use.

Besciamella Sauce

makes about 1 cup

To be used with Bolognese or marinara sauce for any of the baked, stuffed pastas on page 101.

3 tablespoons butter	½ teaspoon salt
3 level tablespoons flour	Pinch of white pepper
½ cup milk	A few gratings of nutmeg
½ cup heavy cream	

Melt the butter over moderate heat in a small saucepan without letting it brown. Remove the pan from the heat, add the flour, and stir together thoroughly. Add the milk and cream, and beat with a whisk to dissolve the flour partially. Then return the pan to moderate heat and, whisking constantly, bring the sauce to a boil. When it is quite thick and smooth, reduce the heat to its lowest point and simmer the sauce for 2 or 3 minutes to remove any taste of raw flour. Stir in the salt, pepper, and nutmeg. If the sauce is not to be used immediately, stir it every now and then as it cools to prevent a skin from forming on its surface. Then cover it with plastic wrap and refrigerate. It will solidify when cold. Reheat it to tepid, stirring constantly, before using. Thin it with a little more milk or cream if it seems thicker than it was originally.

Primavera Sauce

for 1 to 1½ pounds of vermicelli, enough to serve 4 to 6

For *vermicelli*, preferably, but may be used to sauce *linguine*, spaghettini, or any of the more delicate homemade string pastas.

3 pounds (8 medium size) ripe tomatoes, *peeled, seeded,*	*finely chopped, and drained (about 4 to 4½ cups)*

6 tablespoons (¾ stick) butter
About 12 young scallions, including at least 2 inches of their
green tops, *to make 1½ cups
thinly sliced*
Fresh basil, *enough to make 3
tablespoons coarsely cut,* or
1½ tablespoons dried basil,
crumbled

Flat-leaf parsley, *enough to make
4 tablespoons coarsely cut*
Salt
Freshly ground black pepper
Freshly grated imported Parmesan
cheese

Because this sauce takes only minutes to compose, it should, ideally, be made while the pasta is cooking. The ingredients themselves should of course be prepared ahead and held in readiness. Most important are the tomatoes. Drop them into a large pot of boiling water and let them boil for about 10 seconds. Drain them at once in a colander and run cold water over them. With a small sharp knife, cut out and discard their stem ends. Then peel the tomatoes carefully, slice them in half crosswise, and squeeze each half firmly to remove its seeds and juices. Chop the tomatoes finely and drain them in a sieve.

Melt the butter over moderate heat in an 8- to 10-inch heavy frying pan. Add the scallions and cook them for 2 or 3 minutes, tossing them about in the hot butter with a wooden spoon. They should not brown but wilt only slightly. Stir in the basil and parsley, cook for 10 seconds, then add the tomatoes. Raise the heat to high and, stirring constantly, bring them to a boil. Then cook the sauce briskly for 2 or 3 minutes until most but not all the tomato juices have evaporated. Do not overcook. Stir in as much salt and freshly ground pepper as you think it needs, and, following the procedures on page 92, drain the pasta, toss it in the hot butter, and pour the hot sauce over it. Taste for seasoning and add the extra salt and pepper it will undoubtedly need. Serve at once with a bowl of freshly grated Parmesan cheese.

NOTE: If you must, you may make the sauce ahead of time but in that event, reheat it without any further cooking lest its fresh, fragrant flavor be dispelled.

Butter, Cheese, and White Truffle Sauce

for 1–1½ pounds of pasta to serve 4–6

8 tablespoons (¼ pound, 1 stick) butter, *softened*
Imported Parmesan cheese, *enough to make 1 cup grated: ½ cup for the sauce and ½ cup to be served with the pasta*

⅓ cup heavy cream
Salt
Freshly ground black pepper
1 or 2 canned white truffles, *drained and sliced paper-thin or coarsely chopped*

In a mixing bowl, cream the butter by beating and mashing it with a large spoon until it is smooth and fluffy. Beat in the ½ cup of the grated Parmesan and then the cream, adding it about 1 tablespoon or so at a time and beating well after each addition. (If you plan to make the sauce ahead of time, cover and refrigerate it, but let it return to room temperature for about 1 hour before serving.)

Following the directions on page 92, cook the pasta, drain it, and place it in a heated bowl, but omit tossing it with the melted butter. Instead, add the butter-cheese sauce, the salt, and liberal grindings of black pepper, then, with two forks, toss the pasta until every strand is coated with the glistening mixture. Taste for seasoning; it will undoubtedly need more salt. Then gently stir in the truffles or scatter them over the top and serve at once.

NOTE: If the truffles are unavailable, omit them. Although the sauce will scarcely be the same without them, it will be far superior to other sauces of its type.

Garlic, Oil, and Parsley Sauce

enough for 1–1½ pounds pasta to serve 4–6

For any of the string pastas, either the commercial or freshly made types.

¾ cup olive oil
Peeled garlic cloves, *enough to make 2 tablespoons finely chopped*
½ teaspoon hot red-pepper flakes
Parsley (preferably the flat-leaf

Italian variety), *enough to make 4 tablespoons finely chopped*
½ teaspoon salt
Freshly ground black pepper

While the pasta is cooking, warm the olive oil over low heat in a small skillet or saucepan. Stir in the garlic and the pepper flakes and simmer for 3 to 4 minutes, being careful not to let the garlic brown. Remove the pan from the heat and add the chopped parsley.

Following the procedure described on page 92, drain the pasta, toss it in hot butter, and pour over the sauce. Add the salt and a liberal amount of freshly ground pepper and, with two forks, mix the pasta and sauce together thoroughly, lifting the pasta up from the bottom of the bowl so that the strands are thoroughly coated with oil, garlic, and parsley. Taste for seasoning, add the extra salt and pepper the pasta will undoubtedly need, and serve at once.

Pesto

*to make 1½–2 cups
for 1–1½ pounds of pasta
to serve 4 to 6*

Peeled garlic cloves, *enough to make 2 teaspoons finely chopped*
1 teaspoon salt
Fresh basil leaves, *stripped from their stems and finely chopped, enough to make 2 cups (tightly packed)* or use flat-leaf parsley, *enough to make 2 cups finely chopped,*

and 2 tablespoons dried basil leaves
Pine nuts or walnuts, *enough to make 2 tablespoons finely chopped*
1–1½ cups olive oil
Imported sardo or Parmesan cheese, *enough to make 1 cup grated: ½ cup for the sauce and ½ cup to be served with the pasta*

With a large pestle, pound the garlic and salt to a paste in a mortar. (Or use the back of a wooden spoon to mash it to a paste in a heavy bowl.) A small amount at a time, pound in the fresh basil (or the parsley and dried basil), and when it is reduced to a purée, pound in the pine nuts or walnuts. Now beat in the olive oil, a few tablespoons at a time, and continue adding oil (up to 1½ cups, or even more, if necessary) until the *pesto* is thin enough to run sluggishly off a spoon. Stir in ½ cup of the grated cheese.

Thin the *pesto* with 3 tablespoons of the hot spaghetti water, then stir about half the sauce into the freshly cooked, drained, and buttered pasta (as described on page 92). Taste for seasoning and add as much salt and freshly ground pepper as you think it needs. Serve at once accompanied by the remaining *pesto* served in a sauceboat and the rest of the freshly grated cheese passed in a bowl.

NOTE: To make the *pesto* in an electric blender, combine 1 cup of the oil and all the other ingredients except the cheese in the blender jar and blend at high speed until reduced to a smooth purée. Stop the blender every now and then and scrape the herbs down from the sides of the jar with a rubber spatula. If the sauce seems too thick and clogs the machine add more oil, using all of it or even more if necessary. Transfer the *pesto* to a bowl and stir in the cheese. Thin with the spaghetti water and serve as described above.

cooking with
wines and spirits

cooking with wines and spirits

Wine is one of the oldest alcoholic drinks known to man, and the refinements he has introduced in making it have always paralleled the development of fine cooking. Perhaps this accounts for the great cuisines of the countries that produce their own wines, and for the relatively unsophisticated food of those that do not. Certainly the culinary excellence of at least two of the most important wine countries, France and Italy, is beyond dispute.

In America during the eighteenth and early nineteenth centuries, domestic wines other than herbal, dandelion, or berry wines—not really wines at all—were unknown. Our upper classes imported European vintages at great expense, and served them at elegant dinners. Such wines were used only sparingly in the kitchen and had little influence on American cooking. Farmers and members of the working class drank hard cider, corn whisky, rum, and bourbon. It was not until 1870 that California began to produce wine in any quantity, and it was hard going to convince the average American to drink it, let alone cook with it. By the early 1900's, however, wine was being produced in California in excess of 30,000,000 gallons a year, and French food cooked in wine began to appear in New York establishments less grand than Sherry's, Rector's, and Delmonico's. Under the influence of new cookbooks and ladies' magazines, housewives began to experiment with wine cookery. What the results tasted like we will never know, but if the good women were laboring under some of the present-day misconceptions about wine cookery, their dishes probably left much to be desired.

Cooking with alcohol in any of its drinkable forms can frequently transform a prosaic dish into a masterpiece, or almost as frequently ruin it. Paradoxically, cooking with alcohol, once shorn of its mysteries, proves to be more a matter of cooking *away* the alcohol than cooking *with* it. For in food the taste of alcohol is harsh and unpleasant; the usefulness of wine, beer, spirits, and liqueurs in cooking depends on knowing how to control the alcohol in each of them.

More culinary crimes have been committed with wine than with any other food. (And that wine is a food has yet to be generally recognized; a pint-and-a-half bottle of table wine has approximately the caloric value of a quart of milk, a pound of bread, or two pounds of potatoes.) Table wine contains 10 to 13 per cent alcohol, the result of natural fermentation. When the wine is subjected to heat, however, the alcohol at once begins to evaporate, and leaves in its wake a raw, acrid liquid that must then be fully cooked to be edible.

Many American and English cookbooks speak of "cooking" wines. There is no such thing. There are only wines that are fit or not fit to drink. Cooking a poor wine with food doesn't camouflage the wine's imperfections but, by reduction and concentration, intensifies them. A thin, rough wine will be even thinner and rougher when cooked, and its only effect upon the food cooked with it will be to spoil it.

Cooking with a good wine doesn't necessarily mean cooking with a great one. In fact, the ephemeral bouquet of a rare vintage wine will vanish irretrievably at the first touch of heat. A wine to be cooked with should have fullness of body and a decided flavor. In most European countries, particularly France, the *vin du pays,* or local wines, meet this description admirably and have been the inspiration for any number of fine regional dishes. Fortunately for us, many of these dishes can be made successfully with other wines, including those from California and New York State.

Two of the most popular French dishes in America today are *coq au vin* and *boeuf bourguignon.* Recipes for them in one form or another appear in almost any cookbook, and the wines suggested range from Italian Chianti to California Pinot Noir. Any reasonably good red wine will do the job quite well. When the dishes don't succeed, I have discovered it is not the wine that is at fault but the cooking methods. Most American recipes for *boeuf bourguignon* work infinitely better than those for *coq au vin.* The reason is simple; it takes considerably longer to cook stewing beef than it does a young chicken. Consequently the wine in the *boeuf bourguignon* is fully cooked, whatever the dish's other deficiencies, while that in the *coq au vin* is undercooked. The classic *coq au vin à la bourguignonne* was always made with an old cock (and the bird's blood, as well), and it usually took a couple of hours of stewing, at least, to make it edible. The wine in the sauce would then be properly cooked. Now French cooks achieve the same result by pre-cooking the wine, reducing it to about half its original volume, before cooking a young and tender chicken in it.

Rather than repeat the classic *coq au vin à la bourguignonne* as published in an earlier book of mine (*Michael Field's Cooking School*), I have devised another *coq au vin* using Riesling rather than Burgundy. In France this is a common practice, the French housewife thriftily cooking with whatever good wine—or even combinations of wine—that she may have on hand. In my *coq au vin Riesling* on page 124 you will notice that I have carried the principle of precooking not only the wine itself but combining it with chicken backs, giblets, necks, wing tips, including any other chicken oddments I happen to have at hand. The wine-chicken stock produced by this method is suave and winey in the best sense of the terms. It intensifies, as all good cooking with wine should, the natural flavor of the food rather than overpowering it. You can, if you like, add the mushroom garniture typical of the Burgundian version, but I think my *coq au vin Riesling* is better without it.

The Swiss with their great culinary genius and their superb *vin du pays* (few of which, unfortunately, are exported to America) have elevated cooked wine to a position of eminence in their national dish, cheese fondue. This is the hot, communal dunking dish composed of Switzerland or Gruyère cheese, melted in hot wine then laced with Kirsch, a cherry *eau de vie*. Chunks of crusted French bread are speared on long fondue forks, swirled about in the fragrant cheese mixture, then eaten forkful by forkful without more ado. Many a skier half frozen after a day on the slopes has been grateful for its warming effects, as I have on blustery cold days in the Swiss Alps even though I don't ski. I have, at least on one occasion, felt less grateful—when the fondue had been poorly made, that is, with insufficiently cooked wine, the aftertaste of the hot uncooked wine streaking across my tongue like a lash. But I knew how to resolve the problem; I waited until my obviously less discerning or perhaps hungrier skiing friends had greedily consumed half the bubbling fondue before claiming my share. By that time, the fondue had simmered long enough for the wine to have cooked through sufficiently to reach the point of finesse a fine fondue should have.

In my discussion of the classic Swiss fondue on page 37 I have ex-

plained in some detail the difficulties American cooks frequently en-
counter when they slavishly follow Swiss fondue recipes in cookbooks
written by authors who have evidently never attempted to cook the
dish themselves or have curious misconceptions about it.

Switzerland's French neighbors in the Jura mountains, culinarily
competitive as always, have never, evidently, approved at all of the
classic *fondue neuchâteloise,* however well the Swiss made it. The
French developed a version of their own, not only cooking the wine but
reducing it to almost a third of its original volume, then smoothing it to
a velvety sheen with a little butter and thick cream before adding the
Kirsch; their *fondue jurasienne* is in every way different from its Swiss
counterpart, and my recipe for it appears in my book *Michael Field's
Cooking School*—it is really a matter of taste which of the two you
prefer.

As in the *fondue jurasienne,* fully cooked wine is also the secret of
the great French sauces, particularly those composed almost wholly of
wine. One of the most notable is *sauce marchand de vin*—literally, wine
merchant's sauce. In France, it is almost indispensable to a grilled
steak. Its preparation is again based on reduced wine, cooked down together with minced shallots to half its original volume. In restaurants
devoted to classical French cooking, this ambrosial liquid is finished off
with a *sauce espagnole,* more commonly known as brown sauce. But a
quite respectable *marchand de vin,* as you will see on page 128, can be
made at home without the *espagnole*—a complex and time-consuming
preparation.

A generally misunderstood function of wine is its place in a marinade. Marinades were devised primarily to tenderize and preserve
meat; flavoring it was a secondary consideration. Although marinades
may be composed of lemon or lime juice, both of which contain tenderizing enzymes, wine (often combined with wine vinegar) does a
better job in certain preparations. Wine in a marinade will tenderize
the lowliest cut of meat, an old indifferently endowed fowl or a tough
haunch of venison. Unlike commercial tenderizers—whose enzymatic
action on meat tends to break down its cell walls and to produce a
pulpy rather than a pliable texture—wine gently tames the meat into
tractability and subtly flavors it at the same time. Even an ordinarily
tough cut of beef like chuck steak, usually braised or, in other words,
cooked with moist heat, will be tender enough to serve broiled as a
London broil if it is first marinated in a mixture of wine, wine vinegar,

and herbs for 12 hours or so. If you have doubts about this, follow my recipe for broiled marinated chuck steak on page 129, but be certain to pay careful attention to my carving instructions as well. I think you will find the flavor of the chuck (provided you buy a fine cut, comparatively free of fat and gristle) in many ways comparable, if not sometimes superior, to a more expensive cut of beefsteak.

Less familiar forms of wine cookery employ the aristocratic fortified wines; that is, wines fortified after fermentation with added alcohol or brandy. Of them all, Port, Madeira, and Marsala are the finest for cooking. When they are of the best quality, these are wines of such distinction that their cooking should be approached not only respectfully but with some trepidation. Unlike table wines, most fortified wines should never be cooked for any length of time because intense heat destroys their penetrating and distinctive bouquet. But in most dishes except those with a thickening agent used in the Cumberland sauce on page 146, if they are heated to just below the boiling point, all taste of alcohol will be gone and the wines will bloom at their peak of flavor.

A couple of tablespoons of fine Madeira stirred into a spinach purée will lift that ordinary green to Olympian heights (see my version on page 130), and a well-made Madeira sauce can make even a precooked canned ham seem exciting. Port, too, does remarkable things for food, particularly when it is used to marinate fruit.

Cooking with sherry is on the whole an Anglo-American invention and, frankly, not one of the best. For me, at least, traumatic memories of lobster Newburgh and chicken à la king made with a cloying "cooking" sherry keep me from cooking anything with sherry, even a superior one. Fine French and Spanish chefs seldom cook with sherry—except for a few special dishes—and they have known the wine much longer than we have. They wisely drink it instead.

On the other hand, the Italians have a fine way with Marsala, which is more robust than the other fortified wines, and can be cooked somewhat more strenuously without losing its character—as in the celebrated *veal scaloppine Marsala*, my version of which appears on page 131. The Marsala in *zabaglione*, however, is barely cooked and is perhaps all the better for it. Impalpable as air, *zabaglione* (see my recipe on page 132) is something of a relief after a substantial Italian dinner. In fact, the Italians quite sensibly think of it as a restorative.

Champagne is neither a table wine nor a fortified wine—in the hierarchy of wines it occupies a place all its own. At its best, it is perhaps the noblest of them all. But the French province of Champagne, unlike those of Burgundy or Bordelais, has never developed an important cuisine based on its wine. And with good reason. Champagne does not lend itself to cooking, clever chefs and enterprising restaurateurs not withstanding. A *ris de veau au Champagne* listed on a restaurant menu may attract customers, but, truth to tell, this dish of *La Grande Cuisine* would be equally as magnificent made with a good dry white wine as I have suggested in the recipe on page 134. The effervescence of champagne, no matter how rare or special its vintage, is dissipated at the first touch of heat; the flat wine remaining has little left to recommend it but its basic flavor and its illustrious name.

In fruit desserts, however, chilled champagne may be used with scintillating effect. I often steep peeled peaches, apricots, or plums, fresh strawberries or raspberries in a little Cognac for an hour or so, present them in chilled glasses, then pour the best champagne I can afford over each serving of fruit at the table.

Although champagne and beer are hardly to be mentioned in the same breath, they do have one thing in common: their effervescence. The effervescence in beer is as ephemeral as that in champagne, but beer is made of sterner stuff. Like a table wine, it can be cooked for hours and emerge only the better for it. Because of its flavor of malt and hops, uncompromising to say the least, beer should only be used in dishes stalwart enough to stand up to it. Such a dish is the Belgian *carbonnade à la flamande*. This beef-in-beer stew is made with such a staggering quantity of onions that at first sight it seems the most improbable of culinary constructions. But it is an extraordinary dish, the onions, beef, and beer merging at the end of long, slow cooking to produce a sauce quite as original as the elements that went into it. And cooked with American beer—or even Stout—instead of Belgian beer, my version on page 137 of a *carbonnade* is in some ways better I think than many of its Flemish prototypes.

Like wine in a marinade, beer has functions in cooking other than that of flavoring. The tenderizing action of the alcohol in the beer will lighten a frying batter perceptibly. The French have known this for a long time, as their delicate fruit *beignets* clearly testify. Welsh rabbits use beer, in greater amounts, for the same purpose, but here the beer adds flavor to the melted cheese as well.

Cooking with wine or beer, whatever the problems and subtleties they present, is considerably less dramatic than cooking with distilled spirits. When you cook with these properly, you are literally playing with fire. A routine French cooking practice has lately become so popular in America that we have borrowed the French word *flamber,* that is, "to flame," to describe it.

High alcohol content is necessary for effective flaming. A spirit—whether it is Cognac distilled from wine, Calvados from apples, gin from grain, rum from sugar cane, or aquavit from potatoes—more than meets this requirement; it contains at least 40 per cent alcohol by volume—80 proof as we in the U.S. describe it. But the basic cooking problem remains the same: how best to evaporate the alcohol in the spirit you are using and yet retain the flavor that led you to choose it in the first place.

Burning the alcohol away is the simplest solution and a fast, spectacular one. But there are other methods. Because the flavoring elements in spirits are on the whole quite stable, comprising as they do various fruits, roots, herbs, barks, berries, and condiments, their basic character is not easily altered. Gin, for example, can be flamed easily, but its alcohol can be almost as quickly evaporated by boiling, without destroying its characteristic flavor of juniper. I never hesitate to substitute gin in recipes that call for juniper berries, which are often difficult to find. It works wonderfully in a *choucroute,* the braised sauerkraut preparation so beloved by the Alsatian French; to some American admirers of the dish, gin is even preferable. After the requisite four or five hours of slow cooking, the gin is tamed and thoroughly absorbed by the sauerkraut, but its juniper flavor remains. The *choucroute* with spareribs on page 140 that I have adapted from an old Alsatian recipe not only uses gin but Kirsch—again unflamed—as well.

However, flaming a spirit has a number of advantages in dishes that require less cooking than a *choucroute.* A chicken sauté is one of them. During the first stages of the sautéing or browning process, intensely flavored bits of dark crust will collect on the bottom of the pan. Flaming the chicken at this point with Cognac, gin, Calvados, or any other spirit will flavor the bird exquisitely; furthermore, the blazing alcohol will burn away any excess fat, dissolve the crust in the pan and form the glaze as it is called for the base of a fine sauce. The chicken *en cocotte Vallée d'Auge,* on page 142, a superb example of Norman cooking, quite naturally employs the Norman apple brandy, Calvados. It must be sadly noted, however, that old Calvados (the only type to consider) is rare these days. If I don't have old Calvados on hand, I substitute a good American applejack; it does the job with almost equal success.

Flaming cooked foods at the table has little to recommend it, and the manner in which it is done in many restaurants has even less. As I have so frequently observed it is an empty theatrical gesture that often has an unfortunate effect on the dish being flamed. It cannot be denied, of course, that *crêpes Suzette,* plum pudding, dessert omelettes, and even cherries Jubilee, among other things, are all the better for being flamed at the last moment with a suitable spirit. But the rite must be performed competently. Although it is not necessary or even desirable that the spirit be fully cooked, any alcohol remaining will insidiously penetrate the food and give it an almost medicinal aftertaste. I consider it imperative that the alcohol be allowed to burn itself out completely. This is best accomplished by heating the spirit to luke-warm in a small pan before setting it alight, and whenever appropriate to the dish— *crêpes Suzette,* for example—first sprinkling the food with a little sugar to add extra fuel to the flame.

Liqueurs are less difficult to cook with than spirits but I think their special intensity of flavor demands discretion and control. Flaming them publicly or privately is really a waste of time. Although the alcoholic content of liqueurs is as high as that of spirits and sometimes higher (Pernod is 90 proof) their flavors are so concentrated that I tend to use only a small amount of a liqueur, whatever its flavor, to achieve the effect I want. Consequently, the little alcohol present is not unpleasant when it is not entirely dispelled.

Heavily sweetened liqueurs are generally effective in desserts such as soufflés. These may be flavored with almost any sweet liqueur, and the most popular is surely Grand Marnier. An even more unusual liqueur-flavored soufflé, however, is one I make with crème de cacao amplified with coffee. A soufflé is a considerably less hazardous culinary operation than is commonly supposed, and my crème de cacao–mocha soufflé, as I call it, on page 144, is easier and more effective than most. Because it contains no flour, milk, or butter but only eggs, sugar, crème de cacao, and coffee, the soufflé has a texture unlike that of most dessert soufflés.

For some tastes, orange liqueurs such as Grand Marnier, curaçao, Triple Sec, among others, are indispensable to the preparation of roast ducks and their sauces. In my view, this can be a successful alliance only if the sweetness of the orange liqueur is tempered with a substantial quantity of fresh lemon juice.

The less sweet liqueurs (and there are a number in which the taste of sugar is barely apparent) may be used successfully in a wider variety of preparations. One of the most original is oysters Rockefeller, made with a purée of green herbs and vegetables flavored with Pernod or its Louisiana equivalent Herbsaint. Southerners will hotly deny it (Creoles claim it as their very own), but the origin of this curious dish is indubitably French by way of the Italians, oysters having been baked with spinach and *mornay* sauce in France since the days the gourmandizing Catherine de Medici journeyed from Florence to France with her retinue of Italian cooks when she married the future King Henry II.

Even with all our proliferating culinary literature, our many cooking schools, and the general elevation and refinement of our eating and drinking habits, cooking with wines and spirits is still approached by many Americans with uncertainty, confusion, and, often, downright suspicion. By and large, American regional cooking, indifferent to the example of cuisines in wine-growing countries, remains almost the same as it was a hundred years ago. Despite the strong culinary influence of the French from the time of Lafayette to the present, the lustier contributions of the wine-loving Italians, the increasing variety and quality of our own viniculture—despite all this, our native American cooking remains as unsullied by alcohol as any teetotaler could ask. Whether the remarkable cooking of the Pennsylvania Dutch and the Shakers, both pervasive influences in our culinary history, has anything to do with this, makes for interesting speculation. Although these farming people were much given to "putting up" fruits in brandy, and to drinking staggering amounts of beer with their meals, they never cooked with anything more potent than vinegar.

To foster the cause of American alcohol cookery, we need not douse our native flapjacks with applejack—maple syrup is infinitely preferable. But short of flaming everything on a sword, the many good and imaginative cooks in this country could make better use of our wines, beers, and whiskies. We are no slouches when it comes to drinking the stuff. For the sake of sobriety alone I wish that more of it were being cooked.

Coq au Vin Riesling   *serves 4*

3 cups Riesling or any other
    Moselle or Alsace or Rhine
    wine (1 bottle)
A 3-pound chicken, *cut into 4*
    pieces (*back bone and wing*
    tips removed), *the legs left*
    attached to the thighs to pre-
    vent the meat from shrinking
    from the bones; they can be
    cut apart, if you wish, just
    before serving
The chicken giblets, neck, and any
    other odd pieces
1 medium-size onion, *peeled and*
    thinly sliced
2 medium-size carrots, *scraped*
    and thinly sliced
2 large unpeeled garlic cloves,
    bruised with the flat of a
    large wide-bladed knife

A bouquet consisting of 4 sprigs
    parsley, 1 large leek (white
    part only, *well washed to rid*
    it of sand), 1 celery top with
    its leaves, and 1 large bay
    leaf, *tied together with string*
½ teaspoon leaf thyme, *crumbled*
Chicken stock, fresh or canned
    (optional)
¼ pound lean, mildly cured salt
    pork, *rind removed and dis-*
    carded, and the pork cut into
    ¼-inch dice
12–16 small white onions, each
    about 1 inch in diameter,
    peeled
Salt
White pepper
¼ cup cognac
2 level tablespoons flour

Pour the wine into a 2-quart enamel or stainless-steel saucepan. Add the chicken back (cut into 2 or 3 pieces), the giblets, neck (and other fresh or frozen chicken giblets or chicken oddments you may have on hand), the onion, carrots, garlic, and the bouquet. Bring the wine to a boil over high heat, meanwhile skimming off the scum and the foam as they rise to the top. Stir in the thyme, reduce the heat to its lowest point, and simmer the stock with the pan partially covered for about 40 minutes, or until it has reduced to about 2 cups. (Don't worry if you have miscalculated and end up with less; simply bring it to the proper amount by adding fresh or canned chicken stock.) Strain it through a fine sieve into a bowl and set it aside.

Render the salt pork by frying it over high heat in a heavy 10-inch

Coq au Vin Riesling

sauté pan or enamel or stainless-steel skillet, stirring it occasionally. When the pork bits have given off all their fat, remove them from the skillet with a slotted spoon and set them aside on paper toweling to drain.

Preheat the oven to 350 degrees. Reheat the fat in the skillet until it sizzles, then drop in the little white onions. Shake the pan with a back-and-forth motion so that the onions roll around in the fat and brown on all sides. (Don't carry this too far or the outer layer of the onion skin will come off.) Scoop the onions out of the pan with a slotted spoon and place them in a small baking dish just large enough to hold them snugly in one layer. Add enough of the browning fat to film the bottom of the baking dish and bake the onions in the middle of the oven for about 30 minutes, or until they feel tender but still slightly resistant when you press them with your fingers. Remove them to a double thickness of paper toweling to drain.

Pat the chicken pieces dry with paper toweling (they won't brown well if they are damp) and sprinkle them liberally with salt and, more discreetly, with pepper. Heat the pork fat remaining in the skillet until it sizzles (add a little vegetable oil if the fat doesn't film the bottom of the pan entirely). Add the chicken pieces, skin-side down, and brown them rapidly, regulating the heat so that they brown fairly quickly without burning. Turn them with tongs and brown the other sides for a somewhat shorter period, again adding more oil to the pan if necessary. Turn off the heat, and with a bulb baster, remove most but not all the fat from the pan. Heat the Cognac to lukewarm in a small pan, then set it alight with a match. Pour the flaming Cognac a little at a time over the chicken, sliding the skillet back and forth on the range until the flames subside. Remove the chicken to a plate and set it aside while you make the sauce.

Stir the flour into the dark mahogany glaze remaining in the skillet. Stirring constantly, simmer the *roux,* as this mixture is called, over low heat, for about 1 minute (watch carefully for any signs of burning), then pour in the 2 cups of the strained reserved wine stock. Beating with a whisk, bring the sauce to a boil over high heat, whisking constantly until the sauce is thick and smooth. Return the chicken, skin-side up, to the sauce (include any juices that have accumulated on the plate) and bring to a boil. Then, with the heat at its lowest point and the skillet tightly covered, simmer the chicken for about 30 minutes, or until it is tender enough to be easily pierced with a fork. Now add the reserved browned onions and the browned pork bits; simmer for 5 minutes more to heat them through, and taste for seasoning. (If the sauce is too thick for your taste, thin it slightly with a little fresh or canned chicken stock.) Serve at once. It might be useful for you to know that the *coq au vin* can be made ahead and reheated successfully. Simply bring it to a boil, covered, lower the heat, and simmer the chicken for a few minutes until it is heated through.

Pièce de Boeuf à la Bourgignonne

serves 8–10

4 pounds beef rump, bottom round, or chuck of beef, not less than 5 inches around: *have the butcher encase it in a ¼-inch layer of fat, preferably from the kidney, and tie it with 4 or 5 loops of string around its width*

1 large clove garlic, *peeled and cut into 4 or 5 one-eighth-inch slivers*

½ pound fresh pork fat, *diced and rendered,* or 6–8 tablespoons vegetable oil

24 small white onions, each about 1 inch in diameter, *peeled and left whole*

1 large onion, *to make 1 cup finely chopped*

1 small carrot, *scraped, to make ½ cup finely chopped*

4 level tablespoons flour

1 cup beef stock, fresh or canned

3 cups dry red wine, preferably a French Burgundy or an American Pinot Noir

½ teaspoon dried thyme, *crumbled*

Freshly ground black pepper

A bouquet consisting of 4 sprigs parsley, 1 celery top with leaves, 1 large leek, white part only (well washed to rid it of sand), and 1 large bay leaf, *tied together with string*

1 pound medium-sized fresh mushrooms, *quartered*

Preheat the oven to 325 degrees. Meanwhile, with the point of a small sharp knife, make 4 or 5 deep incisions in the meat and insert a sliver of garlic in each, then set the meat aside. If you plan to use pork fat instead of vegetable oil (and the extra effort involved will give the

meat a deeper color and finished sauce a finer flavor than the oil),
render it by frying it over high heat in a heavy enameled casserole large
enough to hold the meat comfortably. When the pork bits have browned
and given off all their fat, remove them with a slotted spoon and discard them. Heat the rendered fat in the casserole (or 6 tablespoons of
the oil) over high heat until it literally sizzles, then drop in the whole
onions. Slide the pot with a back-and-forth motion over the heat so
that the onions roll around in the fat and brown lightly on all sides.
With a slotted spoon, transfer them to a small baking dish just large
enough to hold them snugly in one layer. Add enough of the browning
fat from the casserole to barely film the bottom of the baking dish, and
bake the onions in the middle of the oven for about 30 minutes, or until
they feel tender but still slightly resistant when you press them with
your fingers. Remove them from the baking dish to paper toweling to
drain, then set them aside.

Pat the meat dry with paper toweling, then heat the fat remaining
in the casserole to sizzling (if the fat doesn't completely film the bottom
of the pot, add the pork fat from the dish in which you cooked the
onions or the remaining oil). Add the meat and brown it well on all
sides, regulating the heat so that the meat takes about 20 minutes to
reach its proper mahogany hue. Then remove the meat to a plate, and
add the chopped onions and carrots to the casserole. Stirring occasionally, cook the vegetables for about 8 minutes until they color lightly,
and stir in the flour. Stirring constantly, cook the mixture over low heat
until the flour turns the color of dark caramel, but be careful not to let
it burn or your final sauce will be bitter and unpleasant. Then pour in
the beef stock and the wine. Beat with a whisk over high heat until the
sauce comes to a boil and thickens. Return the browned meat (and any
juices that have accumulated around it) to the casserole, add the thyme
and a few grindings of black pepper, and submerge the bouquet in the
sauce. Again bring the sauce to a boil, cover the casserole tightly, and
braise in the lower third of the oven for 2 hours. Turn the meat over
after the first hour, and continue to braise for the second hour (tougher
cuts of beef, such as chuck, naturally, will take longer) until the meat
can be easily pierced with a fork. Fifteen minutes or so before you think
the beef will be done, add the mushrooms and the reserved little white
onions, cover, and braise for the remaining quarter hour.

To serve, remove the beef to a carving board and cut away the
strings. Skim and discard as much fat from the surface of the sauce as

you can, and taste for seasoning. If the sauce seems thin and lacks flavor, reduce it by boiling it rapidly, uncovered, until it reaches the consistency and flavor you like. If the sauce is too thick, thin it with a little beef stock (*not* wine). Carve the meat into ¼-inch-thick slices, arrange them slightly overlapping down the center of a large platter, and scatter the mushrooms and onions around it. Then moisten the meat and vegetables with a few tablespoons of the sauce, and serve the remaining sauce separately in a sauceboat.

Marchand de Vin Sauce for Broiled Steak, Roast Beef, or Hamburger   serves 6

8 medium shallots, *to make ½ cup finely chopped*	1 teaspoon flour
1½ cups dry red wine	1 teaspoon fresh lemon juice
2 teaspoons meat glaze (preferably the brand called BV)	Chives or parsley, *enough to make 2 tablespoons finely cut*
	Salt
8 tablespoons (¼ pound, 1 stick) unsalted butter, *softened*	Freshly ground black pepper

Combine the shallots (onions will *not* do) and wine in an 8-inch enamel or stainless-steel skillet and bring to a boil over high heat. Reduce the heat to low and simmer, uncovered, until the wine has cooked down to about ¾ cup. (When you measure it, don't worry if the amount is a little less or a little more than ¾ cup.) Stir in the meat glaze and simmer until it dissolves. Strain the mixture through a fine sieve set over a bowl, pressing down hard on the shallots with a spoon to extract all their juices before throwing them away.

With a wooden spoon (or in an electric mixer equipped with a paddle or pastry arm), beat and mash the butter in a bowl until it is smooth and fluffy, and beat into it the teaspoon of flour. Then beat in, drop by drop, the lemon juice, and finally the chives or parsley. Put aside (in the refrigerator, if it must wait for longer than ½ hour) until ready to serve.

Just before serving, bring the wine to a simmer over low heat and beat into it, a little at a time, the butter mixture (softened again if it has been refrigerated). Simmer the sauce for a minute or two until it thickens lightly. Taste for seasoning. Commercial meat essences tend to be salty, so add salt to the finished sauce with a light hand. Freshly ground pepper may be added with more abandon. Serve in a heated sauceboat.

Broiled Marinated Chuck Steak   *serves 4*

2 pounds best-quality chuck   *skewer together any split*
    steak, cut 1 inch thick: *ask*   *seams in the meat*
    the butcher to either sew or

THE MARINADE

½ cup vegetable oil   1 large bay leaf
¼ cup dry red wine   2 large cloves garlic, *peeled and*
1 tablespoon red wine vinegar   *thinly sliced*
2 teaspoons soy sauce   Parsley, *enough to make 1 table-*
½ teaspoon salt   *spoon finely chopped*
½ teaspoon peppercorns, *coarsely*
    ground

Plan to marinate the steak for 6 to 7 hours at room temperature or, if your kitchen is very warm, for 8 hours (or even longer) in the refrigerator. To make the marinade, pour the oil, wine, wine vinegar, soy sauce, and salt into a small bowl and beat them together vigorously with a whisk until the seasoning liquids are fully incorporated in the oil. Stir in the peppercorns, bay leaf, garlic, and parsley and pour the mixture into a shallow glass, stainless-steel, or enamel baking dish just large enough to hold the steak snugly. Dip the steak into the marinade, turning it over 2 or 3 times to moisten both sides thoroughly. Then lay it flat, spoon over some of the marinade, and cover with plastic wrap. Turn the steak over every 2 hours or so.

Remove the broiler pan and grid, turn on the broiler, and allow as much time as your particular broiler needs to reach its maximum heat. Remove the steak from the marinade, pat it dry with paper toweling, and broil it 2 inches from the heat for about 3 minutes. Brush it lightly with the liquid marinade, broil 1 minute longer, raising the rack 1 inch closer to the heat if the steak has not yet turned a golden-brown. Turn the steak over with tongs, broil for about 1 minute, brush with the marinade, and broil for about 1 minute longer. If the steak is not to be chewy or tough, it should not be broiled much beyond the medium-rare stage. Serve at once, carving the slices against the grain of the meat with a thin, very sharp carving knife held at about a 45-degree angle to the steak. This diagonal slicing, contrary to popular misconception, will not make the slices more tender than they essentially are, but will produce exceedingly thin slices with a much wider surface than you could possibly achieve were you to slice the steak directly down.

NOTE: The marinating procedure described above may be applied to other types of steaks known as London broils: particularly a flank steak, or the top round of beef. Broiling times, naturally, will vary with the thickness of the particular steak. Whatever the type of steak you use, the diagonal slicing procedure is essential to its success.

Purée of Spinach with Madeira
serves 4

3 tablespoons butter: *2 for sautéing the spinach and 1 for mixing into the spinach before serving*
2 ten-ounce packages of frozen spinach, *defrosted, squeezed completely dry, and chopped fine*, or 1 pound fresh spinach, *cooked, squeezed dry, and finely chopped*
1 level tablespoon flour
¾–1 cup heavy cream
½ teaspoon salt
⅛ teaspoon white pepper
A few gratings of nutmeg
2 tablespoons dry Madeira

Over moderate heat, melt 2 tablespoons of the butter until it begins to froth but not brown. Add the chopped spinach and toss it about with a fork to break up any clumps. When the spinach is well coated with the butter, sprinkle the tablespoon of flour over it and stir until all traces of flour disappear. Cook the spinach for a minute or so, then add ¾ cup of the cream, the salt, white pepper, and a few gratings of nutmeg. Stir constantly until the mixture comes almost to the boil and thickens perceptibly. Then reduce the heat to its lowest point, stir in the Madeira, stirring occasionally, and simmer the spinach for 2 or 3 minutes to remove any taste of raw flour, and to cook away the alcohol in the Madeira. If the purée is too thick for your taste, stir in as much of the remaining cream as you like (even more, if necessary), simmer a moment longer, and taste for seasoning. Serve with any unsauced fish, fowl, or meat.

Scaloppine al Marsala   *serves 4*

1½ pounds of veal scallops (cut, preferably from the rump), *each sliced ⅜ inch thick and pounded with the side of a cleaver or a meat pounder between waxed paper to a ¼-inch thickness*
Salt
Freshly ground black pepper
½ cup flour
5 tablespoons butter, *softened:*

3 for sautéing the scallops and 2 for the sauce
2 tablespoons olive oil
½ cup dry Marsala
½ cup chicken stock, fresh or canned
A few drops of fresh lemon juice
Parsley (preferably the flat-leaf Italian type), *enough to make 1 tablespoon finely chopped*

Immediately before sautéing the scallops, sprinkle them liberally on both sides with salt and more discreetly with pepper. Then dip them into the flour and shake each scallop vigorously—almost as if you were waving a flag—to remove the excess. There should be only the lightest coating of flour on each piece of veal.

Melt 3 tablespoons of the butter and the oil over high heat in a heavy 10- to 12-inch skillet. When the fat begins to turn ever so lightly brown, add 3 to 6 of the scallops (depending on their size) and brown them for 2 or 3 minutes on each side, turning them with tongs. Watch

Scaloppine al Marsala

carefully for any sign of burning, and regulate the heat so that they color quickly and deeply without burning. Transfer the scallops to a plate and brown the remaining ones in a similar fashion.

Quickly deglaze the pan by pouring off all but a thin film of its fat, adding the Marsala, and bringing it to a boil over high heat, meanwhile with a wooden spoon scraping in any browned particles clinging to the bottom of the pan. Add ½ cup of the stock and bring to a boil again. Boil briskly for 2 minutes or so until the sauce thickens to a slightly syrupy consistency. Then return the veal to the skillet. Reduce the heat to low, baste the scallops with sauce, and cover tightly. Simmer for 2 or 3 minutes to heat the veal through. The scallops should be tender and show no resistance when pierced with the point of a small sharp knife; if they seem tough (they won't be, if the veal is of good quality), cover the pan tightly and simmer them over low heat for a few minutes longer.

To serve, arrange the scallops, slightly overlapping, on a heated platter, add a few drops of lemon juice to the sauce in the skillet, taste for seasoning, and stir in the remaining 2 tablespoons of softened butter. Pour the sauce over the veal and serve at once, sprinkled with the parsley, if you like.

Hot Zabaglione

serves 4

1 whole egg plus 5 egg yolks
2 tablespoons sugar
½ cup sweet Marsala or, less
    traditionally, sherry, Madeira,
    or Port

Cinnamon or freshly grated nutmeg (optional)

Combine the yolks, whole egg, and the sugar in a 3-quart stainless bowl and beat the mixture vigorously for a minute with a wire whisk, rotary beater, or electric hand beater (the last by far the least arduous instrument of the three) until the eggs begin to thicken slightly. Place the bowl in a 10-inch skillet half full of simmering water and, over low heat and beating constantly, slowly pour in the wine. Continue to beat until the mixture is hot and has thickened into a frothy custard, dense enough to barely hold its shape in a spoon. This may take as long as 10 minutes of continuous beating. (If the mixture appears to be heating too rapidly, remove the bowl from the skillet, beat a minute or two to cool the custard, then return the bowl to the simmering water, beating as before.)

Immediately spoon the *zabaglione* lightly into sherbet or large wine glasses and serve at once. Dust each serving lightly with cinnamon or a few gratings of nutmeg, if you like.

COLD ZABAGLIONE

The preceding zabaglione
½ cup heavy cream

Follow the same procedure as described in the master recipe, but instead of serving the *zabaglione* hot, immediately transfer it to another bowl and place it in a large bowl filled with crushed ice or ice cubes submerged in a couple of inches of cold water. Continue beating as before until the *zabaglione* is cold.

Quickly beat the heavy cream in a chilled bowl until it clings in soft peaks to the beater when it is lifted out of the bowl. With a rubber spatula, gently stir the cream into the cold *zabaglione*, using an up-and-under folding motion to keep the mixture light, and continue to fold until the cream is absorbed. Do not overfold. Serve at once in chilled sherbet glasses or cover the bowl with plastic wrap and refrigerate for no longer than 1 hour before serving. Dust each serving with a little cinnamon or a few gratings of nutmeg.

NOTE: You may, if you prefer, omit the cream altogether and serve the *zabaglione* when it is cold. It will not keep successfully, however, without the cream, and should be served the moment it is chilled.

Veal Sweetbreads with Champagne Sauce

RIS DE VEAU AU CHAMPAGNE　　　　　　　*serves 4–6*

2½–3 pounds veal sweetbreads
Salt
White vinegar
10 tablespoons butter: *4 for sauté-
    ing the vegetables, 4 for
    sautéing the mushrooms, and
    2, softened, for the sauce*
1 medium onion, *peeled and
    finely chopped*
1 medium carrot, *scraped and
    finely chopped*
About ⅛ pound boiled ham, *to
    make ¼ cup diced*
¾ cup dry white wine
1 cup chicken stock, fresh or
    canned

A bouquet consisting of 6 parsley
    sprigs, 1 celery top with its
    leaves, and 1 large bay leaf,
    tied together with string
½ teaspoon thyme, *crumbled*
1 tablespoon fresh, strained lemon
    juice
¾ pound fresh mushrooms, *thinly
    sliced*
½ cup flour
6 tablespoons clarified butter (see
    NOTE at end of recipe)
1 cup (1 split) flat champagne
    or use 1 cup good dry white
    wine
1 cup heavy cream

Wash the sweetbreads under cold running water, then let them soak in a bowl of cold water for 30 to 40 minutes. Change the water three times or simply let the tap water trickle into the bowl for the entire period. Place the sweetbreads in an enamel or stainless-steel pan just large enough to hold them, cover them with cold water, and stir in about 1 teaspoon of salt and 1 tablespoon of white vinegar for every quart of water. Bring to a boil over high heat and boil the sweetbreads rapidly, uncovered, for 2 minutes. Immediately drain them and plunge them into a bowl of cold water and soak again for 5 minutes, or until the sweetbreads are cool enough to handle. Separate each pair of sweetbreads with a small sharp knife and cut away any thick or hard tissue and pieces of fat. Carefully pull off as much of the outer membrane as you can with the aid of the knife, but don't carry this too far lest the sweetbreads tear and fall apart. (Refrigerate, covered, if you don't plan to cook them immediately; sweetbreads are extremely perishable.)

Preheat the oven to 325 degrees. Over moderate heat, melt the 4 tablespoons of the butter in a 4-quart heavy enameled casserole and stir in the onion, carrot, and ham. Reduce the heat to low and, stirring occasionally, cook the mixture for about 8 minutes until it is soft but not brown. Add the wine and boil it over high heat until it has almost completely cooked away. Then stir in the chicken stock and ¼ teaspoon salt, bring to a boil again, and remove the casserole from the heat. Immediately arrange the sweetbreads side by side in the casserole, add the bouquet and thyme, and cover tightly. Place the casserole in the middle of the oven and braise the sweetbreads undisturbed for 15 minutes.

Meanwhile, melt 4 tablespoons of the remaining butter in an 8-inch skillet, stir in the lemon juice, and add the sliced mushrooms. Toss them about to coat them thoroughly, cover the pan, and cook over moderate heat for 3 or 4 minutes until they have given off their juices. Transfer the mushrooms with a slotted spoon to a bowl and reserve the juices in the skillet.

When the sweetbreads have cooked their allotted 15 minutes, remove them to a plate to cool, and pour into the casserole the reserved mushroom juices. Bring the casserole to a boil over high heat, uncovered, and boil briskly until the liquid has cooked down to ¼ cup—more or less. Strain the entire contents of the casserole through a sieve set over a bowl, pressing down hard on the vegetables to extract all their juices before throwing them away. Skim the surface of the liquid of all fat and reserve the liquid.

Now carefully slice the sweetbreads into neat ¼-inch-thick slices. Sprinkle them with a little salt, then coat them lightly with flour and shake off the excess. Melt the 6 tablespoons of clarified butter (see NOTE) over high heat in a heavy enamel skillet, preferably one with a nonstick surface. When the butter begins to turn ever so lightly brown, add the sweetbreads and brown them lightly for 3 or 4 minutes on each side. Remove them to a heated platter, cover loosely with foil to keep them warm, and pour the champagne or white wine into the fat remaining in the skillet. Bring to a rapid boil over high heat, meanwhile scraping into it any brown sediment clinging to the bottom of the pan. Boil briskly for about 3 minutes, uncovered, or until the champagne or wine has almost completely cooked away. Then pour in the reserved sweetbread liquid and the cream. Bring to a boil again and boil for about 3 minutes longer; the sauce should now be thick enough to coat a spoon lightly. If it seems too thin, boil it for a minute or two longer. Quickly stir in the reserved mushrooms (do not include any juices that may have accumulated around them) and taste for seasoning. Off the heat, swirl in the 2 tablespoons softened butter and pour the sauce over the waiting sweetbreads. Serve at once.

NOTE: To clarify ¼ pound butter, cut it into small pieces and melt it slowly over low heat without letting it brown. Remove it from the heat, skim off the surface foam, and let the butter rest for 2 or 4 minutes. Then carefully spoon off the clear butter, discard the solids (the whey) settled at the bottom of the pan.

Macédoine of Fruit with Fresh Ginger and Port

serves 4–6

1 small can frozen pineapple chunks
1 package frozen sliced peaches
1 package frozen raspberries
Fresh ginger root, *enough to make 1 teaspoon scraped and grated,* or use 2 scant table- spoons candied ginger root,

well washed, dried, and finely chopped
Lemon rind: *the lemon thinly peeled with a swivel-bladed vegetable peeler, then finely chopped, enough to make 1 teaspoon*
¼ cup Port wine

Drop the frozen pineapple, sliced peaches, and raspberries into a large sieve set over a bowl and let them defrost thoroughly at room temperature. Discard the accumulated juices and place the defrosted fruit in a large stainless-steel or glass bowl. Gently stir in the fresh or candied ginger root, lemon rind, and Port, and mix until the fruit is well saturated with the wine. Refrigerate, covered with plastic wrap, for at least 1 hour before serving in chilled compote dishes.

NOTE: Other frozen thoroughly defrosted and drained fruits (totaling about 4 cupfuls) may, of course, be prepared and served in the same manner as described above.

Carbonnade of Beef Flamande   serves 6–8

8 tablespoons (¼ pound, 1 stick) butter, *cut into small pieces*

About 3 pounds yellow onions, *peeled, to make 8–10 cups thinly sliced*

2 teaspoons sugar

4–6 tablespoons rendered fresh pork fat or use an equivalent amount of vegetable oil

3½–4 pounds beef chuck or rump, *well trimmed of all fat, and cut into ½-inch-thick sym-metrical slices*

Salt

Freshly ground black pepper

3 level tablespoons flour

2 cups beer, preferably Stout, but any domestic beer will do (leftover flat beer will do equally as well if not better than freshly opened beer)

1 cup beef stock, fresh or canned

½ teaspoon leaf thyme, *crumbled*

A bouquet consisting of 4 sprigs parsley, 2 celery tops with their leaves, and 1 large bay leaf, *tied together with string*

1–2 tablespoons wine vinegar

Melt the butter over moderate heat in a 12-inch skillet, add the onions and stir them about with a large spoon until they glisten. Stirring occasionally, cook for 20 to 30 minutes, or until the onions are quite brown; lower the heat if they appear to be browning too quickly. When they are the deep golden color you are aiming for, stir in the 2 teaspoons sugar, raise the heat and, stirring constantly, cook for about 5 minutes, or until the sugar melts, carmelizes, and turns the onions a deep mahogany brown. Watch for any sign of burning, and regulate the heat accordingly.

While the onions are cooking (or after they are done, if you feel you can't cope successfully with two culinary operations at the same time), pat the slices of meat completely dry with paper toweling. Sprinkle each side of the meat liberally with salt, and more discreetly, with black pepper.

Preheat the oven to 325 degrees. In a heavy 12-inch skillet, set over high heat, bring the 4 tablespoons of rendered pork fat (or oil) almost to the smoking point. Add the meat slices and brown them deeply 3 or 4 at a time, for about 3 minutes on each side. Then transfer them with tongs to a platter. If you find it necessary, add more fat or oil to the pan as you proceed to brown the remaining meat. Now stir the flour into the fat remaining in the pan (if the bottom of the pan is not thinly filmed with fat, again add a little more fat or oil) and, stirring constantly, cook the mixture until the flour turns a deep, dark brown. Proceed carefully here. This browning operation will give the final sauce its characteristic color, and if the cooking is done too quickly or carelessly, the flour will surely burn and the *carbonnade* will have a bitter, unpleasant taste. Pour in the beer and stock, raise the heat to high and, stirring constantly with a whisk, bring the sauce to a boil, whisking until the sauce is thick and smooth. Then stir in the thyme and let the sauce simmer slowly as you proceed to construct the *carbonnade* in the following fashion.

Spread a thin layer of the browned onions on the bottom of a heavy 4- to 6-quart casserole equipped with a tightly fitting cover. Spread a layer of the browned meat slices, side by side, over it, then mask them with a few tablespoons of the sauce. Continue to build up succeeding layers of onions, meat and sauce, devising the proportions so that the last layer of meat is topped with onions. Pour the remaining sauce in the skillet over the onions and place the bouquet on top.

Bring the casserole to a boil on top of the stove, cover it securely, then braise the *carbonnade* in the lower third of the oven for about 2 hours, or until the meat is tender. Test the meat for tenderness after about 1 hour (some cuts take less time to cook through than others). And don't let the meat overcook lest it shred unattractively. When you think the *carbonnade* is done, add to it 1 tablespoon of vinegar; taste, then add more vinegar, salt, and pepper if you feel it needs it. I think it almost always does. Serve the *carbonnade* directly from the casserole.

Because the *carbonnade flamande* is braised it may successfully be made ahead and reheated on top of the stove or in a 350-degree oven. I might point out that reheating the *carbonnade* will not improve its flavor, old wives' tales to the contrary. But it won't spoil it either, if you have followed my instructions precisely from the start.

Apple Beignets (Fritters)   *serves 4-6*

THE BATTER

1 egg, *separated*

3 tablespoons vegetable oil

¾ cup flat beer

1 cup flour, *sifted before measuring*

⅛ teaspoon salt

THE FILLING

4-6 medium-size firm, tart apples

1 teaspoon fresh, strained lemon juice

Sugar

2-4 tablespoons Calvados, apple-

jack, Kirsch, or Cognac (optional)

Vegetable oil for deep frying

Powdered sugar

Two hours or so before you intend to make the fritters, combine in the jar of an electric blender the egg yolk, oil, beer, flour, and salt, and blend at high speed for about a minute. Then turn off the blender, scrape down the sides of the jar with a rubber spatula, and blend again for another minute. Pour the batter into a 2- or 3-quart mixing bowl, cover with plastic wrap, and let it rest at room temperature for about 2 hours. Meanwhile, peel and core the apples, and cut them into ½-inch rounds or into quarters or eighths. Place the apples in a glass bowl and sprinkle them with the lemon juice and as much sugar you think they need. Toss them about to coat them thoroughly and stir in any of the optional liquors. Cover with plastic wrap and let the apples macerate until you are ready to coat and fry them.

A few minutes before frying, beat the egg white until it forms firm, unwavering peaks and carefully fold it into the batter. Heat at least 3 inches of oil in a deep fryer until it registers 375 degrees on a deep-fat frying thermometer. Drain the apples and gently pat them dry. Four or five at a time, drop them into the batter, and when they are well coated, plunge them into the hot fat. Turn them gently about in the fat with a slotted spoon until they are well puffed and brown on all sides. Then drain them on paper toweling while you coat and fry the remaining fritters similarly.

Apple Beignets (Fritters)

The apple fritters are at their best and crispest if served the moment they are done, but they may be kept warm in a 250-degree oven for 10 minutes or so if they must wait. In any case, sprinkle them lightly with powdered sugar just before serving.

NOTE: Canned, drained pineapple slices patted dry may be treated precisely in the same fashion as the apples described above.

Alsatian Choucroute with Spareribs

serves 6

2 tablespoons rendered goose fat, if you can get it, or use 2 tablespoons rendered fresh pork fat or lard

1 large onion, *to make 1 cup coarsely chopped*

Peeled garlic cloves, enough *to make 2 teaspoons finely chopped*

⅓ cup gin

4 pounds sauerkraut, fresh if possible, otherwise canned or in plastic bags, *soaked for 15 minutes in cold water, then drained, squeezed through the fingers, and pulled apart to separate the strands*

2 medium baking potatoes, *coarsely diced (about 1 cup)*

2 cups dry white wine, preferably the Moselle type

1–1½ cups chicken stock, fresh or canned: *if you use the concentrated canned type, dilute it with an equal amount of water*

A bouquet consisting of 6 sprigs parsley and 1 large bay leaf, *tied together with string*

1–1½ pounds mildly cured lean salt pork, in one piece or, if necessary two pieces

3 pounds meaty pork spareribs, *cut into fairly large serving pieces*

1 tablespoon vegetable oil

2 tablespoons Kirsch

6–12 medium new potatoes, *scrubbed, freshly boiled*

Fresh parsley (preferably the flat-leaf Italian type), *enough to make 2 tablespoons finely chopped*

Over moderate heat, melt the 2 tablespoons of the fat in a 6- or 7-quart casserole, add the onions and garlic, and, stirring occasionally, cook for about 8 minutes, or until the onions are lightly colored but not really brown. Add the gin, raise the heat, and boil rapidly until the gin has all but disappeared. Add the sauerkraut and diced potatoes. With a long pronged fork, lift up the strands of sauerkraut and the potatoes and stir them about until they are well coated with the fat. Pour in the wine and a cup of the chicken stock and, stirring constantly, bring the liquid to a boil. Then submerge the bouquet and the salt pork in the sauerkraut, cover the casserole tightly, and reduce the heat to low. Simmer the mixture for about 1 hour, checking it from time to time to make certain all the liquid hasn't cooked away. If it has, add the remaining ½ cup of stock (and even more, if the sauerkraut seems excessively dry).

While the sauerkraut is simmering, partially roast the spareribs in the following fashion: preheat the oven to 475 degrees. Arrange the ribs, fat-side up and in one layer on a rack in a shallow roasting pan. Brush the surface of the ribs lightly with the vegetable oil and roast them undisturbed in the upper third of the oven for 15 to 20 minutes, or until they turn golden-brown. Remove them from the pan and spread them out on a double thickness of paper toweling to drain. Turn the oven down to 300 degrees.

After the sauerkraut has simmered for its allotted hour, add the spareribs to the casserole, imbedding them beneath the surface of the sauerkraut. Cover tightly and braise in the center of the oven for about 30 minutes. Then with a bulb baster, remove as much of the surface fat from the casserole as you can, tipping the casserole slightly in order to get at it. Sprinkle the sauerkraut with the 2 tablespoons of Kirsch, cover the casserole again, and braise for ½ hour longer.

When the *choucroute* is done, mound the sauerkraut in the center of a large, deep, heated platter, place the spareribs on top and surround the whole with the freshly boiled potatoes with their skins left on, or peeled if you prefer. Sprinkle with parsley and serve at once.

Chicken en Cocotte Vallée d'Auge   *serves 4*

A 3-pound chicken
7 tablespoons butter: *2 softened for bird, 4 cut into small pieces for browning bird, and 1 softened for sauce*
¾ teaspoon fresh, strained lemon juice: *½ for butter mixture and ¼ for sauce*
1 teaspoon salt: *½ for butter mixture and ½ for sauce*
⅛ teaspoon white pepper
2 tablespoons vegetable oil
⅓ cup Calvados or use ⅓ cup applejack
2 medium-size tart apples, *peeled,*

cored, and cut into 1-inch dice
1 medium-size onion, *peeled and cut into quarters*
1 medium carrot, *scraped and cut into 1-inch chunks*
1 celery stalk, *to make ½ cup coarsely chopped*
½ teaspoon leaf thyme, *crumbled*
½ teaspoon salt
1 teaspoon arrowroot, *dissolved in 1 tablespoon Calvados or applejack*
2 egg yolks
½ cup heavy cream

Cream 2 tablespoons of the butter by beating and mashing it against the side of the bowl with a spoon until it is light and fluffy. Then beat in ½ teaspoon of the lemon juice, ½ teaspoon of the salt, and the pepper. Pat the chicken thoroughly dry inside and out with paper toweling, and rub the cavity with the creamed butter mixture, spreading it as evenly as you can. Truss the bird securely with white kitchen cord, and preheat the oven to 325 degrees.

In a small casserole, preferably an enamel oval cocotte equipped with a tight lid and just large enough to hold the chicken snugly, melt 4 tablespoons of the remaining butter and oil together over high heat. (The size of the casserole is important; if it is too large, the juices the chicken gives off later will evaporate too quickly and burn.) When the fat begins to turn ever so lightly brown, add the chicken, breast-side down, and brown it well, turning it from side to side, and regulating the heat so that the bird becomes golden on all sides without burning. The entire browning process should take about 15 minutes. Turn off the heat, then with a bulb baster or spoon remove all but a thin film of the fat from the casserole.

Heat the Calvados or applejack in a small pan to lukewarm, then set it alight with a match. Pour the flaming brandy over the chicken in a thin stream, sliding the pot back and forth rapidly on the range until the flame subsides, leaving a dark-brown glaze on the bottom of the pot. Scatter the apples, onions, carrots, celery, and thyme around the chicken and sprinkle the bird evenly with the remaining ½ teaspoon of salt. Set the casserole over high heat until you hear it sizzle, then cover it tightly, place the casserole in the center of the oven and braise the chicken for 50 to 60 minutes; baste it every 15 minutes or so with the juices that will soon accumulate around it. (Turn the heat down to 325 degrees or even 300 degrees if at any point the chicken seems to be cooking too rapidly; the movement of the pan liquid should be barely perceptible.)

Test the chicken for doneness by piercing the fleshy part of a thigh with the point of a small sharp knife. The juice that trickles out should be a pale yellow; if it is pink, braise the chicken for 10 or 15 minutes longer. When the chicken is done, carefully transfer it to a heatproof platter, remove the trussing strings and cover the bird loosely with foil to keep it warm while you make the sauce.

Quickly strain the entire contents of the casserole through a fine sieve into a small saucepan pressing down firmly on the vegetables before throwing them away. With a large spoon skim off and discard as much of the surface fat as you can, then bring the juices to a boil, uncovered, over high heat. Continue to boil briskly, undisturbed, until the liquid has cooked down to about ½ cupful. Meanwhile, in a small bowl, dissolve the arrowroot in a tablespoon of Calvados or applejack and stir in the egg yolks. Slowly pour the reduced chicken juices into the egg yolks, stirring constantly. Return the mixture to the saucepan, and over low heat, slowly simmer the sauce (it must not boil or it will curdle) until, as you continue to stir, it thickens enough to coat a spoon lightly. Off the heat, add the remaining ¼ teaspoon of lemon juice, taste for seasoning, then gently stir in the tablespoon of softened butter.

Pour off and discard any juices that may have accumulated around the waiting chicken and strain the sauce over the bird, masking it completely. Serve at once, surrounded, if you like, with the apple *beignets* described on page 139, substituting, if you prefer, a similar amount of dry white wine for the beer in the batter. If you are sufficiently adept with a carving knife to perform publicly, carve the bird at the table. Or you may, for safety's sake, prefer to carve the chicken in the kitchen, arranging the pieces attractively on a heated serving platter, then straining the sauce over them.

Crème de Cacao–Mocha Soufflé   *serves 4–6*

1 tablespoon butter, *softened*
7 tablespoons sugar: *2 for sugaring the soufflé mold and 5 for the soufflé base*
7 eggs: *5 yolks for the soufflé base and the 7 whites for the soufflé*

¼ cup crème de cacao, dark or light
1 tablespoon instant coffee, preferably instant espresso
¼ teaspoon cream of tartar
Powdered sugar
1 cup heavy cream, *chilled*

Preheat the oven to 425 degrees. With a soft pastry brush, thoroughly coat the inside of a 2-quart soufflé dish or charlotte mold with the tablespoon of softened butter. Then pour in 2 tablespoons of the sugar, and holding the mold sideways over a sheet of waxed paper, slowly rotate it so that the sugar spreads evenly over all of the buttered surfaces. Invert the mold and tap it gently to dislodge any excess sugar. The inside of the mold should look like finely grained sandpaper.

In the top of a stainless-steel or enamel double boiler (aluminum will not do; it will discolor the eggs unattractively), beat the egg yolks and the remaining 5 tablespoons of sugar with a whisk, rotary beater, or electric handbeater (the last by far the least arduous of the three instruments) until they flow sluggishly off the beater in a thick stream when the beater is lifted from the pan. Place the pan over barely simmering water. Stirring constantly with a rubber spatula (concentrate on the creased sides of the pan where coagulated egg is likely to form), heat the mixture until it thickens to a dense custard, and when tested feels almost too hot to the finger. Immediately remove the pan from the hot water, stir in the crème de cacao and instant coffee, and continue to stir until the mixture is cool or at least lukewarm (this mixture may be made anywhere from 6 to 8 hours before you plan to cook the soufflé;

if so, then cover it with plastic wrap and refrigerate. It will tend to separate after a couple of hours, but don't be concerned; merely stir the mixture vigorously with a whisk to recombine it just before making the soufflé).

For the best results, beat the egg whites in a bowl of unlined copper, if you have one; the quality of your beaten egg whites, it is well to know, is the crucial factor in all soufflés. But any bowl except an aluminum one will do, if it must; however, your soufflé will not rise as high or as spectacularly as it should. Beat the whites and the cream of tartar with a clean balloon whisk or a rotary beater (*not* an electric mixer) until they foam thickly and gradually form stiff, unwavering peaks on the beater when lifted from the bowl. With a rubber spatula, vigorously stir 3 heaping tablespoons of the whites one at a time into the crème de cacao sauce, and when they are thoroughly absorbed, pour the mixture over the remaining egg whites. Fold the two together using a rubber spatula to bring the heavier mass over the lighter whites, thus, in effect, enfolding the two instead of mixing them. Continue folding in this fashion until only the faintest streaks of egg whites still remain, although it will not be disastrous if they completely disappear. Do not overfold, however, lest you lose the air you have so laboriously beaten into the whites to inflate them. Immediately pour the mixture into the sugared mold and smooth the surface gently with the spatula. (If you like, quickly run the spatula around the rim of the dish, inserting it about an inch from the sides and an inch deep to create a vaguely defined circle. As the soufflé bakes, the center should rise into a large, decorative crown.)

Bake the soufflé in the lower third of the oven for about 2 minutes, then turn the heat down to 375 degrees and bake undisturbed for 20 minutes if you prefer the center of the soufflé soft, as I do. Or bake it for 10 or 15 minutes longer. (Whatever the baking time you decide on, the soufflé will have risen at least 2 or 3 inches above the rim of the dish if you have followed my instructions precisely.) Meanwhile, beat the cream in a chilled bowl until it forms soft peaks. Serve the soufflé at once, sprinkled lightly with powdered sugar and accompanied with the bowl of whipped cream.

Cumberland Sauce

makes about 1 cup

1 large lemon
1 large orange
⅓ cup Port
2 tablespoons red-currant jelly

1 teaspoon sugar
2 level teaspoons cornstarch
1 tablespoon cold water

With a swivel-bladed vegetable peeler, remove the skin of the lemon and orange in long paper-thin spirals. Cut the peels into match-like strips about 1 inch long and ⅛ inch wide, and drop them into enough boiling water to cover them completely. Cook briskly, uncovered, for 5 minutes, drain in a sieve and run cold water over them to cool them quickly and set their color. Spread the peel on paper toweling and pat them dry.

Squeeze the lemon and orange and strain the juices through a fine sieve into a small saucepan. Add the Port, currant jelly, and sugar and, stirring constantly with a whisk, bring the mixture to a boil over high heat. Reduce the heat to low and simmer uncovered and undisturbed for 5 minutes.

Dissolve the cornstarch in the cold water and whisk it into the simmering sauce. Raise the heat and stir until the sauce comes to a boil, thickens and clears. Strain the sauce through a fine sieve into a bowl and stir in the lemon and orange peel. Refrigerate for at least 2 hours or until thoroughly chilled.

Cumberland sauce is traditionally served with mutton, venison, and smoked ham. Less traditionally, I often serve it with the pistachioed roast loin of pork (cold, or more properly at room temperature of course) on page 345.

THE LEMON

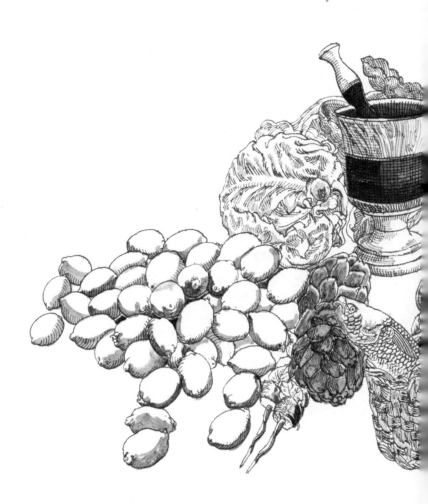

tHE lEMON

Surely, the lemon's seductive fragrance and its bright, sunlit color must have inspired Goethe's nostalgic line, "Knowest thou the land where the lemon-trees bloom?," evoking for the more fanciful and poetic among us visions of flowering lemon groves in romantic, faraway places.

It is a confirmed historical and botanical fact that the American continent, even in its southernmost latitudes, never produced any citrus fruit until Columbus carried lemons and their seeds from the Canary Islands to Haiti, on his second voyage to the New World, in 1493. The trees soon spread to the other islands of the West Indies and then, inevitably, found their way to the American mainland. There, as if to make up for a slow start, they proliferated so quickly that, by now, California and Arizona alone produce more lemons than the greatest lemon-producing countries of Europe, notably Italy and Spain; in fact, these American states account for at least forty-five per cent of the world's lemon crop. And what an unending crop it is! Because the lemon tree can produce buds, blossoms, and fruit at the same time, thus encompassing a whole life cycle simultaneously, lemons can be harvested month after month, twelve months of the year. In the face of this extraordinary natural phenomenon, one can readily understand the attraction the lemon tree has had for poets, botanists, and lemon growers alike.

But from my view naturally, it is the cook who has the most to gain from the lemon. And the manner in which cooks of all nations use the fruit is as intriguing to me as its history.

When most of us think of the lemon, we quite naturally think of its juice. Its piquant and invigorating acidity has become for some palates as important a seasoning for certain foods as salt. Indeed, many doctors suggest fresh lemon juice as an alternative to salt in a prescribed salt-free diet. But too few cooks are aware of what else this extraordinary juice can accomplish. Among other things, it can "cook" fish without any heat, tenderize the toughest cuts of meat, and stabilize the color of easily discolored fruits and vegetables. If this weren't endowment enough, lemon juice contains an impressive amount of antiscorbutic Vitamin C.

While scientists don't yet know precisely why certain foods blacken upon exposure to air (maybe they really do know, but their complex technical explanations still elude me), they recognize that the Vitamin C in lemon juice inhibits the discoloring process as soon as it begins. Fresh artichokes, for example, will never have that gray forlorn look if each of the areas you trim, as you prepare the vegetables for cooking, is rubbed at once with the cut half of a lemon or sprinkled with its juice. The juice will keep the exposed areas from darkening, no matter how long the artichokes must wait before they are cooked. Fruits like bananas, peaches, pears, and apples, if they are peeled and exposed to air for any length of time, will respond just as magically to similar treatment, whether you cook the fruits or not.

I have discovered however that green vegetables cooked in water acidulated with an appreciable amount of lemon juice will turn an unaccountable unattractive brown. Yet potatoes, cauliflower, and rice cooked in similarly acidulated water retain their original color, and the juice seems to act as a bleach, as well. Yellow vegetables, on the other hand, appear to be impervious to the action of the fruit in any way. But red cabbage, which often turns an unpleasant blue when cooked in the excessively alkaline or hard water typical of many localities, can be quickly restored to its pristine state by merely sprinkling it with lemon juice while it is cooking, as you will see when you make the braised red cabbage on page 159.

Lemon juice performs quite as dramatically in other areas, too, particularly when it takes the leading role in a marinade. As a marinade for fish, for example, its effect is remarkable. So remarkable, in fact, that raw strips of firm, white-fleshed fish, after steeping in fresh lemon juice from eight to twenty-four hours, emerge from their citric bath tasting as if they had been really cooked.

The Japanese, South Sea Islanders, Mexicans, South Americans, and Scandinavians—all of whom are addicted to raw fish—thus marinated—serve it as a form of hors d'oeuvre, under a variety of names

(*seviche* is one of them; my recipe for it appears on page 160) and
flavor it according to their national tastes. The South Americans and
Mexicans season their versions of the dish with onions, green and red
chilies, tomatoes, and almost always with fresh coriander; this parsley-
like herb has a singular (and for some tastes, unpleasant) flavor that is
never appreciated as it should be by many otherwise culinarily cultivated people I know. Inevitably, the Scandinavians use a preponderance of dill in the dish; the Japanese and Chinese, fresh ginger root; the
South Sea Islanders, coconut. But whatever the seasoning and garnish
(added sometimes before and sometimes after the marinating process),
the enzymatic action of the lemon juice on the raw fish actually breaks
down its tissues and gives the fish a far more interesting texture than if
it had been literally cooked.

A similar reaction takes place when meat is marinated in lemon
juice. The connective tissues of most meats are tough and fibrous and
therefore more resistant than those of fish to breakdown. Although a
lemon-juice marinade will surely tenderize tough meat, it needs the
assistance of heat to complete the job. To observe the effectiveness of
lemon as a tenderizer, try using lemon instead of wine to marinate the
broiled chuck steak as described in my recipe on page 129.

Middle Eastern cooks, like the Greeks, Armenians, and Turks,
know all about what a good marinade will do for the lamb that they
raise so extensively. Certainly, one of their finest culinary achievements
is shish kebab: chunks of lamb marinated for hours in lemon juice,
olive oil, and herbs, then threaded on skewers and broiled. Marinated
and broiled in this fashion, a tough piece of lamb, whatever the cut,
becomes as docile as a lamb is proverbially said to be.

Whether lemon juice is used in a marinade or in any other manner,
it is its uncompromising acidity that gives it its special effectiveness.
Consequently, those lemons with the greatest degree of acidity (and
it does vary) are much to be preferred. If you can find lemons with a
slightly greenish cast, don't pass them by. They will in all likelihood
have a sharper, more characteristic lemon flavor than bright yellow
ones.

All lemons today, I think you should know, are picked while they
are still green and are allowed to ripen in storage under carefully controlled physical conditions. Contrary to what you might expect, curing,
as this procedure is called, produces lemons that have a better flavor
and more juice than do those that have been tree-ripened. Although

most lemons that go to market today are of the highest quality, it is advisable, nonetheless, to search out fruit that feels heavy for its size and is sheathed in finely textured skin. Avoid coarse, shriveled, or excessively thick-skinned lemons and those that feel soft and spongy to the touch. If you are economy-minded (as I, alas, seldom am), you might take a tip from commercial lemon juice producers. Although, from my view, their bottled or canned products leave much to be desired, these enterprising people have devised a way to extract more juice from their lemons than household cooks can. The lemons are dropped into boiling water, blanched for about two minutes, then removed from the water, and allowed to cool slightly. When squeezed, the yield is gratifyingly half again as much as that of an unblanched lemon.

Slightly green lemons are, to my surprise, often confused with limes. Limes do have a more than passing kinship to the lemon; but it should be recognized that they belong to a distinct, highly developed species of their own, albeit in the citrus category. They may, in certain instances, be substituted for lemons. They are somewhat sweet, however, and the juice should be added to food with considerable discretion if you plan to use them in place of lemon juice.

Apart from acidity, there are few fruit flavors with as definite and uncompromising a taste as that of the lemon. For this reason, its use in cooking should never be careless or casual, but carefully considered. The French, past masters in the art of sauce-making, think of lemon juice as a seasoning and cook with it sparingly, but with maximum effect. For the most part, they add it to their white sauces—*béchamels, veloutés,* and *suprêmes,* for example—literally drop by drop, not for the purpose of giving the sauces a lemon flavor (which a good French cook would consider disastrous), but to heighten the basic flavor of the sauce itself. And for the same reason, they sprinkle the juice lightly over fish before broiling it, and sometimes over meat before roasting it. The lemon flavor is never apparent; but the natural taste of the food is curiously intensified.

There are many dishes outside the orbit of French cooking in which the flavor of the lemon is meant to be perceived—not overpoweringly, to be sure, but as a foil to the food it accompanies. Certainly, our national habit of squeezing lemon over poached, baked, and fried fish is a case in point, and an admirable one. Admirable, that is, compared with our deplorable practice of dunking our magnificent oysters and clams into overpowering cocktail sauces, instead of sprinkling them with a few drops of lemon juice and a grating or two of black pepper, as the French do.

We might take a tip from the Italians who often serve their cold shellfish with a lemon flavored green sauce called *salsa verde,* my version of which appears on page 161. And *salsa verde* goes just as well, if not better, with cold boiled beef, chilled asparagus, among others.

The Greeks are apt to use lemon juice more forthrightly than the Italians. They have created with it two important dishes, one a soup and the other a sauce. Both are called *avgolemono* and are notable for the ease with which they can be prepared and the unusual effect they create. A detailed recipe for the sauce appears in one of my earlier books, *Michael Field's Culinary Classics and Improvisations,* so I have not included it again here. The Greeks use it on almost everything: broiled lamb, fish, chicken, and vegetables. One particular advantage of this versatile *avgolemono* sauce is that it contains no fat other than the insignificant amount in the egg yolks, which makes it an ideal sauce for the calorie-conscious. I often use it as a substitute for hollandaise in many dishes quite successfully and without apology.

Largely ignored by our cooks, if not by our bartenders, lemon peel is a surprisingly important ingredient in fine European cooking. It is most often encountered in soups, stews, sauces, and as a garnish for vegetables. The French, in fact, think so highly of the lemon peel that they have given it a graphically descriptive name, *zeste*. And with their usual precision in culinary matters, they make a nice and necessary distinction between the *zeste* and the bitter white pith beneath it, which they call, almost sneeringly, the *ziste* and which, needless to say, they scrupulously avoid ever using. Separating the *zeste* cleanly from the *ziste* has always been something of a struggle even for the French; but with the invention (by an American) of the swivel-bladed vegetable peeler, the problem is solved. Now it is possible to strip the *zeste* from the *ziste* without any white pith adhering to it. The almost-transparent peel can then be slivered or julienned, or chopped and used as directed in my recipes that require it.

In the United States, we use the peel, when we cook with it, almost exclusively in cakes and pies. Surely one of the most original examples of American cooking, our lemon meringue pie, fine as it frequently is, would be even better if American cooks could be persuaded to adopt my method of peeling and then finely chopping—instead of grating—

the lemon peel they add to the pie in such generous quantities. The faint, elusive bitterness resulting from the small amount of pith that almost always adheres to the grated rind would thus be eliminated and the lemon meringue pie would have the clean, acid taste of the lemon it should ideally have.

Would that I could say the same for the general quality of most of the lemon meringue pies produced in this country. Their fillings are either too gummy or too fluid and inevitably the moisture from the egg white sinks to the bottom of the pie and turns the crust sodden. This phenomenon has never, to my knowledge, been adequately coped with by any American cookbook published since the pie made its appearance when cornstarch was first produced in this country. Commercial bakers, of course, use special stabilizers unavailable in markets, and although they do indeed stop the seepage ("weeping," as this maddening effect is technically called), they make meringues taste as if they were made of white wet wool. I was determined to conquer this problem. After laborious research and consultation with our country's leading food chemists, I was about to accept that the problem seemed to be insoluble when a particularly imaginative scientist, Dr. Paul Buck, associate professor of Food Science at Cornell University, hazarded the guess that a calcium phosphate powder of some kind might do the trick. But since he never really cooks, he hadn't the faintest idea how much to use, how to use it, or how long to cook it. Determined to solve the chemical mystery, and using Dr. Buck as a guide, I went to work and experimented with the powder* combined with cream of tartar in pie after pie for days until I found the solution. To end this tale on an immodestly triumphant note, I have evolved a lemon meringue pie (see the recipe page 163) that seldom "weeps," except on occasion—and then only slightly—when the weather is excessively humid. I have also provided a safeguard to absorb that possible leakage—a sprinkling on the crust of crushed ginger snaps, which in addition to its absorptive value, adds to the flavor of the pie as well.

But, when all is said and done, it is again the Italians who employ the peel of the lemon most creatively. One of their Milanese dishes, *osso buco,* composed of stubby pieces of veal shank braised in wine,

* Calcium phosphate powder (or pills which may be crushed to a powder) is available as a U.S.P. or food grade phosphate product in about twenty varieties in drugstores throughout the United States. There is one in particular called Di-Cal which I especially recommend.

vegetables, and tomatoes, is garnished, when it is served, with a color-ful mélange of finely chopped lemon peel, garlic, and parsley. Called *gremolata*, this inspired mixture transforms *osso buco*, an essentially rough and lusty dish, into a masterpiece. In the hands of imaginative cooks, *gremolata* is often used to garnish other braised and sautéed veal dishes and, on occasion, is even sprinkled over broiled or sautéed fish. In my recipe for *osso buco* on page 27 I have taken the liberty of add-ing chopped orange peel (prepared in the same way as the lemon peel) to the *gremolata*. It makes for an interesting variation on what might otherwise be a typical Italian *gremolata*. Of course, if you are a purist, you may omit the orange peel.

You can introduce similar variations in your lemon dishes as I have in my own. Hopefully, you may discover in this fashion how really ver-satile this piquant fruit can be.

Boiled Artichokes with Lemon Butter

serves 6

1 large lemon, *cut in half cross-wise*
6 thirteen- to fourteen-ounce fresh, firm artichokes

6 quarts water
3 tablespoons salt

LEMON BUTTER

½ pound (2 sticks, 1 cup) butter, *cut into small pieces and clarified according to directions on page 136*

3 small lemons, *cut in half cross-wise*

With a large sharp knife, trim the stems of the artichokes flush with their bases to prevent them from wobbling when you stand them upright. Bend and snap off the small bottom leaves and any badly bruised or torn outer leaves. Immediately rub the cut areas with half the lemon to prevent them from discoloring. One at a time, lay the artichokes on their sides and, grasping them firmly, slice about an inch or so off their tops. Rub with a lemon half. With a pair of scissors, cut off the sharp points of each artichoke leaf. Again rub with lemon.

You can now boil the artichokes in their present state, or remove their hairy inner chokes. Although this is a fairly arduous operation, I think it worth the effort. For one thing, it will reduce the cooking time; for another, it will make eating the artichoke a less messy procedure. And finally, you can, if you wish, use the hollowed out center of the hot cooked artichoke as a container, in effect, for the sauce of your choice, be it lemon butter, hollandaise, or *béarnaise*, among others. Or if you decide to serve the cooked artichoke cold, it can be filled with a simple French dressing, the *rémoulade* sauce on page 230, or the *salsa verde* on page 161.

To remove the chokes before cooking, gently spread the outer layers of the artichoke leaves apart as far as you can without tearing them, and grasp the inner core of leaves securely. (Watch out for their sharp points!) Twisting and turning the core with your fingers, pull it out. If it doesn't come out in one piece—it rarely does—pick out any small stray leaves clinging to the sides of the choke. Now dig down into the center of the artichoke with a longe-handled small spoon—an iced-tea spoon is ideal—and scrape away the choke, digging deeply enough to reach solid bottom. Run the spoon around the inside edges of the base to get at any hidden fuzz, then poke around with your finger to remove the rest. When you are certain you have removed all the choke, squeeze a little of the lemon juice into the openings of each artichoke and rub it into the core with your finger. Gently squeeze and pat each artichoke back into its original shape. The artichokes are now ready for boiling.

Bring 6 quarts of water to a turbulent boil over high heat in an 8-quart enamel or stainless-steel casserole or pot (aluminum will *not* do; it will discolor the artichokes). Stir in the salt and drop in the artichokes. Push them beneath the surface so that they fill with water and let them boil rapidly, *uncovered,* turning them over from time to time until their bases show only the slightest resistance when pierced with the tip of a small sharp knife. (Thirteen- to 14-ounce artichokes, with their chokes removed, should take about 20 minutes to cook; those with their chokes left in, about 40 minutes.)

Remove them from the pot with tongs and drain them upside down for 2 or 3 minutes on a large deep platter. Serve with small individual bowls of hot clarified butter, each accompanied by a lemon half. (If you have the time, remove any exposed lemon seeds from the halves with the tip of a small knife, or better still, wrap each lemon half in a square of cheesecloth and twist the ends together to make a neat bundle, so that it can be squeezed into the butter seedlessly and without squirting.) These artichokes are delicious hot, but are just as good served cold.

Marinated Shish Kebabs of Lamb

serves 4

2 pounds boneless lamb, *prefer-
ably cut from the leg,*   *trimmed of excess fat and
cut into 2-inch cubes*

Marinated Shish Kebabs of Lamb

MARINADE

¼ cup fresh, strained lemon juice
½ cup olive oil
1 teaspoon salt
½ teaspoon crumbled oregano, *dried*
1 large onion, *peeled and sliced into thin rounds*

3 large cloves garlic, *peeled and smashed with the side of a large, flat knife*
Parsley, *enough to make 2 table-spoons finely chopped*
15–20 large bay leaves

In a glass or stainless-steel baking dish or bowl just large enough to hold the lamb comfortably, beat together with a whisk the lemon juice, olive oil, salt, and oregano. Add the onions, garlic, parsley, and lamb and toss with your hands or a large spoon until the lamb is thoroughly moistened. Marinate at room temperature for at least 6 hours or in the refrigerator for 8–10 hours.

These kebabs may be broiled on a charcoal grill or in the broiler of your oven. Light a layer of coal in a charcoal broiler and let them burn until a white ash appears on the surface. Or preheat your household broiler to its highest point.

String the lamb on 4 skewers—each skewer about 14 inches long—dividing the pieces of meat in equal amounts between them. Thread a piece or a whole bay leaf between each chunk of lamb. And for the best results, push the lamb pieces close together on the skewers; this will allow the outside surface of the meat to become crisp and brown and keep the interior of the meat moist. To broil the lamb, lay the skewers directly on the pre-greased grid of the broiling pan.

Broil the meat about 3 inches from the source of the heat, turning the skewers from time to time, to brown the meat evenly. For my taste, at least, the lamb should be broiled about 10 minutes in all and be pink inside when done. However, you may cook it longer if you wish, but don't overcook it or it will be dry and tasteless.

To serve, either present the skewered lamb at the table or slide the pieces off the skewers in the kitchen and serve them on heated plates. A fine accompaniment for these kebabs would be saffron rice, a bowl of chopped scallions, and quartered lemons.

Braised Red Cabbage   serves 6–8

A 2- to 2½-pound head red cabbage
⅓ cup fresh, strained lemon juice
⅓ cup water
4 tablespoons (½ stick) butter,
   cut into small pieces

1 tablespoon sugar
1 teaspoon salt
¼ cup red-currant jelly
A peeled and cored tart apple, *to
   make 2 tablespoons finely
   grated*

Wash the cabbage under cold running water and strip off the tough outer leaves. With a large sharp knife, cut the cabbage into quarters from top to bottom, and cut away the core. Lay each quarter flat-side down on a chopping board and slice it crosswise as finely as possible. There should be about 9 cups of shredded cabbage.

Preheat the oven to 325 degrees. Combine the lemon juice, water, butter, sugar, and salt in a heavy stainless-steel or enamel 4- to 5-quart casserole equipped with a tightly fitting cover. Bring the liquid to a boil over high heat and, when the butter has melted completely, add the cabbage. Toss the shreds about with two large spoons or forks until they are completely coated with the lemon mixture. Then return the liquid to a boil over high heat, cover the casserole tightly, and braise the cabbage in the middle of the oven for about 2 hours. It is unlikely that the cabbage will become dry, but play it safe and check the casserole occasionally. Add a tablespoon of boiling water to the cabbage every now and then if you think it necessary; the cabbage should be fairly moist (but not swimming in liquid) during the entire period.

When the cabbage has braised its allotted time, stir in the jelly and grated apple, cover tightly again, and braise 15 or 20 minutes longer. Taste for seasoning and serve.

NOTE: It is said by the Germans who ostensibly invented this dish that its flavor will improve if the braised cabbage is allowed to rest for a day in the refrigerator, and then reheated either on top of the stove or in a 325-degree preheated oven. My contention, however, is that it really doesn't make any difference—that is, if you have braised the cabbage perfectly to begin with.

Seviche

¾ cup fresh, strained lemon juice

¾ cup fresh, strained lime juice

Peeled garlic cloves, *enough to make ½ teaspoon finely chopped*

1 tablespoon chili powder

Fresh ginger root, *scraped, enough to make 1 tablespoon finely chopped,* or 1½ teaspoons dried cracked ginger, *finely pulverized with a mortar and pestle*

½ teaspoon hot red pepper flakes

1 teaspoon salt

Freshly ground black pepper

2 pounds fresh (*not* frozen) sole fillets or any other firm, white *delicately textured fish, skinned, separated into 2 halves lengthwise, then cut crosswise into approximately 2-inch pieces*

2 medium-size red onions, *peeled, sliced ⅛ inch thick, and separated into rings*

2 heads Boston or Romaine lettuce, *separated into individual leaves, washed and thoroughly dried*

Fresh coriander (cilantro) or parsley, *enough to make 2 tablespoons finely chopped*

Combine the lemon and lime juices in a shallow glass or ceramic baking dish just large enough to hold the fish in one layer comfortably. Add the chili powder, garlic, ginger, red pepper flakes, salt, and a liberal amount of freshly ground black pepper, and beat with a whisk until the ingredients are thoroughly mixed. Lay the fish pieces in the marinade, side by side, and scatter the onion rings on top. If the marinade doesn't quite cover the fish and onions completely (and it may not, if your dish is too large), add more strained lemon and lime juice in equal amounts. Cover with plastic wrap and refrigerate for at least 6 hours, or until the fish is firm, white, and opaque, indicating that it is fully "cooked." Covered and refrigerated, *seviche* may be safely kept for as long as 2 or 3 days; in fact, the longer marination enriches the flavor. It is well to note, however, that very thin fillets such as young flounder will tend to disintegrate if marinated too long. Fillets, at least ¼ inch thick are advisable in any case.

To serve, shape several lettuce leaves into a cup on individual chilled plates. With a slotted spoon, place a portion of the *seviche* in each cup and garnish it with a few of the onion rings. Moisten the fish with a little of the marinade and sprinkle it with the fresh coriander or parsley.

Salsa Verde

4 medium scallions, including 2 inches of the green tops, *to make ½ cup finely chopped*

Parsley (preferably the flat-leaf variety), *enough to make ½ cup finely chopped*

Fresh basil, *enough to make 1 tablespoon finely chopped,* or use 1 teaspoon dried basil, *crumbled*

Sour dill pickles (preferably the imported French *cornichons*), *enough to make 2 tablespoons finely chopped*

Peeled garlic cloves, *enough to make 1 teaspoon finely chopped*

About 6 flat canned anchovies, *drained, to make 1 tablespoon finely chopped*

1 medium potato, *cooked, cooled, and finely chopped (not mashed), to make about ¼ cup*

3 tablespoons fresh, strained lemon juice

½ cup olive oil

Freshly ground black pepper

For the success of this extraordinarily piquant sauce, it is imperative that all the solid ingredients be chopped as finely as possible. Do not be tempted to use the blender; the results will be disastrous.

Combine in a glass or stainless-steel mixing bowl the chopped scallions, parsley, basil, pickles, garlic, anchovies, and potato. Stir together gently but thoroughly, then add the lemon juice, a tablespoonful at a time, stirring after each addition, and then finally, the olive oil. Add a few grindings of black pepper; stir, and taste for seasoning. It is most unlikely that it will need salt but if you think it does, add it discreetly. Chill before serving with such hot and cold foods (among others) as hot or cold boiled beef; the deep-fried scallops on page 230, etc.; or the cold artichokes on page 156.

Greek Lemon Soup

AVGOLEMONO   *serves 4–6*

6 cups chicken stock, fresh or
    canned: *if you use the con-*
    centrated canned type, dilute
    it with an equal amount of
    water
6 tablespoons raw rice, *not* the
    precooked or converted
    variety
4 large eggs

3–5 tablespoons fresh, strained
    lemon juice
A pinch of white pepper
Salt
Fresh mint leaves, *enough to*
    make 2 tablespoons finely
    cut, or use an equal amount
    of fresh parsley (preferably
    the flat-leaf variety)

In a 3- to 4-quart enamel or stainless-steel saucepan, bring the stock to a turbulent boil and add the rice. Stir once or twice, turn the heat down to low, and partially cover the pan. Simmer the rice for about 20 minutes, or until it is quite soft.

With a whisk or a rotary beater, beat the eggs until they froth (don't overbeat) and stir in the lemon juice. A tablespoon at a time, stir in 4 tablespoons of the simmering stock, then, in a slow stream, return the mixture to the simmering soup, stirring constantly. Still stirring, simmer the soup over low heat for 3 minutes, or until it thickens into a very light custard-like consistency. Under no circumstances allow the soup to come to a boil or it will most surely curdle. Taste it now for seasoning. Add the pinch of white pepper, as much salt as you think it needs, and 1 or 2 more tablespoons of the lemon juice if you prefer the soup really tart. Pour the *avgolemono* soup into a tureen or individual soup plates, sprinkle the top with the mint (or parsley) and serve at once.

NOTE: The *avgolemono* may be made hours in advance. When you reheat it, however, be especially careful, as before, not to let it boil. Should the soup curdle (and with all your care it *can* happen), strain it through a fine sieve into another pan and beat it vigorously with a whisk to recombine it as best as you can. Run hot water over the rice in the sieve to remove any cooked egg particles and return the rice to the soup. This *avgolemono* will be thinner in texture and somewhat less than perfect, but it will be close enough to the real thing to make it worth serving.

Lemon Meringue Pie

makes a 9-inch pie

THE PASTRY

1¼ cups flour

4 tablespoons vegetable shortening or lard, *chilled*

2 tablespoons butter, *chilled, cut into ¼-inch pieces*

⅛ teaspoon salt

3 tablespoons ice water

THE FILLING

¾ cup granulated sugar

¼ cup cornstarch, packed down by tapping the measuring cup sharply on a table, then filling it to the specified amount

⅛ teaspoon salt

1¾ cups cold water

6 large eggs: 6 *yolks for the filling and ½ cup whites for the meringue*

2 tablespoons butter, *softened, cut into small pieces*

⅓ cup strained, fresh lemon juice

Lemon rind: *the lemon thinly peeled with a swivel-bladed vegetable peeler, then the rind finely chopped, to make 2 tablespoons*

Ginger snaps, *enough to make 2 tablespoons finely pulverized (use an electric blender or wrap the snaps in a towel and crush them with a rolling pin)*

THE MERINGUE

½ cup egg whites, at room temperature

½ cup granulated sugar

½ level teaspoon cream of tartar

½ level teaspoon calcium phosphate powder (preferably Di-Cal, see page 154)

Lemon Meringue Pie

The Pastry:

Combine the flour, shortening or lard, butter, and salt in a large mixing bowl. With your thumbs and fingertips rub the flour and fats together until they look like flakes of coarse meal. Don't let the mixture get oily. Now pour in the water, and with your hands toss the mixture about to moisten the dough thoroughly, then knead it gently until you are able to gather it into a compact ball. If it crumbles, add a teaspoon or so more of water and mix until the particles adhere. Dust the dough lightly with flour, wrap it in waxed paper or foil, and refrigerate it for at least ½ hour.

Preheat the oven to 400 degrees.

With a pastry brush, lightly butter the bottom and sides of a 9-inch pie tin (a glass pie plate will *not* do). On a lightly floured surface, pat the dough into a thick round, then roll it out into a circle about ⅛ inch thick and about 13 to 14 inches in diameter. Drape it over your rolling pin, lift it up, and unroll it over the pie plate, leaving enough slack in the middle of the pastry to enable you to line the plate without pulling or stretching the dough. (Any such manipulation of the dough will make it shrink as it bakes.) Trim the excess pastry with a sharp knife or a pair of scissors to within ½ inch of the pan and fold the extra ½ inch under to make a double thickness all around the rim of the plate. With the back tines of a fork, press the pastry all around its circumference to secure it to the rim of the pan. To hold the pastry in place, spread a sheet of lightly buttered foil across the pan and press it gently into the edges and against the sides of the pan. Bake the shell in the middle of the oven for 10 minutes, then remove the foil; lower the heat to 350 degrees, prick any bubbles in the pastry with the point of a small knife, and bake 15 to 20 minutes more or until the pastry has lightly browned and is fully cooked. Let the shell cool in its pan.

The Filling:

Combine in a 2-quart enamel or stainless-steel saucepan the sugar, cornstarch, salt and 1¾ cups water. Stir with a whisk until the cornstarch and sugar are dissolved, then cook over moderate heat, whisking constantly, until the mixture thickens heavily and comes to a boil. (At one point, the cornstarch may separate into small globules. Don't be alarmed; simply remove the pan from the heat and whisk the mixture briskly until the lumps disappear.) Lower the heat and simmer, stirring almost constantly for 2 minutes. When the mixture is thick and almost translucent, again remove the pan from the heat, and beat the egg yolks into it, one at a time. Then return the mixture to the heat for the last time; add the chopped lemon rind and simmer it over low heat for about 5 to 7 minutes until it becomes a smooth, very thick, dense yellow custard. (Again if it turns lumpy at any point beat with a whisk until smooth.) Off the heat, beat in the butter, and then the lemon juice, a tablespoon at a time. Let the custard cool to room temperature, whisking it every now and then. Sprinkle the bottom of the pie shell evenly with the ginger snaps. Then spoon the filling over the crumbs into the pie, smoothing it out with a rubber spatula.

The Meringue:

Preheat the oven to 325 degrees.

First sift together the sugar, cream of tartar, and calcium phosphate powder. Then beat the egg whites with a balloon whisk, rotary beater, or in an electric mixer until they are thick and foamy. Beating constantly, slowly add the sugar mixture a few tablespoons at a time and continue to beat until the meringue is firm enough to hold stiff, almost rigid peaks on the beater when it is lifted out of the bowl. If you have any doubts about its consistency, overbeat rather than underbeat it.

Spoon the meringue on the custard, mound it in the center, and make decorative swirls on top with a spatula. Make sure the meringue covers the filling completely but leave part of the pastry rim exposed. Bake in the upper third of the oven for 25 to 30 minutes or until the meringue is a golden brown. Let the pie cool for at least 2 hours (*not* refrigerated) and serve at room temperature.

NOTE: Any left over pie may be refrigerated; but let it come to room temperature for about an hour before serving it again.

Lemon Soufflé with a Meringue Topping

serves 4–6

If the meringue part of this recipe strikes you as fraught with too much potential disaster (although I assure you it works if you follow my directions to the letter), simply omit it altogether. Instead, simply sprinkle the fully baked soufflé with powdered sugar and serve at once with a bowl of whipped cream.

THE SOUFFLÉ

4 tablespoons (½ stick) butter, *softened: 1 to coat the mold and 3 for the soufflé base*

7 tablespoons sugar: *2 to coat the buttered mold, 4 for the soufflé base, and 1 for the beaten egg whites*

4 level tablespoons flour

¾ cup milk

6 large eggs (not "extra large" or "jumbo"): *4 yolks for the soufflé base and the 6 whites for the soufflé*

¼ cup fresh, strained lemon juice

1 tablespoon Grand Marnier or other orange-flavored liqueur

Lemon peel: *the lemon peeled, paper-thin, with a swivel-bladed vegetable peeler, then very finely chopped, enough to make 1 tablespoon*

THE MERINGUE

3 egg whites

⅛ teaspoon cream of tartar

6 tablespoons superfine sugar

1 cup heavy cream, *chilled, stiffly whipped (optional)*

The Soufflé:

With a pastry brush, evenly butter a 2-quart charlotte mold or ceramic soufflé dish with 1 tablespoon of the softened butter. Then pour in 2 tablespoons of the sugar, and holding the mold sideways over a sheet of waxed paper, slowly rotate it so that the sugar spreads evenly over all the buttered surface. Invert the mold and tap it gently to dislodge the excess sugar. The inside of the mold should look like finely grained sandpaper. Put the pan aside while you make the sauce.

Melt the remaining butter (without letting it brown) in a 2-quart enamel or stainless-steel saucepan. Off the heat, stir in the flour to make a smooth *roux,* then pour in all at once the milk. Beat with a whisk to partially dissolve the *roux,* then, over high heat, bring the mixture to a boil, whisking constantly until the sauce is smooth and very thick. Turn down the heat to low, stir in 4 tablespoons of the remaining sugar, and simmer the sauce, stirring it constantly for 1 or 2 minutes. Remove the pan from the heat and, one at a time, quickly whisk the egg yolks into the hot sauce, then stir in the lemon juice, liqueur, and the chopped lemon peel.

About 45 minutes before you plan to serve the soufflé, preheat the oven to 400 degrees. Beat the egg whites (in an unlined copper bowl, and with a balloon whisk, if possible) until they foam. Add the remaining tablespoon of sugar, and continue to beat until the whites are stiff enough to grip the beater firmly and their small white peaks stand firmly upright. Be careful not to underbeat. Thoroughly mix 2 large spoonfuls of the whites into the warm lemon sauce. Then, with the aid of a rubber spatula, immediately pour the mixture over the remaining egg whites in the bowl. Fold the two together, using the spatula to bring the heavier mass over the lighter whites, thus, as it were, enfolding the two instead of mixing them. Continue folding in this fashion until only the faintest streaks of egg whites still remain. Do not overfold, lest you lose the air you have so laboriously beaten into the whites to inflate them. Immediately pour the mixture into the sugared mold and smooth the surface with the spatula. Bake in the lower third of the oven for 2 minutes, then turn the heat down to 375 degrees, and continue to bake for about 30 minutes, or until the soufflé has risen at least 2 inches above the rim of its mold. (You may bake the soufflé 5 or 10 minutes longer if you prefer a firmer consistency, as so many Americans do.)

The Meringue:

While the soufflé is baking, make the meringue in the following fashion. Beat the egg whites with the cream of tartar until they foam. Still beating, add the sugar, a tablespoon at a time, and continue to beat until the

Lemon Soufflé with a Meringue Topping

whites are literally stiff. Because of the large amount of sugar added to them, these whites will have a decidedly different consistency (that might be described as marshmallow-like) than the whites you folded into the soufflé. Spoon them into a large pastry bag fitted with a large plain or decorative tip; twist the ends of the bag tightly together and put the meringue aside, unrefrigerated, until you are ready to use it.

Five minutes or so before the soufflé is done to your taste, open the oven door, raise the heat to 450 degrees, and gently slide the rack out halfway. Quickly pipe the meringue in decorative swirls on top of the soufflé (don't take too long or the soufflé may collapse) and slide the rack back into place. Gently, close the oven door and bake the soufflé for 5 to 8 minutes or until the top of the meringue is lightly browned. Serve at once with or without the whipped cream.

cooking with chocolate

cookiNq with chocolate

Few things we eat have as outspoken a flavor as chocolate, yet when it is used as a seasoning—as it often is in cuisines other than our own—its character is subdued and one often has a hard time identifying what the subtle flavor is that the chocolate imparts to a dish.

The suave, rich chocolate we know today is a far cry from the crude chocolate first brought from Mexico to Europe by the explorer Cortez in the sixteenth century. Europeans then found the flavor of the cocoa beans far too bitter for their taste, and it was not until an enterprising cook thought of sweetening the chocolate with sugar that the strange new food began to be taken seriously—so seriously, in fact, that chocolate became one of the most popular drinks in Europe and, as a cooking ingredient, profoundly affected the repertory of every important cuisine in the Western world.

Until the middle of the nineteenth century, chocolate was coarse and grainy in texture, comparatively rare and formidably expensive. With the invention of special processing machinery and new refining techniques, however, the quality of chocolate began to improve steadily, until today we live in virtually a chocolate paradise. Available to us everywhere are chocolates of every degree of richness and sweetness. And if that weren't largesse enough, most domestic brands are divided or wrapped in individual one-ounce squares, for precise measuring. Cooking with chocolate now offers us numberless opportunities to make unusual dishes, many of which I present on pages 176–191. All the more reason, then, for you to be aware of the unpredictable and insidious ways in which chocolate sometimes behaves. Household cooks who have infrequently cooked with chocolate would suppose, not unreasonably, that the melting of chocolate—a first step necessary to all but one of my recipes—would be the simplest of tasks. And usually it is, if care is taken to melt the easily scorched chocolate as slowly as possible in a pan or a bowl over hot water, or in a slow oven, or more precariously over direct heat in a heavy pan, stirring it constantly and never allowing the chocolate to boil. But it is disconcerting to discover that, despite your care, the melting chocolate sometimes unaccountably turns into a stubborn, sticky mass, which no amount of stirring or beating will budge or break up.

Fortunately, the solution is simple. Rather than throw the chocolate away, as you may be tempted to do, stir into it one tablespoon of vegetable shortening for every six ounces of the recalcitrant chocolate. Miraculously, the chocolate will become fluid, docile, and manageable again. And to avoid a recurrence of this frustrating phenomenon—"tightening," as it is called—you might find it useful to know why it occurs.

To melt successfully, chocolate must be either absolutely dry or combined with no less than two tablespoons of liquid—water, coffee, or almost anything else—for every ounce of chocolate. If it is melted dry—and that is the more foolproof method—even an insignificant drop of water lurking in the melting pan, a wet mixing spoon or a little vanilla innocently added to the melting chocolate may cause it to tighten. But curiously enough, once the chocolate is subdued, you can stir any amount of liquid into it with impunity. For mysterious chemical reasons, the cocoa butter in an ounce of chocolate tends to resist absorbing any liquid less than two tablespoons, so that if you are melting it with a liquid, you must use at least that much.

You will never be confronted with the problem of chocolate's tightening in a chocolate sauce for example. Because these essentially simple preparations usually require enough liquid to make the sauce fluid enough to pour, liquid and chocolate may be safely combined and cooked together from the start. Although good cookbooks offer a multitude of respectable chocolate sauces to choose from, a couple of the more original and useful ones deserve to be better known.

The Scandinavians make an extremely effective sauce with what is called Dutch-process cocoa (that is, cocoa scientifically treated to deepen its color and increase its water solubility). Three quarters of a cup of water mixed with one cup of sugar are brought to a rapid boil and boiled for precisely two minutes. The pan is then removed from the heat, and a cup of unsweetened cocoa is beaten into it with a whisk. A few minutes of persistent beating produce a smooth, shiny, and thick bittersweet sauce, which can be flavored, if you wish, with vanilla, cinnamon, mint, cognac, or a liqueur and served either hot or cold.

A considerably richer and more heavily textured sauce, devised by the late Helen Evans Brown, is made with sour cream and can be used as a cake frosting as well as a sauce. I use it with great success in my recipe for New England Chocolate Cake on page 176. When the frosting is cool, you can spread it smoothly on a cake as I do or, with a pastry tube, pipe it into the most intricate swirls, swoops, and curlicues, which will retain their shape whether the cake is refrigerated or not.

The frosting becomes a sauce merely by thinning it with hot water, milk, or sweet cream. In both the frosting and the sauce, the slight acidulation of the sour cream is always faintly apparent to the taste and adds a new and pleasantly dissonant note to the familiar taste of the chocolate. If you wish, you may flavor the frosting or sauce with any of the spices or liqueurs I suggested above for the Scandinavian sauce.

Special as chocolate is in sauces, it is probably in cakes that it fulfills its highest culinary destiny. And surely no chocolate cakes (our own brownies, devil's food, and other fine chocolate cakes notwithstanding) compare in sheer grandeur with those European masterpieces, the fondant-frosted Austrian *Sachertorte* and the chocolate-cream-filled Hungarian Dobos torte. I have evolved my own version of a *Sachertorte* recipe that really works; it does quite frankly depart from what are accepted as standard classic versions in almost every respect, but I make no apologies because the original recipe has undergone so many changes through the years as to be virtually unrecognizable. As for the Dobos torte, the true version is exceedingly difficult to do and should more properly be made by a professional pastry cook.

Disappointingly, the density of chocolate that gives chocolate cakes their charm has quite the reverse effect in chocolate soufflés. Although chocolate soufflés look more or less like ordinary dessert soufflés, they seldom, if ever, have the same ephemeral lightness. In fact, chocolate soufflés, even when prepared by experts, are usually woolly, pudding-like affairs, because cocoa butter is the natural enemy of stiffly beaten egg whites and tends to break them down no matter how gently the chocolate and whites are combined. Since it is the air in the beaten whites that expands when the soufflé is baked and causes it to rise, a chocolate soufflé is almost deflated from the start. I have worked with this challenge for years and I finally give you a recipe for a chocolate

soufflé on page 180, which I think solves that particular problem at
least.

Despite my aversion to most other chocolate soufflés, one type does
have a culinary function, nonetheless, and that is when it collapses and
becomes a chocolate roll. In this admirable creation, popularized by
that extraordinary cook Dionne Lucas a chocolate-soufflé mixture is
baked on a jelly-roll pan and allowed to collapse and cool. It is then
turned out and rolled up, jelly-roll fashion, with a lavish filling of sweetened vanilla- or in my own version of it on page 182 with coffee-
flavored whipped cream. And to intensify its chocolate flavor further
(and incidentally camouflage any cracks on its surface), the finished
roll is lightly dusted with unsweetened cocoa. Because the chocolate
roll contains no flour, its texture, although cakelike, has an aerated
lightness few ordinary cakes can approach. The chocolate roll's superi-
ority to the usual hot chocolate soufflé is apparent at the first mouthful.

A chocolate *mousse,* in any form, is something else again. Lightness of texture is not crucial to it, and for many tastes, the denser it is,
the better. A recipe that has come to be known as a standard chocolate
mousse is simplicity itself to make and even easier to remember: four
egg yolks beaten into four ounces of hot, melted semisweet chocolate,
then four stiffly beaten whites folded in. To gild the lily, the *mousse*
may be flavored with chopped candied orange peel or any of the orange
liqueurs, for which chocolate seems to have a particular affinity. I have
departed somewhat from this simple formula in my recipe for a choco-
late-orange *mousse* on page 185 and have made the orange flavor of the
mousse quite predominant.

But however you prepare a *mousse,* remember that it will be at its
best if you let it come almost to room temperature before serving it.
Most chilled chocolate desserts suffer a distinct loss of flavor if they are
served too cold. A successful *mousse* may be made with almost any type
of cooking chocolate, adding more sugar to the chocolate when necessary. But to assume that one type of chocolate may be substituted at
will for another or that cocoa may be used in place of chocolate (even
with the addition of extra fat) is a serious error. In complex chocolate
recipes, particularly good ones, substitutions can often produce catastrophic results. Different cooking chocolates contain varying amounts
of cocoa butter and substitution is at best a chancy business. Needless
to say, only unsweetened chocolate should be used in chocolate-
flavored preparations other than drinks, confections, and desserts.

Few American cooks are aware of the intriguing, mysterious flavor unsweetened chocolate, used discreetly, can give fowls, meats, and sauces. The Mexicans, as one might expect from their illustrious chocolate heritage (their Mayan and Aztec ancestors were the first to use chocolate as a food), employ it with particular effect in dishes they call *molés*. These are sauces composed of crushed chili peppers, peanuts, almonds, garlic, tomatoes, raisins, various spices, and ground bitter chocolate, in which pork, chicken, and, most often, turkey are cooked. They are so popular in Mexico that, I have heard it said there, every Mexican has two ambitions: to win the national lottery and to eat turkey *molé* on his birthday.

A *molé* is indeed a festive dish; but as the Mexicans traditionally make it, laboriously pounding the ingredients by hand to a paste, it is not a task to embark upon lightly. In the past few years, however, with the improvement of the electric blender, a good *molé* can be made now in a short time, as you will see when you make my fairly traditional version of turkey *molé* on page 186.

Adventurous French cooks have also developed a few main-course chocolate-flavored dishes of some consequence. Notable among them is the rabbit with almonds and chocolate sauce on page 189 among others. Even we culinarily conservative Americans have made a small foray in this direction by daringly adding, on occasion, small amounts of grated bitter chocolate to an otherwise conventional beef stew, with fine effect.

In time, many chocolate-flavored dishes of this type and others will undoubtedly evolve and find greater acceptance. As new foods go, chocolate, after all, hasn't been with us very long. When one considers that, according to a recent survey, the taste of chocolate is still unknown to almost three quarters of the world's population, cooking with chocolate is still in its infancy.

New England Chocolate Cake with Chocolate– Sour-Cream Frosting

serves 8 (more or less)

THE CAKE

13 tablespoons unsalted butter, *softened: 1 tablespoon for the baking pan and 12 tablespoons (1½ sticks) for the cake*

2 level cups plus 2 tablespoons all-purpose flour: *the 2 tablespoons for flouring the pan and the 2 cups* (not *packed down*) *for the cake*

6 one-ounce squares unsweetened chocolate, *coarsely chopped*

1½ level teaspoons double-acting baking powder

¼ teaspoon salt

2½ cups sugar

4 large (not extra large or jumbo) eggs

1 teaspoon vanilla extract

1½ cups milk

THE CHOCOLATE FROSTING

6 ounces (1 package) semisweet chocolate bits

1 cup commercial sour cream

The Cake:

Preheat the oven to 350 degrees.

With a pastry brush, spread 1 tablespoon of the butter on the bottom and sides of an 8-by-12-inch baking pan, 2 inches deep. Add the 2 tablespoons of flour, and holding the pan sideways over a sheet of waxed paper move it from side to side so that the flour spreads evenly over all the buttered surfaces. Invert the pan and tap it sharply to dislodge the excess flour.

Melt the chocolate over low heat in a small saucepan, stirring it constantly. Under no circumstances allow it to boil, and watch carefully for any sign of scorching. When the chocolate is smooth and fully melted, let it cool to room temperature.

Sift the 2 cups of flour, the baking powder, and the salt through a sifter (or shake it through a fine sieve) into a bowl and set aside.

New England Chocolate Cake with Chocolate–Sour-Cream Frosting

In a deep mixing bowl, cream the remaining 12 tablespoons of butter with the sugar by mashing and beating them against the sides of the bowl until the mixture is light and fluffy. (If you own an electric mixer equipped with a paddle or pastry arm, the creaming and subsequent procedures will be considerably easier to manage.) Beat in the eggs one at a time, making sure the egg is fully incorporated in the butter before adding the others in similar fashion. Beat in approximately ⅓ cup of the flour mixture and then ¼ cup of the milk, beating vigorously after each addition. Continue to add the remaining flour and milk alternately in ⅓ and ¼ cups, beating vigorously until the batter is smooth. (Don't overbeat.) Stir or beat in the cooled chocolate and the vanilla. Then pour the silky, mocha-colored batter into the waiting baking pan and smooth it to the edges with a rubber spatula.

Bake in the middle of the oven for about an hour or perhaps a few minutes more, or less, depending upon your oven. The finished cake will have risen to the top of the pan and feel springy to the touch. A more reassuring test for doneness is to insert a table knife into the center of the cake—it should emerge clean; if the knife has any chocolate batter clinging to it, bake the cake for a few minutes more.

You may remove the pan from the oven and in the old-fashioned American way, let the cake cool in the pan before frosting it. But a more effective method, if perhaps a precarious one, is to first run a long sharp knife all around the edges of the cake to loosen the sides, and then place a wire cake rack on top and invert the cake onto it. In either case, the cake should be fully cooled before you frost it.

The Chocolate Frosting:

While the cake is cooling (or, in fact, any time you like), make the frosting. Melt the chocolate bits in the top of a double boiler set over or into boiling water. (If you don't have a double boiler, melt the chocolate, over low direct heat, watching it carefully; it must not boil.) Stir in the sour cream, a few tablespoons at a time, and continue to stir until the mixture becomes a smooth dark glossy cream. Refrigerate for at least ½ hour, or until it becomes thick enough to spread.

If you have left the cake in the pan, simply pour the frosting over it and with a spatula spread it out over the entire surface. If you have turned the cake out on a rack, transfer it from the rack to a rectangular plate and frost the sides as well as the top. Cut into any shapes you like and serve.

NOTE: Do not refrigerate this chocolate cake; it will give it a woolly texture. Naturally, if you plan to serve the cake a day or so after making it—not the most sensible planning—refrigerate it, but let it come to room temperature for at least ½ hour before serving it. One final note: when I remove the cake from the pan, I cut away the crusty sides of the cake before frosting it.

Sachertorte

serves 8

THE CAKE

2 tablespoons butter, *softened*

6 ounces semisweet chocolate, *coarsely chopped*

10 large (not extra large or jumbo) eggs: *8 yolks for the cake and the 10 whites to fold into the batter*

1 teaspoon vanilla extract

8 tablespoons (¼ pound, 1 stick) unsalted butter, *melted and cooled*

⅛ teaspoon salt

¾ cup sugar

1 cup all-purpose flour, *precisely measured and not packed down*

THE GLAZE AND FILLING

3 ounces unsweetened chocolate, *coarsely chopped*

1 cup heavy cream

1 cup sugar

1 teaspoon corn syrup

Heavy cream, *whipped— unsweetened (optional)*

1 whole egg, *lightly beaten in a small bowl*

1 teaspoon vanilla extract

½ cup apricot jam, *rubbed through a sieve with the back of a large spoon*

The Cake:

Preheat the oven to 350 degrees.

Line the bottom of two circular pans 9 inches in diameter and ½ inch deep with individual circles of waxed paper. With a pastry brush, coat each circle and the sides of the pan with the softened butter and set them aside.

Stirring frequently, melt the semisweet chocolate in a saucepan over low heat. When it has become a smooth, thick cream, let it cool to lukewarm. Then, one by one, beat in the 8 yolks (beat vigorously with a small sauce whisk until smooth if the mixture appears to be "tightening" in the slightest). Beat in the vanilla and the melted butter a few tablespoons at a time.

With a wire whisk or rotary beater (and preferably in an unlined copper bowl—but *never* an aluminum one), beat the 10 egg whites with the salt until they foam thickly. Beating constantly, add the ¾ cup of sugar, a few tablespoons at a time, and continue to beat until the whites are stiff enough to form unwavering peaks on the beater when it is lifted from the bowl.

Mix about 1 cup of the whites into the chocolate mixture and when they are absorbed, pour the mixture over the remaining whites. Sieve the flour over the top and fold the three ingredients together with the spatula, bringing the heavier mass over the lighter whites and flour, thus enfolding the three instead of mixing them. There should be no flour or whites showing when you finish. Be careful, however, not to overfold or your cake will not be as light and delicate as it should be.

Immediately divide the batter as evenly as you can between the two cake pans and smooth the tops with the spatula. Bake in the middle of the oven for about 30 minutes, or until the cakes have risen somewhat above the pans and a cake tester, or small knife, inserted in the middle of each comes out clean.

Remove the cakes from the oven, let them rest for 2 or 3 minutes, then run a sharp knife around the sides of each cake to loosen it from the pan. Turn them out on wire racks, peel off the waxed paper circles, and let the cakes cool to room temperature before glazing them.

The Glaze:

While the cakes are baking (or earlier if you like), make the glaze. Combine the unsweetened chocolate, heavy cream, sugar, and corn syrup in a 1- or 2-quart heavy enamel or stainless-steel saucepan. Set it over moderate heat and bring the mixture to a boil, stirring constantly with a spoon, until the chocolate has completely dissolved. Still stirring, cook the mixture fairly briskly for 5 to 8 minutes, or until it reaches a temperature of 220 degrees on a candy thermometer, or until ¼ teaspoon of the mixture forms a soft ball-shaped mass immediately after it is dropped into a glass of cold water. Cooking the glaze can be a precarious procedure. Because it scorches easily, watch it constantly, and lower the heat if at any point it appears to be sticking to the bottom of the pan.

When the glaze has reached the proper consistency, mix 2 or 3 tablespoons of it into the lightly beaten egg. Then stirring the glaze constantly, slowly pour the egg into the pan, reduce the heat to low and, still stirring, simmer the glaze for about 3 or 4 minutes, or until it thickens enough to coat the spoon heavily. Remove the pan from the heat, stir in the vanilla, and pour the glaze into a bowl. Cool to room temperature before frosting the cake.

Meanwhile, prepare the cakes for frosting by trimming off any ragged or coarse edges with a sharp knife. Place one of the racks with cake onto a jelly-roll pan, and spread the sieved apricot jam evenly over the cake. Set the other cake on top. Pour the cooled glaze in a slow stream over the layered cakes, holding the bowl about 2 inches above and moving it slowly around the layers so that the glaze spreads evenly and drips down the sides. With a rubber spatula, pick up any glaze that may have dripped through the rack onto the pan, and spread it on the sides. Don't disturb the top.

Place the cake, still on its rack, in the refrigerator, and let it chill for about 3 hours, or until the glaze is firm and glossy. With two wide metal spatulas, carefully transfer the cake to a plate and serve.

NOTE: Although my version of the *Sachertorte* bears little resemblance to the somewhat leaden concoction served in Vienna today, you might nonetheless wish to stick to tradition and serve a bowl of unsweetened whipped cream with it.

Chocolate Soufflé   *serves 4–6*

2 tablespoons butter, *softened: 1 for the soufflé mold and 1 for the soufflé base*
7 tablespoons sugar: *2 for the mold, 3 tablespoons for the*

soufflé base, and 2 for the egg whites
1 level tablespoon cornstarch
½ cup milk
2 tablespoons strong coffee (left-

over coffee will do—or dissolve 1 teaspoon instant coffee in 2 tablespoons boiling water)
1 tablespoon Grand Marnier or other orange-flavored liqueur
⅓ cup semisweet chocolate bits
or 2½ ounces semisweet chocolate, *coarsely chopped*
6 eggs: *4 yolks for the soufflé base and the 6 whites for the soufflé*
Confectioners' sugar
1 cup heavy cream, *unsweetened, whipped into soft peaks*

Preheat the oven to 400 degrees.

With a pastry brush, thoroughly coat the inside of a 2-quart soufflé dish or charlotte mold with 1 tablespoon of the softened butter. Then pour in 2 tablespoons of the sugar and, holding the mold sideways over a sheet of waxed paper, slowly rotate it so that the sugar spreads evenly over all the buttered surfaces. Invert the mold and tap it gently to dislodge any excess sugar. The inside of the mold should look like finely grained sandpaper.

In a 1-quart enamel or stainless-steel saucepan, beat the cornstarch into the milk with a small whisk. Whisking constantly, bring the milk to a boil over high heat, lifting the pan occasionally from the heat to prevent scorching as the mixture begins to thicken into a pasty mass. Stir in the coffee, Grand Marnier or liqueur, 3 tablespoons of the remaining sugar, chocolate, and the remaining tablespoon of butter. Lower the heat and simmer the mixture slowly, stirring constantly until the chocolate has completely dissolved. Then remove the pan from the heat. One by one, whisk in the 4 egg yolks, and return the pan to low heat again. Still whisking, simmer the mixture (under no circumstances let it come to a boil) for 2 or 3 minutes until it thickens enough to coat a spoon rather heavily. Set aside off the heat.

For the most predictable results, use a bowl of unlined copper in which to beat the egg whites—the crucial element, it is well to know, in all soufflés. But any bowl, except an aluminum one, will do if it must; however, your soufflé will not rise as high or as spectacularly as it should. Beat the whites with a clean balloon whisk or a rotary beater (*not* an electric mixer) until they foam thickly, add the remaining 2 tablespoons of sugar, and continue to beat until the whites gradually form stiff, unwavering peaks on the beater when it is lifted from the bowl. With a rubber spatula, vigorously stir 4 heaping tablespoons, one at a time, into the lukewarm soufflé base, and when they are thoroughly absorbed, pour the mixture over the remaining egg whites. Fold the two together using a rubber spatula to bring the heavier mass over the lighter whites, thus, in effect, enfolding the two instead of mixing them. Continue folding in this fashion until only the faintest streaks of egg whites still remain. Do not overfold, however, lest you lose the air you have so laboriously beaten into the whites to inflate them. Immediately pour the mixture into the sugared mold, and smooth the surface with the spatula. (If you like, quickly run the spatula around the rim of the soufflé, inserting it about an inch from the sides and about an inch deep to create a vaguely defined circle. As the soufflé bakes, the center should rise into a large decorative crown.)

Bake the soufflé in the lower third of the oven for about 2 minutes, then turn the heat down to 375 degrees and bake undisturbed for 30 minutes, if you prefer the center of the soufflé soft, as I do; or bake it for 10 to 15 minutes longer if you like a firmer texture. (Whatever the baking time you decide on, the soufflé will have risen at least 2 or 3 inches above the rim of the dish if you have followed my instructions precisely.) Serve at once, sprinkled lightly with powdered sugar and accompanied with the bowl of whipped cream.

NOTE: The soufflé base may be made hours before you plan to cook the soufflé. Simply cool it to lukewarm, cover it with plastic wrap, and set it aside at room temperature. It is important to remember that the base for this soufflé must be heated to lukewarm before the egg whites are folded in.

Souffléed Chocolate-Mocha Roll   *serves 10–12*

THE SOUFFLÉ ROLL

2 tablespoons softened butter: *1 to coat the pan and 1 to coat the waxed paper lining*

8 ounces (½ pound) semisweet chocolate, *coarsely chopped*

¼ cup strong coffee: *leftover coffee will do or dissolve 2 teaspoons instant coffee—*

instant espresso, if you prefer —in ¼ cup boiling water

7 large (not extra large or jumbo) eggs: *the yolks for the cake base and the whites to fold into it*

1 cup sugar

THE FILLING

1½ cups heavy cream, *chilled*
3 tablespoons confectioners' sugar
2 tablespoons instant coffee

powder (instant espresso, if
you prefer)
⅓ cup unsweetened cocoa

The Soufflé Roll:

Preheat the oven to 350 degrees.

With a pastry brush, butter the bottom and sides of a 12-by-18-inch (or an inch more or less) jelly-roll pan. Then spread a sheet of waxed paper over the pan, but cut it long enough to allow 2 inches to extend over each end. Pat it down securely and brush the paper evenly with the remaining tablespoon of butter, ignoring the overhanging edges.

Stirring constantly with a spoon, melt the chocolate in a small saucepan over low heat (or in a double boiler set over simmering water, if you want to play it safe). Then stir in the coffee and simmer, still stirring, until the chocolate is smooth and fairly fluid. (Beat it for 1 or 2 minutes with a whisk if it seems lumpy.) With a rubber spatula, scrape the chocolate into a small metal bowl and let it cool to lukewarm.

Meanwhile, separate the eggs and drop the yolks into a mixing bowl and the whites into another bowl, preferably one made of unlined copper, or any bowl other than one of aluminum. Beat the yolks with a sauce whisk, or rotary beater for a minute or two, then slowly pour in the sugar, beating constantly until the mixture flows thickly off the beater when it is lifted from the bowl. Slowly beat in the lukewarm chocolate and continue to beat until the mixture is glossy and smooth.

Now beat the whites with a balloon whisk or the washed rotary beater until they form stiff, unwavering peaks on the beater when it is lifted from the bowl. With a rubber spatula, vigorously stir 3 or 4 heaping tablespoons of the whites into the chocolate batter and when they are thoroughly absorbed, pour the batter over the remaining whites. Fold the two together, using the spatula to bring the heavier chocolate mass over the lighter whites, thus, in effect, enfolding the two instead of mixing them. Continue to fold in this fashion until the whites no longer show. Do not, however, overfold the mixture, lest you lose the air you have laboriously beaten into the whites to inflate them.

Immediately pour the batter into the jelly-roll pan and tip it gently from side to side so that it flows evenly into every corner of the pan.

Bake in the middle of the oven for about 18 minutes, or until the cake has puffed and a small knife inserted in the center comes out clean.

Remove the cake from the oven and immediately place a strip of waxed paper over its surface, patting it down to cover the cake. Drape a dry kitchen towel over the pan and let the cake rest at room temperature (don't refrigerate it) until cool.

The Filling:

Whip the cream in a chilled bowl until it thickens slightly, then add the sugar and continue to whip until stiff. Add the instant powdered coffee and fold together with the spatula until the coffee grains dissolve.

To unmold and fill the roll, proceed in the following fashion: spread a triple thickness of waxed paper—cut a few inches longer than the paper in the pan. Remove the towel from the pan and gently strip the waxed paper off the top of the cake—the crusty cake surface will cling and come away with it, which it is meant to do—and sift the cocoa through a fine sieve evenly over the cake. Carefully turn the cake over onto the triple-layered waxed paper. (The cake will not fall out of the pan as you might expect.) To remove the waxed paper without the cake crumbling, hold one end of the protruding paper securely down on the table with one hand, and with the other, lift the short end of the pan slowly away from the cake. Remove the paper covering the cake with care.

With a small sharp knife, cut away the crusty edges of the cake and with the spatula spread the cream over the entire surface of the cake. With one of the long sides of the cake in front of you, use the bottom layers of waxed paper to help roll the cake over, aiming the lifted end toward the center of the cake. The cake will inevitably split slightly into a "sandwich," as it were, but don't be concerned. Make the second roll precisely as the first, but this time lift up and roll the "sandwich" onto the exposed half of the cake, pulling the ends of the paper tautly toward you to gently force the cake into a compact cylinder.

Now pull back the waxed paper from the top of the cake, and with scissors, cut away all the exposed paper along the sides of the roll, leaving the exposed narrow ends intact. Using the ends as handles, lift up the roll, cradle-like, and carefully set it on a jelly-roll board or large platter. Cut off the protruding ends of paper with scissors, then slice the roll (at the table, preferably) crosswise into individual portions, and serve at once.

NOTE: You may, if you like, camouflage any serious cracks in the roll by dusting the exposed cream with a little more sifted cocoa. Don't, however, refrigerate the roll; plan to fill and roll it no more than an hour or even less before serving it. Refrigeration will stiffen the chocolate and the roll will lose its characteristic airy texture.

Chocolate-Orange Mousse   serves 6–8

4 large (not extra large or jumbo) eggs: *the yolks for the base of the mousse and the whites to complete the mousse*
2 tablespoons sugar
1 tablespoon orange peel (SEE BELOW), *very finely chopped*
6 ounces semisweet chocolate, *coarsely chopped*
2 tablespoons Grand Marnier
1 large navel orange: *the peel removed in paper-thin strips*

with a swivel-bladed vegetable peeler, the orange then squeezed and the juice strained
3 tablespoons fresh, strained orange juice (SEE ABOVE)
8 tablespoons (¼ pound, 1 stick) unsalted butter, *cut into small pieces and softened to room temperature*
½ cup heavy cream, *chilled, whipped into soft peaks (optional)*

Combine the egg yolks and the sugar in a stainless-steel mixing bowl and beat them with a whisk, rotary or electric beater until they thicken enough to fall back on themselves in a sluggish ribbon when the mixture is lifted from the bowl. Stir in the chopped orange peel.

Place the bowl in a skillet filled with enough hot water to come to about 2 inches up the sides of the bowl. Place the skillet over low heat (the water must simmer, never boil) and resume beating the egg mixture until it foams thickly and when tested feels almost too hot to the finger. (This should take about 3 or 4 minutes.) Remove the bowl from the skillet and place it in a larger bowl filled with crushed ice or ice cubes covered with an inch or so of cold water. Beat for 3 or 4 minutes longer, or until the mixture is cold, thick, and creamy.

Stirring constantly with a wooden spoon or a rubber spatula, melt the chocolate in a small saucepan set over low heat. Do not at any point allow it to boil and watch it carefully; it scorches easily. Remove the pan from the heat and with a sauce whisk beat into it, 1 tablespoon at a time, the Grand Marnier and then the 3 tablespoons of orange juice. Bit by bit, beat in the butter. When the mixture is smooth and glossy, stir it into the cold egg-yolk mixture.

Beat the whites with a clean balloon whisk or rotary beater (not an electric mixer) in an unlined copper bowl, preferably, but any bowl not of aluminum will do if it must. Beat them until they foam, then continue beating until they form soft, wavering peaks on the beater when it is lifted from the bowl. The whites must not be too stiffly beaten or the *mousse* will be spongy rather than creamy. With a rubber spatula, mix about ½ cup of the whites into the *mousse,* then pour it over the remaining egg whites, and gently but thoroughly fold the two together.

Pour the *mousse* into a 1-quart soufflé dish, smooth the top, and cover with plastic wrap. Refrigerate for at least 6 hours or until the *mousse* is fairly firm.

Serve, accompanied with the bowl of whipped cream if you like.

NOTE: An especially festive way to serve the *mousse* is to whip the cream stiffly and pipe it on top in swirls or kisses through a pastry bag fitted with a decorative tip. Decorate the cream with a few candied violets if you can get them.

Turkey Molé   *serves 8–10*

THE TURKEY AND THE STOCK

A 9- to 10-pound turkey
7–8 quarts water
2 medium onions, *peeled*
2 medium carrots, *scraped*

1 large bay leaf
3 stalks celery with their leaves
20 or so whole black peppercorns
1 tablespoon salt

THE MOLÉ SAUCE

6 tablespoons chili powder
5 tablespoons sesame seeds: 3 for

the sauce and 2 to sprinkle over the finished molé

¾ cup blanched almonds, *whole or slivered*

1 tortilla (canned), *crumbled or torn,* or use ¼ cup Fritos or other corn chips, *crumbled*

½ cup seedless raisins

2 medium cloves garlic, *peeled*

½ teaspoon anise seeds

½ teaspoon cinnamon

½ teaspoon powdered cloves

½ teaspoon coriander seeds or ground coriander

3 medium-size ripe tomatoes, *coarsely chopped,* or use 1 cup *drained and finely chopped* canned tomatoes

3 medium onions, *peeled and quartered*

2 teaspoons salt

½ teaspoon whole black peppercorns

4–5 cups turkey stock or use canned chicken stock

1½ ounces unsweetened chocolate, *grated and coarsely chopped*

4–8 tablespoons lard

As formidable as the list of ingredients for this turkey *molé* may appear, in reality the construction of the dish takes little effort. An electric blender, however, is indispensable to its execution.

Ask the butcher to dissect the turkey, or do it yourself. Cut the legs and thighs away from the body of the bird and leave the legs attached to the thighs. Cut off the wings but don't separate the breast. Chop the neck into 2-inch sections and cut the gizzard and heart in half. Save the liver for some other purpose.

In a 10- to 12-quart casserole or soup pot, combine the turkey, its giblets, the onions, carrots, and celery. Pour in 7 quarts of water (8, if the water doesn't cover the bird by at least 2 inches) and bring it to a boil over high heat. With a large spoon, skim off and discard the foam and scum as it rises to the top, then lower the heat. Add the peppercorns and salt and cover the pot. Simmer as slowly as possible for about 45 minutes, or until the turkey is almost but not quite tender. At the end of the cooking time, a leg or a thigh should show a slight resistance when pierced with a fork. At that point, transfer the turkey pieces to a board and cut the meat away from the bones into fairly large serving pieces; if possible, leave as much of the skin on the pieces intact as you can. Return the turkey bones, carcass, and any stray bits of meat to the pot and let the stock cook fairly briskly over moderate heat, uncovered, while you make the *molé* sauce.

In a large mixing bowl, combine the chili powder, 3 tablespoons of the sesame seeds, the almonds, tortilla or either of the substitutions, the

raisins, garlic, anise seeds, cinnamon, cloves, coriander, tomatoes, onions, salt, peppercorns, and 2 cups of the stock taken from the simmering
pot and strained. About 2 cupfuls at a time, add the ingredients (including some of the stock) to the jar of an electric blender and blend at
high speed until the mixture is thoroughly puréed and smooth. Pour the
purée into a 12-inch sauté pan or a 4-quart casserole. Purée the remaining *molé* in similar amounts, adding it to the pan as you proceed. When
all the *molé* has been puréed, stir into it 2 more cups of strained turkey
stock and bring the mixture to a boil. (You can now remove the pot of
stock from the heat and put it aside.) Then lower the heat, add the
grated chocolate and, stirring occasionally, let the *molé* simmer (but
not boil) quietly while you fry the cooked turkey meat.

Melt 4 tablespoons of the lard over high heat in a 10- to 12-inch
heavy skillet until the fat is quite hot but not smoking. Add the turkey
pieces, skin-side down, but don't crowd the pan—the turkey can be
fried in two, and if necessary, three batches. Cook the turkey for about
3 or 4 minutes on each side, turning the pieces cut with tongs, until they
are golden-brown on both sides, adding more lard to the pan whenever
necessary. As you proceed, transfer the browned turkey to the simmering *molé*, and continue frying the remaining turkey and add it to the
sauce. Cover the pan or casserole, reduce the heat to low, and simmer
the turkey in the sauce for about 20 minutes, or until the meat is tender.
Don't at any point allow the sauce to boil. If the sauce seems too thick,
thin it by adding a tablespoonful of the reserved stock whenever necessary. The *molé* sauce should have the consistency of heavy cream when
the turkey is done. Taste for seasoning, then transfer the turkey to a
large, deep platter, pour the sauce over it and sprinkle with the remaining 2 tablespoons of sesame seeds. Serve at once.

NOTE: Two 4- to 5-pound roasting chickens or capons may be prepared
in precisely the same fashion as the turkey.

Braised Rabbit with Almonds and Chocolate Sauce in the Spanish Manner

serves 4

3 tablespoons vegetable oil

¼ pound mildly cured lean salt pork, *rind removed and reserved, and the pork cut into ⅛-inch cubes*

16–20 small white onions, each about 1 inch in diameter, *peeled*

A 2½- to 3-pound rabbit (thoroughly defrosted, if frozen), *cut into 6 or 8 neat serving pieces*

Salt

Freshly ground black pepper

½ cup flour

¾ cup dry red wine

1½ cups chicken stock, fresh or canned: *if you use the canned concentrated kind, dilute with an equal amount of water*

½ teaspoon dried thyme, *crumbled*

Fresh parsley (preferably the flat-leaf type), *enough to make 4 tablespoons chopped*

1 medium-size bay leaf

½ cup blanched, untoasted almonds, *finely pulverized in a blender or with a mortar and pestle*

2 tablespoons unsweetened chocolate, *grated*

¼–½ cup heavy cream

The rabbit should be braised, preferably in a 12-inch heavy sauté pan equipped with a tightly fitting cover, but a shallow 4-quart enamel casserole will do almost as well, if it must.

Pour the oil into the pan and set it over moderate heat. Add the salt-pork cubes and stir frequently with a wooden spoon; cook for at least 10 minutes, or until the pork pieces are brown and crisp and have rendered all their fat. Scoop them out with a slotted spoon and spread them out on paper toweling to drain.

Add the onions to the fat in the pan and raise the heat to high. Move the pan back and forth across the burner so that the onions roll around on their own and brown fairly evenly and quickly. Don't let them burn. Remove them from the fat with the slotted spoon and put them in a bowl.

Braised Rabbit with Almonds and Chocolate Sauce

Now pat the pieces of rabbit thoroughly dry with paper toweling and sprinkle them liberally on all sides with salt and, more discreetly, with pepper. One at a time, dip them in the flour and shake them vigorously to remove any excess. Heat the fat in the pan until it is very hot but not smoking. Add as many pieces of rabbit, fleshy-side down, as it will hold comfortably. Brown them to a golden hue—about 3 to 5 minutes on each side—then remove them with tongs and place them on a platter. (Fry any remaining rabbit pieces similarly, adding 1 tablespoon of oil or so to the pan if it seems dry, and transfer them to the platter.)

Pour off and discard all but the thinnest film of fat from the pan and pour in the wine. Bring it to a boil over high heat, meanwhile scraping into it any brown sediment clinging to the bottom of the pan. Continue to boil briskly, uncovered and undisturbed, until the wine has almost completely, but not quite, cooked away. Pour in the chicken stock, stir thoroughly, and bring to a boil. Add the thyme, 2 tablespoons of the parsley, the bay leaf, and the pieces of rabbit, including any juices that may have collected around them. Make sure the rabbit pieces don't overlap—they will, if your pan is too small—and immerse the onions in the sauce between and around them.

Cover the pan tightly, lower the heat—the sauce should barely simmer—and cook the rabbit for about 1 hour, turning the rabbit pieces and the onions over after about 30 minutes. (If the onions are tender but still intact at this point, which is unlikely, remove them from the pan and return them to their bowl; otherwise, let them cook until done with the rabbit for the remaining 30 minutes.) When you can easily pierce a leg of the rabbit with a fork, it is done.

Now remove the rabbit and the onions (if you haven't removed them earlier) from the pan. Tip the pan and, with a large spoon, skim off and discard as much of the surface fat as possible. Bring the remaining juices in the pan to a boil over high heat, and stir in the almonds. Then lower the heat and stir in the chocolate. When it has completely dissolved (the sauce *must not* boil at this point or thereafter), return the rabbit and the onions to the pan. Baste them well, and scatter the drained brown salt-pork bits over the top. Simmer the rabbit for a few minutes to heat it through. Taste the sauce for seasoning.

Arrange the rabbit pieces on a large heated platter, surround them with the onions and pour the sauce over the top. Sprinkle with the remaining chopped parsley and serve at once.

Figs Stuffed with Chocolate and Almonds in the Portuguese Manner

makes 2 dozen

⅔ cup whole blanched almonds
24 large dried figs

1-ounce square of semisweet chocolate

Preheat the oven to 350 degrees.

Spread the almonds in one layer on a baking sheet and, turning them over occasionally, toast them in the upper third of the oven for about 10 minutes, or until they color lightly. Set 24 of the almonds aside and finely pulverize the rest in an electric blender or with a mortar and pestle. Grate the chocolate with a Mouli grater or the fine side of a hand grater and stir it into the pulverized almonds, mixing or pounding them together to form a fairly dry paste.

With scissors or a small sharp knife, cut the stems off the figs. Then, with your fingers or the handle of a small spoon, make a deep depression in the stem end of each fig (be careful not to tear it) and stuff about a teaspoon of the chocolate-almond mixture into it, packing it in tightly. Pinch the openings firmly closed with your fingers.

Arrange the figs, pinched-sides up, side by side, on an ungreased baking sheet. Bake undisturbed in the center of the oven for 8 minutes, turn them over and bake for 8 minutes more. Press a toasted whole almond gently but firmly into the outside of each fig and serve warm (not hot) or at room temperature.

NOTE: These charming confections are traditionally served in Portugal after dinner, accompanied by a glass of fine old Port.

THE EGG

tHE EGG

Samuel Butler was somewhat partial to eggs and maintained irrever-
ently in "Life and Habit" that the hen was only an egg's way of making
another egg. I agree entirely. Eggs are not only one of the most delectable of foods with magical powers when combined with other foods, but
nutritional powerhouses as well. Because an egg contains protein of the
highest quality (nutritionists use it as a standard by which they measure other proteins), all the essential vitamins (except Vitamin C), saturated and unsaturated fatty acids, a preponderance of important min-
erals and a minimum of carbohydrates, the egg is, as it were, an almost
complete food, with the added advantage of averaging only 72 calories.

Perhaps the highest level of our national health is due in part to the
fact that we consume over 60 billion eggs a year, considerably more
than any other country in the world. Reasonably, you would think that
by now we would have developed a highly sophisticated egg cuisine;
but in reality the reverse is true. If our average restaurant menus are
guides, we eat our eggs uncomplainingly for breakfast day after day
and in the same old way: boiled, fried, scrambled, or poached; sometimes with bacon, ham, or sausage; frequently alone. That eggs can be
more artfully cooked and served in other ways—and for other meals—
rarely seems to occur to us.

Not that all our egg dishes are to be disdained. Far from it. Our
eggs Benedict, for example, is an extraordinary construction. And a traditional Southern breakfast composed of fried eggs, a thick slice of
broiled country ham, hominy grits, and freshly baked biscuits is a meal
I especially like. But when I think of cuisines somewhat older than ours,
it is clear that the egg, even when it is simply cooked, can reach heights
of culinary elegance far removed from our own.

For the most part, hens' eggs are common to almost all cuisines, although the oilier duck and goose eggs are often used in their place on many privately owned farms which produce them. But whatever the egg, cooking it is not the simple matter it is often said to be. Boiling an egg would hardly appear to offer a challenge to even a neophyte cook. Yet one of the great basic cookbooks of France, *Livre de Cuisine*, by Madame St. Ange, lists five methods for this elementary procedure. And each produces a perceptibly different result.

The best, for my taste, is the method of simply placing the egg (at room temperature, of course) in a pan of boiling water, removing the pan from the heat and covering it tightly, then letting the egg rest in the hot water from five to eight minutes—depending on its size—before serving it. The result should be a soft-cooked egg with a smooth and creamy white and a yolk still fluid but cooked just long enough to give it some density. But Madame St. Ange stresses sternly: "A true boiled egg must have been laid the day it is to be eaten." And, as anyone who has eaten one knows, of course, that she is right. Nothing can compare with the special fresh-egg taste of a newly laid, perfectly cooked egg.

Freshness is an even more important consideration when the egg is to be poached the way the French do it. That is, stirring a pan of simmering, acidulated water with a large spoon to form a whirlpool, into which the egg is then slipped, so that the revolving water turns the white of the egg round and round the yolk, to clothe it finally in the most filmy and delicate of veils. Eggs past their prime develop thin, watery whites, which float free of their yolks as soon as they touch hot water. Consequently, an egg more than one or two days old usually can't be poached at all. On page 202, in my recipe for eggs Benedict, I have described another, and I think simpler, poaching method, but both ways are equally effective.

Poaching an egg is not to be confused with steaming it, which is exactly what happens to it in a mechanical so-called egg poacher. This pan, with its nest of molds, predictably produces neatly shaped rectangular or circular eggs, which look as if they had been stamped with a die, their whites almost always overcooked and quite rubbery in texture. Needless to say, an egg poached in this fashion needn't be particularly fresh. Because the white and its yolk are safely contained in their own receptacle, there is no danger of separation. From my view, these insidious pans are best avoided.

Whether or not you are addicted to poached eggs, it is worth searching out fresh eggs and learning to poach them, in order to make that greatest of cold egg dishes, *oeufs en gelée,* or eggs in aspic. Despite its glamorous reputation, the dish is merely perfectly cooked poached eggs, chilled, then immersed in a clear, tarragon-flavored aspic and unmolded on a bed of salad greens. Visually spectacular in this simple form, eggs in aspic are even more so when they are molded with slices of *pâté de foie gras,* ham, or fancifully cut truffles. If you follow my recipe precisely for this glorious dish on page 204, you will spare yourself the exasperating experience of having the egg float to the top of the aspic instead of remaining firmly encased in a jewel-like fashion within it.

If you can't get really fresh eggs (and you probably can't unless you are in the country) and must forego the poaching of them, it may be consoling to know that older eggs have their uses. Their whites (at room temperature) can be beaten to a greater volume than really fresh ones. And if you use an unlined copper bowl and a steel balloon whisk with which to beat them, you will discover that they will have an infinitely better texture than whites beaten in other bowls and by other means. The chemical reaction that takes place because of the copper— a scientist friend called it "electrolytic"—affects the whites in some mysterious manner so that your soufflés rise higher than you ever dreamed possible and your meringues are more stable. I stress this important point in all my soufflé and meringue recipes, such as *oeufs à la neige* on page 210. I warn you too not to beat your whites, for whatever purpose, in an aluminum or plastic bowl; aluminum will turn your whites gray and most plastics will decrease their volume. If you don't have a copper bowl (and it's worth the investment if you are a serious cook), use a glass or stainless-steel bowl. Make doubly certain then, that the whites you use come from older eggs.

Older eggs have other uses too. Hard-cooked eggs should never be attempted with eggs that are too fresh. Even if you go through the time-honored procedure of plunging them into cold water the moment they are done, fresh eggs will still be impossible to peel. Because the results are more predictable, I prefer to hard-cook eggs that I am sure are 4 or 5 days old. However, those of you who live in our larger cities will never be confronted with this problem. Whatever you are told, the eggs you buy in most supermarkets today are at least 4 or 5 days old to start with, if not older.

Naturally, after a certain point, slight deterioration does set in. Al-

though an old egg may still be edible, its yolk will rupture easily and
its white will have thinned so markedly that its performance in many
dishes may well be catastrophic.

How to determine the freshness of an egg has perplexed consumers
for years. Most foods displayed in the market offer easily read clues to
their condition, but the shell of an egg is literally blank and inscrutable.
Unless it is cracked (a serious matter because of the possibility of bac-
terial entry), an egg defies any type of examination except candling, a
process used by the egg industry to look through an egg as it passes
over a strong light. Now electronically controlled, candling provides a
high degree of consistency in the grading of eggs, and for the most
part, the grades are clearly marked on each box. But seldom, if ever, is
the degree of the eggs' freshness specified. Too often, cold-storage eggs
—which have been stored anywhere from six months to a year—are sold
as fresh ones, and although they are perfectly wholesome and function
well enough in most preparations—as when their yolks are used to
thicken sauces—they leave something to be desired when the pure flavor of the egg in a dish is an important consideration.

Whatever else the differences may be in highly developed cuisines,
the flavor of eggs remains a constant culinary factor. But, interestingly
enough, the Chinese, with considerable daring, age eggs the way we
do cheese, with the deliberate purpose of actually changing their flavor.

For this delicacy, newly laid eggs, ducks' eggs more often than not,
are smeared with a mixture of mud and lime, wrapped in rice husks or
some similar moisture-proof covering, and put away to ripen. Euphe-
mistically, the Chinese call them thousand-year eggs, but of course they
are nothing of the kind. Six or seven weeks is usually the amount of
time allotted for them to reach maturity, although they can be aged for
as long as a year. Adventurous eaters may buy them already cured in
many Chinese food stores. Not to everyone's taste—I like them—the
eggs make unusual and colorful hors d'oeuvres, the whites a satiny
black, the yolks a deep orange-green. Because the flavor is bland, I usually serve them as the Chinese do: with a dipping dish of soy sauce.

Less startling, perhaps, but equally attractive is another Chinese
egg preparation, called tea eggs. Hard-cooked eggs, simmered for
about half an hour, are plunged into cold water, and their shells are
gently cracked all over but not removed. They are then simmered again
for about three hours, this time in very strong, lightly salted tea, flavored with star anise, or orange rind when the anise is unavailable.

Oddly enough, despite the long cooking period, the texture of these eggs is far more tender than of those of ordinary hard-cooked eggs, and the sepia-tinted imprints left on their whites by the cracked shells are beautifully intricate and weblike.

The French, too, have their way with eggs and, from some points of view, the best. By conservative estimate, French cooks have devised over seven hundred ways to serve them. Many of the recipes are quite complex and require the use of puff paste, *espagnole* sauce, and other embellishments of *La Grande Cuisine;* they cannot even be considered for the average American- or even French-household kitchen. Other French egg dishes, however, are so inspired that it behooves us, as cooks of the greatest egg-producing country in the world, to learn more about them.

Fried eggs, as we generally cook them, are almost unknown in France—and everywhere else, for that matter. And with good reason. Of all our egg dishes, this surely can be the worst. In the hands of a skillful cook, of course, fried eggs can be superb—the eggs fried slowly, hovered over and basted constantly with butter, so that they cook through evenly without toughening or burning. But much too often, particularly in many restaurants, frying an egg is a slapdash operation. The yolks are sometimes broken and usually overcooked, and the whites are brittle and burned, with "edges like some dirty kind of starched lace and a taste part sulfur and part singed newspaper," in the words of the witty and knowing M. F. K. Fisher.

The French fry eggs differently, and their method produces a more attractive and foolproof result. They call them *oeufs sur le plat.* Quite simply, their secret consists in slowly frying the eggs, with a cover. Because they are usually cooked in individual dishes, in which they are also served, there is no danger of the yolks breaking. For most of us, when all is said and done, an unbroken, still-liquid yolk is the only reason for frying an egg in the first place. Although the French apply all types of refinement to this dish, *oeufs sur le plat* are really at their best when they are cooked quite simply. Shirred eggs, called *oeufs miroir* in French, are very much like *oeufs sur le plat,* except that they are broiled instead of fried. On page 207, I have suggested the various garnishes to serve with them. Shirred eggs seem to lend themselves to more elaborate treatment than fried ones.

Surely one of the greatest contributions to egg cookery is the plain omelette, at once, perhaps, the simplest and quickest preparation in all

French cooking—simplest because all an omelette requires is two or three fresh eggs, a little salt and pepper, and about a tablespoon of butter; and quickest because it takes less than a minute to cook, from start to finish. It has always been the contention that only a well-seasoned omelette pan, never washed and never used for anything else, was indispensable to the production of the perfect omelette. With the development of a non-scratch, non-stick-surfaced pan today, this is no longer true, whatever the purists may say.

The making of omelettes can be traced back for centuries in various cuisines, among them the Chinese, Roman, Spanish, Italian, German, and French. Each country makes its omelettes in somewhat different ways. The Italian *frittata,* such as the one on page 209 for instance, is quite different from a sweet puffed omelette (page 207). But only the French omelette can still provoke violent arguments among amateurs and even professionals as to the proper way to prepare it. Omelette cooks, however else they may differ, do agree that omelettes should be cooked over high heat. But from then on out, omelette cooking fragments into a multitude of schools, of which the following two are the most vociferous.

One school pours the beaten eggs into a hot, buttered pan and, with a spatula or fork, quickly pushes the outer portion of cooked eggs toward the middle of the pan, forcing the still-liquid center to flow into the space cleared for it. This maneuver is repeated until the omelette is cooked to the desired state of doneness, whereupon it is folded or rolled and served. In skillful hands, omelettes of this type emerge with lightly browned crusts and, ideally, creamy centers.

Whatever its merits, this procedure is dismissed as amateurish by proponents of the second school, to which I distinctly belong. Our omelette is called, precisely, *l'omelette brouillée,* or scrambled omelette, and it employs the traditional omelette techniques set forth in Escoffier's *Guide Culinaire, Larousse Gastronomique,* and other classic cookbooks. Indeed, Escoffier describes it academically as "scrambled eggs enclosed in a coating of coagulated egg."

Perplexing and ambiguous as it sounds, that is exactly what this omelette is. Lightly beaten eggs (never more than three) are poured into a hot, buttered eight-inch pan, then stirred rapidly with the flat of a fork held in one hand, while the other hand slides the pan back and forth over the heat, to shake the eggs continually free (with a pan coated with the latest, unscratchable, non-stick Teflon, I no longer find it necessary to use a special omelette pan or to slide the pan over the range when I make my omelettes; and they *never* stick). In about thirty seconds, the bottom layer of eggs will have solidified ever so lightly, while the upper layers are still being stirred. A few seconds later, the omelette will be done. It is rolled at once, turned onto a heated plate and served. The light, imperceptibly layered egg texture produced by this difficult method is impossible to achieve by any other means.

The variations possible with omelettes, however they are made, are imposing: fresh herbs, grated cheese, bits of fish, poultry, meat, or vegetables, usually creamed and *always* cooked or warmed separately first, can be placed in the center of the omelette before it is rolled. Similar variations can be used in my dessert omelette on page 207 if you omit the sugar and vanilla.

An easier alternative to omelette in any of its forms is scrambled eggs, and they have their passionate partisans, too. In fact, Escoffier, whose enthusiasm for the classic omelette can hardly be questioned, described scrambled eggs, in an unguarded moment, as "the finest of all egg preparations."

Although they take no special culinary skill to prepare, they do require care and patience. Unlike the omelette, scrambled eggs can be soft and creamy only if they are cooked as slowly as possible, some purists going so far as to say they should be cooked in a double boiler over barely simmering water. More practical cooks, however, are able to achieve identical results and from my view, better ones, by starting the eggs in a cold—or slightly warm—buttered frying pan, again if possible with a non-stick surfaced pan. Then they are stirred continuously, so that they heat through slowly and evenly. When done, they are a velvety, custard-like mass. The French device of stirring into them a tablespoon or so of heavy cream or a bit of soft butter before they are removed from the pan stops their cooking at once and, at the same time, enriches and smooths them.

Oversimplified as it may sound, the key to successful egg cookery is the cook's ability to stop the cooking of the egg at precisely the point when it is neither undercooked nor overcooked. Boiling, poaching, frying, scrambling, omelette-making and the innumerable variations on these procedures, to say nothing of sauce-thickening, clarifying, soufflé-making and the rest, are irrevocably dependent on this sense of timing. I know few other foods, however they are used, that demand such special care and attention.

Eggs Benedict   serves 2 or 4

THE POACHED EGGS

4 very fresh eggs
Cold water
1 tablespoon distilled white

vinegar for every quart of
water used
No salt

THE HOLLANDAISE SAUCE (made in an electric blender)

8 tablespoons unsalted butter
(¼ pound, 1 stick), *cut into
½-inch pieces*
3 large egg yolks, 4 if the yolks
are small
2 teaspoons fresh, strained lemon
juice

½ teaspoon dry mustard
(optional)
⅛ teaspoon salt
A pinch of cayenne pepper

THE BENEDICT INGREDIENTS

4 slices good white bread, *cut
into 3-inch crustless rounds,
or 2 English muffins, split in
half*
4 teaspoons butter, *softened*

4 quarter-inch slices cooked ham
(preferably Virginia ham)
*cut into rounds 3 inches in
diameter*

The Poached Eggs:

Before poaching the eggs, have ready a bowl of warm—not hot—water, to receive them the moment they are done. This will keep the eggs warm while you make the hollandaise sauce for the eggs Benedict. (Alternatively, have a bowl of cold water at hand in which to quickly cool the poached eggs if you intend to use them for the *oeufs en gelée* on page 204.)

Pour 6 to 8 cups of water into a 10- or 12-inch enamel or stainless-steel skillet, or enough water to come about 2 inches up the sides of the pan. Stir in the appropriate amount of vinegar (but don't add any salt or, for mysterious reasons, your poached eggs will have tiny pin pricks over their surface), and bring the water to a boil over high heat. Then lower the heat so that the water barely simmers. Break one of the eggs into a small dish and carefully slide it into the pan. With a wooden spoon or a small spatula, immediately lift the whites over the yolk. Do this once or twice (a few wisps of the white will inevitably come away from the mass, but if the eggs are really fresh, most of the whites will adhere and wrap themselves around the yolks like cocoons). Quickly follow the same procedure for the remaining eggs, then let them simmer quietly, undisturbed, for about 3 or 4 minutes, or until the whites are set and the yolks feel soft when you prod them gently with your finger. Lift the eggs out of the water with a slotted spoon and drop them into the bowl of warm water (or the cold water if you are poaching them for *oeufs en gelée*).

The Blender Hollandaise:

Melt the butter in a small skillet set over low heat, so low, in fact, that the butter is in no danger of becoming the least bit brown as it melts. Meanwhile, combine the egg yolks, lemon juice, mustard (if you have decided to use it), salt, and cayenne in the jar of your electric blender. Cover the jar and blend at high speed for about 4 seconds. Then turn off the machine, scrape down the sides with a rubber spatula, and blend for 4 seconds more. Quickly raise the heat under the butter to high and when it begins to foam (but still not brown), turn the blender to high speed, remove the cover, and very slowly pour in the butter, holding the cover sideways over the top of the jar to prevent the sauce from splattering all over you. In a short while, as you pour, the sauce will turn thick and heavy. Turn off the machine, taste for seasoning (you might want to stir into it more salt, lemon juice, or cayenne), and set the jar in a bowl of lukewarm water to keep warm while you construct the eggs Benedict.

The Benedict Ingredients:

Toast the bread or English muffins lightly on both sides and spread each half with about a teaspoon of softened butter. Arrange them on individual heated plates and place the ham rounds on top. With a slotted spoon, remove the eggs from their bowl of warm water, place them on a towel, and gently pat them dry. Trim any ragged egg whites with scissors if you wish (though it is really not necessary) and set one egg in the middle of each round of ham. Spoon the warm hollandaise over each serving, masking the egg and ham completely. Serve at once.

NOTE: The order of preparation I have suggested is not necessarily the one you must follow. There are others. You may, for example, find it easier to toast the bread, make the hollandaise sauce and keep it warm while you poach the eggs. All you need do then is omit dropping them in the bowl of warm water, and simply pat them dry and trim them before constructing the dish as I describe it above.

Oeufs en Gelée   *serves 8*

8 poached eggs, as small as possible, *trimmed and chilled* (*page 202*)

THE ASPIC

4 cups chicken stock, fresh or canned, *thoroughly skimmed of all fat*

2 envelopes (2 tablespoons) unflavored gelatin

½ cup cold water

1 large, fresh ripe tomato, *coarsely chopped*

About 4 scallions, including 1 inch of the green stems, *to make ½ cup coarsely chopped*

2 celery tops with their leaves

Fresh tarragon, *enough to make 1 tablespoon coarsely cut*, or 1 teaspoon dried tarragon, *crumbled*

8 whole black peppercorns

2 egg whites

ASPIC SUBSTITUTE

4 cups canned, jellied chicken consommé

Fresh tarragon, *enough to make 1 tablespoon coarsely cut*, or

1 teaspoon dried tarragon, *crumbled*

Salt

Poach the eggs as described on page 202 and chill them in the refrigerator while you make the aspic.

Sprinkle the 2 envelopes of gelatin into the ½ cup of cold water and let it rest for about 5 minutes. Pour the chicken stock into a 2- or 3-quart saucepan, stir in the softened gelatin, and add the tomato, scallions, celery tops, fresh or dried tarragon, and peppercorns. Beat the egg whites to a somewhat thick froth and stir it into the stock. Now bring the stock to a boil over high heat, stirring constantly with a whisk. The aspic will soon begin to froth and slowly rise. Continue to stir until the foam has almost risen to the top of the pan, then immediately turn off the heat. The froth will soon subside. Let the aspic rest undisturbed for 5 minutes, then pour it into a deep bowl through a fine sieve lined with a dampened kitchen towel. Do not disturb the aspic at any point as it drains or the aspic will be cloudy instead of brilliantly clear. Discard the debris in the sieve and let the aspic cool to room temperature.

You may eliminate this entire procedure by using canned jellied chicken consommé that has already been clarified. I think it is wise in this case, however, to amplify its usually pallid flavor (no matter how good the brand), by simmering it for a few minutes with fresh or dried tarragon, then simply straining it through a fine sieve and letting it come to room temperature without refrigerating it. Taste for seasoning and stir in some salt if you think it needs it.

To make the eggs in jelly, choose either 8 oval metal egg molds (those used traditionally by the French), or use any small circular glass or ceramic dish that will hold ½ to ¾ cup of liquid. Making eggs in jelly properly takes some patience, but you will see that the results are definitely worth it. Spoon enough cool aspic into the bottom of each mold to come about ¼ to ⅜ inch up the sides. Refrigerate until firm. Then place the traditional two tarragon leaves in a cross over the top of the chilled surface of the aspic and place a poached egg—best-looking-side down—on top. Now do *not* fill the mold with the remaining aspic but pour, perhaps 1 or 2 teaspoons of the still-liquid aspic around the eggs. Return the eggs to the refrigerator until the liquid aspic has firmed and secured the egg and its decoration to the bottom layer of the aspic. It is only at this point that you can safely spoon into the molds the rest of the liquid aspic without having the egg and its decoration float to the top. Now return the molds to the refrigerator and chill them for at least 4 hours, or until the aspic is firmly set. Any remaining aspic may be chilled until firm and then chopped or cut into fanciful shapes to surround the decorated, unmolded eggs.

To unmold the eggs, one at a time dip their bottoms in hot water for 2 or 3 seconds. Then run a knife around the edge of the jelly and place a small, chilled serving plate on top of the mold. Grasping mold and plate together, invert them, rap the plate once sharply on the table and the egg should come out easily. Garnish with any extra aspic you may have on hand and refrigerate until ready to serve. A sprig of watercress on each plate makes an attractive addition.

NOTE: There are other ways to construct these egg masterpieces. For those of you accustomed to working with aspic in the professional manner, that is, chilling it to a jelly-like consistency over ice, the procedure I describe above still holds. But I think my method less demanding if more time consuming. You may, as I have suggested earlier, decorate the first layer of chilled aspic not only with tarragon leaves but with a thin slice of *foie gras,* a truffle cutout, ham, or what have you. But the technical procedure remains the same.

Shirred Eggs with Cream

OEUFS MIROIR   *serves 4*

8 eggs	¼ cup heavy cream
8 teaspoons butter, *softened*	Fresh parsley, chives, dill, or
Salt	tarragon, *finely chopped*
Freshly ground black pepper	(*optional*)

For the most satisfactory results, the eggs should be shirred in shallow, individual ceramic ramekins about 4 inches in diameter, but any shallow dish of approximately the same size will do, if it must.

Preheat the broiler to its highest point. Place 2 teaspoons of the butter in each ramekin, then, one dish at a time, melt the butter over moderate heat, but don't let it brown. Drop two eggs into each dish, sprinkle them liberally with salt and more discreetly with pepper, and cook the eggs, undisturbed, for a few seconds until the whites form the thinnest of opaque layers on the bottom of the dish. Put the dish aside while you proceed to precook the remaining eggs in similar fashion. (The eggs in this state may wait for 2 or 3 minutes before completing the dish.)

Just before serving, pour 2 teaspoons of the cream over the eggs and place the dishes on your broiler rack, set about 1 inch from the source of heat. Leave the broiler door open and broil the eggs for about 1 minute, basting with the cream (using a small spoon or bulb baster) every few seconds until the whites are set and the yolks still soft. Serve at once, sprinkled with a little chopped parsley, if you wish, or any other finely chopped herb of your choice—among them: chives, dill, tarragon, and the like.

NOTE: There are, of course, infinite variations on this dish. You may sprinkle the cream with a little freshly grated Parmesan cheese before broiling the eggs. Or the cream may be omitted altogether, and the eggs merely basted with their butter as they broil. Or sprinkle each pair of eggs with ½ teaspoon or so of red or white vinegar just before they are done. This dish, and other versions of it, is sometimes rather morbidly called eggs in hell. As for the garnishes, you may serve the shirred eggs—whatever the initial variation—with broiled bacon or ham, sautéed chicken livers or mushrooms or literally anything else that strikes you as suitable.

A Sweet Puffed Omelette

serves 1 or 2

2 large eggs	2 tablespoons unsalted butter
1 teaspoon superfine sugar	Confectioners' sugar
¼ teaspoon vanilla extract	

For this incredibly simple yet spectacular omelette, a 10-inch pan (measured from the edge of the rim of the pan) with sloping sides is almost indispensable to its success. A non-stick finish on the pan is preferable but not imperative as it is for the *omelette brouillée* described on page 200.

Separate the eggs cleanly, and drop the yolks into one small bowl and the whites into another. With a whisk or rotary beater, beat the whites until they are stiff enough to cling solidly to the beater like a skein of wool when the beater is lifted out of the bowl. Immediately add the sugar and vanilla to the bowl of yolks and beat them with the un-

A Sweet Puffed Omelette

washed beater until they thicken—which they will do after about a minute or so of incessant beating.

With a rubber spatula, scrape the whites over the yolks (or the other way around, if you wish) and fold the two together, bringing the heavier yolks over the whites with the spatula, until the two are combined. A few stray streaks of white still showing in the mixture is desirable, but not essential.

Over high heat, melt the butter in the non-stick frying pan. When the butter begins to turn ever so lightly brown, pour in the mixture, smoothing it out to fill the pan evenly. Lower the heat to moderate and cook the omelette until the edges begin to turn the lightest brown. (If you are using an ordinary frying pan, slide it back and forth over the burner occasionally to prevent the omelette from sticking to the bottom of the pan.) To make sure the omelette is not cooking too quickly and burning, lift the edge slightly with the spatula and peek under it. When you are sure the bottom is a golden brown, and the top of the omelette has puffed somewhat—it won't rise like a typical soufflé—turn it out on a heated platter in the following fashion.

Remove the pan from the heat, and tilting it—an inch or so above, and at the edge of the plate—allow the omelette to slide out of the pan of its own accord on to the plate. When it is about halfway out, use the edge of the pan to help you fold the remaining half in the pan over the omelette half already lying on the plate. The finished omelette should have the shape of a puffed golden-brown pocketbook. Sprinkle it generously with confectioners' sugar and serve at once.

NOTE: Before proceeding with this intricate-sounding but, in reality, easy folding maneuver, you may, if you like, spread the top of the omelette with a jam or jelly of any kind. Or allow your imagination some play and spread the bottom half of the omelette with any slices of heated canned or frozen (thoroughly defrosted and drained) fruit before folding the top of the omelette over it.

Zucchini Omelette in the Italian Manner

FRITTATA   *serves 4*

About 2 medium, firm, unpeeled zucchini, *to make 1 cup diced —the dice should be approximately ¼ inch in size*

2 tablespoons fresh white bread crumbs, *pulverized in an electric blender or pulled into very fine shreds with a fork*

3 tablespoons cold milk

Imported Parmesan cheese, *enough to make 5 tablespoons freshly grated: 4 for the omelette mixture and 1 for the top*

Lemon peel: *the lemon peeled with a swivel-bladed vegetable peeler, then finely chopped, to make ¼ teaspoon*

¼ teaspoon salt

4 large eggs

2 tablespoons butter

Preheat your broiler to its highest point. Blanch the diced zucchini by dropping them into a 1-quart saucepan of turbulently boiling water and letting them boil, uncovered, for 3 minutes. Drain them immediately in a sieve and run cold water over them to cool them quickly. Then spread them out on paper toweling and pat them dry. Soak the bread crumbs in the milk for about 5 minutes.

Combine the zucchini, the soaked bread crumbs, 4 tablespoons of the grated cheese, the lemon peel, and salt. Toss them gently together with your hands or stir them with a wooden spoon until they are well mixed. In another bowl beat the eggs with a whisk or fork only long enough to combine them. (Don't let them reach the point of foaming.) Pour over them the zucchini mixture and stir until the eggs coat all the ingredients thoroughly.

To make the *frittata* (which should be done just before you serve it), melt the butter over moderate heat in a heavy 10-inch skillet, preferably one with a non-stick surface. When the butter begins to turn ever so lightly brown, pour the entire contents of the bowl into the pan, spreading it out evenly with a rubber spatula. Cook the omelette—still over moderate heat—sliding the pan back and forth over the burner occasionally to prevent the omelette from sticking to the bottom of the pan. (Of course, you will have no such problem with a Teflon or other similarly coated pan.) Lift one edge of the omelette after about 2 minutes; if it has not yet begun to brown, raise the heat slightly and cook for another minute or so until it does. Sprinkle the top evenly with the remaining tablespoon of Parmesan cheese, then place the skillet under the broiler—about 2 or 3 inches from the source of heat. Broil for about 1 minute or so to brown the top lightly.

Slide the omelette out of the pan onto a small heated platter, cut it into four pie-shaped wedges, and serve at once.

Oeufs à la Neige

EGGS IN SNOW   *serves 8–10*

THE MERINGUE
6 egg whites
½ cup powdered sugar (*sifted, if lumpy*)

3 cups milk
2-inch piece of vanilla bean or use 1 teaspoon vanilla extract

THE CUSTARD SAUCE
6 egg yolks
⅓ cup granulated sugar

2 cups milk (from poaching meringues)
1 teaspoon vanilla (optional)

¼ cup semisweet chocolate, *cut into slivers or curls*, or toasted almonds, *slivered* (*optional*)

The Meringue:

Place the egg whites (at room temperature, preferably) in a large unlined copper or stainless-steel mixing bowl, and beat with a balloon whisk, rotary beater, or in an electric mixer until the whites thicken perceptibly and hold soft peaks. Slowly add the powdered sugar and continue to beat until the meringue is firm enough to hold stiff, almost rigid peaks on the beater when it is lifted out of the bowl. If you have any doubts about its consistency, overbeat rather than underbeat it.

Pour the milk into a 10-inch enamel or stainless-steel skillet. Add the vanilla bean (or vanilla extract) and heat the milk until small bubbles begin to form around the edge of the pan. Then lower the heat and keep the milk simmering gently while you poach the meringues in the following fashion: with either a teaspoon or a small tablespoon, scoop up the meringue. With another spoon inverted over it, shape it gently into the form of an egg and slide it off the first spoon into the milk. Continue in this fashion until the surface of the milk is almost but not quite covered with the egg-shaped meringues. Let them simmer undisturbed for about 2 minutes, then gently turn them over with the spoon and poach the other sides for about a minute or two, or until the meringues feel fairly firm to the touch. (Don't overcook them or they will collapse.) Lift them out of the pan with a slotted spoon and lay them side by side on a linen kitchen towel to drain. Make another batch of meringues in the same way until all the uncooked meringue has been used. After the meringues have drained for a few minutes, transfer them from the towel to a large platter and chill until ready to serve. Reserve the poaching milk.

The Custard:

Meanwhile, make the custard. With a whisk, rotary or electric beater, beat the egg yolks with the sugar until they thicken enough to run off the beater in a sluggish stream when the beater is lifted from the bowl. Strain the poaching milk through a sieve into a pint measuring cup, discarding any excess milk or adding fresh milk to make up the 2 cups. Slowly pour the milk into the egg yolks, stirring all the while. Then pour the entire mixture into a 2-quart enamel or stainless-steel saucepan. Stirring constantly, simmer over low heat until it thickens enough to coat a spoon lightly. Do not let the custard come anywhere near the boil or it will curdle. As soon as it reaches the consistency you like, pour (or strain) it into a large shallow glass serving bowl. Let the custard come to room temperature, then chill until ready to serve.

Just before serving, float the meringues on top of the custard and sprinkle them with shaved chocolate or slivered, toasted almonds, if you like.

facts and fancies about shellfish

fACTS ANd fANCiES
AbOUT shellfish

The high cost of shellfish today appears to make little difference in the staggering amounts of it we buy. We consume, in fact, more lobsters, shrimp, crabs, scallops, oysters, and clams per capita than any country in the world, and we have created with them shellfish dishes of great distinction. Where else in the world can you find such unusual dishes peculiarly American in their simplicity as our oyster stews, seafood gumbos, steamed soft-shelled clams, fried soft-shelled crabs, and clam chowders? But despite these culinary achievements, I find that there are still too many American cooks who approach the handling, cooking, and even eating of shellfish with an apprehension based more often on hearsay than on fact.

Why, for example, are most of us afraid to do anything with a lobster other than to drop it, live but securely pegged, into a pot of boiling water to cook until done? Particularly when there are so many sophisticated lobster dishes—like stuffed or unstuffed baked lobster, lobster *fra diavolo*, lobster *à l'Américaine*, among others? Flatly, the answer is that all these delectable recipes require that the lobsters be split and cut up while they are still alive, an operation that sounds too harrowing to the averge American cook. But there is no alternative; lobsters are at their best only if they breathe their last either in the dish in which they are cooked or moments before they are added to it.

That most American women—as well as many men I know—are unable to cope with the problem of slaughtering the lobster seems clear; otherwise, these not too complicated lobster dishes would appear on our tables at home more often than they do.

Scientists long ago demonstrated that crustaceans have nervous systems of such simplicity that they scarcely feel pain as we do. Nevertheless, it might reassure you to know that a lobster can be completely anesthetized by severing its spinal cord. This is quickly done by turning the lobster on its back, grasping it securely with a towel and, with a small sharp knife, cutting a deep crosswise incision at precisely the point where the body and tail are joined. Although the lobster will continue to thrash about alarmingly, it will feel nothing at all (as far as we know), whether it is split along its length for broiling, cut into medallions for dishes like lobster *à l'Américaine* (as described in my book, *Michael Field's Cooking School*) or simply dropped into a pot of boiling water.

The only dodge for cowards is to settle for less than culinary perfection and ask your fishman to dissect the live lobster for you. Or you may, of course, buy a cold cooked lobster. Make sure, however, that the lobster was alive when it was cooked. The one way to tell (don't let your fishman dissuade you) is to observe whether the lobster's tail is coiled tightly against its body; a flat, flaccid tail is a certain indication that the lobster was dead before it entered the pot. Although such a lobster may be safely eaten, provided you know that it met its end naturally (and was refrigerated no longer than twenty-four hours before it was cooked), a flat-tailed lobster whose history you don't know can be a precarious investment indeed.

Many cooks unfamiliar with lobsters can find cleaning them, either cooked or uncooked, a perplexing task. Fortunately, only two of the lobster's organs, although harmless, are inedible and should be removed. These are the small gelatinous stomach sac, set in the head directly behind the eyes, and the long black (sometimes white) intestinal vein attached to it. The liver, a greenish-brown mass near the stomach, is a great delicacy, as is the roe, frequently found in female lobsters, known as the coral (because it turns red after it has been cooked) Both the coral and the liver of cooked lobsters are often pounded to a paste, or rubbed through a sieve mixed with mayonnaise and served with a lobster, shrimp, or crabmeat salad.

Crabs share the distinction of being the only other crustacean sold alive. I am talking primarily about the small Eastern blue crabs, which, for all their sweetness and magnificent flavor, are really not worth coping with at home, or at least I, for one, don't think so. What little meat they contain is so difficult to extract that you are better off buying canned or frozen crabmeat taken, usually, from the superb Dungeness crab of the Pacific Coast. Or, better still, try to find the luxurious refrigerated lump crabmeat sold in containers.

Live soft-shell crabs (actually blue crabs after they have shed their hard shells, preparatory to growing new ones) are something else again. Fortunately for those of us averse to handling them, the crabs (and they *must* be alive) are almost always—or should be—cleaned for cooking by fishmongers at the very moment you buy them. After they are cooked, all parts of the dressed crabs are edible, including the paper-thin shells. In whatever fashion the crabs are prepared—and they lend themselves especially to frying, deep-frying, and broiling—they seldom take more than three to five minutes to cook through and must be watched carefully lest they overcook.

The crustaceans that doubtless suffer most from being overcooked are shrimp. Fresh or frozen shrimp should be cooked only long enough for them to turn pink, lose their gelatinous gloss, and feel firm to the touch. Depending on their size, this should take between two and five minutes. And when shrimp are to be simply boiled (or, more properly, simmered), for shrimp cocktails, salads, and other cold dishes, it is a waste of time and material to cook them in anything but well-salted water. If the shrimp are simmered for the short time they should be, *court-bouillons* or any other highly seasoned liquids will have no effect at all on them. As for the so-called scampi listed on American restaurant menus, they are simply large shrimp masquerading as scampi; true scampi are native to the Adriatic and are never available in the United States.

We are constantly being told to remove the black veins from our cooked and uncooked shrimp. This is not standard practice in other countries, where less finicky cooks seldom bother with this extra chore. The veins are harmless and have no taste, and it is entirely a matter of choice whether you remove them or not.

If culinary misconceptions abound about shrimp, they are equally plentiful about scallops. Because dressed scallops look so much like small chunks of fish, many Americans frequently forget that scallops are shellfish. In fact, my novice students at least are often astonished to learn that the small, delicately flavored bay scallop and the larger, more coarsely textured sea scallop belong to the mollusk family, which numbers among its distinguished members oysters, clams, and mussels.

The scallop, unlike other mollusks, is an active swimmer and gets around by noisily snapping its large shells together. During this process, it develops an oversize muscle, the creamy white kernel of flesh we, rather inaccurately, call the scallop. For some unexplained reason, our fishermen discard—or use as bait—the fine-flavored coral attached to it and market only the muscle or "eye" as it is called. Europeans, more thriftily and sensibly, buy and eat the whole scallop and, moreover, use the exquisitely fluted shells as cooking and serving dishes.

Since our native scallops come to us already cleaned, cooking them is a comparatively simple matter. You need only wash and then poach them in slightly salted and acidulated water for two or three minutes. This is the classic French method for cooking scallops that are subsequently meant to be served sauced, like the famous *coquilles St.-Jacques à la Parisienne,* a rich dish of scallops and mushrooms, poached in a white wine *court-bouillon,* then masked with a *mornay* sauce and gratinéed.

More to American tastes, however, are sautéed, deep-fried, or broiled scallops; not one of these methods takes any notable culinary skill, if overcooking is avoided. And even easier, scallops—the bay type especially—can be served raw, merely sprinkled with a little lemon juice, salt and pepper—or with, perhaps, a *sauce rémoulade* as I describe it on page 229.

The only other mollusks we Americans eat raw are oysters and clams. But oysters are equally impressive cooked. Whatever their types —and there are many—they can all be cooked the same way: poached for a moment or two in their own liquor until their edges curl; fried; baked with a stuffing on the half shell; even smoked. Some fine seafood cooks think one of the best ways of all is to bake the oysters unopened (but thoroughly scrubbed, of course) for five to seven minutes in a 450-degree oven until, barely cooked, they open enough for you then to pry off their shells easily. Served with melted butter, lemon juice, fresh herbs or any seasoning you prefer, these baked oysters make a memorable beginning for any meal, or even a meal itself.

There is a persistent myth that oysters are unsafe to eat during the months whose names lack the letter "r." It is during these warm months that oysters breed, and it is to ensure their spawning undisturbed that taking them at this time is forbidden in many states. They would be perfectly safe to eat were you able to buy them, but I must admit that their flavor leaves much to be desired.

Probably because we have so many more clams than oysters, they

have never been subject to the same superstition. But clams have managed to acquire a curious set of myths all their own.

We undoubtedly eat more clams than do the people of other countries. And well we might, for our native varieties are among the best in
the world. Yet for all their virtues, American clams are just like their
foreign cousins in their ability to secrete sand.

One widely held notion is that soaking clams in a mixture of cold
water and cornmeal will force them to disgorge their sand and ob-
ligingly replace it with an equal amount of nourishing cornmeal. That
this is patently false is apparent to anyone who has taken the trouble to
try it. And I have. Not only does the sand obstinately remain in the
clam no matter how long it is soaked, but the clam, taken from the sea,
drowns in the fresh water to which it is unaccustomed. (This, by the
way, is also true of live lobsters left for any appreciable time in cold
fresh water.)

The most forthright way to cope with sand in clams (and not all
clams are sandy, by any means) is to scrub each one thoroughly with a
small, stiff brush, or, better still, a soapless steel or copper pad, making
sure to get into any small crevices where sand may possibly be hidden.
If you insist on taking your chances with steamed clams, usually called
"steamers" (and sand or no sand, the clams are incomparable), serve
them with separate bowls of hot clam broth, into which you can swirl
each clam free of its sand before dipping it into melted butter spiked
with a little fresh lemon juice before eating it.

Most clam and oyster recipes can be used interchangeably; but
clams, unlike oysters, may open slightly before they are cooked. They
should close at once when the shells are pressed together; if they don't,
they should be discarded.

Mussels—in their black and silvery oval shells (I describe them
only because so many Americans are woefully ignorant of this delicacy)
—are never eaten raw except on occasion in European countries, share
many of the characteristics of clams, and can be, initially at least, prepared the same way. They, too, may gape open before they are cooked;
but ordinarily they won't close at once when their shells are handled.
Test the mussels further by running cold water over them, but, like
clams, never soak them. If the mussels remain open they must be
thrown away. Another note of warning: should you have the opportu-
nity to forage at the shore for seaside mussels on your own, it would be
wise to make sure that they come from government-certified unpolluted

waters, and that the mussels, wherever you find them clustered, are submerged and exposed continuously with the rising and falling of the tides.

Because most mussels tend to be heavily encrusted with hardened sand, mud, and barnacles, scrubbing them clean (like clams, with soapless steel or copper pad or stiff brush) can be a fairly demanding task. But for those who love the plump orange (or sometimes light yellow) flesh, it is worth every minute of extra effort. The characteristic beard, or byssus, attached to the mussel can easily be pulled out or cut away; any that are too resistant can be removed after the mussels are cooked. They are, in any case, harmless.

As a nation of ardent seafood lovers, we owe it to ourselves to become more familiar with our hordes of sadly neglected mussels. My mussel recipes on pages 240–8 should give you an idea of how extraordinary these delicious mollusks can be and, hopefully, stimulate you to use them in other creative ways.

Lobster Fra Diavolo

serves 4

2 live 1½- to 2-pound lobsters,
    each split in half lengthwise
    (*page 216*)
½ cup olive oil
1 small onion, *to make ½ cup*
    finely chopped
Peeled garlic cloves, *enough to*
    make 2 teaspoons finely
    chopped
2 cups dry white wine
2 pounds firm ripe tomatoes,
    peeled, seeded, and finely
    chopped (*page 109*) (*about*
    3 cups), or use 3 cups *drained*
    and finely chopped canned

tomatoes (*preferably Italian*
    plum tomatoes)
Parsley (preferably the flat-leaf
    type), *enough to make 1 ta-*
    blespoon finely chopped
Fresh basil, *enough to make 2 ta-*
    blespoons finely cut, or use 1
    teaspoon dried basil, *crum-*
    bled
1 teaspoon dried oregano, *crum-*
    bled
¼ teaspoon crushed hot red pep-
    per
½ teaspoon salt
Freshly ground black pepper

Following the directions on page 216, split the lobsters in half and remove their gelatinous sacs and the long intestinal veins attached to them. With a small spoon, scoop out the greenish-brown tomalley and the black coral, if there is any, and set aside in a small bowl. Twist or cut off the claws and, with a large sharp knife, gash the flat underside of each claw. Cut off and discard the antennae and the thin, small legs attached to the body.

Heat the olive oil in a heavy 12-inch skillet equipped with a tightly fitting cover, add the lobster pieces and, turning them frequently with tongs, cook them for 3 or 4 minutes until the shells begin to turn pink. Transfer the lobster to paper toweling to drain. (If necessary, do the browning process in two batches, adding a little more oil to the pan if you think it needs it.)

Pour off all but a thin film of oil from the skillet and add the onions and garlic. Stirring frequently, cook over moderate heat for 5 minutes, or until the onions are soft and transparent but not brown. Pour in the wine and, stirring occasionally, boil it briskly for 2 or 3 minutes, or until it has cooked down to about a cupful. Stir in the tomatoes, parsley, basil, oregano, red pepper, and salt and bring to a boil again. Return the lobsters to the sauce in the skillet and with a large spoon baste them thoroughly. Then cover the pan tightly and simmer over moderate heat for about 20 minutes, basting two or three times more.

To serve, transfer the lobster pieces to a large heated platter with tongs or a slotted spoon. With the back of a large spoon, rub the tomalley and coral (if any) through a fine sieve directly into the sauce remaining in the skillet and, stirring constantly, simmer over low heat for 1 minute or so. Taste the sauce for seasoning; it will doubtlessly need more salt and possibly a few more grindings of black pepper. When the flavor of the sauce suits you, pour it over the lobster and serve at once.

Baked Lobster with Dill or Tarragon Stuffing

serves 2 or 4

2 two-pound live lobsters

The tomalley and coral (if any) of the lobsters

¾ pound (3 sticks) butter: *½ pound for the stuffing and 8 tablespoons (¼ pound) melted and cooled to dribble over lobsters*

About 1 small onion or 2 medium scallions, including about 1 inch of the green tops, *to make ½ cup chopped*

Peeled garlic cloves, *enough to make 1 teaspoon finely chopped*

2 cups (loosely packed) fresh bread crumbs, *made in the electric blender from good, fresh or day-old, homemade-type bread (crusts removed) or torn apart and shredded with a fork*

Fresh tarragon or fresh dill, *enough to make 1 tablespoon finely cut*

1 teaspoon dry mustard

½ teaspoon salt

2 teaspoons fresh, strained lemon juice

8 tablespoons (¼ pound, 1 stick) butter, *melted and cooled*

Lemon quarters (optional)

Baked Lobster with Dill or Tarragon Stuffing

Place the lobsters on their backs and with a sharp, heavy knife, split the lobsters directly in half, lengthwise, using a hammer to drive the knife through the shells if necessary. (If you find this task too unpleasant, ask your fishman to do it for you.) Crack the claws with a sharp blow of the knife. With scissors, cut off the antennae and the eyes, remove the gelatinous sac and the intestinal vein (as described on page 216) and with a small spoon, scoop out all the tomalley and coral, if any. With the back of a large spoon, rub the tomalley and coral through a fine-meshed sieve into a small bowl and set aside.

For the stuffing, slowly melt the ½ pound of the butter in a 10- to 12-inch skillet. Add the onions (or scallions) and the garlic, and stirring frequently, cook them for about 3 or 4 minutes, or until they are transparent and limp, but not brown. Add the bread crumbs and toss them about with a spoon to coat them evenly with the butter and onions. Cook over moderate heat for about 5 minutes, stirring them frequently. When they are slightly dry, and the crumbs have separated but not browned, scrape them into a large mixing bowl. Add the tarragon or dill, the mustard, salt, and lemon juice, then taste for seasoning. Any of the herb or seasoning ingredients can at this point be altered to your taste—but with discretion. Stir in the puréed tomalley and coral and the lobsters are now ready to be stuffed.

Drain the lobster halves of any liquid and brush them—flesh and shell sides—with four tablespoons of the melted butter, making sure to dribble a little butter into the cracked claws. Pack the stuffing into all the open cavities of the lobster and spread the remaining stuffing over the tail sections, packing it down with a spatula to make it adhere. (You may now refrigerate the lobsters for anywhere up to 3 or 4 hours before baking them.)

Preheat the oven to 400 degrees. Arrange the lobsters side by side, stuffed sides up, on a rack set in a shallow roasting pan. Dribble the remaining melted butter over each lobster half and bake in the lower third of the oven for about 30 minutes. If you have any doubt as to when they are done, pierce the flesh in the tail section with a small skewer or the tip of a small sharp knife. If the flesh seems too resistant, bake the lobsters a few minutes longer, but guard against overcooking them if you would have your lobsters moist, tender, and succulent. Serve immediately, with lemon quarters, if you like.

Crabmeat and Parmesan Cheese Soufflé

serves 4–6

4 tablespoons (½ stick) butter:
  1 softened to coat the soufflé dish, and 3 for the soufflé base
Imported Parmesan cheese,
  enough to make 8 tablespoons finely grated: 2 to coat the soufflé dish, 4 for the soufflé base, and 2 for the topping
4 level tablespoons flour
1 cup milk
6 eggs: *4 yolks for the soufflé base and the 6 whites to fold into it*

¼ teaspoon dry mustard
½ teaspoon salt
1 teaspoon fresh, strained lemon juice
6–8 drops Tabasco
½ pound fresh crabmeat, *coarsely shredded,* or a 7¾-ounce can crabmeat, *all cartilage and bits of shell removed and the crabmeat thoroughly drained*

With a pastry brush, evenly butter a 2-quart charlotte mold or ceramic soufflé dish with the tablespoon of the softened butter. Scatter 2 tablespoons of the cheese into the mold and, holding it over a strip of waxed paper, turn the pan from side to side to spread the cheese over the buttered surfaces to coat them completely. Then invert the mold, rap it gently on the waxed paper to dislodge any extra cheese. Put the mold aside while you make the sauce.

Melt the remaining butter (without letting it brown) in a 2-quart enamel or stainless-steel saucepan. Off the heat, stir in the flour to make a smooth *roux,* then pour in, all at once, the cup of milk. Beat with a whisk partially to dissolve the *roux,* then over high heat, bring the mixture to a boil, whisking constantly, until the sauce is smooth and thick. Lower the heat and simmer the sauce, stirring occasionally, for 2 or 3 minutes. Remove the pan from the heat, and one at a time, quickly whisk in the egg yolks, then stir in the 4 tablespoons of the remaining cheese, the salt, lemon juice, and tabasco. With a spoon, gently stir in the shredded crabmeat, and taste for seasoning. It will probably need more salt, and possibly more Tabasco. Remember that a soufflé base

should be slightly overseasoned if the soufflé is to have any character
when the beaten egg whites are folded in. (This base may be made
ahead, covered with plastic wrap, and refrigerated for as long as 12
hours if you don't plan to make the soufflé at once. Then, heat it gently
to lukewarm again before beating the egg whites.)

About 45 minutes before you plan to serve the soufflé, beat the egg
whites (in an unlined copper bowl, and with a balloon whisk, if possible) until they are stiff enough to grip the beater firmly and their small
white peaks stand upright on the beater when it is lifted from the bowl.
Be careful not to underbeat. Thoroughly mix 2 large spoonfuls of the
whites into the warm crabmeat sauce, then with the aid of a rubber
spatula pour the sauce over the remaining egg whites in the bowl. Fold
together gently but thoroughly until no streaks of white show through
the mixture, but be careful not to overfold or your soufflé won't rise as
it should.

Pour the mixture into the mold or soufflé dish and smooth the top
with a spatula. Sprinkle the top of the soufflé with the remaining 2 tablespoons of cheese and bake the soufflé in the lower third of the oven
for 30 to 40 minutes until it is well puffed and golden brown. Serve at
once with hollandaise, *béarnaise* sauce.

Curried Crabmeat Pâté

1 cup fresh crabmeat or an 8¾-
 ounce can crabmeat, *thoroughly drained*
½ small onion, *to make ¼ cup
 coarsely chopped*
½–¾ cup heavy cream
6 tablespoons (¾ stick) butter,
 softened

1 teaspoon curry powder
¼ teaspoon salt
1 teaspoon fresh, strained lemon
 juice
6 drops Tabasco

Remove and discard any cartilage or pieces of shell from the crabmeat, shred the meat, and place it in a jar of an electric blender. Add
the chopped onions and ½ cup of the cream. Blend at high speed for

about 1 minute, then turn off the machine and scrape down the sides of the inside of the jar with a rubber spatula. Blend again, adding the remaining cream, if necessary, to prevent the machine from clogging. Continue to blend until the crabmeat becomes a smooth purée. (Don't be concerned if the mixture is quite fluid; it will firm up later.)

Cream the butter with the curry powder by beating and mashing it against the sides of a bowl with a large spoon until smooth and fluffy. Little by little, beat into it the crabmeat purée, then stir in the lemon juice and the Tabasco. If you are a perfectionist, you can now rub the *pâté* through a sieve with the back of a spoon, but if you are not, simply taste the *pâté* and add any more seasoning you think necessary. Spoon the *pâté* into a crock and chill covered with plastic wrap for at least 3 hours or until firm. Serve with crackers or buttered toast as an accompaniment to drinks.

NOTE: The same procedure may be used to make a shrimp or lobster *pâté* with equal success. Simply substitute 1 cup cooked or canned, drained shrimp or lobster for the crabmeat.

Shrimp Mousse
serves 4

1 tablespoon vegetable oil (flavorless)

1 envelope (1 tablespoon) unflavored gelatin

¼ cup cold water

½ cup chicken stock, fresh or canned, *thoroughly skimmed of any fat*

¼ cup dry white wine

1 pound shelled raw shrimp, *deveined if you prefer*

1 small onion, *to make ½ cup finely chopped*

Fresh tarragon leaves, *enough to make 1 tablespoon finely cut, or 1 teaspoon dried tarragon, crumbled*

1 tablespoon tomato paste

1 tablespoon fresh, strained lemon juice

1 teaspoon salt

White pepper

1 cup heavy cream, *chilled*

Brush the bottom and sides of a 1½-quart decorative mold (a fish mold, if you have one) with the oil, then turn it upside down to drain on paper toweling.

Sprinkle the gelatin into the cold water and let it soften for about 5 minutes. Bring the stock and wine to a boil in a small enamel, or stainless-steel saucepan and drop in the shrimp. Let the liquid return to the boil then cook the shrimp briskly, uncovered, for 3 or 4 minutes until they turn pink. With a slotted spoon, transfer them to a plate. Stir the softened gelatin into the stock and when it has dissolved completely cool to room temperature.

With a whisk, rotary or electric beater, beat the cream only long enough to hold soft peaks on the beater when it is lifted out of the bowl. (Stiffly beaten cream will give the *mousse* too dense a texture.) Chop the shrimp coarsely and combine with the stock, onions, and tarragon in the jar of an electric blender. Blend at high speed for 30 seconds, then stop the machine and scrape down the sides of the jar with a rubber spatula. Blend again until the mixture becomes a smooth purée. Scrape it into a bowl, stir in the tomato paste, lemon juice, salt, and pepper and taste for seasoning. Remember that cold dulls flavor and that a *mousse* of this type should be highly seasoned.

Place the bowl of puréed shrimp over a larger bowl or pan filled with ice, and, with a spatula, stir until the purée begins to thicken ever so slightly. (Be careful not to let it thicken too much.) Immediately fold in the whipped cream, and continue to fold until traces of white no longer show. (See NOTE!) Pour the mixture into the mold and spread it out evenly with a spatula. Refrigerate the *mousse* for at least 2 hours, or until it is firm to the touch.

To unmold and serve the *mousse,* run a knife all around the inside edge of the mold and dip the bottom in hot water for a few seconds. Place a chilled platter upside down on top of the mold and, grasping platter and mold firmly together, invert them. Rap the platter sharply on a table, the *mousse* should slide out easily. Garnish with parsley or watercress sprigs and slices of lemon and either refrigerate or serve at once with a bowl of mayonnaise or with the *rémoulade* sauce on page 229, substituting tarragon, if you have it, for the dill.

NOTE: Should you have miscalculated and allowed the mixture to thicken too much, beat in the whipped cream with a whisk instead of attempting to fold it in.

Grilled Shrimp in the Italian Style

serves 4–6

2 pounds (32 to 40) large fresh
shrimp in their shells
1 cup olive oil
2 tablespoons fresh, strained
lemon juice
4–6 drops Tabasco
1 tablespoon tomato paste
Parsley, *enough to make ¼ cup
finely chopped*

1 tablespoon dried oregano,
crumbled
Peeled garlic cloves, *enough to
make 1 tablespoon finely
chopped*
1 teaspoon salt
Freshly ground black pepper
Hot French or Italian bread (optional)

Shell the shrimp but leave the last segment of the shell and the tail attached to each shrimp. With a small sharp knife, devein the shrimp by making a shallow incision down the back and lifting out the intestinal vein with the point of the knife. (If you wish, you may dispense with the deveining process altogether.) Wash the shrimp thoroughly under cold running water and pat them dry with paper toweling.

Combine in a deep bowl the olive oil, lemon juice, Tabasco, tomato paste, parsley, oregano, garlic, salt, and a liberal grinding of pepper. Stir until thoroughly combined, then taste for seasoning. Add the shrimp and turn them about with a spoon until they are thoroughly saturated with the marinade. Cover with foil or plastic wrap and marinate at room temperature for about 2 hours, turning the shrimp once or twice to keep them moistened on all sides.

Preheat the broiler to its highest point. Arrange the shrimp in a shallow baking dish just large enough to hold them snugly in one layer, then pour the marinade over them. Broil 3 or 4 inches from the heat for about 3 minutes, then turn the shrimp over with kitchen tongs or a slotted spoon, baste them with their marinade, and broil for 3 to 5 minutes longer. The shrimp are done when they have browned lightly and feel firm to the touch. Be careful not to overcook them.

Serve the shrimp directly from the baking dish, and even at the risk of seeming inelegant, dunk hot French or Italian bread in the sauce.

Bay Scallops with
Dilled Rémoulade Sauce

serves 6–8

2 pounds fresh bay scallops

THE RÉMOULADE SAUCE

2 teaspoons dry mustard

2 teaspoons fresh, strained lemon juice

1 teaspoon capers, *drained and finely chopped*

Fresh dill, *enough to make 2 tablespoons finely cut*

Parsley, *enough to make 1 tablespoon finely chopped*

Peeled garlic cloves, *to make ½ teaspoon finely chopped*

1 egg, *hard-cooked and finely chopped*

2 cups freshly made mayonnaise or use a good unsweetened commercial mayonnaise

Salt

⅛ teaspoon cayenne pepper

Only very fresh and tiny bay scallops are tender and delicate enough to be served raw. For this recipe, do not use sea scallops or frozen bay scallops. Wash the scallops quickly under cold running water and pat them dry with paper toweling. They will be at their best if thoroughly chilled.

In a deep bowl, stir the mustard and lemon juice together until the mustard is completely dissolved. Add the capers, dill, parsley, garlic, and chopped egg, and when they are well combined beat in the mayonnaise. Stir in the salt and cayenne and taste for seasoning.

To serve, arrange the scallops attractively on a chilled plate and pierce each one with a decorative pick. Spoon the *rémoulade* sauce into a bowl and pass it separately as a dip for the scallops.

NOTE: The *rémoulade* sauce can be used with fine effect as a dip for cold shrimp or as a sauce for a crabmeat or lobster cocktail.

Sautéed or Deep-Fried Scallops   serves 4

1½ pounds bay or sea scallops
½ teaspoon salt
⅛ teaspoon white pepper
¾ cup flour

3 eggs
1 tablespoon vegetable oil
1–2 cups very fine dry bread
   crumbs

IF YOU INTEND TO SAUTÉ THE SCALLOPS

4 tablespoons butter   3 tablespoons vegetable oil

IF YOU INTEND TO DEEP-FRY THEM

3–4 inches of oil for deep frying

Wash the scallops quickly under cold running water and pat them thoroughly dry with paper toweling. Sprinkle them liberally with salt and a little white pepper and toss them about with your hands to season them evenly. Now pour the flour into a strong paper bag, add the scallops, and shake the bag vigorously (twisted closed at the top, of course) to coat the scallops with the flour. Empty the entire contents of the bag into a coarse sieve and shake the excess flour through, leaving the scallops covered with only the slightest film of flour. With a whisk or fork, beat the eggs and oil together only long enough to combine them, and spread the bread crumbs out on a long strip of waxed paper. Working quickly, dip the floured scallops, a few at a time, into the egg mixture, then roll them in the crumbs; pat the crumbs into place, if necessary, with a spatula or with your fingers. Line the breaded scallops side by side on a cake rack to dry for 10 to 15 minutes before either sautéing or deep-frying them.

To Sauté the Scallops:

Choose a heavy skillet—preferably with a non-stick finish—large enough to hold the scallops in one layer. Set the pan over high heat, add the butter and oil, and when the butter has melted and has begun to turn ever so slightly brown, add the scallops. Slide the pan back and forth over the heat to keep the scallops in constant motion as they brown on all sides. (Or, if you prefer, turn them about almost constantly in the pan with a large wooden spoon or a spatula.) Bay scallops should be done in 2 or 3 minutes and larger sea scallops (adding more oil to the pan, if necessary) in 4 or 5 minutes. Serve at once with quartered lemons, or more elaborately, if you like, with *salsa verde* (page 161) or hazelnut sauce (page 342), or the dilled *rémoulade* (page 229).

To Deep-Fry the Scallops:

Preheat the oil in your deep fryer to 375 degrees on the deep-frying thermometer. Add the scallops, a batch at a time (if you crowd the frying basket, the temperature of the fat will go down too quickly and the scallops will absorb to much oil), and deep-fry them for about 3 minutes or until golden brown. As they fry, turn them about occasionally in the oil with a large spoon. Drain on double thicknesses of paper toweling and serve at once with either the lemon quarters or any of the other sauces suggested above.

NOTE: To sauté the scallops more simply, you may, as is often done, omit the breading process and merely season the scallops with salt and pepper, then coat them with the flour precisely as I have described above. From my view, this is not a satisfactory precedure. Almost inevitably, the excess moisture in the scallops seeps through into the pan and the result is likely to be more a stew than a sauté.

Coquilles St.-Jacques
à la Parisienne   *serves 4*

1 cup fresh or canned chicken stock: *if you use the concentrated canned type, dilute it with an equal amount of water*

1 cup dry white wine

2 large shallots, *peeled and thinly sliced,* or 3 scallions, *cut into 1-inch lengths*

A bouquet consisting of 3 parsley sprigs, 1 celery top with its leaves, and 1 small bay leaf, *tied together with string*

1 pound whole bay scallops or 1

Coquilles St.-Jacques à la Parisienne

pound sea scallops, *cut against the grain into ½-inch slices*	½ cup milk
	1 egg yolk
½ pound fresh mushrooms, *thinly sliced*	¼–½ cup heavy cream
	A few drops of fresh lemon juice
4 tablespoons (½ stick) butter: *3 for the sauce and 1 for buttering the shells*	Salt
	A pinch of white pepper
	Switzerland cheese, *enough to make ¼ cup grated*
4 level tablespoons flour	

In an enamel or stainless-steel 10- to 12-inch skillet, bring the chicken stock, wine, shallots or scallions, and the bouquet to a rapid boil. Add the scallops and the mushrooms, lower the heat, cover, and simmer for about 5 minutes. Do not let the scallops overcook lest they toughen. With a slotted spoon, transfer the scallops and mushrooms to a bowl and bring the liquid in the pan to a rapid boil once more. Continue to boil, uncovered, until the broth has cooked down to a cupful. Strain it, then, into a bowl. (If you have miscalculated and have less than a cupful, amplify it with a little more chicken stock; if you have a little more, save it to thin the sauce later, if necessary.)

Make the sauce in a 2- to 3-quart enamel or stainless-steel saucepan. Melt 3 tablespoons of the butter over moderate heat (don't let it brown), then, off the heat, thoroughly stir in the flour. Pour in the cupful of reduced broth and the half cup of milk and beat with a small whisk to dissolve the flour partially. Return the pan to moderate heat and, whisking constantly, bring the sauce to a boil. Still whisking, let it boil until it is quite smooth and thick. Lower the heat and beat in the egg yolk, and then ¼ cup of the heavy cream. Simmer slowly for about 1 minute, stirring constantly. The sauce should be dense enough to coat a spoon fairly thickly. If it is too thick, thin it with as much of the remaining cream (and/or any extra broth or stock you may have) that you need. Season the sauce to your taste with salt and a pinch of so of white pepper and a few drops of lemon juice.

Lightly butter 4 large scallop shells, and preheat the oven to 375 degrees. Pour off and discard all the liquid that has accumulated around the waiting scallops and mushrooms (this is important!) and in its place, pour in all but 4 tablespoons or so of the sauce you just made. Stir the mixture about with a spoon, then divide it among the 4 scallop shells. Spread a tablespoon of the reserved sauce over the top of each shell and sprinkle each with 1 tablespoon of the grated cheese. (At this point, you may, if necessary, cover the shells with plastic wrap and re-frigerate them for as long as 8 hours until you are ready to bake them.)

Place the shells on a baking sheet and bake in the upper third of the oven for 10 to 15 minutes, or until the sauce begins to bubble. Slide the shells under the broiler for a few seconds to brown their tops and serve at once.

Baked Oysters in the Italian Manner

serves 4–6

7 tablespoons butter: *1 softened for buttering the dish, 4 for sautéing the crumbs, and 2 cut into ¼-inch bits for the top*
Peeled garlic cloves, *enough to make 1 teaspoon finely chopped*
1½ cups fresh white bread crumbs, *made from Italian or French bread, trimmed of crusts and pulverized in a blender, or torn apart and shredded with a fork*

Parsley (preferably the flat-leaf Italian variety), *enough to make 2 tablespoons finely chopped*
2 dozen fresh oysters, *shucked,* or 2 dozen defrosted frozen oysters, *thoroughly drained*
Imported Parmesan cheese, *enough to make 3 tablespoons freshly grated*

Preheat the oven to 450 degrees.

With a pastry brush, spread the tablespoon of softened butter over the bottom and sides of an ovenproof platter or shallow baking-serving dish just large enough to hold the oysters in one layer.

Over moderate heat, melt 4 tablespoons of the remaining butter in a small skillet, and stir in the garlic. Cook for 10 or 15 seconds without letting it brown; then add the bread crumbs. Tossing them about with a spoon or fork, fry the crumbs for 2 or 3 minutes, until they have absorbed all the butter and have colored lightly. Remove the skillet from the heat and stir in the parsley. Spread about half the crumbs evenly over the bottom of the buttered dish, and arrange the oysters side by side on top. Stir the grated cheese into the remaining crumbs, sprinkle them over the oysters, and dot with the remaining 2 tablespoons of butter cut into small bits.

Bake the oysters in the upper third of the oven for 10 to 15 minutes or until the crumbs brown lightly. Serve at once.

NOTE: You may, if you like, slide the oysters under the broiler for a few seconds (no longer) to brown the crumbs more deeply but watch carefully for any sign of burning.

Clams in White Wine in the Spanish Manner

serves 4

⅓ cup olive oil

1 small onion, *to make ½ cup finely chopped*

1½ pounds ripe fresh tomatoes, *peeled, seeded, and coarsely chopped (page 109) (about 2 cups), or use 2 cups drained and coarsely chopped* canned tomatoes

Fresh or day-old white bread, *trimmed of crusts, enough to make ¼ cup coarsely crumbled*

2 eggs, *hard-cooked, the yolks sieved and the white finely chopped*

Peeled garlic cloves, *enough to make 2 teaspoons finely chopped*

4 dozen small hard-shell clams, *washed and thoroughly scrubbed*

2 cups dry white wine

Salt

Freshly ground black pepper

Fresh parsley (preferably the flat-leaf Italian variety), *enough to make 2 tablespoons finely chopped*

1 lemon, *cut lengthwise into 8 wedges*

Pour the oil into an 8- to 10-inch heavy skillet set over moderate heat, add the onions and, stirring constantly, cook them for about 5 minutes until they are soft and transparent but not brown. Stir in the tomatoes, bread, egg yolks, and garlic. Mashing and stirring with a spoon, cook fairly briskly for about 5 minutes more until most of the liquid in the pan has cooked away and the mixture has become a thick, somewhat smooth purée. Remove from the heat.

Place the clams in a 4-quart casserole or pot equipped with a tightly fitting cover. Pour in the wine and bring to a boil over high heat. Cover tightly, reduce the heat to moderate, and steam the clams for 5 to 10 minutes or until they open. Discard those that remain persistently closed, although you might give them a moment or two longer, first removing the already opened clams, of course, lest they overcook and become tough.

With tongs or a slotted spoon, place the clams on a deep, heated platter. Working quickly, strain the clam broth left in the skillet through a fine-meshed sieve (lined with a double layer of cheesecloth if possible) directly over the tomato mixture. Bring to a boil, stirring constantly. Taste, then season cautiously with salt and more liberally with pepper and pour the sauce over the clams. Sprinkle the top with chopped egg whites and parsley and garnish the platter with the lemon wedges. Serve at once.

Clam Soup in the Italian Manner

serves 4

2 pounds fresh ripe tomatoes, *peeled, seeded, and finely chopped* (*page 109*) (*about 3 cups*), or use 3 cups *drained and chopped* canned tomatoes (preferably Italian plum tomatoes)

½ cup olive oil

Peeled garlic cloves, *enough to make 1 teaspoon finely chopped*

½ cup dry white wine

1 cup water

2 dozen small hardshell clams, *thoroughly washed and scrubbed*

Fresh parsley (preferably the flat-leaf Italian variety), *enough to make 2 tablespoons finely chopped*

Hot French or Italian bread

Drop the fresh tomatoes into a pan of boiling water and boil briskly for 10 minutes. Drain and run cold water over them, then peel them with a small sharp knife. Cut out the stems and slice the tomatoes in half crosswise. Squeeze the halves gently to remove the seeds and juice and chop the pulp coarsely. There should be about 3 cups of pulp. (The canned tomatoes need only be drained, chopped, and measured.)

Heat the olive oil in a 2- to 3-quart saucepan. Drop in the garlic and, stirring constantly, cook over moderate heat for 10 to 15 seconds to color it lightly but without letting it burn. Stir in the wine and the tomatoes and bring to a boil. Reduce the heat to low, partially cover the pan, and simmer for about 10 minutes, stirring occasionally.

Meanwhile, pour enough water into a heavy 12-inch skillet equipped with a tightly fitting cover so that it is about ⅛ inch deep. Bring the water to a boil over high heat. Drop in the clams, cover the pan tightly, and steam over high heat for 5 to 10 minutes, or until the clams open. Those that remain persistently closed should be discarded, although you might give them a moment or two longer, first removing the already opened clams lest they overcook and become tough.

With tongs or a slotted spoon, transfer the clams, still in their shells, to four heated individual soup plates. Line a fine sieve with a double thickness of cheesecloth and strain the clam broth remaining in the skillet through the sieve into the simmering tomato sauce. Boil briskly for a minute or two, taste for seasoning, then pour the soup over the clams. Sprinkle the top with parsley and serve immediately with hot French or Italian bread.

Steamed Clams in the Algarve Manner, Hotel Alvor Praia

½ pound *linguisa* or *chorizo* or other highly seasoned, garlic-flavored smoked pork sausage

½ cup olive oil

4 medium onions, *peeled and* *sliced paper-thin (about 3 cups)*

¼ pound prosciutto or other cooked smoked ham, *finely chopped*

Steamed Clams in the Algarve Manner, Hotel Alvor Praia

1 pound fresh ripe tomatoes, *peeled, seeded, and coarsely chopped (page 109) (about 1½ cups)*, or use 1½ cups *drained and chopped* canned tomatoes

Fresh parsley (preferably the flat-leaf Italian variety), *enough to make ½ cup finely chopped*

½ cup dry white wine

Peeled garlic cloves, *enough to*

make 1 tablespoon finely chopped

1 large bay leaf, *crumbled*

1 teaspoon paprika

¼ teaspoon crushed hot red pepper

Freshly ground black pepper

24–36 small hard-shell clams, *washed and thoroughly scrubbed*

Remove the casings of the sausage with a small sharp knife, and with your fingers crumble the meat finely into a sieve. Plunge the sieve into a pan of boiling water and cook briskly for 1 minute. Then spread the sausage meat out on a double thickness of paper toweling to drain, and pat it dry with some more toweling.

Pour the oil into a large casserole equipped with a tightly fitting lid and set it over moderate heat. Add the onions, and, stirring frequently, cook them for about 10 minutes, until they are soft and transparent. Don't let them brown. Then stir in the sausage meat, ham, tomatoes, parsley, wine, garlic, bay leaf, paprika, red pepper, and a liberal grinding of black pepper. Bring to a boil over high heat and, stirring occasionally, cook briskly until most of the liquid in the pan cooks away. Watch for any signs of burning, lowering the heat a bit if necessary.

Place the clams, hinged-sides down, on top of the meat and tomato mixture, cover tightly, and cook over moderate heat for 5 to 10 minutes, or until the clams open. Those that remain persistently closed should be discarded, although you may find it worth your while to cook them a minute or two longer, first remove the already opened clams lest they overcook and become tough. Taste the sauce for seasoning (return any clams you may have removed to the pot) and serve at once.

Clams Casino   *serves 6*

2½–3 dozen cherrystone or little-
   neck clams
3–4 slices lean bacon, each about
     ⅛ inch thick
¼ pound (1 stick) unsalted butter, *softened to room temperature*
1½ tablespoons fresh, strained
   lemon juice
About 4 shallots or scallions
   (white part only), *to make 4
   tablespoons finely chopped*
2 tablespoons canned or bottled
   pimientos, *drained and
   chopped*
Peeled garlic cloves, *enough to
   make 1 teaspoon finely
   chopped*
1 small green pepper, *to make 4
   tablespoons finely chopped*
Fresh parsley, *enough to make 3
   tablespoons finely chopped*
6 or more drops Tabasco
2–4 tablespoons fine dry bread
   crumbs

Have your fishman shuck the clams, put them in a container with their juices, and ask him to give you the empty shells. Separate the shells, save the deeper halves and throw the rest away. Scrub the shells thoroughly under cold running water with a stiff brush, dry them inside and out, and arrange them side by side on one or two jelly-roll pans.

Fry or broil the bacon until half done; that is, do not allow it to become crisp nor render all its fat. Then cut the bacon into 2½ to 3 dozen ½-inch squares, and set them aside on paper toweling to drain.

Cream the butter in a large mixing bowl (or in an electric mixer equipped with a paddle) by beating and mashing it against the sides of the bowl with a large spoon until it is smooth and fluffy. Beat in the lemon juice, and when it is all absorbed, stir (don't beat) in the shallots or scallions, pimientos, garlic, green pepper, parsley, and Tabasco. Taste for seasoning and add more Tabasco if you like.

To construct the clams casino, place a clam (washed in its own juices or even water, if it feels sandy, and then patted dry) in each shell half. If you feel extravagant, and the shells are large enough, use 2 clams for each shell. Dot each filled shell with about a teaspoon of the seasoned casino butter, and place a bacon square on top. Sprinkle the tops with a few bread crumbs and either refrigerate the clams (safely up to 8 hours) or bake at once.

Preheat the oven to 450 degrees. Bake the clams in the upper third of the oven for about 10 minutes, or until the butter has melted completely and the bacon has begun to crisp. If the topping doesn't seem brown enough at this point, slide the clams briefly under the broiler, but watch them carefully. They must not overcook or burn. Serve at once.

NOTE: There is a recipe in my book, *Michael Field's Cooking School*, for clams Rockefeller in which the initial preparation of the clams is described as it is above. The same procedure using the clams Rockefeller topping can be applied with equal success to make oysters Rockefeller.

240

mussels

The following mussel recipes have one thing in common apart from the obvious fact that they all contain mussels or their broth. They are based on the culinary principle of steaming the scrubbed, washed, and bearded mussels in a mixture of wine, water, and herbs until they open. Once you have learned this simple technique, few mussel recipes—mine, your own inventions, or those in other cookbooks—should hold any terror for you. It would be foolish indeed for me to pretend that cleaning fresh mussels is an easy task. It is, in fact, time-consuming and laborious. But if you attempt the operation as I describe it on page 220, it must be done precisely, lest you find your mussel broth, the basis of many mussel dishes, heavily laden with sand. It is important, too, that you discard in the process those mussels that feel too heavy for their size or make a rattling sound when you shake them; in all likelihood, they will be filled with mud or pebbles and the result should they open while cooking would be disastrous to say the least.

This recipe for *moules marinière*, my version of the famous French classic, is the key to most of the mussel recipes that follow.

Moules Marinière   *serves 4–6*

5 pounds medium-sized mussels (about 6–7 dozen), *washed, scrubbed, and beards removed*
2 cups dry white wine
1 cup water
4 tablespoons unsalted butter, *cut into small pieces*
2 medium onions, *peeled and cut into quarters*, or 8 large shallot cloves, *peeled*
A bouquet consisting of 6 sprigs parsley, 2 celery tops with their leaves, and 1 large bay leaf, *tied together with string*
½ teaspoon thyme
A strip of lemon peel about 3 inches long and 1 inch wide
10 whole black peppercorns
Fresh parsley (preferably the flat-leaf Italian variety), *enough to make ¼ cup coarsely chopped*

Combine the wine, water, butter, onions (or shallots), the bouquet, thyme, lemon peel, and peppercorns in a 6-quart heavy enamel or stainless-steel casserole equipped with a tightly fitting cover. Bring the liquid to a boil with the casserole uncovered, then lower the heat, partially cover the casserole and simmer the *court-bouillon* (as the French call it) for about 10 minutes. It is useful to know that the *court-bouillon* can be made hours before you intend to cook the mussels and simply set aside.

Plan on about 10 minutes in all to cook the mussels and strain the sauce. Be fairly precise about this; the *moules marinière* to be at their best must be served the moment they are done. Bring the *court-bouillon* to a turbulent boil, uncovered, and drop in the mussels. Cover the casserole tightly and boil briskly for 3 to 5 minutes, or until the mussels open. To distribute heat evenly, French cooks grasp the ends of the casserole with a pot holder in each hand and, holding the cover in place securely with their thumbs, lift the casserole from the heat, bringing it toward themselves with a tossing motion. This enables the mussels to cook evenly in their broth and open hopefully all at the same time. If these culinary calisthenics strike you as potentially disastrous (and they can be), forget the whole thing, and let the mussels cook undisturbed until they open on their own.

When all the mussels have opened (throw away those that remain tightly closed), pick them up with tongs and immediately transfer them to a large, heated serving tureen or attractive, heated casserole. Quickly strain the mussel broth over the mussels (there will be about 4 cupfuls). Use the finest sieve you have. If you think your sieve too coarse (most American ones are), line it with a double thickness of cheesecloth and strain the broth through that. Only with these devices (the cheesecloth is preferable even to the finest sieve) can you be sure that the broth will be entirely free of sand. Taste the sauce for seasoning; it is most unlikely that you will have to add any salt since the mussels themselves are naturally quite salty.

Quickly scatter the chopped parsley over the mussels, stir gently with a large wooden spoon, and rush the mussels and their broth to the table. Serve in deep soup plates accompanied by crusty, hot French or Italian bread.

NOTE: If you like, you may sauté about ¼ cup finely chopped shallots in 2 or 3 tablespoons of butter. When the shallots are soft but not brown, scatter them over the hot mussels before sprinkling on the parsley.

Billi-Bi   serves 6–8

Follow the recipe for *moules marinière* precisely but omit the butter in the *court-bouillon*. After the mussels have opened, place them in a bowl and strain the broth (preferably through cheesecloth) into a 2-quart enamel or stainless-steel saucepan. You now have 4 cups of mussel broth as a base for *Billi-Bi*, this glorious masterpiece created, so it is said, by Maxim's in Paris, for William (Billy) B. Leeds. To make the soup, have the following additional ingredients at hand:

4 egg yolks
1 cup heavy cream
A pinch of white pepper or cayenne pepper

1 recipe *moules marinière,* omitting the butter in the *court-bouillon*

In a small bowl, mix the egg yolks and cream together with a small whisk only enough to combine them. Bring the mussel broth almost to the boil and stir 2 tablespoons of it into the cream-egg mixture. Then reverse the process, and whisking constantly, pour the mixture in a slow stream into the hot mussel broth. Now switch to a wooden spoon, reduce the heat to low, and stirring constantly—particularly around the inside creases of the pan—cook the *Billi-Bi* until it thickens ever so slightly. Forget everything you've ever heard about the soup coating the spoon; it won't, and moreover, it shouldn't. But whatever else you do, do not allow the soup to come anywhere near the boil or it will curdle. Stir in the pinch of white pepper or cayenne and taste for further seasoning. Because of the natural saltiness of the mussel broth it is unlikely that you will have to add salt. Serve the soup hot (with a few mussels thrown in, if you like, though purists frown at the idea) and sprinkle the top with a little finely chopped parsley. Or chill the soup and serve it icy cold—again, with or without the mussels added. In any case, the cold soup can be enlivened if you wish by sprinkling it with a fresh herb of some kind: chives, dill, tarragon, parsley, or even a little finely chopped watercress or fresh sorrel.

Moules Glacé in the Manner of Café Chauveron
serves 4–6

1 recipe moules marinière, omitting the butter in the court-bouillon (page 241)
4 tablespoons (½ stick) butter
8 level tablespoons flour
¾ cup milk
1 cup heavy cream
1 cup reduced mussel broth

Imported Parmesan cheese, *enough to make 4 tablespoons grated*
White pepper or cayenne pepper (optional)
1–2 tablespoons fine dry bread crumbs (optional)

After the mussels have opened place them in a bowl and strain the broth (preferably through cheesecloth) into an enamel or stainless-steel 12-inch skillet or 2-quart saucepan. Bring the broth to a rapid boil and boil it, uncovered, until it has cooked down to 1 cupful. This reducing process can take anywhere from 10 to 20 minutes depending upon the pan you use (the skillet with its wider-exposed surface will cause more rapid condensation). Watch the broth carefully as it begins to reach the amount you want. Measure it from time to time; if you reduce it too much it will become almost intolerably salty. When it has reduced to 1 cup, set it aside.

Over moderate heat, in the enamel or stainless-steel saucepan, melt the butter without letting it brown. Off the heat, stir in the flour to make a *roux*. Then pour in the milk, ¼ cup of the cream (reserve the other ¼ cup), and the reduced mussel broth. Beat with a whisk to dissolve the *roux*, and return the pan to the heat. Whisking constantly, bring the sauce to a boil and still whisking, continue to boil until the sauce is very thick and smooth. It will be quite thick, and if you have whisked consistently, very smooth. Now lower the heat and slowly simmer the sauce, uncovered, for about 10 minutes, stirring or whisking it occasionally.

Meanwhile, remove and discard ½ of each mussel shell (leaving the mussel itself attached to the other half of its shell). Arrange the mussels side by side, in a baking dish just large enough to hold them snugly in one layer. If you don't have a large enough dish, use two baking dishes. There is even another alternative: use individual ramekins, or coquille shells.

To construct the *moules glacé*, first preheat the broiler to its highest point. Stir the Parmesan cheese into the simmering sauce. If the sauce seems too thick (it should coat a spoon fairly lightly) thin it with the remaining cream (and even a little more if necessary), stirring it in by the tablespoonful. Taste the sauce for seasoning; it will probably need no salt because of the intense flavor of the reduced mussel broth, but a speck of white pepper or a little cayenne might liven it up a bit. Spoon a little of the sauce over each exposed mussel, and if you like, sprinkle the surface lightly with a few bread crumbs, or for that matter, even a little more cheese. Glaze the *moules* under the broiler about 3 inches from the source of the heat, watching it carefully for any sign of burning. In a minute or two, the surface of the sauce should be lightly speckled with brown and the sauce bubbling. Serve at once.

NOTE: If you take certain precautions, you may prepare the *moules* ahead; that is, up to the point before glazing them. You must do the following: cool the sauce after you stir the cheese into it. Then pour it over the mussels. (If the sauce were hot it would cook the mussels further.) Cover the baking dish or dishes with plastic wrap or foil and refrigerate until ready to glaze. Because the mussels will be cold, you will have to bake them for a few minutes before glazing them. Preheat the oven to 425 degrees and bake the mussels for anywhere from 5 to 8 minutes, or until the sauce begins to bubble. Glaze them quickly under the broiler and serve at once.

Stuffed Mussels with Rémoulade Dill Sauce

1 recipe moules marinière (page 241)
2 cups of the dilled rémoulade sauce on page 229 (use fresh tarragon in place of the dill if you prefer)
Fresh dill, tarragon, or flat-leaf parsley leaves

Remove the cooked mussels from their shells (save the deeper halves of the shells), place them in a bowl and refrigerate, covered, until thoroughly chilled. Fill the shells with the *rémoulade* sauce and half submerge a chilled mussel in each. Top, if you like, with a dill, tarragon, or parsley leaf and refrigerate again until ready to serve.

NOTE: If 6 to 7 dozen mussels seems a formidable amount, make half the *marinière* recipe and 1 cup of *rémoulade* sauce. It might be useful for you to know, if you are planning to make these delicious morsels for a large cocktail party, that 1 cup of *rémoulade* sauce will fill approximately 3 dozen medium-size mussel shells.

Cold Stuffed Mussels in the Turkish Manner

MIDYA DOLMAS

6 dozen medium-size mussels, *washed, scrubbed, and beards removed as described on page 220*

About 4 medium onions, *to make 3 cups finely chopped*

1 cup olive oil

½ cup pine nuts (pignolias, page 340)

1½ cups rice, *not* the converted or parcooked type

¼ cup dried currants

½ teaspoon ground cinnamon

¼ teaspoon ground allspice

1 teaspoon salt

4 cups water

Lemon wedges

With a small sharp knife, open the mussels but leave the shells hinged together. If this task seems beyond you, ask your fishman to do it for you.

To make the stuffing, set a 10- to 12-inch heavy skillet over moderate heat and pour in the oil. Add the onions and, stirring constantly, cook them for 8 to 10 minutes, or until they turn a delicate golden brown. Watch carefully for any sign of burning, and lower the heat if necessary. Stir in the pine nuts, cook for a moment or two with the onions, then add the rice, currants, cinnamon, allspice, salt, and 2 cups of the water. Bring the mixture to a rapid boil over high heat, stirring occasionally, then lower the heat, cover the skillet tightly, and simmer for 20 minutes, or until all the water has been absorbed by the rice. Uncover the skillet and cool the stuffing to room temperature. Taste for seasoning.

To stuff the mussels, pour off and discard any liquid that may have collected in the shell (to say nothing of any specks of sand you come upon), and fill each mussel loosely with a tablespoon (more or less—depending on the size of the shell) of the stuffing. Press the shells together firmly and tie them around their centers securely with a short length of white kitchen string. Arrange the mussels side by side in a casserole just about large and deep enough to hold them compactly in two layers. Pour in the remaining 2 cups of water and bring the casserole to a boil over high heat. Then reduce the heat to its lowest point, cover the pan tightly, and simmer (or more precisely, steam) the mussels for about 20 minutes. Uncover the casserole and let the mussels cool in their own liquid. Remove the mussels with kitchen tongs, cut off the strings, and serve the mussels as an hors d'oeuvre with wedges of lemon.

Mussel Soup in
the Italian Manner   serves 6

1 medium onion, *peeled*
2 stalks celery
4 large cloves garlic, *peeled*
½ cup olive oil
Fresh basil leaves, *enough to make 2 tablespoons finely cut* or 1 tablespoon dried basil, *crumbled*
Freshly ground black pepper
1 cup dry white wine
3 cups canned Italian plum tomatoes preferably (including their liquid), *cut into small pieces,* or use 2 pounds fresh ripe tomatoes, *peeled, and coarsely chopped (about 3 cups)*
Lemon peel: *the lemon peeled with a swivel-bladed vegetable peeler, then finely chopped, to make 1 tablespoon*
5 pounds medium-size mussels (about 6 or 7 dozen), *washed, scrubbed, and beards removed (page 220)*

With a large sharp knife, chop the onion, celery, and garlic together as finely as you can. Or more easily, if less traditionally, first chop them separately and then together.

Heat the olive oil in a 6- to 8-quart casserole or enamel or stainless-steel pot. Add the chopped vegetables, basil, and a liberal grinding of black pepper. Cook for 8 to 10 minutes, stirring frequently and regulating the heat so that the vegetables color lightly and evenly without burning. Pour in the wine and, stirring constantly boil briskly, uncovered, for 2 or 3 minutes until the liquid is reduced to about half of its original quantity. (Don't worry about precision here.) Then add the tomatoes and their liquid and, stirring frequently, simmer, still un-covered, over moderate heat for 20 minutes, or until the mixture is thick enough to hold its shape lightly in a spoon.

Drop in the prepared mussels, cover the pot tightly, and steam over high heat for about 10 minutes, following the pan-shaking procedure, if you wish, as described in the recipe for *moules marinière* on page 241. When all the mussels have opened, the soup is done; if a few resistant mussels remain closed, cook the soup for 1 or 2 minutes longer to give them another chance before discarding them.

Ladle the mussels, still in their shells, into six heated individual soup plates or a large tureen. Taste for seasoning and ladle the soup over them. Sprinkle with the chopped lemon peel, and serve at once.

Seafood Stew with Fried Saffron Toast in the Portuguese Manner

serves 8–10

2 pounds fresh ripe tomatoes, *peeled, seeded, and coarsely chopped* (page 109) (*about 3 cups*), or use 3 cups *drained and coarsely chopped* canned tomatoes

2 medium green peppers, *to make 1 cup finely chopped*

2 medium onions, *to make 1½ cups finely chopped*

Peeled garlic cloves, *enough to make 2 teaspoons finely chopped*

½ teaspoon salt

Freshly ground black pepper

¾ cup olive oil: *½ cup to sauté the vegetables and ¼ cup to fry the bread*

3 dozen hard-shell clams, *washed and thoroughly scrubbed*

3 pounds fish (cod or haddock or a combination of the two), *skinned, boned, and cut into 2-inch cubes*

1½ cups dry white wine

⅛ teaspoon powdered saffron

8 slices French or Italian bread, *cut ¼ inch thick*

Fresh parsley (preferably the flat-leaf Italian variety), *enough to make ¼ cup finely chopped*

Seafood Stew with Fried Saffron Toast in the Portuguese Manner

Put the tomatoes, green peppers, onions, garlic, and salt in a bowl, add a liberal grinding of black pepper, and toss together until they are well combined.

Pour ½ cup of the olive oil into a 5- to 6-quart heavy casserole and tip the pot to spread the oil evenly. Lay the clams in the bottom of the casserole and scatter half the vegetable mixture over them. Add the cubes of fish and scatter the remaining vegetables on top. Pour in the wine, bring to a boil over high heat, cover tightly, and lower the heat. Simmer undisturbed for 20 minutes, or until the clams open and the fish flakes easily when prodded gently with a fork. (Discard any unopened clams.) Taste the soup for seasoning.

While the stew is simmering, heat the remaining ¼ cup of olive oil in a large skillet and stir in the saffron. Add the bread and fry it over high heat for a minute or two on each side, or until the slices are a golden brown. Add a little more of the oil to the pan if necessary.

To serve, place two slices of fried bread in each of eight heated soup plates. Arrange the clams and fish on top of the bread and ladle the soup over them. Sprinkle with parsley and serve at once.

THE ONION AND
ITS FAMILY

tHE ONiON ANd iTS fAMily

Of all the vegetables cultivated and consumed by man, the onion is one of the few universally used today. There is scarcely a country in the world whose cooking has not in some way been influenced by its singularly pungent and assertive flavor.

Unlike cooks of other nations who consider the onion an edible vegetable in its own right, we tend to use it mainly for seasoning. And that it performs this function admirably can hardly be disputed. But to think of these versatile vegetables as seasoners alone is to minimize their value. In knowing hands onions can be transformed into the most subtle of sauces and the heartiest of soups; they can be served sautéed, deep-fried, poached, braised, or baked and used as a garnish for other foods; stuffed, as they infrequently are, they can proudly stand alone.

Because there are so many different kinds of onions available today, choosing one type for a specific purpose is often a perplexing problem, I confess. Onions can be yellow, white, red, or brown; flat, round, or oval. Moreover, their textures can be dry or moist and their flavors mild to bitingly intense.

The most popular onion in the United States is the yellow or white globe. It accounts for at least 75 per cent of all onions grown here and, for this reason indeed, is the vegetable most of us mean when we speak of onions at all. Called an all purpose onion, the globe is characterized by its moderate size, a decidedly strong aroma and taste, and a firm, crisp texture. Although its growers claim that it can be used in any dish requiring onions, these stalwart specimens are really at their best as an aromatic base in long-cooking stocks, soups, or stews. I find, for inexplicable reasons, that the globe seems able to survive hours of simmering with its flavor still intact; this is not always the case with most other onions whose intensity is usually diminished during any lengthy cooking process.

Because of its sustaining power, the globe does well also in more intricate preparations like the French *soubise*. This remarkable vegetable dish is described in most French cookbooks in great detail, but the best version, by far, is the one in which a large quantity (at least 2 pounds) of thinly sliced onions and ½ cup of parboiled rice are braised in butter in a slow oven until the rice is soft and the onions have literally dissolved in their own juices. Thinned with a little cream and judiciously seasoned with salt and pepper (and occasionally with grated cheese, mustard, or a good curry powder), this savory, thick purée makes a most effective accompaniment to any lamb, veal, or chicken dish. And the *soubise* can easily be transformed into a *sauce soubise* by first puréeing it further (through a sieve or in a blender) and then adding it to a rich cream sauce. It can be used with surprising effect in place of an ordinary cream sauce, particularly in those dishes meant to be gratinéed or in other words browned under a broiler. I have discussed *soubise* and given a precise recipe for it in one of my earlier books, *Michael Field's Culinary Classics and Improvisations*. There, it is used as an ingredient for the classic gratin of Veal Orloff, but the *soubise* as I describe it can be modified by you in any of the ways I have suggested above.

The thrifty French, who have wrought culinary magic with the onion in so many ways, use even its peel miraculously, tossing a few onions, unpeeled, into a soup or stock to darken it. Onion peels—except for the white varieties—have the capacity to color any hot liquid to which they are added, and at Easter, eggs are dyed yellow by simply hard-cooking them with a handful of the dry, papery skins. English cooks, following an ancient tradition, carry this process a step further. They wrap the eggs individually in a husk of the peels, enclose them in cheesecloth bags and cook them until they are hard. Unwrapped, the eggs emerged mottled, striped, or marbled, and when they are rubbed with a little oil or butter, have the soft glow of old alabaster.

Whatever the cuisine, onions have always been an important element in soup-making, from the crude bread-water-onion *gazpacho* of the Andalusian peasant to the invigorating onion soup of the French and the piquant onion tart of Provence. Interestingly enough, while the French use the globe onion or its French equivalent for many of their soups, their classic onion soup is almost always made with yellow Spanish onions. Spanish onions—or Bermuda onions, as they are sometimes called—are notable for their moist, silky texture and faintly sweet mildness. They usually contain more sugar than other types and when slowly sautéed in butter (an indispensable step in the preparation of this onion soup) the sugar carmelizes and gives the soup not only its exquisite flavor but its characteristically rich mahogany color as well.

While the role of onions in soup-making can not be overestimated, that of the leek—a distinguished member of the onion family—is of equal importance. In fact, professional cooks would find it virtually impossible to make most of their soups and stocks without them. However, if the scarcity of leeks in most of our vegetable stores and supermarkets is an indication, the average American cook seems unaware of their existence.

Leeks look like huge, overgrown scallions, and the choicest specimens are usually 1½ inches in diameter. Larger ones tend to be pulpy or dry. Generally, only the white part of the leek is used, its layers separated gently from the top, and carefully washed to remove hidden pockets of grit; I consider the flat green stalks of the leeks too coarse for most culinary purposes and almost always discard them, except as I use them in the chicken, tongue, and leek pie on page 270. Exceedingly expensive in the United States when they can be found, leeks are so common in France that they are often called the asparagus of the poor. But taken for granted or not, the French do extraordinary things with them. Leeks are superb if braised like celery, as I do in my own recipe for leeks *provençale* on page 262, or try them baked in a tart with some ham and cheese. And the classic *potage parmentier*—or leek and potato soup—is for my taste superior even to onion soup.

Ironically enough, considering our national indifference to the leek, we have, without knowing it, taken the vegetable to our hearts. I find it curious that many cooks don't know that *vichysoisse*, which we consume in such prodigious quantities during the summer here, is the very same French leek and potato soup which I mention later, but here it is laced with heavy cream, and garnished with chives—another member of the onion family—and served icy cold. I have chosen to add watercress to it in my recipe on page 308, but there is no reason why you can't improvise on the soup in your own way adding to it any herb or cooked vegetable you may have at hand.

The Scotch, too, have their celebrated leek soup, charmingly called cockaleekie. Its simple recipe has remained unchanged for centuries and consists of an old fowl (good Scotch cooks say, the older and tougher, the better), swathed in layers of thinly sliced leeks and simmered for hours as slowly as possible in a few quarts of water. Often, but not always, a handful of barley is tossed in as I do in my recipe for the soup on page 265. The cockaleekie is finished, says that fine English food historian, Dorothy Hartley, when "the bird is rags, and the leeks are pulp, and the broth is lovely."

If the leek has established itself as the autocrat of the soup kettle, the shallot—I think, can be considered the most distinguished member of the onion family—and often plays the same role as the onion in the saucepan. The diminutive shallot, with its clusters of purplish-brown cloves, doesn't taste at all like garlic, as some cooks who have evidently never really tasted it contend. The shallot has a distinction purely its own—something you can't miss when you taste such famous French shallot sauces as *marchand de vin* (page 128), *bércy, beurre blanc,* and *béarnaise.* Or a relatively simple dish like sautéed chicken livers with an abundance of chopped shallots and some Madeira (page 266). It is useless to assume, as has often been suggested, that scallions may be substituted for shallots in these and similar recipes although I do reluctantly suggest it in some of my recipes in this and other of my books because shallots are often difficult to find. When all is said and done, the scallion is still an onion pulled before it reaches maturity, and its flavor, like the shallot's, is very distinctly its own. If you can't find shallots sternly put off making traditional dishes which absolutely require them until you can. And in this and my other books I made it clear which do and which don't.

No such problem will confront you when you shop for little white onions. Fortunately, they are available everywhere. Short of boiling them to the point of disintegration which seems to be their general fate —many cooks I know evidently have no idea what else to do with them. Continental cooks handle these delicate vegetables more skillfully. They don't peel the onions tediously, one by one, in their dry state, but instead, drop them into a kettle of boiling water, count ten slowly, and immediately cool them under cold running water. With the aid of a small knife, the skins peel off as easily as gloves, leaving the onions smooth and unscarred. They are then braised in stock until tender. The braised onions may accompany a main meat or fish course as they do in my recipe among others, for *pièce de boeuf à la Bourguignonne* on page 126. Or they may be added at the last moment to any beef, lamb, or chicken stew. If you like the onions creamed (and they are indispensable indeed to our traditional holiday dinners) blanch them in water, then simmer them, as I do in the creamed onions on page 267, in a *béchamel* or white sauce, enriched with thick, heavy cream. These tiny, delicate vegetables deserve nothing less.

At the other end of the scale, large Spanish or even globe onions, if they are big enough, respond remarkably well to being stuffed, then baked in a little stock or dry white wine. The stuffing may consist of minced cooked poultry, meat, or vegetables, aromatically seasoned with herbs and moistened with cream. (Try my baked Bermuda onions with beef, spinach, and rosemary stuffing [page 268] as an example of this technique.) And, if you wish, any onion pulp, finely chopped and sautéed in butter, may also be added to the stuffing as I do in my specific recipe. It might be well to remember that before being stuffed with any filling of your own devising, the onions should be parboiled for about ten minutes to soften them; then hollow them out, layer by layer, beginning at the root end until the onion's last two layers or so remain, forming a cup.

Despite the undeniable appeal of cooked onions in all their various guises, for some tastes there is nothing quite like the exhilarating flavor of fresh raw onions, whether they are teamed with a hamburger, a salad, or veal or black caviar. Any onion may, of course, be eaten raw, but best, by far, are the mildest white and red Spanish and Italian onions, and the youngest of slender green scallions. Minced or thinly sliced, raw shallots have a place too in a salad bowl, and a sprinkling of freshly cut chives goes with almost anything. And if, for any reason, you need fresh onion juice, a large, unpeeled onion can be cut in half crosswise, and squeezed like an orange on a fruit juicer.

There's not a good cook who doesn't have an onion handy in the vegetable bin, but let's pay more honor to this singular and valuable vegetable and experiment a bit more with it and the various members of its family. In time, if we become demanding enough perhaps American supermarkets will have leeks and shallots as readily available as the more familiar onion.

Gazpacho in the Seville Manner   *serves 6–8*

THE SOUP

6 medium ripe, red tomatoes, *peeled and coarsely chopped*

2 medium cucumbers, *peeled and coarsely chopped*

1 large onion, *peeled and coarsely chopped*

1 medium green pepper, *seeded, deribbed, and coarsely chopped*

4–6 medium garlic cloves, *peeled and coarsely chopped*

French or Italian bread, *trimmed of its crusts, enough to make 4 cups coarsely crumbled*

4 cups cold water

¼ cup red wine vinegar

¼ cup olive oil

1 tablespoon tomato paste

1 tablespoon salt

Freshly ground black pepper

THE GARNISHES

¼ cup olive oil

Bread, *trimmed of its crusts (preferably French or Italian bread), cut into ¼-inch cubes, enough for 1 cup*

1 large onion, *to make 1 cup finely chopped*

2 medium cucumbers, *peeled, to make 1 cup finely chopped, drained of liquid*

2 small red or green peppers, *to make 1 cup finely chopped*

For the soup, combine in a deep bowl the tomatoes, cucumbers, onions, green pepper, garlic, the crumbled bread, and 2 cups of the water. Stir thoroughly, then finely purée the mixture 2 cups or so at a time in the jar of an electric blender. Pour the batches, as you proceed, into another bowl. When all the vegetables have been blended, beat into the purée the remaining 2 cups of water, the vinegar, olive oil, tomato paste, and salt. Taste for seasoning, and add more salt and a few grindings of pepper if you think it needs it. In Seville, at least, this *gazpacho* is always highly seasoned.

(To make the soup by hand, purée the vegetables and bread mixture in a food mill, or rub it through a sieve set over a bowl with the back of a large spoon. Discard any vegetable debris left in the sieve. Then beat in the remaining water, vinegar, olive oil, tomato paste, and salt and pepper.)

Cover the *gazpacho* with foil or plastic wrap and refrigerate for at least 4 hours, or until it is thoroughly chilled.

Meanwhile, pour ¼ cup olive oil into a small, heavy skillet and set it over high heat. When the oil is very hot but not smoking, add the bread cubes and, stirring frequently, fry them until they are crisp and golden. Drain them on a double thickness of paper toweling.

Before serving, whisk or stir the *gazpacho* lightly to recombine it; it tends to separate a bit as it stands. Then ladle it into a large chilled tureen or into individual chilled soup plates, and pass the bread cubes and the vegetable garnishes in small separate bowls to be added to the soup at the discretion of each diner.

Onion Soup in the French Manner, Gratinéed

serves 6–8

4 tablespoons (½ stick) butter
2 pounds onions (preferably Bermuda onions), *peeled and thinly sliced (about 7 cups)*
1 teaspoon salt
1 level tablespoon flour
2 quarts brown beef stock, freshly made or canned: *if you use concentrated canned type, dilute it with an equal amount of water*

Freshly ground black pepper
6–8 one-inch-thick slices of French bread
3 teaspoons olive oil; *2 for the croûtes and 1 for the gratinée*
About 4 ounces Switzerland cheese, *to make 1 cup coarsely grated,* or use equal amounts of Switzerland and imported Parmesan cheese, *freshly grated*

Melt the butter over moderate heat in a heavy 5- to 6-quart casserole, but don't let the butter brown. Add the onions and salt, and stirring occasionally, fry them for 20 to 30 minutes, regulating the heat so that the onions become a deep rich brown within the time I specify. Don't hurry this, or the onions will char and have a particularly unpleasant flavor. Now stir in the flour; cook, stirring constantly for a minute or two, then pour in the stock. Bring the stock to a boil, and reduce the heat to its lowest point; partially cover the casserole, and simmer for 30 to 40 minutes. Taste for seasoning. Depending upon the stock you use, you may have to add considerably more salt than I have indicated to give the soup more body and flavor. I find nothing more distressing than undersalted soup, especially onion soup.

While the soup is simmering, or, in fact, earlier, if you prefer, make the *croûtes*. Preheat the oven to 325 degrees. Arrange the slices of bread side by side on a baking sheet, then slide it into the upper third of the oven and toast them for about 15 minutes. With a pastry brush, lightly coat each side of the bread with equal amounts of olive oil (up to 2 teaspoonfuls). Return them to the oven and bake the *croûtes* until they are crisp and golden brown. Remove the *croûtes* from the oven and set them aside.

When you are ready to serve the soup, preheat the oven to 375 degrees. Arrange the *croûtes* side by side on top of the soup, and sprinkle them evenly with the cheese and the remaining teaspoon of oil. (Or you may prefer to ladle the soup into deep individual ceramic bowls before adding a *croûte* to each, and sprinkling it with the cheese and oil.) In either case, bake the soup in the middle of the oven for 10 to 15 minutes, or until the cheese has melted and formed a light-brown crust. If it is not brown enough for your taste, slide the casserole or the individual bowls under the broiler for a few seconds or so to brown the tops further. Serve at once.

Pissaladière

A PROVENCE ONION AND TOMATO TART   *makes a 10-inch tart*

A partially baked 10-inch pastry
    shell (page 285)
4 tablespoons (½ stick) butter
About 2 pounds onions, *to make 6
    cups finely chopped*
Peeled garlic cloves, *enough to*

*make 1 tablespoon finely
chopped*
3 tablespoons olive oil: *2 for
    cooking the tomatoes and 1
    for dribbling over the top of
    the tart*

2 pounds fresh, ripe tomatoes, *peeled, seeded, and finely chopped* (*page 109*) (*about 3 cups*)

1 tablespoon tomato paste

Fresh basil, *enough to make 1 tablespoon finely cut,* or 2 teaspoons dried basil, *crumbled*

1 teaspoon dried oregano, *crumbled*

1 teaspoon salt

Freshly ground black pepper

1 tablespoon dry bread crumbs

24 flat anchovies, *drained of all their oil*

24 black olives (the black Mediterranean type if possible)

Parsley (the flat-leaf Italian type if possible), *enough to make 1 tablespoon finely chopped*

Over moderate heat, melt the butter in a heavy 10- or 12-inch skillet. Stir in the onions, and when they are well coated with the butter, cover the pan and simmer them for about 10 minutes, stirring occasionally. Uncover the pan, then add the garlic and cook over low heat for about 30 minutes, stirring periodically until all the liquid in the pan has evaporated and the onions are soft, translucent but not brown. Meanwhile pour 2 tablespoons of the olive oil into another skillet and set it over high heat. Add the chopped tomatoes and bring them to a boil. Stirring frequently, let them boil briskly, uncovered, until all their liquid has cooked away and the tomatoes have become dense enough to hold their shape almost solidly in a spoon. (Watch carefully for any sign of burning, and lower the heat a bit if necessary.) Off the heat, stir in the basil, oregano, and tomato paste. When both preparations are finished (it doesn't matter in which order you do them but it *does* matter that in both all liquid has been cooked away), combine them in a mixing bowl. Stir in the salt and a few grindings of black pepper and taste for seasoning. Provençale preparations of this type—like their southern Italian antecedents—are usually highly seasoned, so that you may add more salt (discreetly because of the anchovies to be added later) and pepper, basil and oregano with a fairly heavy hand if you wish.

Preheat the oven to 375 degrees. Place the partially cooked pastry shell (still in its pan) on a cooky sheet or jelly-roll pan. Sprinkle the bottom of the shell evenly with the bread crumbs (to absorb any excess liquid and to prevent the tart from becoming soggy), then spoon in the tomato-onion mixture, smoothing it to the edges of the circle with the flat side of a knife or spatula. Make a latticework on top of the tart with the flat anchovies, spreading them end to end. Place an olive in each resulting square, and dribble the tablespoon of olive oil over the top as evenly as you can. Bake the tart in the center of the oven for 30 to 40 minutes or until the onion-tomato mixture is ever so lightly browned. Remove the tart from its pan by placing it on the top of a coffee can and sliding off the outside rim. Serve either hot, tepid, or at room temperature. In either case, sprinkle the tart lightly with the chopped parsley just before serving.

Braised Leeks Provençale

HOT OR COLD   *serves 4*

10–12 leeks, their bases each about   2–3 cups cold water
    1 inch in diameter   1 teaspoon salt
½ cup olive oil

THE SAUCE

1 pound fresh ripe tomatoes,   1 tablespoon fresh, strained
    peeled, seeded, and chopped   lemon juice
    (*about 1½ cups*) (*page 109*)   ½ teaspoon salt
2 tablespoons olive oil   Freshly ground black pepper
Peeled garlic cloves, *enough to*   Parsley (preferably the flat-leaf
    make 1 teaspoon finely   Italian variety), *enough to*
    chopped   *make ½ cup finely chopped*
                     Lemon quarters

Trim the leeks so that each one is approximately 6 inches long. Then carefully cut off the dangling roots but not so deeply as to separate the white leaves; the base of each leek should be smooth and disc-like. Wash each leek with care; leeks are notorious for the sand they secrete so insidiously—and after washing, although they may seem to be clean you may discover to your dismay after braising them that hidden pockets of sand have escaped you. To ensure their being sand-free, gently spread the green leaves apart (cutting, stripping, or trimming away those that appear coarse or wilted), and run cold water through them. As a final precaution, it is not a bad idea to soak them leaves-side down in a bowl of cold water for at least 10 minutes, or until you are ready to braise them. Then wash them once more.

Preheat the oven to 350 degrees. Lay the leeks in a shallow baking dish just large enough to hold them side by side snugly in one layer. Mix the olive oil, 2 cups of the water, and the salt together in a small bowl, and pour it into the baking dish. The liquid should almost, but not quite cover the leeks. Add more of the water if necessary.

Bring the liquid in the baking dish to a boil over high heat, then cover the top of the dish slackly with a large sheet of foil (don't secure it to the edges or the steam will not be allowed to escape, and the leeks will wilt depressingly; on the other hand, if you omit the foil altogether, the leeks will brown, which is not your intention at all).

Place the leeks in the center of the oven and braise them for about 30 minutes, turning them over gently with tongs from time to time. They are done when their bases show only a slight resistance to the tip of a skewer or the point of a small sharp knife. Don't let them overcook. In fact, they will be considerably more attractive and flavorful if they are slightly undercooked.

While the leeks are braising, make the sauce. Pour the 2 tablespoons of olive oil into an 8- or 10-inch skillet set over moderate heat. Add the garlic and, stirring constantly, simmer for a moment or two (don't let it brown) before adding the chopped tomatoes. Raise the heat to high and, stirring almost constantly, cook the tomatoes briskly until their moisture has almost completely boiled away. Stir in the lemon juice, salt, and a few grindings of black pepper. Remove the pan from the heat and add the parsley. Taste for seasoning.

When the leeks are done, thin the tomato sauce with 4 tablespoons of the braising liquid, then pour off and discard the remaining liquid. Spread the tomato sauce over the leeks and serve either hot, or let them cool to room temperature. You may refrigerate the leeks if you plan to use them another time, but before serving remove them from the refrigerator and let them return to room temperature, their flavor will be muted if they are too cold. Garnish the leeks with lemon quarters.

Leek Tart   *serves 6–8*

A partially baked 10-inch pastry
    shell (page 285)
5 tablespoons butter: *4 for brais-*
    ing the leeks and 1, cut into
    small bits, for dotting top of
    pie
About 1 pound leeks, *to make 2*
    cups (packed down) coarsely
    chopped (well-washed white
    parts only)
4 eggs: *2 whole eggs and 2 egg*
    yolks for the custard

1½ cups heavy cream
¾ teaspoon salt
Freshly ground black pepper
About ¾ pound lean ham
    (preferably Virginia ham),
    to make 1⅓ cups coarsely
    diced
Imported Parmesan cheese,
    enough to make 2 tablespoons
    freshly grated

Preheat the oven to 375 degrees.

Over low heat, melt 4 tablespoons of the butter in a 10- to 12-inch heavy skillet. Add the leeks. Stirring frequently, simmer them slowly, uncovered, for about 8 minutes and regulate the heat so that they soften without coloring. Drop the 2 whole eggs and the 2 yolks into a large mixing bowl and, with a whisk, beat them only long enough to combine them. Slowly pour in the cream, stirring all the while. Then add the salt and a few grindings of black pepper, and taste for seasoning. Add more salt and pepper, if necessary.

Place the prebaked pastry shell (still in its pan) on a cooky sheet or a jelly-roll pan. Spread the sautéed leeks evenly over the bottom of the pie with a rubber spatula and scatter the ham over the top. Slowly pour in the egg and cream mixture, sprinkle the surface with the grated cheese, and dot with the tablespoon of butter bits.

Bake the tart undisturbed in the upper third of the oven for about 30 minutes, or until the custard is firm—but not too firm—and the top lightly browned. Serve at once, hot or lukewarm, following the directions for unmolding the tart on page 262.

NOTE: The leek tart may be baked ahead, cooled and then reheated when you are ready to serve it, in a preheated 350-degree oven for about 10 minutes.

Cockaleekie   *serves 8–10*

12 large leeks, each about 1½
   inches in diameter
A 5- to 6-pound stewing fowl,
   any large chunks of fat re-
   moved from the cavity and
   the bird securely trussed,
   the giblets and the neck cut
   into 1-inch pieces (reserve
   the liver for another use)

5–6 quarts cold water
½ cup pearl barley, *washed in a*
   sieve under cold running
   water until the draining
   water runs clear
1 tablespoon salt
Fresh parsley (preferably the flat-
   leaf Italian variety), *enough*
   to make ¼ cup finely chopped

With a sharp knife, cut away the roots of the leeks, and strip away any withered leaves from the stems. Cut off and discard all but about 3 inches of the green tops. Then split the green parts in half, lengthwise, stopping where they begin to shade into white. Carefully spread the leaves apart and wash the leeks under cold running water to rid them of any hidden pockets of sand. Lay the leeks on the table and slice them crosswise into ½-inch-thick rounds. There should be at least 8 cups of leeks, perhaps 10, depending upon their size.

Place the fowl and the giblets in a 10- to 12-quart casserole or soup pot, and pour over them 5 quarts of the water. The water should cover the bird by about 2 inches; if it doesn't, add any of the remaining quart of water or even more, if necessary. Bring to a boil, uncovered, over high heat; meanwhile, with a large spoon, skimming off the foam and scum as they rise to the top. When the surface seems fairly clear, add the leeks, barley, salt, and lower the heat. Partially cover the pot and let it simmer undisturbed (the water should barely move except for small bubbles bursting on the top every few seconds or so) for about

3 to 3½ hours, until the bird has literally begun to fall apart. If the fowl is a venerable one, you may have to simmer it even longer.

When "the bird is in rags, and the leeks are pulp, and the broth is lovely," to repeat Dorothy Hartley's charming description I quoted in the introduction to this chapter, carefully transfer the fowl to a platter, and turn off the heat under the pot. Let the broth rest while you remove the skin of the fowl and pull off the meat still clinging to the bones. Discard the skin and bones, and cut the meat into shreds about 1 or 2 inches long.

Now, with a large spoon, carefully skim off and discard as much fat as you can from the surface of the broth. Return the strips of chicken to the soup, taste for seasoning—it will doubtlessly need more salt— and simmer for a moment or two to heat the chicken through.

Serve in a large, heated tureen or in deep individual soup plates, and sprinkle the top with chopped parsley.

Sautéed Chicken Livers in the Spanish Manner with Shallots and Madeira

serves 3

4 tablespoons butter: *2 for sautéing the shallots and 2 for the livers*

About 10–12 shallot cloves, *to make ½ cup finely chopped*

Peeled garlic clove, *enough to make ¼ teaspoon finely chopped*

1 level tablespoon flour

¾ cup chicken stock, fresh or canned

Fresh parsley, *enough to make 1 tablespoon finely chopped*

1 tablespoon vegetable oil

1 pound chicken livers, *trimmed and patted thoroughly dry with paper toweling*

¼ cup dry Madeira

A few drops fresh lemon juice

In an 8-inch heavy skillet, melt 2 tablespoons of the butter over moderate heat and add the shallots. Stirring occasionally, cook slowly for about 5 minutes, or until the shallots are soft but not brown. Stir in the flour, simmer for a few seconds, then pour in the chicken stock all at once. Bring to a boil over high heat, stirring constantly with a spoon or whisk. When the sauce is quite thick, add the parsley, lower the heat and simmer slowly, uncovered, for about 10 minutes. Set aside off the heat.

Heat the remaining 2 tablespoons of butter and oil in a heavy 12-inch skillet, preferably one with a non-stick surface. When the butter has melted completely and has begun to turn ever so faintly brown, add the livers. Sprinkle them liberally with salt and a few grindings of pepper. Sauté them briskly for about 5 minutes, turning them about in the pan with a large spoon or spatula until they are lightly brown but still pink in the center. Cut into one to make sure.

Quickly scoop the livers out of the pan with a slotted spoon, set them on a plate. Pour the Madeira into the pan drippings and bring it to a rapid boil over high heat, meanwhile scraping into it any brown bits or sediment clinging to the bottom of the pan. Boil briskly, uncovered, until the wine has cooked down to about half its original volume (this should take 2 or 3 minutes), then stir in the shallot sauce. Stirring constantly, bring the combined sauces to a boil, add the livers (and any juices that have collected around them), and simmer for a minute or two to heat the livers through. Taste for seasoning, sprinkle with lemon juice, and serve at once, preferably with rice pilaf or boiled buttered rice.

Creamed Little White Onions   *serves 4–6*

2 dozen little white onions, each about 1 inch in diameter
1 teaspoon salt
2 tablespoons butter
2 level tablespoons flour

½ cup milk
¼–½ cup heavy cream
A few gratings of fresh nutmeg
A pinch of white pepper

Drop the unpeeled onions into a large pot of turbulently boiling water. Boil them briskly for 30 seconds or so, then drain them immediately in a colander and run cold water over to cool them quickly. With the help of a small sharp knife, slip off the paperlike skins. Trim the root ends, but be careful not to cut too deeply or the outer layers of the onions will fall away as they cook.

Place the onions in a 1- to 2-quart saucepan and add ½ teaspoon of the salt and enough cold water to cover them by 1 inch. Bring the water to a boil over high heat, then reduce the heat to its lowest point. Partially cover the pan and simmer the onions for 15 to 20 minutes, or until they are tender but still slightly resistant to the point of a small knife. Drain the onions in a sieve set over a bowl, reserving the cooking water.

In the same saucepan, melt the butter (without letting it brown) over moderate heat. Stir in the flour to make a *roux*. Pour in ½ cup of the reserved onion water, the milk, and ¼ cup of the cream. Beat with a whisk and bring the sauce to a boil over high heat. When the sauce is thick and smooth, lower the heat and simmer it slowly for 2 or 3 minutes. Then stir in the remaining ½ teaspoon of salt, a few gratings of nutmeg, and the pinch of white pepper, and taste for seasoning. Stir in more salt, nutmeg, and pepper, if you think it needs it. Now add the well-drained onions and simmer for a few minutes to heat them through. Add the remaining cream by the tablespoonful if you find the sauce too thick for your taste, and simmer a few seconds. Serve at once.

Baked Bermuda Onions with Beef, Spinach, and Rosemary Stuffing

serves 6

6 large, firm Bermuda onions, each about 3 to 4 inches in diameter

5 tablespoons butter: *1 to coat the baking pan, 3 for sautéing the onions, and 1, cut into bits, for the topping*

Peeled garlic cloves, *enough to make 1 tablespoon finely chopped*

1 small green pepper, *enough to make 2 tablespoons finely chopped*

Baked Bermuda Onions with Beef, Spinach, and Rosemary Stuffing

1 small celery stalk, *to make ¼ cup finely chopped*

1 teaspoon dried rosemary, *crumbled*

½ pound fresh spinach, *cooked, then squeezed dry and finely chopped,* or use a 10-ounce package of frozen chopped spinach, *thoroughly defrosted and squeezed dry, then finely chopped*

1 pound finely ground lean beef

1 tablespoon vegetable oil

1 teaspoon salt

½ cup fresh bread crumbs, *pulverized in a blender or torn apart and shredded with a fork*

4–6 tablespoons heavy cream

Freshly ground black pepper

½ teaspoon fresh lemon juice

½–1 cup fresh or canned chicken stock: *if you use the concentrated canned type, dilute it with an equal amount of water*

Drop the onions, unpeeled, into a large pot and pour in enough boiling water to cover them by 2 inches. Boil them briskly, uncovered, for about 10 minutes. Drain them in a colander and run cold water over them to cool them quickly. Peel them carefully, starting at the root end, and cut away the short stem ends with scissors. With a sharp knife, cut a one inch slice off the root end of each onion and, with a large fork, pull out the centers of the onions, leaving a hollow cup composed of the last 2 or 3 onion layers. Chop the scooped out onion pulp as finely as you can. Measure 1 cupful of the pulp, pack it down, add more pulp to reach the required amount, and put it aside. Discard the remaining pulp.

Melt 3 tablespoons of the butter over high heat in a 10- to 12-inch heavy skillet. Add the pulp, lower the heat to moderate, and stirring it frequently with a wooden spoon, cook for about 10 minutes, until all its moisture has evaporated, and it has colored lightly. Stir in the garlic, green pepper, celery, and rosemary, and cook for 5 or 8 minutes, then add the chopped spinach. Raise the heat to high and, stirring constantly, cook the mixture briskly until all the liquid in the pan has evaporated, and the spinach has begun to stick almost imperceptibly to the pan. Watch carefully for any sign of burning, and lower the heat a bit if necessary. With a rubber spatula, scrape the entire mixture into a large mixing bowl.

Pour the tablespoon of oil into the skillet and set it over high heat. When the oil is quite hot but not smoking, add the ground meat. Constantly break and mash it to remove any lumps as it cooks. In about 5

Baked Bermuda Onions with Beef, Spinach, and Rosemary Stuffing

minutes, most of the liquid in the pan will have evaporated and the meat should be lightly browned. Immediately transfer the meat into a sieve set over a bowl and let any fat drain off. Discard the fat and add the meat to the spinach mixture. Add the salt and a liberal grinding of black pepper, the lemon juice and 4 tablespoons of the bread crumbs. Toss the stuffing about with your hands or with a large spoon to mix the ingredients well, then mix in 4 tablespoons of the cream. If the mixture seems too dry, stir in the remaining cream and taste for seasoning. It may need more salt, pepper, and perhaps lemon juice.

Preheat the oven to 375 degrees. Pack the stuffing into the onion cups and mound the tops slightly. Spread 1 tablespoon of the remaining tablespoon of butter over a shallow baking dish just large enough to hold the onions comfortably, and in it arrange the onions side by side. Sprinkle the remaining bread crumbs over the top of each onion and top with the bits of butter. Pour ¼ cup of the chicken stock into the dish (if it doesn't cover the bottom of the pan by about ¼ of an inch, add the remaining stock, and even more if necessary).

Bake in the middle of the oven for an hour or even longer, or until the tops of the crumbs on the stuffing are golden brown, and the onions feel somewhat soft—but not too soft when pressed lightly with your fingers. (While the onions are baking, baste them every 15 minutes or so with the stock in the pan to keep them moist.) Serve at once, moistening each onion as you serve it with a little of the pan juices.

Chicken, Leek, and Tongue Pie in the English Manner
serves 4–6

The ingredients for the tart pastry (page 285)

8 large leeks, 1 to 1½ inches in diameter

A 6- to 6½-pound roasting chicken or stewing fowl, *securely trussed;* include the bird's

giblets (save the liver for another use)

1 celery stalk

8 parsley sprigs

1 medium-size bay leaf

½ teaspoon dry thyme, *crumbled*

1 tablespoon salt

Chicken, Leek, and Tongue Pie in the English Manner

½ pound cooked smoked beef
　tongue, *cut into ½-inch dice*
　(*about 1½ cups*)
Fresh parsley, *enough to make*
　1 tablespoon finely chopped

1 egg yolk *lightly beaten with* 1
　tablespoon heavy cream
1½ cups heavy cream

Combine the ingredients for the pastry as described on page 285. Wrap the ball of pastry in waxed paper and let it chill in the refrigerator while you make the filling for the pie.

With a sharp knife, cut away the roots of the leeks and strip away any withered or overly coarse leaves from the stem. Cut off all but 2 inches of the green tops, chop the tops coarsely, and wash 2 cupfuls of them in a sieve under cold running water. Put them aside. Slit the whole leeks in half lengthwise, carefully spread the leaves apart, and wash them thoroughly. Then lay the leeks on their sides, and slice them crosswise into 1-inch rounds. Set aside.

Place the chicken and its giblets in a 6- to 8-quart casserole and pour enough water over it to cover the bird by at least 2 inches. Bring to a boil, uncovered, over high heat, meanwhile skimming off the foam and scum that rises to the top. Add the 2 cups of chopped leeks, the celery stalk, parsley sprigs, bay leaf, thyme, and salt, and reduce the heat to low. Partially cover the casserole and let it simmer undisturbed until the bird is tender but not falling apart. (A roasting chicken may be done in an hour; a stewing fowl may take as long as 2 or more hours, depending on its age and tenderness.)

Remove the chicken from the pot and place it on a platter. Strain the stock through a fine sieve set over a large bowl, and discard the giblets and vegetables. With a large spoon, skim the surface of the stock of as much fat as you can and discard it. Then pour 1½ cups of the stock into a small saucepan, add the cut-up leek rounds, and bring to a boil over high heat. Lower the heat, partially cover the pan, and simmer the leeks for about 5 minutes. Taste the broth for seasoning, and add more salt if it seems too bland. Remove the pan from the heat.

When the bird is cool enough to handle, remove its skin and cut away all the meat from the bones. Discard the skin and bones and cut the meat into approximately 1-inch pieces. Set an inverted bowl, about 3 inches wide and 2 inches deep, in the center of a 9-by-12-inch baking dish about 2 inches deep. Arrange the chicken pieces in the baking dish,

Chicken, Leek, and Tongue Pie in the English Manner

scatter the tongue over them, and add the leek rounds and their broth. Sprinkle the top with the parsley.

Preheat the oven to 400 degrees. On a lightly floured surface, roll the chilled pastry (let it soften a bit, if you find it too difficult to manage) into a rough 12-by-16-inch rectangle. Then, lift it up on your rolling pin, and drape it over the baking dish. With scissors or a small sharp knife, trim the excess pastry to within ½ inch of the dish and fold the extra ½ inch under to make a double thickness all around the rectangle. With the back tines of a fork, press the pastry around the pie to secure it firmly to the dish. (If you wish, you may gather the leftover scraps of pastry into a compact ball, reroll it, and cut into simple leaf and flower shapes. Moisten the undersides of each decoration with the egg and cream mixture and arrange them as decoratively as you like on the pie.) Then, with a small sharp knife, cut ½-inch holes on either side of the centered bowl holding up the pastry, and brush the entire surface of the pie with the remaining egg and cream mixture.

Bake the pie for ½ hour in the lower third of the oven. Then turn the heat down to 350 degrees and bake ½ hour longer or until the crust is golden brown.

While the pie is baking, pour the cream into a small saucepan and bring to a boil over high heat. Reduce the heat to moderate and, stirring occasionally, continue to cook it, uncovered, until it has thickened and cooked down to about 1 cup.

Immediately before serving the pie, insert a small funnel or a large, plain pastry-decorating tip into one of the openings in the crust, and slowly pour in half the cream (reheated, if it has cooled by now). Pour the remaining cream similarly into the other opening and tip the pie from side to side to spread the cream evenly. Serve at once.

NOTE: You may insert small bouquets of parsley or watercress into the pastry openings for a charming decorative effect.

ROOTS

ROOTS

Root vegetables are indispensable to much of our basic cooking and are a part of our melting-pot European heritage. But most American cooks today would hardly recognize, let alone know what to do with, celeriac, salsify, rutabagas, or any of the other curiously named members of this subterranean vegetable kingdom.

Turnips, for some reason, occupy a particularly ignominious place in American cooking. To be sure, their flavor is distinct and uncompromising and not to everyone's taste, but I don't understand the dismay so many people I know feel at the very thought of eating this maligned root, particularly when turnips, knowingly prepared, can have great delicacy and charm.

Almost every cuisine in the world has its individual way with turnips. The Arabs and Egyptians pickle them, the Italians stuff them, the Greeks eat them raw, and the Chinese stir-fry them. But the French I think, prepare them in, probably, the best way of all: they braise them —and usually with a duck. French cooks long ago recognized that turnips braised with a duck would not only absorb a good deal of the rich fat given off by the bird but would, after the process, emerge from the braising sauce sleek and succulent, with a flavor quite unlike that of any other vegetable. Although turnips respond almost as well to being braised with lamb, mutton, or any other fatty meat, as you will see in my recipe for braised lamb with turnips or rutabagas on page 281, it is for the duck that they appear to have the greatest affinity. Braised duck with turnips, or, to give it its classical French name, *caneton braisé aux navets,* is with justification considered one of the glories of the French cuisine. I have not included it in this root chapter for the simple reason that my definitive recipe for it appears in my book, *Michael Field's Culinary Classics and Improvisations.*

No less a culinary achievement is the dish French housewives make by artfully combining puréed potatoes and turnips, beating them together with plenty of butter and cream and serving them garnished with tiny shards of freshly cut chives. And the same combination works equally well if you use turnips and tubers in *potage parmentier,* the classic potato and leek soup, and its cold American counterpart, *vichysoisse,* which I present to you with variations on page 308. The barely perceptible flavor of the turnip used in this fashion gives these familiar soups a new dimension, at least for my taste and I hope, when you try them, for yours as well.

All these turnip dishes, and others, are ours for the serving whenever we want them. Unlike French turnips, which are seasonal and often expensive, American turnips are available the year round and usually at reasonable prices. Don't settle for any but those of the highest quality, and you won't when you are aware of precisely what to look for when you shop for them.

Yellow turnips are perfectly edible but the white-fleshed types are more delicate and therefore preferable. These are generally globular in shape and closely sheathed in smooth white skins splashed at the top with graduated shades of purple. Turnips, like most root vegetables, are at their best young, and the most reliable indications of their youth are leafy tops which are unwilted, crisp, and a fresh bright green. Turnips sold without their tops are more difficult to assess. To be on the safe side, buy those which seem heavy for their size and are firm to the touch.

The same standards of quality apply to the turnip's closest and considerably larger relative, the rutabaga. Often called Swedes or Swedish turnips, these dun-colored roots with wide purple crowns have the unmistakable taste of a turnip but are denser in texture, sweeter in flavor, and generally more assertive in every way. To tame them a bit, peel them deeply first, then blanch them in boiling water for four or five minutes before subjecting them to any other culinary procedure. And this way you can confidently substitute them successfully in any recipe which call for turnips.

If members of the turnip family appear on our tables infrequently, the ever-present carrot more than makes up for their absence. We consume carrots in prodigious quantities, raw and cooked, grated and shredded, in slices, chunks, and curls, and yet, despite our apparent affection for these colorful roots, we never seem to cook or serve them as imaginatively as other countries do.

The French, for example, lovingly trim young slender carrots into small elongated olive shapes—a task not to be undertaken lightly when there are many to be done—and thriftily use the scraps to make a superb carrot soup, delicate soufflés, rich creamy carrot purées, and even desserts. As for the carrots themselves, shaped or not, they should seldom, if ever, be merely boiled, but, more effectively, braised instead. I have described this procedure in some detail on page 284.

The carrot also plays a very important, if more or less anonymous role in most of our cooking, although perhaps we aren't aware of its important functions; because of their large proportion of sugar they are of great value in offsetting the sometimes excessive acidity of many dishes cooked with wine. And the carrot's delicate sweetness, discreetly employed, has an effect on stocks, soups, and sauces, as we well know.

Less well known, however, is the place of carrots in desserts. The Italians grate them raw to make a light, elusively flavored torte reminiscent of a moist spongecake; and the French, going the Italians one better, fill a tart shell with a sweetened purée of carrots mixed with a heavy custard, then top the rich purée with concentric circles of paper-thin sugar-glazed carrots before baking it. Known in France as *flan des carottes à la flamande* (my re-creation of this tart is on page 285), it is served usually as a dessert either hot or cold, copiously dusted with powdered sugar. For variety, the tart is sometimes used as a separate vegetable course, in which event you can make it with considerably less sugar and omit the custard.

The English make similar pies of parsnips, and recipes for them go as far back as Elizabethan times. In my reconstructed version of the pie on page 287, parsnip purée is heavily sweetened with honey, seasoned with ginger, mace, cinnamon, grated orange rind, and lemon juice. Eggs are added and the purée is then baked in a tart shell with a latticework of rich pastry crisscrossed over the top. In England, this parsnip pie is usually served in early spring, gaily decorated, as it has been for over four hundred years, with bright red primroses set at the cross of the lattices.

Cooking parsnips in this fanciful fashion is a far cry from what most of us do with them. Because we seldom serve them as vegetables in their own right and use them mainly to season our soups and stews, many of us have only the faintest notion, if any, of what a parsnip really tastes like. But parsnips have characteristics unlike that of any other root; their flavor is particularly sweet and nutty and their texture fibrous but silkily soft. The English are extremely fond of them and cook them with more originality than anyone else. Apart from using parsnips for desserts (and parsnip pie is one among many), English cooks deep-fry the roots like potato chips, turn them into creamy golden croquettes, and, in what is probably the most satisfying way of all, they blanch them for about 10 minutes, then roast them with ribs of beef until they are a crusty brown and have absorbed as much of the beef drippings as they can hold.

Many roots can, of course, be roasted with meat in similar fashion except, perhaps, one—a singular gray, tapering root called salsify, or oyster plant. And it comes by its alternate name honestly; salsify does indeed have faint overtones of an oyster flavor, which makes it necessary to cook it differently from other roots. Although many cuisines use the root in a variety of ways, the most attractive, for some tastes—and one which seems to intensify its oyster-like flavor—are salsify fritters or *beignets,* as made by the French. They make superb cocktail accompaniments as you will see if you serve them in this fashion. If making the fritters seems too much of a chore, simply sauté the roots (first blanched of course), in butter and season them with a few drops of lemon juice and a little chopped parsley. This is a fine way to create an unusual vegetable course with very little trouble. You should know, however, that salsify, upon being peeled and exposed to air, will darken almost at once unless you immediately immerse it in a bowl of water acidulated with a little lemon juice or vinegar. And to keep the roots white, they should be blanched in what the French call *à blanc,* that is, water combined with lemon juice and flour in the proportion of 1 tablespoon flour and 1 teaspoon lemon juice for each cup of water.

Unfortunately, no such device will work with beets, whose characteristic red color must be conserved in other ways. To prevent beets from fading (or bleeding, as it is literally called) they should not usually be peeled before being cooked; nor should their root ends be cut or their tops closely trimmed. Although the beets can be baked successfully (in fact, they are almost always sold prebaked this way in France), they are more easily simmered until tender in lightly salted water. Plunged at once into cold water their tightly protective skins slip off as easily as gloves.

On occasion, other techniques are used to cook beets in soups, particularly in Russian borscht, perhaps the most inspired dish ever devised with the roots. In my recipe for Ukrainian borscht on page 289, I peel and grate the beets, as many Russian cooks do, before cooking them. But the trick is to compensate for the inevitable loss of the cooked beets color by grating a raw beet into a little cold water and straining the brilliant red beet juice into the completed borscht. This device suffuses the soup with a deep red glow, which is especially dramatic when borscht is served cold with a rosette of white sour cream floating on top.

If I can say nothing else about our canned beets (and thankfully I can with truth, say more) their brilliant ruby color remains constant however they are treated. If the canned beets lack the vigorous taste of the freshly cooked beet, they yet have much to recommend them. And their uses are virtually limitless. Tiny whole beets can be marinated in a vinaigrette sauce or in dill-flavored sour cream or yoghurt, speared on picks, and served as colorful cocktail accompaniments. Slightly larger beets can be gently hollowed out and filled with freshly grated or slivered horseradish root and used as a spectacular and original garnish for boiled beef; and if you want to serve beets as a salad, you can stuff them with minced hard-cooked eggs moistened with tarragon-flavored mayonnaise or, in moments of extravagance, with red or black caviar mixed with a bit of grated onion and sour cream.

There are many other edible roots that can be presented cold with great effect and some require no precooking at all. Celeriac, for example, known in the United States as celery knob (not the root of our table celery but another variety altogether) is more often than not merely peeled, cut into baton-like strips, and marinated in a mayonnaise heavily laced with mustard and lemon juice. I deplore the American, and often the French, practice of blanching the strips before marinating them. For my taste, the crisp texture of the root is destroyed. *Céleri-rave rémoulade,* as this celebrated hors d'oeuvre is called throughout France and in French restaurants all over the world, is an exceedingly simple preparation to make. Moreover, celeriac, although it is not generally recognized, is available in many of our markets throughout the year. This gnarled, knobby root is also delicious cooked and can be prepared in any of my recipes that call for turnips. It is particularly effective puréed and combined with potatoes and served either alone or in a potato-based soup.

Perhaps the noblest fate that can befall an edible root is to find itself in an assortment of raw vegetables the French call *les crudités*. Always served as a first course in lieu of or part of hors d'oeuvres, *les crudités* consists typically of celery, scallions, small tomatoes, and tiny raw artichokes, the root vegetable family represented by bright orange carrots, small young turnips, and radishes, usually the globular red varieties but often the tapering white and black ones as well. And always, the radishes are accompanied by a bowl of cold sweet butter, a dab to be spread on each radish before it is sprinkled with salt and eaten. Your friends may be surprised when you serve them in this fashion, but I assure you they will be enchanted with them.

As a coda to my discussion of edible roots, I would like to add a few brief comments about ginger root. Although it is never cooked as a vegetable in its own right, it nonetheless, plays an important role in many of my recipes—notably the Indian ones—in this book. Fresh ginger root is exceedingly difficult to find in American markets except in those stores located in our Chinatowns or in greengrocers catering to a Japanese, Spanish, or Latin American clientele. The rather fiery and distinctive flavor of the fresh root is, of course, incomparable, but fortunately you can find adequate substitutes for it in many supermarkets throughout the United States. The best is the so-called dried cracked ginger, but don't confuse this product with dried whole ginger root, which is as hard and really almost as flavorless as concrete. As for the powdered ginger you can so easily buy in spice cans, it will not serve as an alternative for the fresh or cracked ginger I call for in my recipes. Its place belongs more properly in cakes, puddings, and similar baked dishes. You will notice that whenever I can't get fresh ginger, I suggest pulverizing "cracked ginger" with a mortar and pestle, a fairly arduous job, compounded by the fact that most of you don't own a mortar and pestle, equipment I think almost indispensable to a well-equipped kitchen. The electric blender will, however, pulverize the ginger successfully for your purposes, but don't pulverize the root too finely, it should retain a bit of its fibrous texture.

Braised Lamb with Turnips or Rutabagas

serves 6

3–6 tablespoons vegetable oil
3 pounds boned shoulder of lamb, *trimmed of all fat and cut into 2-inch chunks*
1 teaspoon salt
Freshly ground black pepper
1 teaspoon dried thyme, *crumbled*
3 level tablespoons flour
1 medium onion, *to make ¾ cup finely chopped*
Peeled garlic cloves, *enough to make 2 teaspoons finely chopped*
3 cups fresh or canned beef stock: *if you use the concentrated canned type, dilute it with an equal amount of water*

1 large ripe tomato, *peeled and coarsely chopped*
A bouquet consisting of 2 celery stalks with their leaves, 6 sprigs parsley, 1 well-washed leek (white part only), *tied together with string*
2 pounds white turnips or firm rutabagas, *trimmed, peeled, and cut into 2-inch chunks or cut into olive shapes*
Fresh parsley (preferably the flat-leaf Italian variety), *enough to make 2 tablespoons finely chopped*

Preheat the oven to 500 degrees.

Pour 3 tablespoons of the oil into a 10- to 12-inch heavy skillet and set it over high heat. When the oil is very hot but not smoking, add 5 or 6 pieces of the lamb and brown them well for about 3 or 4 minutes on each side. As the pieces reach their proper color, transfer them with tongs to a 6- to 8-quart heavy casserole, replacing them in the skillet with the fresh pieces of lamb. Add more oil to the skillet, if necessary, as you proceed. When all the lamb has been browned and safely deposited in the casserole, remove the skillet from the heat and set it aside.

Sprinkle the lamb with the salt, a few grindings of black pepper, and the thyme. With a large wooden spoon, toss the lamb and seasonings together. Then add the flour. Toss the meat again with the spoon until all traces of the flour disappear. The mixture at this point will be fairly gummy. Slide the casserole into the center of the oven and let the lamb brown for about 10 or 15 minutes, stirring the meat every few minutes or so until all trace of gumminess disappears. Watch carefully for any signs of burning and lower the oven heat if necessary.

Meanwhile, reheat the oil remaining in the skillet over moderate heat and add the onions and garlic. Stirring frequently, cook them for about 8 to 10 minutes, or until the onions are soft and lightly colored. Pour in the stock and, stirring constantly, bring it to a boil. Then pour the entire contents of the skillet over the lamb in the casserole. Stir in the chopped tomato, submerge the bouquet in the center of the lamb mixture, and lower the oven heat to 325 degrees. Cover the casserole tightly and braise the lamb in the center of the oven for about 1 hour, until the lamb is fairly tender but not quite done.

Pour the entire contents of the casserole into a large sieve set over a bowl. When all the juices have drained through, let them settle for a few minutes, and with a large spoon, skim off and discard as much fat from its surface as you can. Return the juices to the casserole and taste it. If it seems lacking in flavor and its consistency is too thin, bring it to a rapid boil over high heat and let it boil briskly uncovered until it is as thick and flavorful as you like it, then return the lamb to the casserole and discard the bouquet.

Now add the turnips or rutabagas (the rutabagas blanched for 5 to 8 minutes, if you prefer, as described on page 278; if the rutabagas are young and small, don't bother). Stir the turnips (or rutabagas) into the sauce and stir the mixture gently until the vegetables are well moistened. Then cover the casserole, return it to the oven, and braise for about 25 minutes. Test for tenderness after about 15 minutes, and if the vegetables are done to your taste (ideally, they should not overcook and become pulpy), the dish is done. Sprinkle the top of the lamb with the parsley and serve directly from the casserole. Or if you prefer, you may arrange the lamb in the center of a large platter, then surround it with the turnips, pour the sauce over the top, and sprinkle with the parsley.

Braised Turnips

serves 4

1½ pounds white turnips, *trimmed and peeled; if small, left whole; if large, cut into quarters or olive-shaped cylinders*
1½ cups chicken stock, fresh or canned: *if you use the con-*

centrated canned type, dilute it with an equal amount of water
3 tablespoons butter
½ teaspoon salt
Freshly ground black pepper

Drop the turnips into enough rapidly boiling water to cover them by about 1 inch. Boil steadily over high heat, uncovered, for about 6 minutes, then drain the turnips in a sieve and set them aside.

Pour 1 cup of the chicken stock into a 10- to 12-inch enamel or stainless-steel skillet and bring it to a boil over high heat. Add the butter, ½ teaspoon salt (more or less, depending upon the saltiness of the stock), and a few grindings of pepper. When the butter has dissolved completely, add the reserved, blanched turnips. The stock should come about ¾ inch up the sides of the turnips; if it doesn't, add the remaining (or even more of the) stock, or some water—if you have used all the stock you have on hand. Lower the heat, cover the skillet, and simmer the turnips for 10 to 20 minutes (depending upon their size). Don't overcook them; when done, they should still be slightly resistant to the point of a small sharp knife.

To serve, transfer the turnips from the pan with a slotted spoon to a serving dish. Bring the remaining liquid to a boil over high heat and boil, uncovered, until the juices have cooked down to a thin, syrupy glaze. Pour it over the turnips and serve at once.

Braised and Glazed Carrots   *serves 4*

1 pound (approximately) carrots,
   each about 1 inch in diameter
   at their tops, *scraped and cut
   into 1½-inch lengths or
   trimmed into olive shapes
   (about 2 cups)*
½–1 cup chicken stock, fresh or
   canned: *if you use the concentrated canned type, dilute*

*it with an equal amount of
   water*
2 tablespoons butter
1 tablespoon sugar
¼ teaspoon salt
Mint leaves, *enough to make 1
   tablespoon finely cut, or*
   fresh parsley, *enough to make
   1 tablespoon finely chopped*

Pour the chicken stock into a 10- to 12-inch enamel or stainless-steel skillet equipped with a cover. Add the butter, sugar, and salt and, stirring constantly, bring to a boil. When the butter has dissolved, drop in the carrots. Turn them about in the liquid (it should come about a third of the way up the sides of the carrots; if it doesn't, add more liquid), moisten them on all sides, and cover the pan tightly. Lower the heat and simmer the carrots slowly for 20 to 30 minutes, sliding the pan back and forth over the heat so that the carrots roll around in the liquid on their own. Check the carrots occasionally to make sure the liquid has not entirely evaporated as they cook. If it has, add a couple of tablespoonfuls of stock, and cover the pan again.

When the carrots are tender but still slightly firm, remove the cover from the pan and raise the heat to high. Slide the pan back and forth again, rolling the carrots around until the remaining liquid has almost completely evaporated and coated the carrots with a brilliant syrupy glaze. Immediately transfer them to a serving dish, sprinkle them with the mint or parsley, and serve at once.

Flan des Carottes à la Flamande

makes a 10-inch tart

THE PASTRY

2 cups unsifted flour
8 tablespoons (¼ pound, 1 stick),
    butter, *chilled, cut into ¼-inch
    bits*

3 tablespoons lard or vegetable
    shortening, *chilled*
⅛ teaspoon salt
⅓ cup ice water

THE FILLING

About ¾ pound carrots, *scraped,
    to make 3 cups coarsely
    chopped*
3 tablespoons sugar and 1 table-
    spoon butter, softened, com-
    bined
Orange rind: *the orange peeled
    with a swivel-bladed vege-
    table peeler, then finely*

*chopped, enough to make 2
    tablespoons*
2 whole eggs plus 2 additional
    yolks
1½ cups heavy cream
¼ cup orange marmalade
2 tablespoons butter, *cut into
    tiny bits*

The Pastry:

Combine the flour, butter, lard (or shortening), and salt in a large chilled mixing bowl. With your thumbs and fingertips, rub the flour and fats together until they look like flakes of coarse meal. Now pour in the ice water all at once and, with your hands, toss the mixture about until you are able to gather it into a compact ball. If the dough seems crumbly, add a few more drops of cold water (not too much or the dough will be heavy) and mix again until the flour particles adhere. Dust the ball of dough with a handful of flour, wrap it in waxed paper or foil, and refrigerate for at least 3 hours or even overnight if you prefer.

When you are ready to roll it out, remove the dough from the re-frigerator and let it soften for about 10 minutes, or to the point at which your thumb poked into it leaves a distinct mark.

Flan des Carottes à la Flamande

Preheat the oven to 425 degrees.

Roll the dough on a lightly floured board into a circle about 13 to 14 inches in diameter. Drape it on your rolling pin and drop it slackly into a 10-inch false-bottomed buttered *quiche* pan (preferably, with fluted edges if you can find one). Press the pastry against the sides of the pan (don't stretch it at any point or it will shrink as it bakes) and into the fluted edges, then roll the pastry pin over the rim of the pan, pressing down hard to trim off the excess pastry. To hold the pastry in place, spread a sheet of lightly buttered aluminum foil across the pan and press it gently into the edges and against the sides of the pan. Bake in the middle of the oven for 10 minutes, then remove the foil; lower the heat to 375 degrees and bake for about 5 minutes more, or until lightly brown. The center of the pastry will probably begin to puff up after you remove the foil; simply pierce the pastry bubbles gently with the point of the knife to deflate them. Remove the tart from the oven and let it cool in its pan.

The Filling:

In a 2- or 3-quart saucepan combine the carrots and enough water to cover them by an inch and bring the water to a boil. Reduce the heat to low and simmer, covered, until the carrots are soft enough to be easily mashed against the side of the pan. Drain them thoroughly, and spread them out on paper toweling to remove any excess moisture. Then purée them through a food mill set over a bowl, or force them through a fine sieve with the back of a large spoon. Beat into the purée, the sugar-butter mixture and the chopped orange rind. In another bowl, beat the whole eggs and yolks together with a whisk only long enough to combine them, and slowly stir in the cream. Add the carrot purée, stir thoroughly, and taste for seasoning. You may prefer it sweeter; in that event, add a little more sugar.

Preheat the oven to 375 degrees.

With a pastry brush, evenly coat the bottom of the tart shell with the marmalade. Spoon in the cream and carrot mixture, and dot with the small bits of butter.

Place the tart pan on a cooky sheet or jelly-roll pan and bake the tart in the center of the oven for about 40 minutes, or until the filling is firm. Serve warm or at room temperature.

NOTE: You may, if you like, place concentric circles of thinly sliced oranges over the top of the tart before baking it. In that event, sprinkle the oranges with a tablespoon or so of sugar to give them a slight glaze.

English Parsnip Pie   *makes a 10-inch pie*

A partially baked 10-inch pastry shell (page 285)

3–4 pounds parsnips, *scraped, washed, and cut into 1-inch lengths*

2 tablespoons butter, *softened*

½ cup honey

Orange rind: *the orange peeled with a swivel-bladed vegetable peeler, then finely chopped, enough to make 2 tablespoons*

2 eggs, *lightly beaten*

½ teaspoon cinnamon

½ teaspoon mace

¼ teaspoon allspice

¼ teaspoon powdered cloves

1 teaspoon fresh, strained lemon juice

1 cup heavy cream

Put the parsnips in a 2- to 3-quart saucepan and add enough cold running water to cover them by 1 inch, then bring to a boil over high heat. Reduce the heat to moderate, half cover the pan, and simmer undisturbed until the parsnips are soft enough to be easily mashed against the sides of the pan. Drain them at once, pat them dry with paper toweling, then purée them through a food mill set over a large bowl, or force them through a fine sieve with the back of a large spoon. The parsnips should be quite smooth; if necessary, purée them twice. Measure 3 cupfuls of the purée (packed down) and place it in a large mixing bowl. (Any remaining purée may be put aside, seasoned to your taste, mixed with butter and a little cream, and served hot as a vegetable at another time.)

With a large spoon, beat into the purée the softened butter, the honey, orange rind, eggs, cinnamon, mace, allspice, cloves, and lemon juice, and continue to beat until the mixture is as smooth as you can get it. Taste for seasoning; it should be quite sweet and aromatic. Add more honey, if necessary.

Preheat the oven to 375 degrees.

Spoon the mixture into the previously baked pastry shell, smooth the top with a spatula, and spread a thin film of the remaining honey on top. Bake in the center of the oven for 50 to 60 minutes, or until the filling is quite firm and the top lightly browned. Unmold the pie as described on page 262. Cool to room temperature and serve with a pitcher of heavy cream.

NOTE: You may, if you like, roll out any leftover scraps of pastry into ⅛-inch-thick rectangles. Cut it into 10- to 12-inch strips about ½ inch wide and place them on top of the pie, crisscrossing them lattice-wise and pressing the ends securely to the rim of the shell. Paint the strips with a light coating of heavy cream before baking, to give it a light glaze. As for the primroses I describe on page 277, if there are any around, by all means dot the interslices of the pie with them. However, I can't, in all honesty, suggest that you eat them.

Marinated Deep-Fried Salsify Fritters

serves 4

THE BATTER

¾ cup lukewarm water
½ teaspon salt
1 cup flour, *sifted before measuring*

Vegetable oil
1 egg white

THE MARINADE

3 tablespoons fresh, strained lemon juice
½ cup olive oil or vegetable oil or a combination of both
¼ teaspoon salt

Freshly ground black pepper
1–1½ pounds salsify, *scraped and cut into strips 2 inches long and ½ inch wide*

Vegetable oil or melted shortening for frying

Ideally, the batter should be prepared about 2 hours before you plan to use it, allowed to rest uncovered and unrefrigerated, but you can use it at once if you must. Combine the water, salt, and oil in a mixing bowl, then add the flour, stirring it in little by little, and continue to stir until a smooth paste is formed.

Meanwhile, in another bowl, combine the lemon juice, oil, salt, and a few grindings of pepper and beat them with a small whisk until they are thoroughly combined. Drop the salsify into it immediately after peeling and cutting it, and toss the strips about to coat them thoroughly. Let them marinate at room temperature for 2 hours, or until you are ready to deep fry them.

Just before frying, beat the egg white until it forms stiff peaks on the beater when it is lifted out of the bowl. Fold it into the batter.

Pour at least 3 inches of oil or melted shortening into a deep fryer and heat it until it reaches a temperature of 375 degrees on a deep-frying thermometer. Remove the salsify pieces from the marinade and drain them on a double thickness of paper toweling. Pat them dry, drop them all into the bowl of batter, and stir them about to coat them thoroughly. Then, with a slotted spoon, drop a large tablespoon of them into the hot fat. Stir them about gently with the spoon as they fry, until they are golden brown. Remove them to paper toweling to drain while you fry the remaining salsify similarly. They may be kept warm in a 200-degree oven for 5 or 10 minutes if they must, but the salsify will be at their best if served at once.

NOTE: Parsnips, peeled and cut in the same fashion as the salsify, may be marinated, battered, and deep fried in precisely the same fashion as the salsify. And it might be an interesting variation, on some occasions, to use the beer batter on page 139 instead of the one given here.

Ukrainian Borscht

serves 8–10

6 tablespoons (¾ stick) butter
3 medium onions, *to make 2 cups finely chopped*
Peeled garlic cloves, *enough to make 1 tablespoon finely chopped*

2 pounds (after stalks are removed) whole fresh beets, *peeled and grated on the coarse side of a grater, to make about 4 cups (packed down)*

Ukrainian Borscht

2 medium turnips, *peeled and coarsely grated*
1 medium celery root (celeriac) (if available), *peeled and grated*
1 medium parsley root (if available), *peeled and grated*
4 medium fresh, ripe tomatoes, *peeled and coarsely chopped, to make about 2 cups*
1 teaspoon sugar
2 teaspoons salt
Freshly ground black pepper
½ cup red wine vinegar
2½ quarts fresh or canned beef stock: *if you use canned concentrated type, dilute it with an equal amount of water*
2-pound head of green cabbage, washed, the leaves cut into approximately 2-inch squares, or shredded finely, if you prefer
1 pound boiling-type potatoes, *peeled and cut into 2-inch chunks, to make about 4 cups*
1 pound or more Kielbasa (Polish) or any other smoked sausage, *cut into ½-inch slices (optional)*
1 medium raw beet, *trimmed, peeled, and grated into 3 tablespoons cold water*
2 cups sour cream
Fresh dill leaves, *enough to make ¼ cup finely cut*

Melt the butter over high heat in a 4-quart heavy enamel or stainless-steel casserole. Before it begins to brown, add the onions and the garlic, lower the heat to moderate, and cook, stirring frequently, for 8 to 10 minutes, or until the onions are soft and barely colored. Stir in the 4 cups of grated beets, the turnips, celery root, parsley root, tomatoes, sugar, salt, freshly ground pepper, vinegar, and ½ quart (2 cups) of the beef stock. Bring to a boil, stirring constantly, then lower the heat and simmer undisturbed with the casserole partially covered for about 45 minutes.

Meanwhile, pour the remaining 2 quarts of stock into a 6-quart heavy enamel or stainless-steel casserole or soup pot, and bring it to a boil over high heat. Drop in the cabbage and potatoes, partially cover the pot, and lower the heat. Simmer the vegetables for about 15 minutes, or until the potatoes are almost but not quite tender.

When the beet mixture has simmered its allotted time, pour it into the simmering pot of cabbage and potatoes and add the sausage, if you intend to use it. Again, partially cover the pot, and simmer the soup for about 15 minutes. Then strain the water from the 3 tablespoons of beet-soaking water through a sieve directly into the soup to heighten its color. Taste for seasoning. It will undoubtedly need more salt and perhaps a few grindings of pepper.

Serve from a large, heated tureen and pass sour cream and dill in separate bowls to be added to the individual servings of soup at each diner's discretion.

Céleri-rave Rémoulade

CELERY ROOT SALAD WITH
MUSTARD MAYONNAISE   *serves 4*

1 cup freshly made mayonnaise or a good, unsweetened commercial mayonnaise
2 teaspoons prepared mustard, preferably Dijon or Düsseldorf mustard, but a good domestic brand will do almost as well
½ teaspoon dry mustard
1 teaspoon fresh, strained lemon juice

4–6 tablespoons heavy cream
Salt
Freshly ground black pepper
1½ pounds celery root (celeriac), *peeled, washed, dried, and cut into julienne strips about ⅛ inch thick and 1 inch long*
Fresh parsley (preferably the flat-leaf Italian variety), *enough to make 1 tablespoon finely chopped*

In a large mixing bowl, combine the mayonnaise, the prepared and powdered mustards, and the lemon juice. Beat the mayonnaise with a whisk until it has absorbed the mustards and lemon juice. Then thin it to a consistency fluid enough to run lazily off a spoon by beating the cream into it a tablespoon at a time. Depending upon the thickness of your mayonnaise, you may have to use less or even more than the amount of cream I have indicated above. Taste the sauce for seasoning and increase any of the seasoning ingredients to your taste. The mayonnaise should be tartly flavored and have unmistakable mustard overtones.

Add the celeriac, and with a wooden spoon, toss it with the mayonnaise until the strips are thoroughly coated. The salad may be served at once, sprinkled with the parsley, but it will have a finer flavor if it is allowed to rest at room temperature, covered with plastic wrap, for 1 hour or so.

Poached Celery Root with Lemon and Egg Sauce   *serves 4–6*

2½ pounds celery root (celeriac), *trimmed, peeled, and cut crosswise into ½-inch-wide slices*

2 cups cold water

1 teaspoon salt

6 teaspoons fresh, strained lemon juice: *4 for the blanching water and 2 for the sauce*

12 sprigs parsley (approximately) (preferably the flat-leaf Italian variety), *tied together with string*

1 level teaspoon flour mixed to a paste with 1 tablespoon cold water

1 large egg, *lightly beaten*

Fresh parsley (preferably the flat-leaf Italian variety), *enough to make 1 tablespoon finely chopped*

Drop the celery root slices into a 3-quart enamel or stainless-steel saucepan and pour the water over them. Stir in the salt, 4 teaspoons of the lemon juice, the bunch of parsley, and bring the water to a boil over high heat. Cover the pan, lower the heat, and simmer the celery root for about 20 minutes, or until it is quite tender but still slightly resistant to the point of a small sharp knife. Then discard the parsley, and with a slotted spoon, transfer the slices of celery root to a deep heated serving bowl. Cover the bowl loosely with foil to keep the celeriac warm while you quickly make the sauce.

With a rubber spatula, scrape the flour-and-water paste into the liquid remaining in the saucepan. Bring it to a boil over high heat, stirring the mixture constantly with a whisk until the flour dissolves and the sauce thickens lightly. Lower the heat. Combine the beaten egg with the remaining 2 teaspoons of lemon juice and whisk into it about 4 tablespoons of the simmering sauce. Then slowly pour the mixture into the sauce, whisking constantly. Simmer for a moment or two (don't let the sauce boil), taste for seasoning, and pour it over the waiting celeriac. Sprinkle the top with the chopped parsley and serve at once.

THE POTATO

tHe potato

Grubby and graceless, the potato is an unprepossessing object at best; and yet, it is perhaps the most important vegetable in the world today. It appears on our tables more frequently than any other vegetable. And not least among its virtues is the incredible number of ways it can be successfully prepared. Potatoes can be boiled, steamed, baked, broiled, sautéed, or fried, and, in knowing hands, can be transformed into hors d'oeuvres, soups, main dishes, side dishes, salads, and even desserts.

All of us accept the presence of the potato as if it had been with us always, but the fact is the potato was taken to Europe from South America as late as the sixteenth century, and it was a long time before resistance to using it as a food was overcome. For more than a century after the potato appeared in Europe, the plant itself, with its lovely foliage, was grown in English and Continental gardens merely as a botanical curiosity. By the end of the seventeenth century, however, the impoverished Irish, who were among the first to recognize the tuber's nutritional value, proceeded to cultivate it so assiduously that it soon became the most important crop of their country. But the wealthier classes of Europe would have none of it. They complained that the potato was unattractive, added no style to their tables, and had no culinary history. Their chefs, who should have known better, followed their lead and ignored it.

But the importance of the potato as a means of feeding people cheaply and easily could not be disregarded much longer. The reigning monarchs of France and Prussia prodded their agriculturists to investigation and experimentation, so that by the middle of the nineteenth century, over a hundred new potato varieties had been developed. And by this time, happily, the gifted chefs of France—and, to a lesser degree, of Germany—had come to their senses and began to create an important repertory of potato dishes, which has brought the vegetable to the culinary eminence it occupies in the Western world today.

In our time, potato research in America has been supported mainly by the U. S. Department of Agriculture. Its ambitious and successful programs have resulted in potatoes that are highly resistant to plant disease and have flavor and cooking qualities far superior to those of potatoes produced even as recently as ten years ago. Admirable as this is, it is also something of a mixed blessing, for it gives us too wide a range from which to choose. I have decided preferences in potatoes, but few household cooks know how to buy them—and finding the ones they like is more often a matter of luck than of decision.

There are at present over eighty varieties on the market, and even farmers have trouble telling them apart. Nor are their names of the potatoes much help. Perfect Peachblow, Quick Lunch, Up-to-Date, Mortgage Lifter, Early Epicure, and the like give us little indication of their characteristics or what to do with them. I must admit having seen on occasion bags of potatoes marked "Baking Potatoes"; but that is as far, apparently, as potato growers will go.

Few of us know that a potato's cooking quality is, in large part, determined by its starch content, or specific gravity, as agriculturists call it. You have probably noticed that potatoes with little starch tend when cooked to be dry and firm in texture, and those with large quantities of starch, loosely textured and mealy. It is these qualities that make a potato suitable for one purpose rather than another. A potato without sufficient starch will be dry and disappointing if baked; but the same potato will be perfect boiled. A boiled potato with too much starch will fall apart at the touch of a fork, and you might just as well mash it. In fact, potatoes high in starch make ideal mashed potatoes, light, airy, and almost soufflé-like in consistency.

A study by Cornell University some years ago reported that customers would pay considerably higher prices for packaged potatoes classified and labeled as suitable for boiling, baking, pan-frying, salad-making, and so on. When you consider that potatoes are the most important item on almost every vegetable stand, it is shocking to me, to say the least, how carelessly they are marketed. And I don't think it is enough to call them "boiling" or "baking" potatoes. Although the descriptions have some validity, I think they are far from precise. I have discovered, after countless experiments, that many disparate varieties can be used successfully for either of these purposes. When you go beyond the rudimentary processes of merely boiling and baking potatoes, your choice of particular potato types for more sophisticated dishes assumes greater importance. Too often, the wrong potato in a preparation brings about disaster. Pan-fried potato dishes, like cottage-fried, lyonnaise, O'Brien, and others in this category, can easily turn into unattractive, messy hashes as you have doubtlessly discovered to your dismay if the potatoes have too much starch. French-fried potatoes, on the other hand, must be made with starchy potatoes if they are to be crisp on the outside and moist within. And even starchier potatoes are required for *pommes soufflées,* that *tour de force* of French cooking in which potato oblongs are deep-fried twice and, by some mysterious alchemy, made to explode at the second frying into large, hollow, olive-shaped shells. As you will doubtlessly notice, I have decided to omit a recipe for this unusual dish; the incidence of failure is simply too great. Even skillful cooks I know who attempt them at home usually end up with a few bona fide souffléed potatoes but for all their honest efforts the rest inevitably flatten into plain old *pommes frites.* Although I have had some success with the dish when I come upon those special potatoes necessary to make them—those with a starch content of at least 80 per cent and aged to the point of granitic rigidity—I am firmly convinced that this undeniably spectacular potato dish more properly belongs on a restaurant menu. And as a further deterrent to your attempting them, despite the sanguine assurances of many otherwise reputable cookbook writers, many fine American restaurateurs I know reluctantly admit that failures in their kitchens occur with more regularity than they are publicly willing to say.

Unfortunately, until growers label and describe precisely the cooking characteristics of their potatoes, you must, if you care, test varieties on your own and decide which suit your purposes best. All present-day varieties, whatever else their differences, have two clearly apparent properties: their shapes and colors. They are either round or long, and their skins are brown (white, the growers call it), russet, or red. Knowing this doesn't solve the problem by any means, but at least it provides a point of departure. Many varieties, both round and long, are grown locally and seldom shipped more than a few hundred miles. It might be wise to familiarize yourself with some of the more interesting local potatoes and boil or bake a few of them before you use them in more elaborate dishes.

The two varieties that most nearly approach national distribution are easily recognized, and their cooking qualities are fairly well established. One is the round white Katahdin—thin-skinned, firm-fleshed, low in starch; the other is the long Russet Burbank, somewhat thicker-skinned, mealier, with a high starch content, and commonly known as the Idaho potato, whether it was grown in Idaho or not. Though some growers dispute it, others say that round potatoes tend to have less starch than the long ones do. Be that as it may, a notable exception to this notion is a long white California potato named, precisely for once, the California Long White. Grown in California since the turn of the century and often called the White Rose, the present-day Long White is an extraordinary tuber indeed, and it occupies a category all its own.

If a potato can in any circumstances be called handsome, it is surely the Long White. Its skin is parchment-thin, fawn color, sleek, and smooth, and the eyes, always a nuisance to peel when deep, are barely apparent. Californians proudly call the Long White an all-purpose potato, and although I think the claim is sweeping, it is at least partially true. Because of its unique consistency and its moderate starch content, the Long White may be boiled without losing its shape, mashed into an airy lightness, successfully pan-fried and even French-fried. On the demerit side, for those of you adventurous enough to attempt *pommes soufflées* despite my dire warnings, the Long White if it is aged may be used with only middling success; the Russet Burbank, because of its greater starch content, is really preferable. Baking the Long Whites is also disappointing; California's claims notwithstanding, I find the baked potatoes somewhat dry.

I think you should know, other considerations aside, that mature, or "old," potatoes, whatever their type, contain more starch than younger, or so-called new, potatoes. And new potatoes are not a special variety of the tuber family, as many of us assume, but are simply young potatoes of all types, dug before they have reached maturity. Unlike old potatoes, which are stored for varying lengths of time, new potatoes are shipped directly after being dug. As a consequence, their flavor is fresher and their price higher. But whatever their price, if you love new potatoes, they are more than worth it. What other hot potato dish can possibly compare with small, freshly cooked new potatoes (which by the way needn't necessarily be peeled) swimming in butter and sprinkled with freshly cut herbs? And served, I must add, the moment they are done.

No vegetable so quickly loses its flavor on standing than does a potato, however it is cooked. The deplorable restaurant practice of keeping potatoes warm for untold hours in a steam table and then serving them as freshly cooked is an affront to even the dullest palate. As for leftover potatoes, they should be thrown away. Using them can be justified only on economic grounds, never culinary ones. No matter how clever or skillful the cook, it is impossible to restore the bloom to a reheated potato.

But if recooking a potato is unfortunate, serving it cold is even worse. Stubborn and impenetrable, a cold potato resists absorbing any seasoning, however beguiling it is. Thus, potato salads made with cold potatoes have for me, at least, the flavor and texture of *papier-mâché*. Paradoxically a fresh potato salad is probably the uppermost height to which the lowly potato can aspire. An honest potato salad, be it American, French, or German, should always be prepared with freshly cooked potatoes. In France or Germany, an oval Dutch potato, low in starch and unusually firm in texture, is almost invariably used for salads. Many of our new potatoes, particularly the Long White, will do almost as well, though none seems to approach that characteristic waxiness typical of the Dutch type, unfortunately unavailable here.

Having chosen the firmest potato you can find, all you need do to make a perfect potato salad—really the simplest of dishes—is to slice the potatoes, fresh from the pot, and season and dress them while they are hot. Whatever the dressing—ideally, it should consist of salt, freshly ground pepper, vinegar, olive oil, and fresh herbs as you will see in my recipe on page 306—it will be thirstily absorbed by the warm, receptive potatoes and will mellow and flavor them as they cool. Mayonnaise, if you insist, can be added then. A fine potato salad such as this should never be chilled; it is at its best served at room temperature.

One of the most remarkable attributes of the potato is its ability to absorb and support any number of disparate flavors and still retain its character. Potato salads and simply cooked potato dishes have for me an innocence I find especially attractive. But the complex and extravagant dishes created by inspired cooks have their place, too.

Few Americans have eaten or even heard of the Francillon salad popular in France in the late 1800's. Its history is curious. First described in *Francillon*, a play by Alexandre Dumas fils, salad Francillon soon became the rage of Paris and was served everywhere. Whether

Monsieur Dumas invented it or not is unimportant, but its composition
is fascinating and original. Hot sliced potatoes, first cooked in bouillon
(not water), are marinated in champagne or dry white wine and combined with poached mussels. The potatoes and mussels are then
seasoned and dressed with oil, vinegar, chopped shallots, salt, pepper,
and aromatic herbs, arranged decoratively in a fine crystal bowl and
covered with thinly sliced truffles. This is hardly a potato salad to serve
on everyday occasions, even if one can afford it. My version on page
307 of this extravagant, almost Baroque concoction is a simpler one—
and you don't have to go into hock to make it.

The wildly expensive truffle has its place in other French potato
dishes, too, notably an extravagant version of the by now classic potatoes Anna. Whoever Anna was we shall never know; but she lent her
name, wittingly or not, to a most ingenious culinary construction and
thus perpetuated herself forever. In this dish, as it is made in France,
thinly sliced raw potatoes are arranged in a heavily buttered pan, the
slices slightly overlapping, so they form an orderly, scalloped design.
They are spread with softened butter, seasoned with salt and pepper,
then covered with sliced or chopped truffles. Upon this, another layer
of potatoes is similarly arranged and again buttered, seasoned, and
truffled. This procedure is continued until the pan is filled, whereupon
it is put in a hot oven until the potatoes are tender and the bottom
layer is a deep golden brown. Turned out, bottom layer uppermost,
potatoes Anna are indeed a dramatic sight to behold.

In France, in more opulent days, chefs carried this dish to such
lengths that they devised a special pan in which to cook it. This was a
deep baking cylinder with tightly fitting covers. Thus it was possible to
turn over the pan of potatoes when the bottom layer was brown and
brown the top layer, too. Needless to say, it is perfectly possible to duplicate the dish in an ordinary pan, and, of course, the truffles may be
omitted. But even better and more predictable is to make them in a
non-stick skillet on the top of the stove as I do on page 302. In this
procedure the name of the dish for mysterious reasons known only
to the French is called potatoes Annette.

But truffled or not, the potato has come a long way since its
unpropitious debut in Europe some four hundred years ago. During
that time, it has managed to overcome social rejection and culinary
neglect and has somehow emerged unscathed and triumphant as one
of the great, enduring vegetables of the world.

Shredded Potato Pancakes with Chives or Scallions

serves 4

4 medium baking potatoes, *peeled and covered with cold water*

Fresh chives, *enough to make 2 tablespoons finely cut* or use scallions (green tops only), *enough to make 2 tablespoons finely chopped*

3 teaspoons salt: *2 for the batter and 1 to sprinkle over the finished pancakes*

Freshly ground black pepper

3 tablespoons butter

3 tablespoons vegetable oil

One at a time, pat the potatoes dry with paper toweling and grate them on the shredding side of a grater into a large mixing bowl. Do not drain off the water that will accumulate around them. Quickly stir in the chives, or scallions, 2 teaspoons of the salt, and a few grindings of black pepper. (Cover them with plastic wrap, if they must wait. But if they are allowed to rest for more than 10 minutes or so they will turn an unpleasant brown.)

Combine the butter and oil in a 10- to 12-inch heavy skillet and set it over high heat. When the butter has melted completely and the fat begins to turn lightly brown, make the pancakes by dropping 2 tablespoons of the potatoes in 3 or 4 heaps into the pan, leaving about 2 inches between them. Gently flatten the mounds into thin cakes about 3 inches in diameter, and fry them over moderate heat for about 3 or 4 minutes on each side, turning them over gently with a large metal spatula. As they are done, remove them to paper toweling to drain. Proceed to shape, fry, and drain the remaining potatoes similarly. Serve at once, sprinkled with the remaining salt.

Potatoes Annette *serves 6*

6 medium baking potatoes,
   *peeled and sliced into
   uniform ⅛-inch-thick slices*
   (*6–8 cups*)
8 tablespoons (¼ pound, 1 stick)
   butter, *melted but not
   browned*

Salt
Freshly ground black pepper
Fresh parsley, *enough to make 2
   tablespoons finely chopped*

Almost indispensable to the preparation of this version of potatoes Annette is a heavy 8-inch frying pan (measured across the top) with a non-stick surface—and less imperatively, with sloping sides. Other pans of a similar size will do, of course, but the results will often be unpredictable; for the most part, the potatoes tend to stick to the bottom of an ordinary pan however much butter you use.

Peel the potatoes and drop them into a bowl of cold water as you proceed to prevent their darkening. A half hour or so before you plan to serve the potatoes, pour 2 tablespoons of the melted butter into the non-stick or other pan. One at a time, remove the potatoes from the water and pat them dry with paper toweling. Quickly slice them (with a potato slicer if you have one) into uniform ⅛-inch-thick slices. Without washing or drying the slices (their starch will help them to cling together as they cook), arrange them in concentric, overlapping layers on the bottom of the buttered pan. Sprinkle the layer liberally with salt, more discreetly with pepper, and dribble 1 tablespoon of the remaining butter over them. Add a similar layer of potatoes (you needn't be quite so fussy this time; the inner layers will be concealed when the finished potatoes are turned out), season them, and sprinkle with another tablespoon of butter, and continue layering the potatoes in this fashion until all the potatoes and butter are safely lodged in the pan. The potatoes will probably rise about ½ inch (more or less) above the top of the pan, but don't be concerned—this is as it should be.

Place the pan over moderate heat, and when you hear the butter beginning to sizzle, cover the pan, pressing the lid down firmly to force the potatoes into a compact cake. Continue to cook, covered, for about 5 minutes, then remove the cover and slide the potatoes gently back and forth over the range until the potato cake moves freely, indicating that the bottom has not begun to stick. (With the proper non-stick pan, there will be no such problem, and you can omit the sliding operation altogether.) Re-cover the pan, and lower the heat a bit, and continue to fry the potatoes for about 30 minutes, or until the bottom of the cake is a deep golden-brown (to make sure, peek under it by lifting one side with a spatula) and the top layer can be easily pierced with a fork.

To turn them out, place a circular serving platter, somewhat larger than the diameter of the pan, on top of the potatoes, and grasping the pan and plate firmly together, turn them over. If you have used the proper pan, the potatoes will come out easily. (If your pan is an ordinary one, some of the potatoes may still remain stuck to the bottom of the pan. In that event, simply remove them in one piece, if possible, and patch the section into place on the turned-out cake.) Sprinkle with parsley and serve at once.

NOTE: If you have used a non-stick pan, and are enterprising enough to try it, slide the potato cake, browned-side up back into the pan, raise the heat and brown the under side for about 5 minutes. Then slide it back on its platter, sprinkle it with parsley and serve at once.

Roesti Potatoes in the Swiss Manner

serves 6

6 medium baking potatoes, *washed and scrubbed, (6–8 cups potatoes after grating, as described below)*

8 tablespoons (¼ pound, 1 stick) butter, *melted but not browned*

Salt

Freshly ground black pepper

Fresh parsley, *enough to make 2 tablespoons finely chopped*

Roesti Potatoes in the Swiss Manner

In Switzerland, *roesti* potatoes—a rustic dish—is usually made with fully cooked, cold potatoes. I think my version superior to the original although it requires a little more effort to make.

Drop the unpeeled potatoes into a large pot filled with enough boiling water to cover the potatoes by at least 2 inches. Boil briskly, uncovered, for about 5 minutes, or until the point of a small sharp knife meets decided resistance upon being inserted about ¼ inch into a potato. Drain the potatoes immediately in a colander and let them become cool enough for you to handle them easily. Peel them while they are still warm, and either proceed to fry them in the manner I describe below or let them get completely cold. Because the potatoes are only partially cooked, they won't darken when peeled, as do uncooked potatoes, and will, moreover, suffer no loss of flavor.

About ½ hour before you plan to serve them, grate the potatoes into a small bowl on the shredding side of a stand-up grater; or if you are fortunate enough to own the special *roesti* grater traditionally used in Switzerland, use it instead. This grater is easy to manage because it can be laid flat across the bowl.

Pour 2 tablespoons of the melted butter into a heavy 8-inch skillet (measured across the top), preferably one with sloping sides and a non-stick surface. Spoon a 1-inch layer of the shredded potatoes into the pan and spread it out evenly with a spatula. Sprinkle the top liberally with salt and more discreetly with pepper, and dribble about 1 tablespoon of the remaining butter over it. Add a similar layer of potatoes, season them, sprinkle with another tablespoon of the butter, and continue layering the potatoes in this fashion until all the potatoes and butter are safely lodged in the pan. The potatoes will probably rise ½ inch or so above the top of the pan but don't be concerned—this is as it should be.

Place the pan over moderate heat and when you hear the butter beginning to sizzle, cover the pan, pressing the lid down firmly to force the potatoes into a compact cake. Continue to cook, covered, for about 5 minutes, then remove the cover and slide the pan gently back and forth over the range until the potato cake moves freely, indicating that the bottom has not begun to stick. (With a non-stick pan, there will be no such problem, and you can omit the sliding operation altogether.) Re-cover the pan, and continue to fry the potatoes for about 20 minutes, or until the bottom of the cake is deep golden-brown (to make sure, peek under it by lifting one side with a spatula) and the top layer is fully cooked.

To turn them out, place a circular serving platter, somewhat larger than the diameter of the pan, on top of the potatoes and grasping the pan and plate firmly together, turn them over. The potatoes will come out of the pan easily, brown side up. Serve at once, the top sprinkled lightly with the chopped parsley. Or if you are more daring, you can add 2 more tablespoons of melted butter to the empty pan, and slide the potatoes—browned-side down—back into the pan, raise the heat to high and brown the underside for about 5 minutes or so. When the bottom is as brown as you can get it without burning it, slide the cake out on to the platter, sprinkle it with parsley, and serve. Both methods are equally effective.

Broiled Potato Balls

serves 4–6

2 pounds baking potatoes (about 4 to 5 medium potatoes)
1 teaspoon salt
¼ teaspoon freshly ground black pepper
8 tablespoons (¼ pound, 1 stick)

butter, *melted but not browned*
Parsley, chives, or dill, *enough to make 2 tablespoons finely chopped*

Peel the potatoes, dropping them into a bowl of cold water as you proceed to prevent them from discoloring. Then, one by one, with the large end of a melon baller, scoop out balls and drop them back into the cold water. Don't fret too much about how perfect the balls are; indeed, the charm of this dish is the decorative look of the somewhat half and three-quarter moons many of the shapes achieve.

When you are ready to broil the potatoes, drain and dry them thoroughly with paper toweling or shake them in an old pillowcase. Add the potatoes to the melted butter in a pan and toss them about with a spoon until they are well coated. Stir in the salt and pepper, and then pour the potatoes—butter and all—into a baking dish large enough to hold them more or less in one layer, and slide them under the preheated broiler about 6 inches from the heat. Broil them for about 20 minutes in all, turning them about with a spoon every 5 minutes or so until each ball is a crusty golden brown without and moist within. Naturally, watch the potatoes carefully for any sign of burning, and regulate the heat or the baking pan's distance from the heat accordingly when the potatoes are done (taste one to make sure). Serve at once, sprinkled with chopped parsley, chives, or dill.

French Potato Salad   serves 4

2 pounds small new potatoes, all
    approximately the same size
4 tablespoons chicken stock, fresh
    or canned
2 teaspoons salt
1 teaspoon dry mustard
4 tablespoons wine vinegar
Freshly ground black pepper

½ cup olive oil
About 4 scallions, including 2
    inches of the green stems,
    to make ½ cup thinly sliced
Parsley (preferably the flat-leaf
    Italian variety), *enough to*
    make ¼ cup finely chopped

Scrub the potatoes under cold running water, then drop them into a large pan of boiling water (enough to cover them with about 2 inches) and boil them briskly, uncovered, until they can be easily pierced by the point of a small knife. (Don't overcook them, or the potatoes will fall apart after they are sliced.) Drain and peel them while they are still hot, holding them one at a time in a towel if necessary to protect your hands. Slice them immediately into ¼- to ½-inch rounds and place them in a large mixing bowl. Pour in the chicken stock and stir the potatoes about gently with a rubber spatula until they are thoroughly moistened.

Mix together in a small bowl the salt, mustard, vinegar, and a few gratings of black pepper. Pour it over the still-warm potatoes and again toss them gently to coat them well. Then let them rest for about 10 minutes, stirring once or twice. Now, little by little, stir in the olive oil. Add the scallions and parsley, mix well (gently again, to prevent the potatoes from crumbling), and taste for seasoning. The potatoes will doubtless need more salt. Serve at room temperature. If you must refrigerate any leftover salad to be used at another time, be certain to remove it from the refrigerator at least 2 hours before serving time.

NOTE: The French will occasionally add about ½ cup of coarsely diced celery to the salad for added texture. Do so, if you wish.

My Version of Monsieur Dumas' Salad Francillon

serves 4

The recipe for the French potato salad on page 306, *substituting 1 tablespoon or more of cut, fresh tarragon or finely cut chives for the scallions*
The recipe for moules marinière on page 241, *the mussels removed from their shells*
2 or 3 canned black truffles, *cut into thin slices or into strips 1 inch long and about ¼ inch wide*

When the potato salad has cooled, gently fold in as many of the mussels as you wish. Scatter the truffles on top. Do not add champagne or white wine à la Monsieur Dumas (a deplorable idea, I think); drink it with the salad instead.

NOTE: If you have trouble finding fresh mussels, experiment with some of the canned imported varieties now available, but not the smoked ones. Canned mussels can hardly be compared with the fresh mollusks, but you may find a brand you like. Marinating them in a little white wine for 10 minutes or so will improve them somewhat.

Vichysoisse with Sorrel, Watercress, or Spinach   *serves 6–8*

4 tablespoons (½ stick) butter
Enough leeks, white parts only,
    to make 3 cups thinly sliced
2 scallions, including 2 inches of
    the green stems, *to make ¼*
    cup thinly sliced
1 small celery stalk, *to make ¼*
    cup thinly sliced
⅛ teaspoon curry powder
About 1½ pounds baking potatoes,
    peeled and cut into 1-inch
    chunks, to make 4 cups
6–8 cups chicken stock, fresh or

canned: *if you are using the*
    concentrated canned type,
    dilute it with an equal amount
    of water
Sorrel, watercress, or spinach
    leaves, *enough to make 1 cup*
    (tightly packed) chopped
2 teaspoons salt
A pinch of white pepper
1 to 1½ cups heavy cream
Fresh chives, *enough to make 2*
    tablespoons finely cut, or thin
    rounds of green scallion tops

Over moderate heat, melt the butter in a 3- to 4-quart saucepan, and add the leeks (thoroughly washed to remove any hidden pockets of sand before slicing), the scallions, celery, and the curry powder. Stirring almost constantly, simmer the vegetables in the butter for 3 to 4 minutes without letting them brown, then add the potatoes and 6 cups of the chicken stock. Bring it to a rapid boil, then immediately lower the heat, partially cover the pan, and simmer for 40 to 50 minutes, or until the potatoes and vegetables are soft enough to be easily mashed against the sides of the pan. Now stir in the sorrel (or the watercress or spinach), and simmer for 10 minutes more, then purée the entire mixture through a food mill set over a bowl (or force the mixture through a sieve with the back of a large spoon). In any case, you will have to do the operation twice or even three times to achieve a fairly smooth purée. (Do not, under any circumstances, use the electric blender—it will make the purée much too smooth and your *vichysoisse* will have no character at all.) Stir in the salt, the pinch of white pepper, and 1 cup of the heavy cream. Chill thoroughly. The *vichysoisse* will probably thicken considerably when cold; thin it with more cream if necessary and taste again for seasoning. Cold has the curious effect of deadening the flavor of food and you will probably find that the *vichysoisse* needs more salt. Serve in chilled, small soup plates or bouillon cups, and sprinkle the top of each serving with a few chives or scallion tops.

Portuguese Kale Soup

CALDO VERDE   *serves 4–6*

½ pound fresh kale or 1 ten-ounce package frozen kale, *thoroughly defrosted and finely shredded (about 1 cup)*

3 or 4 medium baking potatoes, *peeled and coarsely diced (about 4 cups)*

6 cups chicken or beef stock, fresh or canned: *if you use the canned concentrated type, dilute it with an equal amount of water,* or use 6 cups of water in place of the stock as the Portuguese do

1 teaspoon salt

Freshly ground black pepper

½ pound linguica, chorizo, or other highly seasoned garlic-flavored smoked pork sausage

3 tablespoons olive oil

Wash the kale (if you are using the fresh) thoroughly under cold running water. Trim away any bruised or blemished spots and strip the leaves from the stems. Discard the stems and bunch the leaves firmly together. Lay the bunch sideways on a chopping board, and with a large sharp knife, shred them as finely as possible.

Combine the potatoes, stock or water, salt, and a liberal grinding of black pepper in a heavy 3- or 4-quart casserole or pot and bring to a boil over high heat. Partially cover the pot and cook fairly briskly for about 15 minutes, or until the potatoes are soft enough to be easily mashed against the sides of the pan. With a slotted spoon, transfer the potatoes to a bowl and mash them to a smooth purée with a fork or potato masher.

While the soup base is cooking place the sausages in a small skillet and prick them in 2 or 3 places with the point of a small sharp knife. Add enough water to cover them completely and bring to a boil over

Portuguese Kale Soup

high heat. Lower the heat and simmer, uncovered, for 15 minutes. Drain the sausages on paper toweling and slice them into rounds about ¼ inch thick. Set them aside to drain on paper toweling.

Return the purée to the casserole and bring the liquid to a boil again, stirring constantly, until the mixture is fairly smooth. Add the kale and olive oil, stir once or twice and cook, uncovered, for 3 or 4 minutes. Now drop in the drained sausage rounds and simmer for 1 or 2 minutes to heat them through. Taste for seasoning and serve at once.

dried legumes

dried legumes

Dried beans, peas, and lentils, of all colors, were among the very first foods cultivated by man and for thousands of years have been an indispensable part of his daily diet; and with good reason. Dried legumes have advantages few other natural foods possess. Virtually indestructable, they can be stored for long periods of time, even years, and still be edible; they keep well after they are cooked; contain large quantities of thiamin, iron, and protein, and to cap it all, they taste good. So good, in fact, that some of the world's greatest dishes are dependent upon them.

Of the numerous legumes available to us in the United States today, dried beans are by far the most popular. We not only use them to the virtual exclusion of other dried legumes but produce them in a profusion and variety few other countries can match. And our beans have names almost as delightfully vivid as their colors: pintos, black turtles, cranberries, white and red kidneys, black eye, yellow eye, and chick peas, marrow, Navy, Great Northern, Mexican pinks, and others too numerous to list.

Not all of these beans, of course, are available all of the time, but I assure you, a more than adequate selection of them can always be found on the shelves of most supermarkets today. Exposed to this array of legumes, those of you unfamiliar with beans can scarcely be blamed for not knowing how to go about choosing or cooking them. It may console you to learn, as I have, however, that all dried beans, whether you know their names or not, are cooked, at least initially, in exactly the same way but for different periods of time. String beans, green peas, fresh lima beans, and other fresh legumes become dried legumes by being allowed literally to wither and dry on the vine. Not unreasonably, then, like most dehydrated foods, they must be soaked or cooked in some sort of liquid to make them edible once more.

Directions on packaged beans and in many cookbooks as well will tell you authoritatively to soak beans overnight before cooking them, but the procedure is really a waste of time. As far back as fifteen years ago, research by the indefatigable United States Department of Agriculture developed a more effective and time saving method: dried beans are covered with liquid, brought to a boil, allowed to boil steadily for two minutes, and then removed from the heat to soak for an hour, the beans are then slowly simmered—not boiled, which would make them burst—in their soaking liquid until done. Although the Agriculture Department oddly enough doesn't suggest it, you may, if you prefer as many European cooks do, not soak the beans at all but simply allow more cooking time. Remember that the older and consequently more dehydrated the beans, the longer it will take for them to reabsorb their lost moisture.

It might be helpful for you to know that dried legumes are chameleon-like and will almost instantly take on the flavor of the liquid in which you cook them. Inevitably, beans—soaked or not—simmered in a good chicken, beef, ham, or even game stock are far more interesting than those cooked in water alone. And when you combine the beans with aromatic vegetables, braised or roast meats, fowl or game, they become the heady stuff from which the great bean dishes of the world are created. And surely one of the greatest is the French *cassoulet*. (A definitive recipe for it—and the one I like the best, appears in an earlier book of mine, *Michael Field's Cooking School*. It is so good, in fact, that I see no reason at this point to try to improve on it.)

Despite its fabled reputation as one of the pinnacles of French Provincial cooking, the *cassoulet* is essentially a rough, hearty, and unpretentious country dish, named after the capacious earthenware casserole, the *cassole d'Issel*, in which it is usually baked. Its ingredients vary according to the particular region in which it is made. But whatever the variety of cooked meats it may contain—mutton, pork, sausage, duck, partridge, or roast or preserved goose—one thing is certain: it is the white beans flavored with goose fat, onions, garlic, and tomatoes that give the *cassoulet* its true character. Anatole France loved the *cassoulet* and called it a "stupendous" dish, which I think indeed it is.

Many of us feel as intensely about our native baked beans as the French do about their *cassoulets*. In Boston, in fact, I find it almost an obsession. Even today, in certain conservative circles, the Puritan ritual of serving baked beans for Saturday-night supper and then again for Sunday breakfast is inviolate tradition (see my recipe on page 318). But don't assume, as many Americans do, that all our baked beans are Boston baked beans. Other sections of the country have their own proud ways with beans, and, for my taste, bake them even better. In the Northwest where beans are consumed in far greater amounts than they are in the East, I have heard Boston baked beans derisively described as effete. Many Southwesterners I know disdain the brown sugar, molasses, and/or maple syrup used by New England cooks to sweeten their beans, and for their own beans prefer to use lustier seasonings like tomatoes, garlic, and chilies, as the Mexicans do. My version of this rather fiery dish appears on page 319.

It is surely because the Mexicans have cooked with beans for so long (some of their best bean dishes can be traced as far back as the Aztecs) that they continue to use them with such authority, ingenuity, and skill. Among the extraordinary bean dishes they make, the most popular (and the one so many of us have taken to our hearts) is *frijoles refritos,* or, literally, refried beans. I assure you, it is a considerably more enticing creation than its prosaic name might indicate. To make it, cooked red or white kidney beans, pintos or pink beans (and more often than not, canned beans of any type), are lightly fried in lard or bacon fat, then gently mashed, fried again with more fat and seasoned with salt, pepper, and chili powder. As I suggest in my recipe for it on page 322, you can serve the beans the way the Mexicans do, either unadorned or garnished copiously with chopped onions, shredded Monterey jack, or Cheddar cheese, or even cold sour cream. In Mexico I discovered that *frijoles refritos* are eaten on every possible occasion: at breakfast, lunch, or dinner, and, in addition, used as a filling for tortillas, tacos, tostados, or in, or on, anything else that will hold them.

No other nationalities carry their passion for beans as far as the Mexicans do, but a few come fairly close to it. The Arabs make a cold, highly flavored bean purée called *hummus,* which they serve at most meals and on social occasions. Prepared by mashing cold, cooked chick peas to a purée with sesame paste (called *taheeni*) then flavoring it with chopped garlic, scallions, lemon juice, and salt, *hummus* is spread lavishly on disks of Arabian bread and consumed without any more ado.

As I present it to you on page 323, you can serve it American fashion as it were, as a mysterious cocktail accompaniment (no one can ever tell what it is), spread on crisp sesame-seed crackers in lieu of the Arabian bread.

Few, if any, substitutions are necessary to make authentic Italian bean dishes, because ingredients for them are available almost everywhere. You can make Tuscan beans and tunafish, one of the great specialities of Florence, by simply opening a couple of cans. Although the fat white beans of Tuscany, freshly cooked of course, are used in Italy to make the dish, any of our canned white beans do almost as well. Drained of their rather obnoxious canning liquid, then washed, and dried, they are first tossed with a little olive oil, lemon juice, parsley, and, if you like, chopped onions, before being garnished with chunks of canned tunafish. You can also make a more elaborate version of this dish, one usually found in Italy's grander restaurants. Simply substitute caviar, fresh if you can afford it, for the tunafish. Curious as these combinations may sound to those of you who have never tried them, they are remarkable creations combining the subtlety, strength, and the elusive piquancy so typical of Italian cooking at its best.

Other dried legumes such as yellow and green split peas and lentils are used throughout the world with similar inventiveness. Most of us in the United States, know them primarily as soup ingredients, and although split peas and lentils do indeed make incomparable soups, as you will see if you make my lentil and split pea soups on pages 329 and 330, the truth of the matter is that these tiny but robust legumes can also be superb vegetables in their own right.

If you love to cook (and I assume you do if you have read this far), you should find dried split peas and lentils especially attractive; they never require soaking (many inaccurate package instructions notwithstanding), and, moreover, you will find they take comparatively little time to cook. A cup of split peas, for example, or lentils (most recipes for them, including my own, are interchangeable), gently simmered in 3 cups of water or stock will produce at least 2 cups of the cooked legumes in 30 or 40 minutes. Puréed, you can then enrich them with butter and a little heavy cream and serve them alone or in place of a so-called starchy vegetable.

You needn't necessarily purée them. Split peas, of course, however slowly and carefully you cook them, will disintegrate to some degree when they are boiled. The best way to ensure their remaining whole is not to boil them at all but to bake them. For predictable results—and I

insist that predictability in cooking can almost always be counted on if
you know what you're doing—first drop the split peas into boiling water
or stock (in the proportion of 1¾ cups of liquid for each cup of peas),
boil for two minutes then let the peas soak, off the heat, for a half hour.
Cover them tightly and bake undisturbed for about thirty minutes in a
preheated 350-degree oven. The split peas will thirstily absorb all their
soaking liquid and emerge at the end of their cooking time tender and
still intact. These full-flavored, mealy morsels offer you any number of
interesting possibilities, not the least of which is to serve them simply as
they are, seasoned with salt and freshly ground pepper with, perhaps,
a few tablespoons of lightly browned butter poured over them. Needless to say, the peas would fare equally well anointed with the *jus,* as
the French call it, of a roast of beef, a leg of lamb, or a roast chicken or
duck.

You can cook most lentils in the same manner as split peas, but you
don't have to bake them in order to retain their tiny, disklike shapes. If
you simmer them gently on top of the stove and don't allow them to
overcook, they will seldom fall apart. For this reason, whole lentils are
particularly successful as salads, particularly my lentil salad mimosa on
page 326. The possibilities, of course, for varying the seasoning in my
recipe and others of its type and combining them with ingredients other
than the ones I suggest are endless.

The same might be said of other dried legumes. With the wealth of
dried beans, split peas, and lentils to choose from, there is no longer any
reason to yearn wistfully for a *cassoulet* in Carcassonne, *hummus* in
Arabia, or *frijoles refritos* in Mexico. It is easier than you think to make
them yourself.

Boston Baked Beans
serves 8–10

2 pounds (4 cups) dried pea
    beans or Great Northern
    beans
3–4 quarts cold water
1 large onion, *to make 1 cup*
    finely chopped
2 tablespoons tomato paste
2 tablespoons cider vinegar
2 teaspoons dry mustard
A pinch of powdered cloves
½ cup dark molasses

2 teaspoons salt
1 teaspoon freshly ground black
    pepper
1½ cups dark brown sugar: *1 cup*
    for the seasoning mixture
    and ½ cup for the topping
½ pound lean, mildly cured salt
    pork, *cut into 2-inch cubes,*
    then washed under cold
    water to remove any salt
    encrustations

Put the beans in a sieve and run cold water over them until the water draining out runs clear. Transfer the drained beans to a 4-quart heavy casserole and cover them with 3 quarts of cold water (the water should rise above the beans by about 3 inches; add more if necessary). Over high heat, bring the beans to a boil, uncovered, and let them boil rapidly for about 2 minutes. Remove the scum from the surface of the water with a large spoon and let the beans soak in the hot water—off the heat—for 1 hour. Then, without any more ado, bring the casserole back to the boil, lower the heat, partially cover the casserole, and simmer the beans for about ½ hour. Adjust the heat so that the simmering water barely ripples. When the beans have simmered their allotted time, drain them through a sieve set over a large bowl, and save the cooking water. Return the beans to the casserole.

Preheat the oven to 250 degrees.

Pour 2 cups of the reserved bean water into a mixing bowl. Stir in the onions, tomato paste, vinegar, mustard, cloves, molasses, salt, pepper, and 1 cup of the brown sugar, and continue to stir until the ingredients are thoroughly combined. Pour the entire mixture over the beans, add the salt-pork cubes, and with a large spoon gently mix the ingredients together.

Cover tightly and bake in the center of the oven for 7 or 8 hours. It might be well for you to check the beans after the fourth hour or so. If all the liquid has cooked away (most unlikely), pour in another cup of the bean liquid, cover again, and return the casserole to the oven.

After the beans have cooked 7 to 8 hours, remove the cover, and sprinkle the surface of the beans evenly with the remaining ½ cup of brown sugar. Bake the beans, uncovered, for another ½ hour (or even longer) until the sugar has melted to a light glaze and the liquid in the casserole has completely evaporated. Serve directly from the casserole with slices of buttered Boston brown bread, if you can find it.

Baked Beans of the Southwest   serves 8–10

2 pounds (4 cups) pea beans or
    Great Northern beans
3–4 quarts cold water
6-ounce can concentrated tomato
    paste
2 teaspoons chili powder
2 large canned hot green chilies,
    drained and finely chopped
2 teaspoons dry mustard
¼ cup red wine vinegar

1 tablespoon salt
Peeled garlic cloves, *enough to*
    make 2 teaspoons finely
    chopped
3 medium onions, *peeled*
¾–1 pound salt pork, *cut into*
    1-inch cubes, rind left on, and
    washed under cold running
    water to remove any salt
    encrustations

Put the beans in a sieve and run cold water over them until the draining water runs clear. Transfer the drained beans to a 4-quart heavy casserole, and cover them with 3 quarts cold water (the water should rise above the beans by about 3 inches; add more if necessary). Over high heat, bring the beans to a boil, uncovered, and let them boil rapidly for about 2 minutes. Remove the scum from the surface of the water with a large spoon and let the beans soak in the hot water—off the heat —for 1 hour. Then without any more ado, bring the casserole back to the boil, lower the heat, partially cover the casserole, and simmer the beans for about ½ hour. Adjust the heat so that the simmering water barely ripples. When the beans have simmered their allotted time, drain them through a sieve set over a large bowl, and save the cooking water. Return the beans to the casserole.

Preheat the oven to 250 degrees.

Measure 4 cups of the bean water into a small bowl and with a small whisk, stir into it the tomato paste, chili powder, chopped green chilies, mustard, vinegar, salt, and garlic. Whisk vigorously until the ingredients are thoroughly combined, then pour it over the beans in the waiting casserole. Stir gently with a large spoon; the liquid should come barely to the top of the beans. Add a little more of the bean water if it doesn't. Now push the onions under the beans and scatter the pieces of salt pork, rind-sides up, on top. Push them down into the beans a bit but only to the point where the rinds peek through the surface.

Bring the liquid in the casserole to a boil on top of the stove, then seal the top with heavy-duty foil and crimp the edges to secure it to the rim of the pot. Put the cover over the foil, making the casserole airtight, and bake, undisturbed, in the middle of the oven for 2 hours. I know it is a nuisance, but you would now do well to undo the whole apparatus and see if the liquid has cooked away. There should be about half as much now as when you started; if there is less, add another cup of the bean water, re-cover the casserole as before, and cook for another hour. You may now remove the cover and foil once and for all, and bake the exposed beans for another half hour or so until the pork rind is brown and the beans absolutely tender but not falling apart.

You can serve them at once, or simply remove the casserole from the heat, put it aside, and reheat it again (covered this time) in a 350-degree oven for 20 minutes or so when you are ready to serve them.

White Beans with
Tomatoes and Garlic   *serves 4*

1½ cups (¾ pound) dried white kidney, marrow, or Navy beans, or use 3 cups drained   canned cannellini or other white beans
2 tablespoons olive oil

White Beans with Tomatoes and Garlic

Peeled garlic cloves, *enough to make 1 teaspoon finely chopped*

½ teaspoon dried sage leaves, *crumbled,* or use a generous pinch of powdered sage

1 tablespoon dried basil, *crumbled*

2 large tomatoes, *peeled, seeded,* and coarsely chopped (*page 109*)

½ teaspoon salt

Freshly ground black pepper

1 tablespoon red or white vinegar

Parsley (preferably the flat-leaf Italian variety), *enough to make 2 tablespoons finely chopped*

Wash the dried beans (if you are using them) in a colander set under cold running water until the water draining out runs clear. Then drop them into a 3- or 4-quart heavy pot and pour in enough cold water to cover them by 2 inches. Bring the water to a turbulent boil and boil briskly for precisely 2 minutes. Immediately remove the pot from the heat and let the beans soak, uncovered, for 1 hour. Again bring the water to a boil. Lower the heat, partially cover the pot, and let the beans simmer, undisturbed, for 1½ hours, or until they are tender but intact. (The beans should be well covered with water throughout their cooking period; if necessary, add more water from time to time.) Drain and spread them out in a single layer, more or less, on double thicknesses of paper toweling. Gently pat them dry with other paper toweling. (Canned beans need no cooking, but it is imperative that they be thoroughly drained of their unpleasant canning liquid, then placed in a colander and washed under cold running water until the water draining out runs clear.)

Pour the olive oil into the pot and set it over moderate heat. When the oil is fairly hot, add the garlic, dried sage, and dried basil and, stirring constantly, cook for about 15 seconds. Watch it carefully; the garlic must not burn. Add the tomatoes, beans, salt, and a few grindings of black pepper. Mix together gently but thoroughly, lower the heat as much as possible, partially cover the pot, and simmer the beans for about 10 minutes, or until they are heated through and have absorbed the flavor of the sauce.

Stir in the vinegar and taste for seasoning. The beans will doubtless need more salt and pepper, and perhaps a little more vinegar. Pour the beans and their sauce into a large serving bowl, sprinkle with parsley, and serve at once.

Frijoles Refritos

REFRIED BEANS   *serves 4–6*

2 cups (1 pound) dried pink
   beans or dried red kidney
   beans
3 medium ripe fresh tomatoes,
   peeled and finely chopped
   (*about 1 cup*), or use 1 cup
   thoroughly drained, then
   chopped canned tomatoes:
   ½ cup for cooking with the
   beans and ½ cup for the
   frying mixture
1 cup (1 large) finely chopped
   onion: *½ cup for cooking with*
   the beans and ½ cup for the
   frying mixture

1 teaspoon finely chopped garlic:
   ½ teaspoon for cooking with
   the beans and ½ teaspoon for
   the frying mixture
2 teaspoons chili powder
1½ teaspoons salt
Freshly ground black pepper
6 cups cold water
8 tablespoons (½ cup) lard: *1*
   tablespoon for cooking the
   beans and the remaining
   lard for frying them

Wash the beans in a colander under cold running water until the water draining out runs clear. Then, in a heavy 4- or 5-quart casserole, combine the beans, ½ cup of the tomatoes, ½ cup of the onions, ½ teaspoon of the garlic, all the chili powder, the salt, and a liberal grinding of black pepper. Pour in the water and bring to a boil, uncovered, over high heat. Partially cover the casserole, lower the heat, and stir in 1 tablespoon of the lard. Simmer, stirring occasionally, for 1½ to 2 hours, or until the beans are soft enough to be easily mashed against the side of the casserole. Then pour the entire contents of the pot into a large sieve and let any liquid the beans have not absorbed, drain off.

In a heavy 12-inch skillet, melt 2 tablespoons of the remaining lard over high heat. When it is quite hot but not smoking, add the remaining ½ cup of onions and ½ teaspoon of garlic. Reduce the heat to moderate and, stirring constantly, fry for about 5 minutes, or until the onions are soft and transparent but not brown. Stir in the remaining ½ cup of tomatoes and simmer the mixture for 2 or 3 minutes more.

Now fry the beans. Add about ½ cup of the drained beans to the skillet. Still over moderate heat, mash and pound the beans vigorously with a long-handled flat potato masher (or lacking that, a fork or the back of a large spoon) until they are fairly smooth. Then stir in another tablespoon of lard, another ½ cup of the beans, mash them, then continue frying as before. If the beans appear to be sticking at any point, lower the heat. Proceed to add the beans and lard, in similar amounts, mashing them after each addition until all the beans and lard have become a fairly smooth purée. If, for some reason, the beans are too moist (they should be fairly dry), raise the heat, and stirring constantly cook until most of the excess moisture has evaporated. Alternatively, if the beans are too dry, stir in a tablespoon or so more of the lard and simmer slowly for a few minutes more or so. In either case, taste the beans for seasoning and lift its flavor, if you think it necessary, with more salt and freshly ground black pepper.

Transfer the beans to a large, heated serving bowl and serve at once. You might accompany them, if you like, with individual bowls of coarsely chopped red onions, shredded Monterey jack cheese, and sour cream—any or all to be used to garnish the beans to the taste of each diner.

NOTE: Needless to say, you can make the *frijoles refritos* hours ahead and reheat them before you serve them. In effect, they can be refried almost endlessly, using more lard whenever necessary to keep the beans from becoming too dry.

Hummus   *makes about 3 cups*

2 cups (1-pound 4-ounce can)
   drained canned chick peas
   (garbanzos)
¼ cup fresh, strained lemon juice
3 medium garlic cloves, *peeled
   and finely chopped*
1 teaspoon salt
Freshly ground black pepper

½–1 cup olive oil
Fresh mint leaves, *enough to
   make 2 tablespoons finely cut,*
   or use fresh parsley (preferably the flat-leaf Italian
   variety), *enough to make 2
   tablespoons finely chopped*

Drain the chick peas in a sieve under cold running water until the water draining out runs clear. Then spread the chick peas out in one layer, more or less, on a double thickness of paper toweling and gently pat them dry with another paper towel.

To make the *hummus* in a blender (the simplest way), combine the chick peas, lemon juice, garlic, salt, a few grindings of pepper, and ½ cup of the oil in the blender jar. Blend at high speed for about 30 seconds. Then stop the machine, scrape down the sides with a rubber spatula, and blend again, this time pouring in sufficient oil to make a purée thick enough to barely hold its shape in a spoon. Taste for seasoning, and add more salt and lemon juice if the *hummus* seems too bland for your taste. *Hummus,* in Arab countries at least, always has a fairly piquant flavor.

(To make *hummus* by hand, force the chick peas and garlic through a sieve with the back of a large spoon or purée in a food mill. Stir in the lemon juice, salt, and a few grindings of pepper, then beat in enough of the oil to give the purée enough body to hold its shape in a spoon. Taste for seasoning.)

Serve the *hummus* in a bowl or shape it into a mound on a small platter. In either case, sprinkle it with the mint or parsley. Traditionally, *hummus* is spread on flat Arab or Syrian bread. If you can find it, by all means serve it. If not, use sesame crackers in its place.

White Bean Salad with Tunafish in the Italian Manner

FAGIOLI TOSCANI COL TONNO   *serves 4–6*

1½ cups (¾ pound) dried white kidney, marrow, or Navy beans, or use 3 cups drained canned cannellini beans

THE DRESSING

½ cup olive oil
2 tablespoons fresh, strained lemon juice
½ teaspoon salt

Freshly ground black pepper
About 2 scallions, including 2 or 3 inches of their green tops, *to make ¼ cup finely chopped*

7-ounce can tunafish (preferably the imported dark meat type, canned in olive oil), *thoroughly drained and divided into 4 to 6 portions*

Fresh parsley (preferably the flat-leaf Italian variety), *enough to make 2 tablespoons finely chopped*
4–6 lemon wedges

Wash the dried beans (if you are using them) in a colander under cold running water until the water draining out runs clear. Then drop the beans into a 3- to 4-quart heavy pot and pour in enough cold water to cover them by about 2 inches. Bring the water to a turbulent boil, and boil briskly for precisely 2 minutes. Immediately remove the pot from the heat and let the beans soak, uncovered, for 1 hour. Again bring the water to a boil. Lower the heat, partially cover the pot, and let the beans simmer for 1½ hours, or until they are tender but still intact. (The beans should be well covered with water throughout their cooking period; if necessary, add more water from time to time.) Drain and spread them in a single layer, more or less, on a double thickness of paper toweling. Gently pat them dry with other paper toweling. (Canned beans need no cooking, but it is imperative that they be thoroughly drained of their unpleasant canning liquid, then placed in a colander and washed under cold running water until the water draining out runs clear.)

The Dressing:

Pour the oil, lemon juice, salt, and a few grindings of pepper into a large mixing bowl and beat them with a small whisk to combine thoroughly. Add the beans (still warm, preferably—naturally, the canned beans will be cold) and toss them about gently with a large spoon until each bean is thoroughly moistened with the dressing. Then stir in the scallions, and set the beans aside, unrefrigerated, to absorb as much of the flavor of the dressing as possible. Although the beans may be topped with the tunafish and served directly after they are cooked, a 2- or 3-hour wait will improve their flavor immensely.

Just before serving the beans, taste them for seasoning. You will doubtless notice that the beans (if they have been allowed to rest) will have absorbed their flavorings to an astonishing degree. Consequently, they will need more salt, pepper, or even a little more lemon juice.

To serve, place a mound of the beans on individual salad plates, arrange the tunafish on top, and sprinkle with parsley. Garnish each serving with a lemon wedge.

NOTE: Similar amounts of black caviar, fresh or pressed, may be used in place of the tunafish.

Lentil Salad Mimosa

serves 4–6

2 cups (1 pound) lentils	2 teaspoons salt

THE DRESSING

4 tablespoons wine vinegar	*make ½ cup finely chopped*
1 teaspoon salt	Peeled garlic cloves, *enough to*
Freshly ground black pepper	*make 1 teaspoon finely*
6 tablespoons olive oil	*chopped (optional)*
About 4 scallions, including 2	2 eggs, *hard-cooked, cooled, and*
inches of the green stems, *to*	*peeled*

Pour the lentils into a colander and wash them under cold running water until the water draining out runs clear. In a 4-quart pot or casserole, cover the lentils with 2 quarts of cold water. Add 2 teaspoons of salt and bring to a rapid boil over high heat. Then lower the heat, partially cover the pot, and simmer the lentils anywhere from 15 to 30 minutes. Test them periodically after 15 minutes. When done they should still be intact, slightly firm but tender. Remember, this is not to be a purée but a salad. When the lentils have reached the point of tenderness you desire, drain them immediately and run cold water over them to cool more quickly. Spread them out, in one layer on a double thickness of paper toweling and gently pat them dry. Transfer them to a large serving bowl.

The Dressing:

Sprinkle the lentils with the vinegar, salt, and a few grindings of black pepper. Stir with a wooden fork, and be careful not to mash the lentils any more than you have to. Then stir in the oil, 1 tablespoon at a time, and, finally, the scallions and garlic.

Cut the shelled eggs in half and separate the whites from the yolks. Chop the whites coarsely into the lentils and let the mixture rest at room temperature for at least 1 hour, then taste it. By then the seasonings will have been absorbed and you will be able to judge better how much more salt, pepper, and even vinegar it may need. The lentil salad may be served in individual portions, in which event, arrange them in mounds on lettuce leaves, and sprinkle each portion with a little of the egg yolks rubbed through a coarse sieve. Or sprinkle the yolks over the bowl of lentils and serve them at the table.

Red Kidney Bean Salad

serves 6–8

1½ cups (about ¾ pound) dried red kidney beans, or use 3 cups drained canned red kidney beans

THE DRESSING

½ cup olive oil or ½ cup vegetable oil or a combination of both in whatever proportions you like
3 tablespoons red wine vinegar
1 teaspoon salt
Freshly ground black pepper
About 8 scallions, including 2 or 3 inches of their green tops, *to make 1 cup finely chopped*
1 green pepper, *to make ½ cup finely chopped*
Peeled garlic clove, *enough to make ½ teaspoon finely chopped*
Parsley, *enough to make ¼ cup finely chopped*

Wash the dried beans (if you are using them) in a colander under cold running water until the water draining out runs clear. Then drop them into a 3- or 4-quart heavy pot and pour in enough cold water to cover them by about 2 inches. Bring the water to a turbulent boil, and boil briskly for precisely 2 minutes. Immediately remove the pot from the heat and let the beans soak, uncovered, in the hot water for 1 hour. Again bring the beans to a boil. Lower the heat as much as possible, partially cover the pot, and let the beans simmer for 1½ to 2 hours, or until they are tender but still intact. (The beans should be well covered with water throughout their cooking period; if necessary, add more water from time to time.) Drain them through a colander and spread them out in a single layer, more or less, on a double thickness of paper toweling. Gently pat them dry with other paper toweling. (Canned beans need no cooking but it is imperative that they be thoroughly drained of their unpleasant canning liquid, placed in a colander, and washed thoroughly under cold running water until the water draining out runs clear. Spread them out on paper toweling as described above, pat them dry and put them aside.)

The Dressing:

Pour the oil, vinegar, salt, and a few grindings of pepper into a large salad bowl, ideally made of glass or ceramic, and beat them briskly with a small whisk to combine them thoroughly. Add the beans (still warm, preferably—naturally, the canned beans will be cold), and toss them about gently with a large spoon until each bean is thoroughly moistened with the dressing. Then stir in the scallions, green pepper, and garlic, and set the beans aside, unrefrigerated, to absorb as much of the flavor of the dressing and vegetables as possible. Although the salad may be served directly after you make it, a 2- or 3-hour wait will improve its flavor immensely.

Just before serving, taste the beans for seasoning. You will doubtless notice that the beans (if they have been allowed to rest) will have absorbed their flavorings to an astonishing degree. Consequently, they will need more salt, pepper, and perhaps even a little more vinegar. Stir in any or all of these additional seasonings to your taste, sprinkle the salad with the parsley and serve.

NOTE: Like most bean salads of this type, this salad is at its best served at room temperature.

Lentil Soup with Scallions

serves 6–8

2 cups (1 pound) lentils
¼ pound lean, mildly cured salt
    pork in one piece
8–10 cups chicken stock, fresh or
    canned: *if you use the con-
    centrated canned type, dilute
    it with an equal amount of
    water*
1 large onion, *peeled and cut in
    half,* or 2 medium onions,
    peeled and left whole
2 medium carrots, *scraped and
    trimmed,* 2 large celery stalks
    with their leaves, and 1 me-
    dium bay leaf, *tied together
    with string*

2 tablespoons butter
A bunch of scallions, including 2
    or 3 inches of their green
    tops, *to make ¾ cup thinly
    sliced*
2 level tablespoons flour
2 teaspoons cider vinegar
Salt
Freshly ground black pepper
Fresh dill leaves, *enough to make
    2 tablespoons finely cut,* or
    fresh parsley, *enough to make
    2 tablespoons finely chopped*
    (optional)

Place the lentils in a sieve and wash them under cold running water until the water draining out runs clear. Then pour them into a 6-quart heavy enamel or stainless-steel casserole or soup pot, add the piece of salt pork, and pour in 8 cups of the chicken stock. Add the onions and the bundle of carrots, celery stalks, and the bay leaf and, stirring occasionally, bring the soup to a boil over high heat. Partially cover the pot, lower the heat, and simmer for about 30 minutes, or until the lentils are tender but still intact.

Meanwhile, melt the butter in a 6- to 8-inch frying pan over moderate heat. Add the scallions, stir them about a bit, and cook slowly for approximately 5 minutes, or until they wilt. Don't let them brown. Now stir in the flour to make a *roux* and, stirring constantly, cook for about 2 minutes. Let the *roux* brown ever so slightly but watch carefully lest it burn.

When the lentils are done, ladle about a cupful of the lentil liquid into the *roux* and stir thoroughly with a whisk until the *roux* dissolves completely. It will become fairly thick. Pour this mixture into the simmering soup, stirring constantly, and scraping in any residue left in the frying pan with the aid of a rubber spatula. Stirring occasionally, simmer the soup, partially covered, for another 10 minutes or so.

Now, with tongs, remove and discard the onions, carrots, celery, and bay leaf. Stir in the vinegar. If the soup is too thick for your taste (personally, I rather like it that way), stir in as much of the extra stock you still have at hand. Salt and pepper the soup to your taste, then pour it into a large tureen and serve. Sprinkle each portion with a little chopped fresh dill or parsley, if you like.

NOTE: If you have any soup left over, refrigerate it and serve it again another time. It will keep quite well for a couple of days, and you may prefer to purée it the second time around. In that case, force the lentils through a food mill or a sieve set over its pot and heat thoroughly. Again, if the soup is too thick for your taste (in this case, it usually is, for mine), thin it with as much stock as you prefer. Serve sprinkled with either of the suggested chopped herbs.

Yellow Split Pea Soup with Salt Pork in the Swedish Manner

serves 4–6

2 cups (1 pound) dried yellow split peas

4–6 cups chicken stock, fresh or canned: *if you use the concentrated canned type, dilute it with an equal amount of water*

1 large onion, *to make 1 cup finely chopped*

1 pound mildly cured, very lean salt pork, *rind removed but the pork left in one piece*

1 teaspoon dried marjoram leaves, *crumbled*

½ teaspoon dried thyme, *crumbled*

Freshly ground black pepper

Salt

Wash the peas in a colander under cold running water until the water draining out runs clear. Then, in a 4- to 5-quart heavy casserole, combine the peas, 4 cups of the stock, the chopped onions, salt pork, marjoram, thyme, and a few grindings of black pepper. Bring to a turbulent boil over high heat, partially cover the casserole, and lower the heat. Simmer, stirring occasionally, for anywhere from 40 minutes to 1 hour, or until the peas have begun to disintegrate and are soft enough to mash. If at any point, the soup becomes too thick, thin it by adding as much additional stock as you like.

Taste for seasoning and add salt and pepper to your taste. To serve, first remove the salt pork from the casserole and cut it into slices about ¼ inch thick. It might be wise at this point to taste it. If the pork is too salty, discard it; if it is the mildly cured pork it should be, return it to the casserole, simmer the soup for a few more minutes, and serve directly from the casserole into individual soup plates with or without a slice of the pork placed in the center of each serving.

NOTE: The soup can, of course, be made hours before you plan to serve it and then slowly reheated. It usually thickens as it stands (especially if it has been refrigerated). Thin it with more stock if necessary, remembering that, traditionally, this pea soup should be fairly thick. If you prefer, you may purée it through a food mill or, with the back of a large spoon force it through a fine or medium sieve set over a bowl. Then return the purée to the casserole and, stirring constantly, bring it almost to a boil over moderate heat before serving.

Chilled Green Split Pea Soup with Mint

serves 6–8

2 cups (1 pound) dried green split peas
6 cups chicken stock, fresh or canned: *if you use the concentrated canned type, dilute it with an equal amount of water*
1 large onion, *to make 1 cup finely chopped*
1 celery stalk, *to make ½ cup finely chopped*
Fresh mint leaves, *enough to make 1 cup finely cut (packed down)*

1 small bay leaf   A pinch of white pepper
½–1 cup heavy cream   6–8 sprigs fresh mint
Salt

Wash the peas in a colander under cold running water until the water draining out runs clear. Then in a 4- to 5-quart heavy casserole, combine the peas, stock, onions, celery, mint leaves, bay leaf, salt and pepper. Bring to a turbulent boil over high heat, partially cover the casserole, and lower the heat. Simmer, stirring occasionally, for anywhere from 1 to 1½ hours, or until the peas have almost completely disintegrated and can be easily mashed against the sides of the casserole with a fork.

Remove the bay leaf, and purée the soup through the finest disk of a food mill set over a bowl, or force it through a fine sieve with the back of a spoon. Stir in ½ cup of the cream, taste for seasoning, and let the soup cool to room temperature. Then cover the bowl with plastic wrap and refrigerate until thoroughly chilled.

The soup will thicken considerably as it chills. Thin it with as much of the remaining cream (or even more) as you think it needs— it should not be too dense; taste for seasoning again, since chilling will have dulled its flavor, and serve in chilled soup plates. Garnish each serving with a sprig of mint.

Black Bean Soup   *serves 8–10*

2 cups (1 pound) dried black   3 or 4 eggs, *hard-cooked, then*
   turtle beans   *coarsely chopped*
10 cups cold water   Salt
1 large onion, *to make 1 cup*   Freshly ground black pepper
   finely chopped   1 lemon, *cut crosswise into paper-*
2 celery stalks with leaves, *to*   *thin slices and all seeds re-*
   make 1 cup finely chopped   *moved with the point of a*
1 small bay leaf   *small knife*
3 smoked ham hocks (pigs' feet)   6–8 small parsley sprigs
1–2 tablespoons red wine vinegar

Wash the beans under cold running water until the water draining out runs clear. Bring the water to a turbulent boil in a 4- to 5-quart heavy casserole, then add the beans, onions, celery, bay leaf, and ham hocks. Let the water return to the boil, stirring constantly. Partially cover the pot, lower the heat, and simmer the beans for about 3 hours, or until they are tender enough to be crushed easily with a spoon.

Remove and discard the ham hocks and bay leaf. Then purée the soup through the finest disk of a food mill or, with the back of a large spoon, force the soup and beans through a fine sieve set over a bowl. If the soup is too thick for your taste, thin with more water, adding it by the tablespoon until it reaches the consistency you like.

Immediately before serving, stir in 1 tablespoon of vinegar (or more, if you like the flavor) and gently stir in the chopped eggs. Taste for seasoning and add as much salt and freshly ground pepper as you think it needs. Serve directly from the casserole or from a tureen into individual soup bowls, float a slice of lemon on each and top with a sprig of parsley.

NUTS

NUTS

Like so many of the products I have been discussing, nuts get very short shrift in the culinary repertoire of this country. They seem to be used primarily as something to nibble or as a relish at Thanksgiving or Christmas, and, of course, they have made their way into desserts. But why not make more interesting use of them in other, more important dishes as so many other countries have? We certainly can't use the excuse that shelling them is too arduous a task; all the popular nuts—almonds, walnuts, peanuts, pistachios—are sold pre-shelled now and come safely vacuum-packed.

Perhaps almonds, more than any other nuts, are beginning to break into main-course dishes. They are particularly rewarding to cook with because their subtle yet pervasive flavor accommodates itself to other foods without overpowering them. Most of the almonds that we use now are grown in California, but for years we imported them from Spain. Spaniards have cooked with nuts for centuries, serving them fried and salted, as *tapas* or tidbits before dinner; stirring them whole into their *paellas* and other rice dishes; pounding them to a paste for their sauces; or turning them into any number of exquisite confections and desserts. I am certain that it must have been those inspired Spanish cooks who first garnished their dishes with cooked vegetables and sautéed fish and meats with slivered almonds browned in butter, although we now, somewhat imprecisely, use the French word *amandine* to describe them.

As for walnuts, the only American dish I can think of which features them is that rather appalling concoction of celery, apples, and walnuts literally doused in mayonnaise, known as Waldorf salad. Perhaps we have been scared off from more important recipes because a number of them require green walnuts—that is, walnuts in which the nut meats are soft, milky, and barely formed. Unless you have a walnut tree growing in your back yard, you are not likely to be able to obtain this precious ingredient in order to make such delicacies as pickled walnuts, walnut catsup, and walnut wine. But for less esoteric dishes, our ripe native walnuts do exceedingly well and are unsurpassed in flavor. The recipe I have for *turator*—a Turkish sauce made with walnuts or hazelnuts and used on shellfish—works as well with our walnuts as it does with the unripe walnuts usually called for.

But the fact is that walnuts—in cooking, at least—are generally at their best when finely ground and used in soufflés, nut rolls, and those ephemeral nut cakes known as *torten*. Despite the supposedly treacherous behavior of *torten*, the truth of the matter is that any cook who can make a simple sponge cake can make a *torte*. The only significant difference in their preparation is that the flour in the sponge cake is replaced in the *torte* by ground walnuts mixed with a proportionate amount (usually half) of bread crumbs.

The manner in which walnuts are ground (or almonds, hazelnuts, or pecans—any of which may be used for *torten*) determines the success or failure of these and similar baked preparations, as you will see when you make my walnut roll on page 343. The electric blender, as seductive a timesaver as it is, should never be used to grind the nuts—it makes them too oily. A hand-operated Mouli grater is far better. This inexpensive little gadget cuts the nuts into tiny dry particles, light and powdery enough to rise with the cake as it bakes and give it its characteristic soufflé-like texture.

Crushed, oily nuts have a purpose, too. Peanut butter, that unequivocally American invention, is nothing more than roasted peanuts crushed into a purée, with a little extra oil. Present-day commercial peanut butters leave much to be desired and you can make a much better version quite easily in your blender (see my recipe on page 345).

Similarly, other nuts can be turned into butters. The oilier nuts, like walnuts, filberts, macadamias, and cashews, work particularly well. And each butter, whatever the nut you use, can be flavored with a different herb or condiment to your taste. In Provence, an intensely flavored walnut butter is made by pounding the nuts with garlic in a mortar, moistening the paste with a little olive oil, and seasoning it with herbs and cayenne. (This can more easily be made in a blender.) When it is spread on squares of toasted bread and accompanied by a glass of red wine, this is an unusual hors d'oeuvre indeed. And then there is, of course, the famous *pesto* which I've discussed on page 89 (recipe, page 111).

Perhaps the only nut that cannot be made into a butter is the chestnut, because it contains more carbohydrate than fat. But as a compensation, its many uses in cooking far exceed those of other nuts. Peeling forty or fifty chestnuts, I will admit candidly, is not a task to embark upon lightly. And if you are short on time you can scarcely be blamed for using the canned nuts. But peeling fresh chestnuts is really worth the effort. All you need—besides the time—are a few pounds of the best-quality chestnuts (that is, heavy nuts with tight-fitting skins), a pot of boiling water, and a small sharp knife. After cutting a small gash across each chestnut, cook them in boiling water for about two minutes. Turn off the heat and, while the nuts are still hot, peel them, three or four at a time. Usually the stubborn inside skins will come away with the shell; but when they don't, pare them off with your knife.

Cooking chestnuts, you will doubtlessly be pleased to know, is easier than peeling them. To serve them as a vegetable, simmer them until tender in a celery-flavored chicken, beef, or game stock. Then purée them with a little butter and cream as a classic accompaniment to roast turkey, goose, and game. Whole chestnuts cooked in this fashion can be added to thick vegetable soups, or combined with other cooked vegetables, such as Brussels sprouts, onions, mushrooms, carrots, or braised cabbage.

For desserts, chestnuts enter a somewhat more exalted sphere. The peeled nuts are first cooked in sweetened milk or water, usually flavored with a large piece of vanilla bean. Drained, they can then be transformed into anything from the simplest of flavored purées to *marrons glacés,* those preserved delicacies most familiar to us in their expensive bottled state. *Marrons glacés* are much too difficult to make at home, but even if you are a novice cook you can turn fresh or canned chestnut purée into any number of attractive desserts.

One of the most impressive is *mont blanc.* Chestnut purée is forced through a ricer into a sugared ring mold. The thin, vermicelli-like strands, as they fall lightly into the mold, intertwine to form a fragile, latticed ring. When the ring is gently unmolded, its center is filled with a snowy-white cone of whipped cream, which gives the dessert its name.

You can also present these same ingredients more simply: spoon the purée into a sherbet glass and top it with whipped cream. Often, this version of the dessert is garnished with thin shavings of bittersweet chocolate; but, untraditional as it is, shredded coconut may be used instead.

Most of us consider fresh coconuts little more than mildly exotic curiosities. When we need coconut for any purpose, packaged coconut does well enough for our layer cakes, cream pies, and the sliced-orange–and–shredded-coconut dessert known as ambrosia. But fresh coconut, because it is not quite as sweet as the packaged variety, is preferable in curries, whether the coconut meat is cooked with the curry itself or is served with it as a condiment. If only for these curries—and their variety is surprising, as you will see if you read the following chapter (pages 353–72)—it is worth trying to find a fresh coconut and literally coming to grips with it.

A coconut has three so-called eyes, one somewhat soft and the others firm. Pierce the soft area and one hard area with an ice pick or screwdriver (you may need a hammer to help you through the hard eye), and perch the inverted coconut on the mouth of a glass or cup. When all the milk has drained through, bake the nut in a preheated 400-degree oven for about fifteen minutes; then wrap it in a towel, and split its shell with a few sharp blows of a hammer. While the coconut is still hot, pare off its brown inner skin with a swivel-bladed vegetable peeler, and grate, shred, or cut the meat into chunks, for whatever purpose you plan to use it.

No such problem will confront you with the diminutive nuts called pignolias, or pine nuts. These creamy-white kernels are always sold unencumbered by any shell or skin and are, consequently, the easiest of all nuts to use. Although I find that they are scarcely known to most American household cooks, pignolias have been for centuries one of the staple ingredients of most Mediterranean and Middle Eastern cuisines. In this country we are more apt to find them in health-food stores (vegetarians have long known of the nut's immense nutritional value) or in groceries carrying imported foods, although recently they seem to be more generally available.

Pignolias can be used in everything from pasta sauces to pastries. As a start, try adding them, lightly toasted or briefly sautéed in butter, to a rice pilaf or a creamy risotto, as the Armenians and Italians do. And for a Spanish touch, fry the pignolias in a little olive oil, and stir them, with a few raisins, into freshly cooked spinach, as I do in my recipe for this dish on page 350. For those of us who love these nuts, it is strange, to say the least, that the pignolias available here are imported from Italy and Spain, while the enormous numbers of pignolia-producing pine trees in the United States are largely ignored.

We must, of course, import those nuts not grown on our shores, notably Brazil, cashew, macadamia, and pistachio nuts. Of the four, the pistachio is unquestionably the most valuable in cooking. Its extraordinary color and flavor make it one of the most dramatic of nuts to cook with, and the French exploit it to the full. As one of many examples, they stud a loin of pork, before roasting it, with forty or fifty of the shelled nuts, and intersect them with tiny slivers of garlic. (My recipe for this unusual dish appears on page 345.) Served hot or cold, this is a dish one does not easily forget. And in their amazing boned-and-stuffed poultry constructions called *galantines,* French chefs arrange pistachio nuts and pieces of black truffle in the stuffing in such a way that when the *galantine* is cut, each slice has the appearance of a brilliant mosaic.

Cooking with nuts in the United States today makes little creative use of the immense variety of native and imported nuts available to us. I think you would do well to explore the culinary traditions of countries that do. I hope the following recipes will convince you to use the immense variety of nuts available to us in far more creative ways.

Hazelnut (or Walnut) Sauce for Cold Shellfish in the Turkish Manner

makes about 1½ cups

1 cup hazelnuts (or walnuts), *pulverized with a mortar and pestle or ground with a Mouli grater (do not use a blender)*

½ cup (loosely packed) soft, fresh bread crumbs, *made in a blender or shredded very finely with a fork*

¼ teaspoon hot red-pepper flakes, *pulverized with a mortar and pestle or in a bowl with the back of a spoon*

Peeled garlic cloves, *enough to make 2 teaspoons very finely chopped*

¼ teaspoon imported sweet paprika

¼ teaspoon salt

2 tablespoons olive oil

3 tablespoons red wine vinegar

2 tablespoons freshly made mayonnaise or an equal amount of a good, unsweetened commercial mayonnaise

The cooked tomalley and coral, if any, of a lobster (optional)

4–6 tablespoons cold water

In a large mixing bowl, combine the ground nuts, bread crumbs, pepper flakes, garlic, paprika, salt, olive oil, and vinegar. With a large spoon, beat together vigorously until the ingredients are virtually indistinguishable from each other. Stir in the mayonnaise. (Or rub the tomalley and coral—if you have them—through a fine sieve with the back of a spoon directly into the sauce, then stir in the mayonnaise.)

The mixture will be quite thick. Thin it to your taste by beating the cold water into it, using as much as you need to give the sauce the density you like. Ideally, it should have enough body to barely hold its shape in a spoon.

Taste for seasoning, and serve cold with cold boiled lobster, cooked shelled shrimp, or, for that matter, with any other shellfish you prefer.

Walnut Roll with Vanilla Whipped-Cream Filling

serves 8–10

2 tablespoons butter
7 large (not extra large or jumbo) eggs, *separated*
1 cup sugar
1 level teaspoon baking powder

¼ teaspoon almond extract
4 ounces shelled (1½ cups, loosely packed) walnuts, *ground with a Mouli grater (not in an electric blender)*

THE FILLING

2 cups heavy cream
5 tablespoons confectioners' sugar: *3 for the cream and 2 to dust over the roll*

1 teaspoon vanilla extract

Preheat the oven to 350 degrees.

With a pastry brush, butter the bottoms and sides of a 12-by-18-inch (more or less) jelly-roll pan with 1 tablespoon of the butter. Then spread a sheet of waxed paper over the pan, but cut it long enough to allow 2 inches to extend over each end. Pat it down securely and brush it evenly with the remaining tablespoon of butter.

Separate the eggs and drop the yolks into a mixing bowl and the whites into another bowl, preferably one made of unlined copper (any except aluminum will do if it must). Beat the yolks with a whisk, rotary, or an electric beater for 1 or 2 minutes, then slowly pour in the sugar, beating constantly until the mixture flows thickly off the beater when it is lifted from the bowl. Beat in the baking powder and almond extract, then beat in the ground walnuts, a handful at a time.

Now beat the whites with a balloon whisk or rotary beater until they form stiff, unwavering peaks on the beater when it is lifted from the bowl. With a rubber spatula, vigorously stir 3 or 4 heaping tablespoons of the whites into the batter, and when they are thoroughly absorbed, pour the batter over the remaining whites. Fold the two together, using the spatula to bring the heavier mass over the lighter whites, thus, in effect, enfolding the two instead of mixing them. Continue to fold in this fashion until the whites no longer show. Do not,

Walnut Roll with Vanilla Whipped-Cream Filling

however, overfold them, lest you lose the air you have laboriously beaten into the whites to inflate them.

Immediately pour the mixture into the jelly-roll pan and tip it gently from side to side so that the mixture flows evenly into every corner of the pan. Bake in the middle of the oven for 18 to 20 minutes, or until the cake has puffed and a small knife inserted in the center comes out clean.

Remove the cake from the oven and immediately place a strip of waxed paper over its surface, covering it completely. Drape a dry kitchen towel over the pan and let the cake rest at room temperature (unrefrigerated) until it is completely cool.

Whip the cream in a chilled bowl until it thickens slightly, then add 3 tablespoons of the sugar and vanilla, and continue to whip until the cream is stiff but not buttery.

To unmold the roll, spread out a triple thickness of waxed paper—somewhat longer than the paper in the pan. Remove the towel from the pan and gently strip the waxed paper off the top of the cake—the crusty cake surface will cling and come away with it, which it is meant to do—and sift the remaining confectioners' sugar through a sieve evenly over the cake. Carefully turn the cake over on to the triple layer of waxed paper. The cake will not fall out of the pan as you might expect, but will probably cling to it instead; to remove without its crumbling, hold one end of the protruding waxed paper securely down on the table with one hand, and with the other, lift the short end of the pan slowly away from the cake. Remove the paper covering the cake with care.

With a small sharp knife, cut away the crusty edges and spread the cake evenly with the whipped cream, reaching every edge. With one of the long sides of the cake in front of you, use the bottom layers of waxed paper to help roll the cake over to make a long, cylindrical log. Now peel the waxed paper back and with scissor cut it from around the long sides of the roll, but leave the protruding short ends. These you will use as handles for lifting the roll and carefully placing it on a jelly-roll board or large platter. Cut off the protruding paper with a sharp knife, then slice the roll (at the table, preferably) crosswise into individual portions, and serve at once.

NOTE: Don't refrigerate the roll at any point; plan to fill and roll it no more than 1 hour or even less before serving it.

Peanut Butter

makes about 1½ cups

2 cups unsalted peanuts (prefer-
    ably the dry-roasted type)

½–¾ cup vegetable oil
½ teaspoon sugar

Drop ½ cup of the peanuts into the jar of an electric blender. Add 2 tablespoons of the oil and purée the nuts at high speed, stopping the machine periodically, scraping down the sides of the jar with a rubber spatula, then puréeing the mixture again and again until it is smooth or as grainy as you like it. Scrape the peanut butter out of the jar into a bowl and purée the remaining nuts and oil in similar amounts until all the nuts are puréed and resting safely in the bowl. (You may, from time to time, add more or less oil than I have suggested, depending upon the original oiliness of the nuts you use. Obviously, if the nuts begin to clog the machine as they blend, you are using too little oil; and, conversely, if the mixture becomes too thin, you are using too much oil.)

When all the peanuts have been puréed, stir in the sugar, and taste the butter. You may want to add some salt, and even more daringly, a few drops of Tabasco; or perhaps omit the Tabasco and stir in a little curry powder; the seasoning possibilities for this peanut butter are virtually endless.

NOTE: Cashews, walnuts, almonds, and other nuts may be prepared and seasoned in the same fashion as the peanuts. For my taste, at least, I like cashew nut butter the best.

Roast Loin of Pork with Pistachio Nuts

serves 6–8

5½-pound loin of pork, center cut,
    if possible
1 large clove garlic, *peeled and
    cut into tiny slivers*

About 2 dozen whole green pista-
    chio nuts, *shelled*
1 tablespoon salt

Roast Loin of Pork with Pistachio Nuts

½ teaspoon coarsely ground black   2 teaspoons dried thyme, *crum-*
pepper   *bled*

Ask your butcher to saw through the backbone or so-called chine of the loin but leave it attached to the loin like a flap. Ask him also to tie the loin crosswise in four or five places to keep the chine in place. This anatomical procedure will enable you to carve the finished loin into neat chops without having to hack your way through the bone.

Preheat the oven to 350 degrees.

With the point of a small sharp knife, make three rows of 1-inch incisions about 1 inch apart along the length of the loin. In each, insert a sliver of garlic and a pistachio nut, forcing them down through the fat with the knife into the center of the meat, and finally patting and pinching each small fatty opening closed with your fingers. Combine the salt, pepper, and thyme in a small bowl and rub the mixture into all sides of the loin.

Place the loin, chine-side down (a rack is unnecessary) in a shallow roasting pan just large enough to hold the meat comfortably. Roast, undisturbed in the center, of the oven for 1 hour. Then turn the loin so that it rests almost tentlike on its rib ends and the side of its chine. Roast, again undisturbed, for ½ hour more. If you have used a meat thermometer inserted in the center of the roast, it should read about 160 degrees. If you haven't, there is little likelihood that the pork will be underdone if your oven is accurately calibrated, and if you have followed my directions precisely.

If you intend to serve the loin hot, let it rest at room temperature for about 10 minutes before carving. For my taste, however, this pistachioed loin of pork is more effective at room temperature. Serve it with the Cumberland sauce on page 146, or more easily, with a sauce composed by simply mixing ⅔ cup of mayonnaise with ⅓ cup of prepared mustard. The potato salad on page 306 would make a fine accompaniment to this attractive dish.

Mont Blanc   *serves 6–8*

2 pounds chestunts, *shelled (as described on page 339)*
1 quart milk
A 3-inch piece of vanilla bean or use 1 tablespoon vanilla extract
1 cup plus 2 tablespoons sugar: *the cup for the chestnut mix-* *ture and the 2 tablespoons for the mold*
⅓ cup water
3 tablespoons unsalted butter: *2, softened, for the chestnut purée and 1 to coat the mold*
1½ cups heavy cream, *chilled*

Combine the chestnuts, the milk, and the vanilla bean (or extract) in a 3-quart enamel or stainless-steel saucepan. Bring the milk to a boil over high heat, then partially cover the pan, lower the heat to moderate, and simmer the chestnuts for about 0 minutes, or until they are tender and almost falling apart. Drain them immediately through a sieve or the strainer of the food mill set over a mixing bowl, then spread them out on paper toweling and pat them dry. Save the milk.

Stir the cup of sugar and the water together in a small saucepan until the sugar has more or less dissolved. Bring the mixture to a boil over high heat, stirring constantly, then let it boil undisturbed for 5 to 8 minutes, or until it reaches a temperature of 220 degrees on a candy thermometer. Immediately pour the syrup into a small bowl and let it cool to lukewarm.

Purée the chestnuts through a food mill, or, with the back of a large spoon, force them through a fine sieve set over a bowl. Beat in the syrup, a tablespoon at a time, and taste the purée from time to time until it is as sweet as you like it. It will be very thick. Thin it, a tablespoon at a time, with the reserved cooking milk. Finally, it should be dense enough to almost—but not quite—hold its shape solidly in a spoon. Then beat in the 2 tablespoons of softened butter.

With a pastry brush, thoroughly coat the inside (including the cone) of a 1-quart ring mold with the remaining tablespoon of butter. Then pour in 2 tablespoons of the sugar, and, holding the mold sideways over a sheet of waxed paper, slowly rotate it so that the sugar spreads evenly over all the buttered surfaces. Invert the mold and tap it gently to dislodge the excess sugar. Place the ring, open-side up, on a fresh strip of waxed paper.

Although there are pastry bags available that are fitted with a special tube capable of producing vermicelli-like strands of purée, an ordinary potato ricer is easier to handle and the effect it creates is the same.

Fill the ricer with the chestnut purée, and holding it directly over the ring mold, press it firmly and move it slowly around the ring so that the vermicelli-like strands of purée fall lightly into it. Proceed in this fashion with the remaining purée, dropping layer upon layer of the strands upon one another until the mold is full. The strands of purée which fall on the wax paper should be lifted up with a spatula and puréed again into the ring through the ricer.

Now place a circular, attractive platter upside down, directly on top of the mold. Grasping the mold and plate together, invert them. Gently lift the mold off the plate. Confronting you, will be a fragile latticed circle of chestnut purée. Refrigerate it, uncovered, until you are ready to serve it.

Just before serving, whip the cream in a chilled bowl with a ballon whisk or rotary or electric beater until it forms soft peaks on the beater when it is lifted out of the bowl.

Spoon the cream into a large pastry bag fitted with a decorative tip and pipe the cream in a mound into the center of the ring. Or, if you wish, simply spoon the cream in the center so that the cream rises to the top in a peak. Serve at once.

NOTE: You may flavor the purée after it is finished with a tablespoon or more of cognac, or in fact any liqueur of your choice. Or scatter shavings of bitter chocolate or even slivers of fresh coconut on top of the unmolded purée.

More easily, of course, but with scarcely comparable results, use 2 cans of sweetened chestnut purée (about 4 cups) in place of the freshly cooked chestnuts. The syrup will then be unnecessary. To make this version of *mont blanc* you need only flavor the purée to your taste and proceed to fill the mold as described above.

Curried Steamed Clams with Fresh Coconut

serves 6

½ cup vegetable oil
Fresh ginger root, *enough to make 1 tablespoon scraped, finely chopped,* or use 2 teaspoons cracked dried ginger, *pulverized with a mortar and pestle*
3 medium onions, *peeled, cut in half lengthwise, then cut lengthwise again into paper-thin slices (about 2 cups)*
2 teaspoons ground cumin
2 teaspoons turmeric
4 dozen small, hard-shelled clams, *washed and thoroughly scrubbed*

1 small fresh coconut, *cracked, drained, peeled and coarsely grated (page 340) (about 2 cups)*
2 tablespoons fresh, strained lemon juice
Coriander (cilantro), *enough to make 1 tablespoon finely chopped,* or use parsley (preferably the flat-leaf Italian variety), *enough to make 2 tablespoons finely chopped*
¼ teaspoon cayenne pepper or hot red-pepper flakes

Pour the oil into a 4-quart enameled or stainless-steel casserole or pot equipped with a tightly fitting cover, and set it over high heat. When the oil is very hot but not smoking, add the ginger and onions, lower the heat to moderate and, stirring occasionally, cook for 10 or 15 minutes, or until the onions are soft and light brown. Watch them carefully for any sign of burning and lower the heat if necessary. Stir in the cumin and turmeric. When the mixture turns a bright orange-yellow, add the clams, and raise the heat to moderate. Cover the casserole tightly and steam the clams for 5 to 10 minutes, or until they open. (Lift the pan with both hands, as professional cooks do, then pressing down the cover with your thumbs, push out and then flip it back toward you with a circular motion, thus allowing the clams to turn over of their own accord in the covered casserole. If this seems too formidable a feat to contemplate, simply remove the cover after 5 minutes, turn the clams about in their liquid, cover again, and continue steaming.) Clams that remain consistently closed should be discarded, although you may find it worth your while to steam the resistant ones a moment or two longer before throwing the closed ones away.

With tongs, remove the clams which remain in their shells to a deep, heated platter. Scatter the grated coconut over them evenly and sprinkle them with the lemon juice, coriander or parsley, and the cayenne or red-pepper flakes. Serve at once in a large deep serving platter.

Spinach with Smoked Ham and Pignolia Nuts in the Spanish Manner

serves 4–6

¼ cup olive oil
2 large cloves garlic, *peeled and cut in half*
½ cup pignolia nuts (pine nuts)
¼ cup diced serrano, prosciutto, or other smoked ham
1 pound freshly cooked spinach,

drained and finely chopped, or use 2 ten-ounce packages of chopped, frozen spinach, *thoroughly defrosted and drained*
Salt
Freshly ground black pepper

Pour the olive oil into a 10- to 12-inch heavy enamel or stainless-steel skillet, and set it over high heat. When the oil is very hot but not smoking, drop in the garlic halves, lower the heat to moderate, and fry them for 1 or 2 minutes before removing and discarding them. Add the pignolia nuts to the oil in the pan and, stirring them constantly, fry them for about 2 or 3 minutes until they turn golden-brown. They burn easily; lower the heat if necessary. Add the ham, and turn it about in the oil until it glistens, then add the spinach. Stirring it gently with a fork to break up any clinging strands, cook the mixture over moderate heat until it is thoroughly heated through. Add as much salt and pepper as you think it needs and serve at once.

CURRY

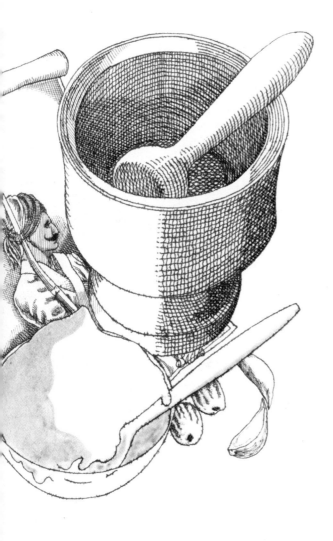

CURRY

Call it wisdom or arrogance, but a knowing French cook rarely attempts to duplicate another country's national dish. Instead, the French borrow its most important characteristic and then, artists that they are, use it as another dimension in their own cuisine. Thus the delicate veal fricassee *blanquette de veau à l'ancienne*, for example, becomes *blanquette de veau à l'indienne* when it is seasoned ever so lightly with curry powder. (My version of both appears in one of my earlier books, *Michael Field's Cooking School.*) American cooks, however, are not generally so prudent. They will douse almost anything—usually a leftover—with a sauce made with commercial curry powder, serve it with rice and an array of haphazard condiments, and call it "Indian" curry. Nothing could be more insulting to the authentic curry. Native Indian curries are lovingly and artfully prepared and belong to a vast culinary tradition Westerners know little about.

Ranging from the most delicately seasoned Hindu vegetable curries to the sharp and vigorous meat and game curries of the Moslems, Indian cooking is much more varied than we commonly suppose. And when we learn that curry is not the name of a specific dish but is only the generic name for spicy sauces, we are obliged to confess that we have a limited idea indeed of Indian cookery.

In the hierarchy of curries, among the most popular in India are the so-called dry curries, or *kebabs,* small chunks of meat steeped in a spiced marinade, then grilled over charcoal; *kormas,* a mild curry in which meat or fowl is marinated in yoghurt and a variety of herbs and spices, as in my lamb kebabs on page 360, before being broiled; and *vindaloo,* a very hot curry made with chicken, duck, goose, or pork and so tart that it is often called sour curry. And then there are, literally, hundreds of others, their ingredients and character determined more often than not by the religious beliefs and economic status of the people in the areas in which they originate.

Although many of us know what curry powder looks, smells, and tastes like, few cooks, even good ones, know that it actually is a blend of from five to fifty spices capable of almost infinite variation. Compare three or four of the better-known commercial blends. All quite properly contain a preponderance of turmeric, which accounts for their golden hue, and lesser amounts of saffron, which is astronomically expensive. But apart from that, each powder differs from the others; their odors alone indicate that each has a personality and life of its own. Imagine how varied, then, are curry powders freshly prepared from whole spices ground or pounded daily, as is almost always done in India. They are mixed according to formulas handed down in families from generation to generation, their secrets guarded as carefully as the liqueur formulas of the Benedictine and Chartreuse monks.

Many of the spices that go into curry powders are relatively unfamiliar to us and deserve to be better known, not only for their particular contribution to curry making but also for their use in cooking generally. Black and white pepper, cayenne, chili, cinnamon, nutmeg, cloves, allspice, poppy seeds—these are, of course, familiar to most cooks. But what of fenugreek, cardamom, mustard seeds, coriander, fennel, cumin, turmeric, ginger, and saffron? Alone, each spice has its unique quality; combined, they react on one another in mysterious fashion. Fenugreek, for example, is bitter and unpalatable by itself. In concert with three or four other spices, its character is changed completely and its acridity disappears almost at once. Allspice, too, is a singular berry, in which are combined the flavors of cinnamon, cloves, nutmeg, and juniper; the French, precise as usual, call it *quatre épices*. Cardamom and cumin are so pleasantly aromatic that they are used in India in curries and in almost everything else. Fennel is employed with more discretion, as its flavor of licorice can be overpowering. Coriander, like turmeric, is one of the most widely used spices in curry, but—except for the Spaniards and Mexicans, who know the herb in its fresh form, *cilantro*—most Westerners find its taste and odor too fetid to be used alone. Indians adore it and, I must confess, I adore it too, albeit in discreet amounts. If you feel sufficiently adventurous to try it, as I suggest in a few of the recipes that follow—you can generally find it in Latin

American, Spanish, or Chinatown markets. And it might be wise to
know that in Chinese markets the herb is called Chinese parsley.

It would be unrealistic, and foolhardy, for me to propose that the
average American cook, unless he is a curry addict, should compose his
own curry-powder formulas and grind them from scratch. For the curry
aficionado—and there are more of them about than you would suspect
—I have indeed suggested in a few of my Indian recipes that they do
just that. For less dedicated mortals, it may be consoling to know that
some present-day Indians use commercial curry powders. I confess I
sometimes do. Follow their lead, and amplify the curry powder with
extra spices, fruit rinds and fresh herbs, such as parsley, tarragon,
thyme, marjoram, fresh coriander, dill, rosemary, aniseed, or garlic. The
addition of finely chopped orange or lemon rind to a sharp curry powder softens its bite a little. Conversely, spiking a mild powder with
ground chili powder or cayenne obviously puts some teeth into it.
Ideally, whichever whole spices you choose, they should be pulverized
with a mortar and pestle, but even modern day Indians—affluent ones,
of course—admit that an electric blender does the job more easily.

Naturally, the choice of additional spices depends on the type of
food being curried, on previous culinary experience with that food, and
finally on the sensitivity of one's palate. Usually, the degree of hotness
of a curry is determined in India by its place of origin—Madras curries,
for instance, are notorious for their blistering intensity. It would seem
a reasonable precept, however, if you are a novice to avoid extremes.
Each heightening of flavor should be thoroughly considered, and any
wild, so-called creative impulses to toss into the pot every spice on the
shelf should be sternly checked. In other words, when in doubt, leave it
out.

It is unfortunate that there have been no native Indian cookbooks
until quite recently and so, only a few in English. For centuries, recipes have been established, like most peasant regional cooking, by
word of mouth. Consequently, most written recipes for curries today,
whatever their excellence, tend to be imprecise, allowing the cook a
dangerous amount of latitude. Moreover, much of traditional Indian
cooking is dependent on native preparations that are impossible to buy
here or for which substitutes are difficult to find: *ghee,* for example—a
type of clarified butter made from buffalo, sheep, or cow's milk; *dhal,* a
coarse purée of dried lentils or unfamiliar beans, of which there are

hundreds of varieties in India; *mustard oil,* so pungent and strong that food prepared with it is nearly intolerable to those who are unaccustomed to it.

Happily, the Indians have numerous curries in which the unfamiliar is piquant rather than startling, and the cooking techniques called for are interesting and useful to know. The *tandooris* as well as *kormas,* which I mentioned, are prepared by first marinating the meat or poultry in yoghurt and spices. Not unlike our Southern device of soaking chicken in buttermilk before frying it, the purpose is the same —to tenderize the meat and at the same time flavor it. But the Indian method is more effective than ours because of the higher proportion of the tenderizing element, lactic acid, in yoghurt, which does a better job than buttermilk in gently breaking down resistant tissues. Moreover, unlike many other dairy products containing lactic acid, yoghurt can be cooked at fairly high temperatures without curdling. And, interestingly enough, the character of yoghurt changes completely after it is cooked; except for the slightest edge of tartness, its presence is barely perceptible.

More than perceptible and often downright unpleasant are curry spices that have not been thoroughly cooked. Native Indian cooks insist, and quite rightly, that spices other than salt and pepper be either "toasted" (without burning, of course) in a hot oven or, better still, cooked in hot fat before being combined with the foods they are to flavor. You will notice, that I follow this principle to the letter. Among the few exceptions are the *kebab* curries in which chunks of meat are marinated in curry powder (and sometimes a little yoghurt, too) before being grilled. But almost every other curry recipe you may come across which pretends to authenticity begins with this preliminary cooking of the spices. (If it doesn't, take matters into your own hands, and cook them anyway.) Frequently, onions and garlic are to be cooked in the hot fat first. Whether you add the spices to the fat before or after this is unimportant. What matters is that the spices themselves be cooked long enough to release all, instead of part, of their volatile oils, thus giving the finished curry a suave rather than a rough, raw flavor—an important consideration quite apart from how hot or mild the final sauce is to be.

The condiments that accompany curries present problems of their own. There are so many different traditions, vague and ill defined, that the widest latitude is possible, limited only by the discretion of the individual cook. Although condiments, except for pickles and chutney, are positively frowned on in many parts of India, the more affluent Indians in the larger cities and in East India go all out in the other direction. The variety of side dishes can be so staggering that the curry itself is often reduced to secondary importance. It is not uncommon to find, on these elaborate tables, that the cook has literally gilded the lily by presenting choice tidbits wrapped in edible gold and silver leaf. Many Indian cooks like Chinese cooks, however, surround their curries with condiments that play supporting rather than starring roles. A sweet accent here, a sour one there—each flavor note, dissonant or consonant, being planned to bring out the special character of a curry, whether it be vegetable, meat or fowl.

The simplest and perhaps the most effective of Indian condiments is cold yoghurt, seasoned with salt and cayenne or with chopped onion, cucumber, pepper, cumin, and fresh coriander. The Indians call this *raita* and, because it is tart and refreshing, they serve it with almost all their curries. My version of *raita* on page 362 contains fresh tomatoes which give it a more colorful note.

More elaborate condiments fall roughly into the following three categories:

Bhurtas, which are highly spiced vegetable purées made of potatoes, eggplant, or tomatoes, each seasoned with chilies, mustard oil, lemon, and lime. (The eggplant *bhurta* on page 363 is an unusual one and is definitely worth trying.) Then there are the sweet, sour, bland, or peppery preparations called *sambals*. These include minced red and green chilies; chutneys; and pickled fish, fruits, and vegetables of all kinds, including pickled walnuts. The third category is Indian bread, which is also considered a condiment and occupies an important position of its own.

Until the advent of the British, yeast was unknown in India, so traditional breads were and still remain unleavened. And because native ovens were exceedingly primitive, breads were always fried. Called *chappatis, parathas, puris,* and *pappadums,* these crisp, wafer-thin pancakes are perhaps the most original of Indian culinary inventions. Most of them are almost impossible to make at home because the necessary ingredients are difficult to find but to our good fortune, the most delicious of the four, *pappadums,* are now available in cans or boxes almost everywhere. It is important to note, notwithstanding package directions to the contrary, that they *must* be deep-fried. Alternative suggestions, such as toasting or merely heating them through, are not enough to bring out their extraordinary taste and texture. In fact, if you don't deep-fry them the *pappadums* will have a soggy, unattractive texture.

Another condiment most of us may have heard about but have never tasted is Bombay duck. This is not a duck at all but a dried fish, native to the Red Sea and called a *bummalo*. Presumably, its habit of skimming over the water like a duck earned the fish its curious and misleading name, or at least that is the straight-faced explanation offered by Indians. To add to the confusion, Bombay duck tastes not unlike salted, crisp bacon. Packed in tall gilt cans, with explicit directions as to its use, it can be purchased in specialty food stores. The contribution of Bombay duck to a meat or vegetable curry might be described as a dissonant one, and it is a perfect foil to a sweet-and-sour condiment such as the tomato chutney on page 364.

Fine commercial chutneys may be bought almost anywhere, but even the best tend to be overly sweet; they are almost all prepared with a base of mangoes. Homemade chutneys offer the energetic cook other alternatives and are surprisingly easy to make as you will see when you try them. Gooseberry, peach, tamarind, tomato, coconut, lime, dates, lemon—the list is endless. Essentially, these are conserves cooked to a thick (or thin) paste and given the characteristic chutney flavor with more or less equal proportions of sugar and vinegar. Usually, other ingredients and spices are also added, for texture and heightened flavor. Some chutneys keep for weeks and make effective accompaniments not only to every type of curry but to cold meats and other foods as well.

Don't assume that all condiments for curry should be exotic or elaborate. Small dishes of chopped hard-cooked eggs, the whites and yolks separate; raisins or dried currants plumped in warm water; slivered almonds or nuts of almost any kind; shredded fresh coconut; sliced scallions; chopped green pepper—these simple things make the less familiar condiments seem even more spectacular.

But the most exquisite condiments for a curry would be wasted were the rice—and it must be rice—short of perfection. Unfortunately, this is too often the case, even though rice is perhaps the easiest of grains to cook successfully. Converted rice presents no problem and is literally foolproof if package directions are followed precisely. On the other hand, adventurous cooks ought to explore other varieties of rice with more interesting textures. And there are many: long-grained Caro-

lina rice; short, stubby grains from northern Italy; long, thin grains from
Patna, India; and many, many others. As each of these grains absorbs a
different amount of water, the best rule for cooking any of them is to
use plenty of boiling salted water; this also washes away the outer coating of rice flour, which causes rice to stick. And as the cooking times
vary, test the rice periodically as it cooks, and stop the cooking precisely when the rice is done—which means when each grain is tender
but still firm.

The Indians also cook rice in other ways. Like the Persians, they
have learned to make remarkable pilafs—highly seasoned rice cooked
in broth and garnished with almonds, sultana raisins, and anything else
that suits the cook's fancy. These pilafs are often served with curry; but
I think them redundant unless they are served as a separate course with
simply broiled meats or fowl. On the whole, plain boiled rice best serves
its traditional purpose of tempering and absorbing the pungency of
most curries.

For the Westerner, the intense flavor of curry poses the sometimes
vexing question of what to drink with it. Many Indians are content, like
the Chinese, to sip innumerable cups of tea with their food. But Americans and Europeans are unused to this. Wines are clearly out of the
question; no wine, no matter how robust, can stand up to a curry.

The English, who certainly eat more curry than most Westerners,
say that the dish should be accompanied by beer and lots of it. They
are unquestionably right. They feel that not only does beer most effectively refresh the palate but aids digestion, besides.

Indian Lamb Kebabs   *serves 4*

2 pounds boneless lamb (preferably from the leg), *trimmed*
*of excess fat, and cut into 2-
inch cubes*

THE MARINADE

1 teaspoon ground cumin
½ teaspoon turmeric
2 teaspoons salt
Fresh ginger, *enough to make 2
  tablespoons scraped and
  finely chopped*, or use 1 teaspoon cracked dried ginger
  root, *pulverized with a mortar and pestle*

1 small onion, *to make ½ cup
  finely chopped*
Peeled garlic cloves, *enough to
  make 1 teaspoon finely
  chopped*
Fresh coriander (*cilantro*) or
  parsley, *enough to make 2
  tablespoons finely chopped*
⅓ cup unsweetened, unflavored
  yoghurt

Combine the lamb, cumin, turmeric, salt, and ginger in a glass or stainless-steel baking dish or bowl just large enough to hold it, and toss the meat about with your hands or a large spoon to coat the pieces evenly with the spices. Add the onions, garlic, coriander, and yoghurt, and thoroughly mix again. Cover loosely and marinate at room temperature for 4 hours or in the refrigerator for at least 6 hours.

Follow the directions for skewering and broiling the lamb as described in the recipe for marinated shish kebabs (page 360). Naturally, omit the optional bay leaves suggested there, but the accompaniments indicated—saffron rice, chopped scallions, and quartered lemons—would do for this Indian dish as well as for the shish kebabs. Another alternative would be to line a large platter with the Indian salad on page 368 and serve the skewers of lamb on it. In any case, the Indians would broil the lamb to the well-done stage rather than to the pink, as I like it.

Pork Curry

VINDALOO   *serves 4–6*

⅓ cup distilled white vinegar
2 teaspoons salt
½ teaspoon black peppercorns,
   coarsely crushed with a mor-
   tar and pestle or rolled in a
   towel and coarsely crushed
   with a rolling pin
3 pounds boneless pork (preferably from the leg or loin),
   cut into approximately 2-inch
   cubes
5 tablespoons curry powder
1 level tablespoon flour
2 tablespoons butter

3–6 tablespoons vegetable oil
2 medium onions, *to make 1½*
   cups finely chopped
Peeled garlic cloves, *enough to*
   make 3 tablespoons finely
   chopped
Fresh ginger root, *enough to make*
   2 tablespoons peeled and
   finely chopped, or use 1 tablespoon dried, cracked ginger, *pulverized with a mortar*
   and pestle
1 cup chicken stock, fresh or
   canned

Pour the vinegar, salt, and peppercorns into a large ceramic or stainless-steel mixing bowl and stir with a spoon until the salt is completely dissolved. Add the pork and toss the pieces about with your hands or a spoon to moisten them completely. Let the pork marinate, uncovered, at room temperature for about 3 hours (or even longer), turning it about occasionally to expose all sides of the meat to the marinade.

When you are ready to make the curry, remove the pork from the marinade and pat the pieces dry with paper toweling. Mix the curry powder and the flour together in a small bowl, and, one at a time, dip a piece of pork into it, making sure the entire surface and all the crevices in the meat (if there are any) are coated with the mixture. Put aside any remaining curry-flour mixture.

Melt the butter with 3 tablespoons of the oil over high heat in a deep 10-inch skillet or sauté pan equipped with a tightly fitting cover. When the fat begins to turn ever so slightly brown, add the pork pieces, but don't crowd the pan unnecessarily. Brown them quickly—that is about 2 minutes or so on each side—and, as they reach the requisite color, transfer them with tongs to a bowl. Replace the browned pork with pieces of the uncooked pork, adding more of the oil to the pan if necessary. The curry coating burns easily; watch it constantly, and regulate the heat accordingly. When all the pork is browned and safely deposited in its bowl, add the chopped onions, ginger, and the 3 (yes, *three*) tablespoons of garlic to the fat remaining in the pan and lower the heat. Stir the onions and garlic about as they slowly begin to fry and, meanwhile, with a metal spatula scrape up all the browned particles on the bottom of the pan. (Stir into the mixture any of the curry-flour mixture you may have left.) Stirring frequently, cook for 10 to 15 minutes, or until the onions and garlic are soft and golden brown. At this point, pour in the stock, raise the heat to high and, stirring constantly, bring the sauce to a boil. It will thicken slightly. Add the browned pork and all the liquid collected around it and stir the pork about until the pieces are thoroughly coated with the sauce. Lower the heat and cover the pan tightly. Simmer the curry for about ½ hour, stirring it occasionally. When the pork can be easily pierced with a fork, it is done. Be careful not to overcook it.

Taste for seasoning—it will be unlikely that you will have to add anything—then transfer the curry to a deep platter and serve with plain hot boiled rice, any of the condiments on pages 356–8, or the *raita* on page 362, one or two of the chutneys (pages 364–6), or a judicious selection chosen from them all. Whatever the condiments I choose for this fairly fiery curry when I serve it, I always include sliced ripe bananas as one of the condiments. Their sweet and velvety texture is an effective foil for the hotness of the sauce.

Raita   *makes about 2 cups*

1 medium firm cucumber
1 tablespoon finely chopped
   onions
1 tablespoon salt

1 small, firm but ripe tomato,
   cored and cut into ¼-inch
   cubes
1 teaspoon powdered cumin

Fresh coriander (cilantro), *enough*   1 cup unflavored yoghurt
      to make 1 tablespoon finely
      chopped

Peel the cucumber and cut it lengthwise. Run a teaspoon down the center of each half and scoop out and discard the seeds. Cut the boat-like shells into ¼-inch cubes. Toss them in a mixing bowl with the chopped onion and salt and let them marinate for about 10 minutes. Then strain through a sieve.

Handful by handful, gently squeeze the cucumbers to rid them of any excess liquid and place them in a glass serving bowl. Add the tomatoes, cumin, and coriander, and mix together thoroughly. Stir in the yoghurt and taste for seasoning. Chill thoroughly before serving as an accompaniment to curry.

Curried Eggplant

BHURTA   *serves 4*

1 large (or 2 small) firm egg-   Peeled garlic cloves, *enough to*
      plants, weighing about 2   *make 1 teaspoon finely*
      pounds   *chopped*
4 medium fresh, ripe tomatoes   1 small onion, *to make ½ cup*
      —washed, stemmed, and   *finely chopped*
      coarsely chopped (1¾ cups,   Ginger root, *enough to make 1 ta-*
      more or less)   *blespoon peeled and finely*
Fresh coriander (*cilantro*) or   *chopped,* or use 2 teaspoons
      parsley, enough to make 3   dried cracked ginger, *pulver-*
      tablespoons finely chopped   *ized as finely as possible with*
2 tablespoons curry powder   *a mortar and pestle*
8 tablespoons (¼ pound, 1 stick)   Salt
      butter, *cut into small pieces*   1 teaspoon fresh, strained lemon
                                                          juice

Preheat the oven to 450 degrees.
With a small sharp knife, make 4 or 5 gashes (about ½ inch deep

and about 1 inch long—this, to prevent the possibility of it exploding as it bakes—in the eggplant and place it in a shallow baking dish. Bake in the middle of the oven for about an hour until the eggplant is soft and almost at the point of disintegration. While it is still warm, cut the eggplant lengthwise into quarters and scrape away all the pulp from the skin with a spoon. Place the pulp in a mixing bowl (discard the skin) and add the tomatoes, 2 tablespoons of the coriander or parsley, and the curry powder. With your hands or a large spoon, mix thoroughly until the ingredients are well combined.

Over high heat, melt the butter (don't let it brown) in a heavy 10- to 12-inch skillet (preferably one with a no-stick finish). Add the garlic, onions, and ginger and, stirring almost constantly, cook them for about 5 minutes, or until the onions are soft and transparent but not brown. Then stir in the curry powder and cook, stirring constantly, for 2 or 3 minutes longer. Add the eggplant-tomato mixture and raise the heat to high. Still stirring, cook the mixture briskly until most of the pan juices evaporate and the *bhurta* is thick enough to hold its shape almost solidly in a spoon. As the mixture begins to thicken watch carefully for any sign of burning and lower the heat if necessary.

Taste for seasoning, and add the amount of salt you think it needs. Pile the *bhurta* in a bowl, sprinkle the top with the lemon juice and the remaining coriander or parsley and serve at once.

Tomato Chutney   *makes about 2½ cups*

3 tablespoons vegetable oil

2 tablespoons yellow mustard seeds

3 medium firm ripe tomatoes (about 1 pound), *cored and coarsely chopped*

1 large onion, *to make 1 cup finely chopped*

1 cup cider vinegar

¼ teaspoon cinnamon

1 tablespoon salt

1 cup (packed down) dark brown sugar

1 tablespoon molasses

Fresh ginger root, *enough to make 2 tablespoons peeled, finely chopped,* or use 1 tablespoon dried, cracked ginger, *finely pulverized with a mortar and pestle*

Peeled garlic cloves, *enough to make 1 tablespoon finely chopped*

¼ teaspoon powdered cloves
2 hot green canned chilies,
    drained and finely chopped

Fresh coriander (cilantro) or
    fresh parsley, *enough to make*
    ¼ *cup finely chopped*

Pour the oil into a small frying pan and set it over high heat. When the oil is quite hot but not smoking, stir in the mustard seeds, fry briskly for about 1 minute, and remove the pan from the heat.

Combine the tomatoes, vinegar, onions, cinnamon, and salt in a 2- to 3-quart heavy enamel or stainless-steel saucepan. Bring to a boil over high heat, stirring constantly. Then stir in the brown sugar, molasses, ginger, garlic, powdered cloves, chopped chilies, and coriander or parsley. Reduce the heat and cook, stirring constantly, for 5 minutes longer. Immediately stir in the mustard seeds, oil and all, to the simmering tomato mixture. Raise the heat to high and bring the mixture to a boil. Stirring almost constantly, boil for 8 to 10 minutes, or until the chutney thickens and most but not all of its liquid evaporates. Watch carefully at the end of the cooking time, and reduce the heat to moderate if the mixture shows any sign of burning.

Taste for seasoning and heighten the flavor of the chutney with more salt if you think it needs it. Pour the chutney into a bowl and cool to room temperature.

NOTE: This tomato chutney, like so many others of its type, may be refrigerated, tightly covered, and safely kept up to 3 or even 4 weeks.

Date and Lemon Chutney   *makes about 1½ cups*

8 ounces pitted dates, *coarsely chopped*
An approximately 6-inch-square piece of peeled, fresh, shredded coconut (page 340), or use ½ cup unsweetened, shredded, packaged coconut
¼ cup fresh, strained lemon juice
Fresh ginger, *enough to make 2*

tablespoons peeled, finely chopped, or use 1 tablespoon dried cracked ginger, *pulverized with a mortar and pestle*
1 tablespoon finely chopped parsley
½ teaspoon fennel seeds
½ teaspoon salt
Freshly ground black pepper

Date and Lemon Chutney

Combine the dates, coconut, lemon juice, ginger, and parsley in a large mixing bowl and toss them about with your hands or a spoon until they are thoroughly mixed. Bruise the fennel seeds with a mortar and pestle (or wrap them in a towel and firmly press and roll a rolling pin on them), and add them to the date and coconut mixture. Add the salt and as much freshly ground pepper as you like, stir thoroughly and taste for seasoning.

NOTE: This chutney may be served soon after it is made or refrigerated, tightly covered, for about a week. Stored much longer, it may spoil.

Curried Cauliflower
serves 4–6

½ cup vegetable oil
1 teaspoon yellow mustard seeds
½ teaspoon cumin seeds (if available)
Fresh ginger root, *enough to make 1 tablespoon peeled, finely chopped,* or use 2 teaspoons dried, cracked ginger, *finely pulverized with a mortar and pestle*
1 small onion, *to make ½ cup finely chopped*
2 teaspoons salt
½ teaspoon turmeric
About 2 pounds cauliflower, *trimmed, washed, and divided into more or less equal-sized flowerets, then dried thoroughly with paper toweling*
1 small, fresh ripe tomato, *washed, cored, and finely chopped*
2 hot green canned chilies, *drained and finely chopped*
1 teaspoon ground cumin (use 2 teaspoons if you have omitted the cumin seeds above)
½ teaspoon sugar
Fresh coriander (cilantro) or parsley, *enough to make 2 tablespoons finely chopped*
1 tablespoon butter, *melted (but not browned)*

Heat the vegetable oil in a 4- to 5-quart heavy enamel or stainless-steel casserole over high heat. When the oil is quite hot but not smoking, stir in the mustard seeds, cumin seeds (if you have them), the ginger and chopped onions. Lower the heat to moderate and, stirring constantly, cook the mixture for about 1 minute before adding in the salt and turmeric. Lower the heat again and simmer the mixture, uncovered, for 3 or 4 minutes.

Now drop the flowerets into the sauce and turn them about with a long spoon to coat them thoroughly. Then stir in the chopped tomato, chilies, ground cumin, sugar, and 1 tablespoon of the coriander or parsley. Cover the pan tightly, and turning them about in the sauce occasionally, simmer the cauliflower for 15 to 20 minutes, or until the flowerets are tender but still intact. Be careful not to overcook them. When finished, they should still show a slight resistance when pierced with the tip of a small sharp knife.

To serve, transfer the entire contents of the casserole to a deep heated platter or bowl and sprinkle the cauliflower with the remaining tablespoon of coriander or parsley, and the tablespoon of hot melted butter.

Curried Lamb
serves 6

3 pounds boneless lamb from the shoulder, *cut into 2-inch chunks*

½ teaspoon hot red-pepper flakes, *crushed with a mortar and pestle*

1 teaspoon salt

Fresh ginger root, *enough to make 1 tablespoon scraped, finely chopped;* or use 1 teaspoon cracked dried ginger, *pulverized with a mortar and pestle*

1 cup unflavored yoghurt

2 tablespoons butter

1 tablespoon vegetable oil

2 tablespoons curry powder

1 teaspoon turmeric

¼ teaspoon freshly ground black pepper

Fresh coriander (cilantro) or parsley, *enough to make 2 tablespoons finely chopped*

A few gratings of nutmeg

In a large mixing bowl, with a spoon or your hands, toss the lamb pieces with the pepper flakes, salt, and fresh or dried ginger. Pour in the yoghurt and toss again, and make sure all the lamb pieces are well moistened. Let the lamb marinate at room temperature anywhere from 2 to 6 hours—the longer the better.

Curried Lamb

Heat the butter and oil (the Indians would, of course, use *ghee*, see page 355), in a 4-quart heavy casserole over moderate heat, but don't let the butter brown. Stir in the curry powder, turmeric, and black pepper, then simmer, stirring constantly for about 1 minute before adding the lamb and all its yoghurt marinade. Raise the heat to high, and, still stirring, bring the marinade to a boil. Immediately lower the heat, cover the casserole, and simmer the lamb for about an hour and 15 minutes until tender. Then stir in the fresh coriander or parsley, cover the casserole, and simmer for 15 minutes more.

When you are ready to serve the curry, transfer the lamb to a large deep platter and carefully skim off and discard all the fat from the surface of the sauce. Taste for seasoning; it may possibly need some salt. Pour the sauce over the lamb and grate a little nutmeg over it. Serve the curry with plain boiled or steamed rice and any chutney or condiment that suits your fancy.

Chicken Tandoori
with Indian Salad

serves 4–6

4-pound chicken, *securely trussed*
⅓ cup fresh, strained lemon juice
2 teaspoons salt
½ teaspoon powdered saffron
2 teaspoons whole coriander seeds
¼ teaspoon dried hot red-pepper flakes
1 teaspoon cumin seeds or powder

2 large cloves garlic, *peeled and coarsely chopped*
Fresh ginger root, *enough to make 1 teaspoon scraped, finely chopped,* or use ½ teaspoon cracked, dried ginger root, *pulverized with a mortar and pestle*
1 cup unflavored yoghurt
4 tablespoons (½ stick) butter, *melted*

THE SALAD

3 medium onions, *peeled and sliced into paper-thin slivers*

12–15 red radishes, *trimmed, washed, and dried*

4 medium-size ripe tomatoes, *cut
into ¼-inch-thick slices*
4 fresh green hot chilies (if available), or use a large green
pepper, *seeded, deribbed,*

*and cut into strips about 2
inches long and 1 inch wide*
2 lemons, *cut into quarters*
Salt
Freshly ground pepper
¼ cup fresh, strained lemon juice

A day before you plan to roast it, marinate the chicken in the following fashion: with a small sharp knife make two ½-inch-deep slits,
about an inch apart in each thigh, and make similar slits in the chicken's
breasts. Place the chicken in a deep casserole just about large enough
to hold it. Stir together the lemon juice, salt, and the saffron, then pour
as much of it as you can into each slit; rub the rest of the mixture all
over the chicken. Place the coriander seeds, the red-pepper flakes, and
the cumin seeds or powder in a small skillet and toast the spices over
moderate heat for about 2 minutes, stirring them constantly. With a
rubber spatula, scrape the entire mixture into the jar of an electric
blender, and add the chopped garlic, the fresh or cracked ginger root,
and 4 tablespoons of the yoghurt. Blend at high speed for about 30 seconds, turn off the machine, scrape down the sides with the spatula, then
blend again until the mixture is thoroughly pulverized. With a spoon,
stir into the purée the rest of the yoghurt and pour it over the chicken.
Turn it about to moisten every part of its skin, cover the casserole
tightly and marinate at room temperature for at least 12 hours or in
the refrigerator for 24 hours. Turn the chicken over in its marinade
every few hours or whenever you happen to think of it.
    Preheat the oven to 400 degrees.
    Choose a shallow roasting pan just large enough to hold the
chicken. (This is important; if the pan is too large, the marinade
and juices will evaporate too quickly, and, more than likely, burn.)
Place the chicken, breast side up, on a rack set in the pan and pour the
marinade over it. Roast for about 10 minutes, then pour on the melted
butter. Roast another 20 minutes, this time basting the chicken with its
marinade every 10 minutes. Now turn the oven down to 350 degrees
and roast for about 1 hour, basting every now and then. Test the
chicken for doneness by piercing a thigh with the tip of a small sharp
knife. The juice that trickles out should be yellow; if it is tinged with
pink, roast 5 or 10 minutes longer.

The Salad

An Indian cook would serve the chicken with the salad in this way: he would scatter the slivered onions all over the surface of a large serving platter, then arrange the radishes, tomatoes, chilies or green peppers, and lemon quarters around the edge of the platter. (He would probably have done this as I do, while the chicken is roasting.) When the chicken is done, it is quickly carved into 6 or 8 pieces, the salt, pepper, and the lemon juice sprinkled evenly over the top, and the chicken pieces then placed carefully and decoratively on the onions. Naturally, the *tandoori* should be served at once.

NOTE: You can, if you prefer, serve the carved chicken without the salad, and accompany it with a rice pilaf instead. In that event, the salad could be served at the same time, but on separate plates.

Curried Lamb Balls Stuffed with Almonds

KEFTAS   *serves 4*

1 pound lean lamb (preferably from the shoulder), *ground twice through the finest blade of a meat grinder*
1 teaspoon salt
½ teaspoon freshly ground black pepper
½ cup chick peas (garbanzos), freshly cooked or canned (page 324)
1 large egg
12 blanched, untoasted almonds

¼ pound (1 stick) butter
1 small onion, *to make ½ cup finely chopped*
Peeled garlic cloves, *to make 1 tablespoon finely chopped*
4–6 tablespoons curry powder
1 cup unflavored yoghurt
4–6 tablespoons vegetable oil
½ cup heavy cream
Salt
Freshly ground black pepper

In a large mixing bowl, combine the ground lamb, salt, and black pepper. With a food mill, or a fine sieve and the back of a spoon, purée

Curried Lamb Balls Stuffed with Almonds

the chick peas directly over the meat. With your hands (an Indian cook would never dream of using a spoon, but you may, if you like) knead the mixture together until it is as smooth as you can get it. In a small bowl, beat the egg only long enough to combine the yolk and white and pour it over the meat. Knead again until it is thoroughly absorbed. If you are not averse to the taste of raw lamb (actually it is quite pleasant), taste the mixture for seasoning and add more salt and pepper if you feel it needs it.

One at a time, make the stuffed meatballs in the following fashion. Drop a tablespoon of the meat on a flat surface, flatten it slightly and put an almond on top. Cover with another tablespoon of the meat. Pick up the sandwich, as it were, and gently pat it into a ball with the palms of your hands, thus enclosing the almond in the center. Arrange the finished meatballs side by side on waxed paper. The meatballs may be made ahead, covered with plastic wrap, and refrigerated until you are ready to cook them.

Before frying the meatballs, make the sauce. Over moderate heat, melt the butter in a deep 12-inch skillet or sauté pan equipped with a tightly fitting cover. Add the onions and garlic, and, stirring almost constantly, fry them for 8 to 10 minutes, or until they are a deep golden-brown. (Lower the heat if the onions appear to be browning too rapidly.) Add 4 tablespoons of curry powder (more, if you like your curries hot) and, stirring constantly, simmer the mixture for about 5 minutes, then pour in the yoghurt, a few tablespoons at a time. Reduce the heat to low and let the mixture simmer quietly, uncovered, while you fry the meatballs.

Heat 4 tablespoons of the vegetable oil in a large 10- to 12-inch frying pan, set over high heat. When it is quite hot but not smoking, add the meatballs (don't crowd them—do them in 2 batches, if necessary, adding the remaining oil if you need it). Fry the meatballs for about 10 minutes in all, turning them over gently from time to time with a spatula until they are a deep mahogany brown. Be careful not to let them burn. As each meatball reaches the requisite color, transfer it with a slotted spoon to the simmering sauce. When all the meatballs are safely settled in their sauce, baste them thoroughly, or turn them about in the sauce to coat them thoroughly, then cover the pan securely. Simmer slowly for about 20 minutes, turning the meatballs over in the sauce every 5 minutes or so.

Immediately before serving, transfer the meatballs to a deep plat-

Curried Lamb Balls Stuffed with Almonds

ter with a slotted spoon. The sauce will appear to have curdled, but don't be concerned. Merely tip the pan slightly towards you, and, with a large spoon, skim off and discard most of its surface fat. Slowly pour in the heavy cream, and stir continuously for a moment or so until the sauce is smooth and thick. If it seems too thick for your taste, thin it with a little more cream, adding it a tablespoon at a time until it reaches the consistency you prefer. Taste for seasoning. It will doubt- lessly need a liberal amount of salt, some freshly ground pepper, and perhaps a few specks of cayenne pepper. Pour the sauce over the wait- ing meatballs and serve with a bowl of plain boiled rice. Any or all the condiments described on pages 356–8 may accompany it, but I think the tomato chutney (page 364) and the *raita* (page 362) served in sep- arate bowls would make even more suitable accompaniments.

Appendix

Index

In planning a menu, it is obvious that you have to take special problems into consideration: the amount of time for preparation that you have at your disposal, the function or significance of a particular meal, the tastes of your guests, the kitchen help you have or don't have, and a host of other factors, not the least of which is the state of your budget. The best recourse is to be frankly yourself. Don't adhere to rigid or conventional formulations: be courageous and devise combinations of dishes that *you* feel belong together. Remember that the element of surprise can be fun.

I offer here a few of my own off-beat menus simply to show you how some of the unusual dishes in this book can be combined with interesting effect. Because so many of the recipes are unfamiliar and scattered throughout the book, I have also listed recipes in fairly convenient categories to help you devise menus of your own.

Menus

A SUBSTANTIAL LATE BREAKFAST FOR 8

Macédoine of Fruit with Fresh Ginger and Port
Eggs Benedict
Cottage-Cheese Pancakes with Strawberry Jam

AN INTIMATE LUNCHEON FOR 4

Moules Glacé Chauveron
Curried Lamb Balls
Date Chutney
Crème de Cacao-Mocha Soufflé

A late supper party for 6

A Large Platter of Chilled Fresh Vegetables with Aïoli
Chicken, Leek, and Tongue Pie
Figs Stuffed with Chocolate and Almonds

A substantial dinner for 8

Boiled Artichokes with Lemon Butter
Turkey Molé
Frijoles Refritos
Chilled Zabaglione

A fairly elaborate dinner for 10

Chilled Shrimp with Hazelnut Sauce
Black Bean Soup
Chicken Tandoori with Indian Salad
Oeufs à la Neige

Recipe Categories

LATE BREAKFAST OR PARTY BREAKFAST DISHES

Sweet Puffed Omelette

Shredded Potato Pancakes with Chives

Freshly Made Peanut or Cashew Butter

Sautéed Chicken Livers in the Spanish Manner

Eggs Benedict

Zucchini Omelette in the Italian Manner

Baked Mushrooms with Duxelles Stuffing

Cheese-and-Bacon Tart (Quiche Lorraine)

Deep-Fried English Cheese Sausages

Veal Sweetbreads with Champagne Sauce

Crabmeat and Parmesan Cheese Soufflé

Apple Fritters

Macédoine of Fruit with Fresh Ginger and Port

Cottage-Cheese Pancakes with Strawberry Jam

Mozzarella in Carrozza with Anchovy Sauce

Welsh Rabbit

Shirred Eggs with Cream

MAIN DISHES FOR LUNCH OR LIGHT SUPPERS

Coquilles St.-Jacques à la Parisienne

Chicken Breasts with Prosciutto and Parmesan Cheese

Mozzarella in Carrozza with Anchovy Sauce

Steamed Clams in the Algarve Manner

Sautéed or Deep-Fried Scallops

Pissaladière

Chicken, Leek, and Tongue Pie

Baked Oysters in the Italian Manner

Moules Glacé Chauveron

Shrimp Mousse

Baked Mushrooms with Crabmeat Stuffing

Grilled Shrimp in the Italian Manner

Curried Lamb Balls Stuffed with Almonds

Curried Steam Clams with Fresh Coconut

Baked Bermuda Onions with Beef, Spinach, and Rosemary Stuffing

Vermicelli and Primavera Sauce

Zucchini Omelette in the Italian Manner

Cheese-and-Bacon Tart (Quiche Lorraine)

Deep-Fried Cheese Sausages in the English Manner

Eggs Benedict

MAIN DISHES FOR LUNCH OR LIGHT SUPPERS (*continued*)

Clams in White Wine in the Spanish Manner
Seviche
Spiedini of Bread, Anchovies, and Mozzarella in the Lugano Manner

Cold Roast Loin of Pork with Pistachio Nuts
Leek Tart
My Version of Monsieur Dumas' Salad Francillon
Welsh Rabbit

COCKTAIL PARTY FOOD

Broiled Mushrooms
Baked Mushrooms Stuffed with Duxelles, Crabmeat, or Spinach
Cheese Beignets
Stuffed Mussels in the Turkish Manner
Cold Bay Scallops with Dilled Rémoulade Sauce as Dip
Cheese Straws
Deep-Fried English Cheese Sausage (small size)
Pissaladière Wedges
Cheese Fondue Neuchâteloise with French Bread

Bacon-and-Cheese Tart (wedges)
Curried Crabmeat Pâté with Hot Toast
Hummus with Sesame Seed Crackers
Mushrooms à la Grecque (with picks)
Deep-Fried Mushrooms in Beer Batter
Deep-Fried Bay Scallops
Marinated Deep-Fried Salsify Fritters
Peanut or Cashew Nut Butter on Melba Toast

DIPS

Aïoli
Skordalia

Bagna Cauda and White Truffles, with Raw Vegetables

SOUPS IN THREE CATEGORIES

HEARTY, FULL-MEAL SOUPS

Soupe au Pistou
Bourride
Mussel Soup in the Italian Manner
Ukrainian Borscht

Portuguese Seafood Stew with Fried Saffron Toast
Zuppe de Pesce (Italian Fish Soup)
Clam Soup in the Italian Manner

SOUPS IN THREE CATEGORIES (*continued*)

HOT FIRST-COURSE SOUPS

*Mushroom Soup with a Garnish of
    Fresh Mushrooms*
Soupe à l'Ail
Cheddar-Cheese Soup
Portuguese Kale Soup
Avgolemono
Cockaleekie

*Onion Soup in the French Manner,
    Gratinéed*
Mushroom Barley Soup
Black Bean Soup
*Yellow Split Pea Soup in the Swedish
    Manner*
Lentil Soup with Scallions

COLD FIRST-COURSE SOUPS

*Vichyssoise with Sorrel, Watercress,
    or Spinach*
Billi-Bi Mussel Soup

Gazpacho
*Chilled Green Split Pea Soup with
    Mint*

HORS D'OEUVRES AND FIRST COURSES FOR DINNERS

COLD

Oeufs en Gelée
Curried Crabmeat Pâté
Seviche
Shrimp Mousse
*Cold Bay Scallops with Dilled
    Rémoulade Sauce*
*Cold Stuffed Mussels in the Turkish
    Manner*

*Stuffed Mussels with Rémoulade
    Dill Sauce*
Mushrooms à la Grecque
*Celery Root Salad with Mustard
    Mayonnaise*
*White Bean Salad with Tunafish in
    the Italian Manner*
Cold Shrimp and Hazelnut Sauce

HOT

Coquilles St.-Jacques à la Parisienne
*Crabmeat and Parmesan Cheese
    Soufflé*
Baked Oysters in the Italian Manner
Boiled Artichokes with Lemon Butter
Moules Glacé Chauveron
Moules Marinière
*Clams in White Wine in the Spanish
    Manner*
Clams Casino
Grilled Shrimp in the Italian Manner

Sautéed or Deep-Fried Scallops
*Broiled Mushrooms Stuffed with
    Garlic Butter on Toast*
*Baked Mushrooms Stuffed with
    Duxelles, Crabmeat, or Spinach*
*Cheese-and-Bacon Tart (Quiche
    Lorraine)*
Pissaladière
Braised Leeks Provençale
Leek Tart

MAIN COURSES FOR DINNERS

Lobster Fra Diavolo
Baked Lobster with Dill or Tarragon Stuffing
Portuguese Seafood Stew with Fried Saffron Toast
Turkey Molé
Braised Rabbit with Almonds and Chocolate Sauce in the Spanish Manner
Curried Lamb
Vindaloo (Pork Curry)
Braised Lamb with Turnips or Rutabagas
Chicken, Leek, and Tongue Pie
Chicken Breasts with Prosciutto and Parmesan Cheese
Bourride with Rouille
Sautéed Chicken Dauphinoise
Italian Pillows of Veal with Cheese and Prosciutto

Osso Buco with Gremolata
Tandoori Murgh with Salat (Chicken Tandoori with Indian Salad)
Curried Lamb Balls Stuffed with Almonds
Roast Loin of Pork with Pistachio Nuts
Roast Chicken Béarnaise
Marinated Shish Kebabs of Lamb
Alsatian Choucroute with Spareribs
Coq au Vin Riesling
Scallopine al Marsala
Pièce de Boeuf à la Bourgignonne
Veal Sweetbreads with Champagne Sauce
Stuffed Pasta with One of Three Fillings
Carbonnade of Beef Flamande
Chicken en Cocotte Vallée d'Auge
Broiled Marinated Chuck Steak

HOT VEGETABLES TO SERVE AS A SEPARATE COURSE OR WITH AN ENTRÉE

Curried Cauliflower
Curried Eggplant
Boston Baked Beans
Braised Turnips
Poached Celery Root with Lemon and Egg Sauce in the Turkish Manner
Flan des Carottes à la Flamande
White Beans with Tomatoes and Garlic
Frijoles Refritos
Braised and Glazed Carrots
Marinated Deep-Fried Salsify Beignets
Braised Red Cabbage

Broiled Potato Balls
Baked Beans of the Southwest
Braised Leeks Provençale
Creamed Little White Onions
Potatoes Annette
Roesti Potatoes in the Swiss Manner
Deep-Fried Mushrooms in Beer Batter
Broiled Mushrooms
Baked Mushrooms Stuffed with Duxelles or Spinach
Purée of Spinach with Madeira
Leek Tark
Spinach with Smoked Ham and Pignolia Nuts

HOT VEGETABLES (*continued*)

Boiled Artichokes with Lemon Butter
English Parsnip Pie

Shredded Potato Pancakes

SAUCES AND RELISHES

Tomato Chutney
Date and Lemon Chutney
Hazelnut Sauce (cold)
Lemon Butter
Aïoli (cold)
Rouille
Salsa Verde
Dilled Rémoulade
Mustard Mayonnaise
Cumberland Sauce
Marchand de Vin Sauce
Skordalia with Almonds

Skordalia with Potatoes
Gremolata
Primavera
PASTA SAUCES
Marinara
Ragù Bolognese
Butter, Cheese, and White Truffles
Marinara with Clams or Mussels,
    Italian Sausage
Lobster Besciamella
Garlic, Oil, and Parsley
Pesto

COLD VEGETABLES AND SALADS

Céleri-rave Rémoulade
Raita
Lentil Salad Mimosa
Red Kidney Bean Salad
Mushrooms à la Grecque

Braised Leeks Provençale
My Version of Monsieur Dumas'
    Salad Francillon
French Potato Salad

DESSERTS

LIGHT DESSERTS

Cottage-Cheese Pancakes
Oeufs à la Neige
Sweet Puffed Omelette
Figs Stuffed with Chocolate and
    Almonds in the Portuguese Style
Zabaglione (hot or cold)

RICH DESSERTS

Lemon Meringue Pie
Souffléd Chocolate Mocha Roll
Walnut Roll with Vanilla Whipped-
    Cream Filling
Chocolate Soufflé
Chocolate Orange Mousse

DESSERTS (*continued*)

LIGHT DESSERTS

Lemon Soufflé with a Meringue
  Topping
Macédoine of Fruit with Fresh
  Ginger and Port
Apple Beignets
Crème de Cacao-Mocha Soufflé

RICH DESSERTS

Ricotta Pie
New England Chocolate Cake with
  Chocolate Sour-Cream Frosting
Cheese Cake
Mont Blanc
Sachertorte

AFTER A DANCE OR THE THEATER

Bagna Cauda and White Truffles,
  with Raw Vegetables
Aïoli or Skordalia, with Raw
  Vegetables and Arab Bread or
  Bread Sticks
Spiedini of Bread, Anchovies, and
  Mozzarella Cheese
Welsh Rabbit
Cheese Fondue Neuchâteloise with
  French Bread

Mozzarella in Carrozza with
  Anchovy Sauce
Pissaladière
Onion Soup in the French Manner,
  Gratinéed
Sweet Puffed Omelette
Bacon-and-Cheese Tart
Broiled Mushrooms Stuffed with
  Garlic Butter on Toast

Index to Recipes

Index to Introductory Essays

A Note About the Author

Michael Field's fame as a superb practitioner and teacher of the art of cooking was established with the publication, in 1965, of *Michael Field's Cooking School*. His reputation has grown steadily over the years through the cooking classes he has held in his New York home, through his writings about food in *Holiday* and *McCall's* magazines, and through his widely discussed critical articles in *The New York Review of Books*. He served as consulting editor for the entire Time/Life Foods of the World Series. *All Manner of Food,* his third book, was originally published in 1970. Mr. Field, who was born in New York City, started his career as a concert pianist and became internationally known as a member of the duo piano team of Appleton and Field. He died in 1971.